The
MEE-OW
SHOW
at 50

From Cultural Rebellion to Comedy Institution

Joseph B. Radding | Paul W. Warshauer

FOREWORD BY **Seth Meyers**

Northwestern University Press
Evanston, Illinois

Northwestern University Press
www.nupress.northwestern.edu

Publisher's Note: This book is based in part on hundreds of hours of interviews with participants in the Mee-Ow Show over the years. Memory, like all things human, is influenced by emotion and perception, both of which can change over time. Occasionally in the text, minor details have been corrected and quotations have been edited for clarity. But for the most part, the authors have let the interviewees speak for themselves, and the result is the dynamic account of a thriving independent theater community at Northwestern University told in the voices of those who created the community. Unless otherwise noted, all images and show memorabilia are from the Northwestern University Archives. Photographers are credited where known.

Quotations from the *Daily Northwestern* appear as originally published and are reprinted with permission.

Printed in Canada

10 9 8 7 6 5 4 3 2 1

Library of Congress Cataloging-in-Publication Data

Names: Radding, Joseph B., author. | Warshauer, Paul W., author. | Meyers, Seth, 1973– writer of foreword.
Title: The Mee–Ow Show at 50 : from cultural rebellion to comedy institution / Joseph B. Radding, Paul W. Warshauer ; foreword by Seth Meyers.
Description: Evanston : Northwestern University Press, 2024.
Identifiers: LCCN 2024017983 | ISBN 9780810148215 (paperback)
Subjects: LCSH: Mee–Ow Show (Northwestern University)—History. | Northwestern University (Evanston, Ill.)—Students. | Comedy.
Classification: LCC PN1922 .R33 2024 | DDC 792.23097731—dc23/eng/20240422
LC record available at https://lccn.loc.gov/2024017983

To Jeff Wilson ('74), our first director. A man with a vision.

And to Viola Spolin, Winifred Ward, and so many other Northwestern gurus who started the "improvisation revolution."

—P.W.W.

To Marilee, my best friend, who married me.

And to my parents Leigh and Anne, who always understood.

—J.B.R.

Contents

We used every floor—
to produce the 1st
Mee-ow show
(Basement for [illegible]
C + 2 for rehearsals
P was McCormick Auditorium
3 was Mee-ow office

Foreword

Seth Meyers

Mee-Ow changed my life twice.

The first time was during new student week of my freshman year. I had heard of but never seen improv, and when a group of Northwestern students bounded on stage to take suggestions for where a scene could take place, my hopes were not high. I remember thinking, "Look at this crew. They have the exhausting energy of the professional yo-yo expert who came to my high school to explain how drugs were bad for—" And before I could finish that thought, I was awestruck. They were brilliant. Immediately brilliant. I couldn't believe I was enrolled at the same school as those kids. The best part was that somewhere in the back of my head I thought, "I can do that."

And so I auditioned my freshman year, and didn't get it.

And auditioned again my sophomore year, and didn't get it.

And then junior year I enthusiastically disproved the adage "Third time's a charm."

Now is the time where I stress—I was in no way wronged. The improvisers blocking my way were, to this day, some of the best I've ever seen. Winer! Weiss! Herbstman! Wenner! Weier! Sandler! Vaillancourt! Villepique! Lamson! They were the 1927 Yankees, and I was a member of the 1928 Yankees, patiently waiting my turn. And my turn would come.

Because senior year I had something new working in my favor—they all graduated.

To this day, I thank my lucky stars none of them were held back a year.

I don't remember auditioning for a fourth time, but I will never forget seeing my name on a cast list pinned to a corkboard in Norris. I floated home. It's the closest I ever felt to being a character in a musical, based on how close I came to breaking into song.

The second time Mee-Ow changed my life was during goodnights of our final show. It was the happiest I had ever been. On stage with my friends, an audience full of peers. And in that moment I had a revelation: “I am going to try to do comedy as a living until they force me to stop.”

I was so excited for me, and I was so heartbroken for my parents. They had paid so much money for a four-year college education just so I could tell them, “I’ve decided to make things up for a living!”

(I have more than made it up to them, FYI. Every time they buy Seth Meyers merch? 15 percent off!)

I’m forever in debt to Mee-Ow, to that first cast I saw new student week, to my fellow cast members, to my fellow cast member and dear friend Pete Grosz, who said, “If we want to do this we should start taking classes in Chicago,” to the student body who came out and made us feel like rock stars, but most important, to the architect of Shanley Pavilion, who said, “I think if we make this building shittier, it will be better for comedy.”

I hope you enjoy reading this book about Mee-Ow as much as I enjoyed doing Mee-Ow, but you won’t.

That would be impossible.

Preface

Stamping our feet to keep warm, we lined up outside Shanley Pavilion, the dimly lit naval training facility that had once served as a classroom, mess hall, bookstore, folk music coffeehouse, and storage dump, and was now repurposed as a performance space. We filed in with the crowd, showing our tickets to the students at the door. As we took off our winter coats and found our seats, the house band played familiar rock classics and people chattered excitedly in anticipation. The stage was a concrete floor, with lighting on stands around the room and the musicians on risers at stage left.

We were there to see the Mee-Ow Show.

In its current form, the Mee-Ow Show at Northwestern University is one-third sketch comedy, one-third improv, and one-third rock and roll. This format has evolved over the show's fifty-year history and will almost certainly see changes as time moves on, but the founding idea of the show remains true: Mee-Ow gives student creators control over their original material, from conception through execution.

Alumni of the Mee-Ow Show include some of the most well-known and awarded names in comedy and entertainment, including Seth Meyers, Julia Louis-Dreyfus, Ana Gasteyer, Kristen Schaal, Dermot Mulroney, Craig Bierko, and John Cameron Mitchell. But there are many more names that people won't recognize: the staff, crew, and musicians who have made Mee-Ow what it was and what it is. Producers schedule performance spaces and manage the expenses and funding. Directors audition the cast and run writing rooms, rehearsals, and improvisation practices. Set and lighting designers and crew plan, construct, and run tech. Musicians and singers develop their skills all year. Publicity staff get people in the door. Graphic designers, photographers, and videographers make posters and social media content.

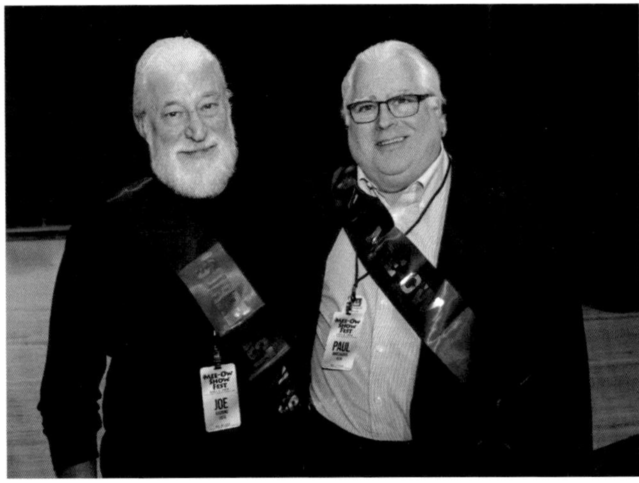

The authors, Joe Radding ("Surrealist-in-Residence") and Paul Warshauer ("Papa Mee-Ow"), at the Mee-Ow Show reunion in 2024

In addition to the cast and staff members over the years who have gone into behind-the-scenes careers in entertainment as writers, directors, producers, and casting agents, there are many more who have taken their skills into other industries, becoming lawyers, doctors, entrepreneurs, and educators.

All these creative, dedicated students come together to produce two unique shows each year. They earn no academic credit for this work, but every person we spoke with emphasized how much they gained from the Mee-Ow Show. Many said they learned more from Mee-Ow than from their classes. Almost everyone said that the confidence they gained was of inestimable value.

Throughout history there are places in time and space that eventually prove to be a nexus of creativity and innovation, attracting like-minded explorers of art. Paris in the 1920s, Renaissance Florence, postwar New York City, and London in the 1960s.

And so, in its own way, was the Mee-Ow Show.

Such a comparison may appear to be hyperbole. Admittedly, Mee-Ow is not the Bauhaus of sketch comedy. But if a place can be measured by the contributions of the people who have passed through it, then Mee-Ow deserves more than a mention.

It deserves a book.

Acknowledgments

Our thanks for your help, guidance, expertise, and support throughout the process of the creation of this book:

Parneshia Jones, director, Northwestern University Press.

Courtney Smotherman, permissions director, Northwestern University Press.

Megan Stielstra, editor, Northwestern University Press.

Kevin Leonard, Northwestern University historian, for steadfast and continued support.

Patrick Quinn, Northwestern University archivist, 1974–2009, who was instrumental in helping Paul Warshauer create the Mee-Ow archives.

Tim Moran, PhD, Wayne State University, for help in crafting interview questions.

Elizabeth J. Kopras, PhD, University of Cincinnati, for help in setting up an online interview permission form.

Kyla Neely, copresident of Out Da Box, for information about that organization.

Laura Hunt Hume, PhD, University of Dayton, for encouragement and suggestions.

Gaylin Walli, pied piper of technical communication, for inestimably important conversations about writing.

Professor Eliza Bent of Northwestern University for information about the Comedy Arts module in the Radio/Television/Film Department.

Drew McCoy for insights and recollections.

The many people of Mee-Ow who have graciously contributed their time, memories, and memorabilia to this effort.

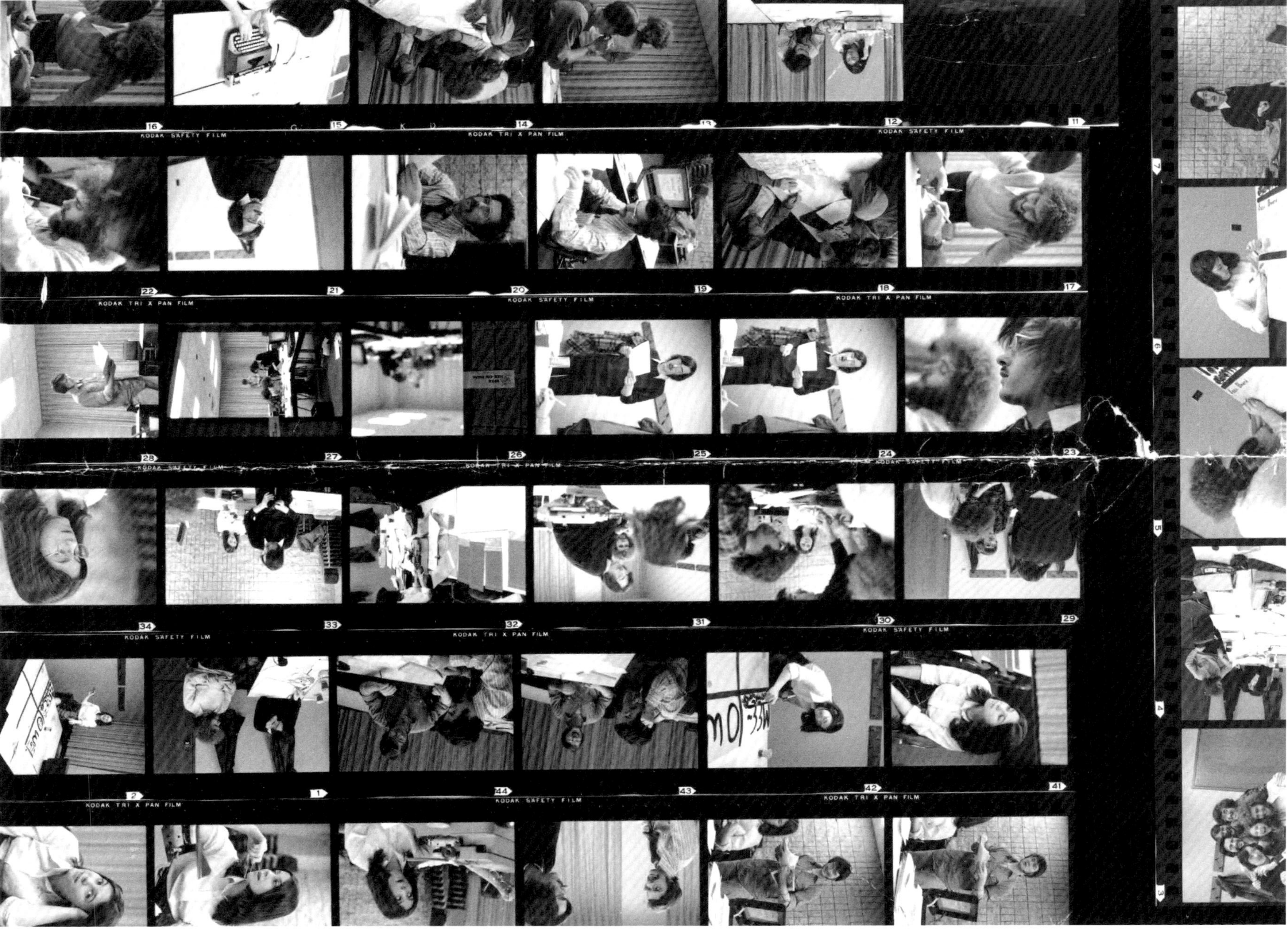

PAUL WARSHAUER AND ROD ORAM

1 Rebellion and Social Change

1974

The first year of the Mee-Ow Show was a wild ride.

With the cultural and political revolutions of the late ’60s and early ’70s swirling around their ears, students at Northwestern University built a performance space that put their ideas and expression at the forefront, a show to both respond and contribute to the world. As with any fledgling arts organization, figuring out what the Mee-Ow Show would become involved all sorts of obstacles, missteps, and a healthy dose of *what in the hell are we doing.*

Mee-Ow is still here because its first players stuck with it. Their hard work and big dreams and caffeine-fueled late nights kicked off the longest-running student-led, student-written, and student-produced improv, sketch comedy, and music show in US history.

Facing page: The first Mee-Ow Show in development

1974

MEE-OW YEAR ONE

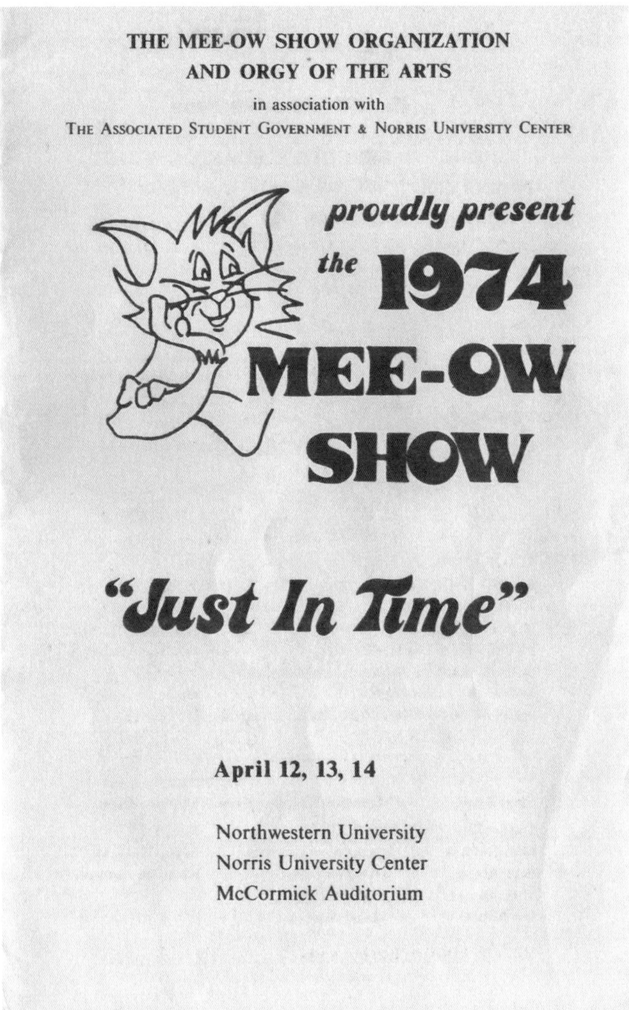

THE MEE-OW SHOW ORGANIZATION
AND ORGY OF THE ARTS
in association with
THE ASSOCIATED STUDENT GOVERNMENT & NORRIS UNIVERSITY CENTER
proudly present
the 1974
MEE-OW
SHOW
"Just In Time"
April 12, 13, 14
Northwestern University
Norris University Center
McCormick Auditorium

Just in Time

Friday through Sunday, April 12–14, at 8 p.m., McCormick Auditorium

The story of Mee-Ow begins with Ruth K. Hill.

Hill was an actor in Off-Broadway productions and took her son Joshua Lazar to musicals, dramas, and controversial avant-garde and African American theater productions. She had been a *Time* and *Life* correspondent during World War II and still had a press pass. "She would show up at the theaters unannounced, flash her press pass, and ask for the two complimentary tickets being held for her—a complete lie—while I cringed nearby," recalled Lazar. She always got them "with apologies from the manager because none of them wanted to make a potential reviewer angry. This went on my entire young adult life. I saw the original productions of everything—*My Fair Lady, Oliver,* Neil Simon plays, you name it. I owe my immersion in the theater to my mother, a great lady, and a wee bit of a con artist."

Lazar came to Northwestern University in the early 1970s in the midst of social and cultural upheaval that included the civil rights movement, years of protests against the war in Vietnam, and the trauma of political assassinations. It was particularly tumultuous on college campuses following the shooting of students at an anti-war rally at Kent State University in 1970 and the ending of draft deferments for full-time college students in September 1971; students with low draft lottery numbers were in class one day and gone the next. At Northwestern, massive student protests, including barricades across Sheridan Road, shut down campus. This resulted in a growing distrust between students and administration, especially in the creative disciplines. Art is a response to the times, and across the country, artists were responding in new and innovative ways. *Hair* debuted on Broadway; *Tommy* was conceived as an album-length rock opera by the Who; and the Beatles' *Sgt. Pepper* changed the understanding of rock and popular music storytelling.

Students were hungry for self-expression. They wanted to be heard. They wanted to write, create, and perform.

THIS YEAR IN HISTORY

Watergate • Vietnam War winding down • Nixon's second term • Comet Kohoutek • Sears Tower • Patty Hearst kidnapped • Dow Jones year-end close 616 • Average new car $4,440 • 1 gallon gas $0.53 • *Blazing Saddles* • Genesis, *The Lamb Lies Down on Broadway*; Joni Mitchell, *Court and Spark*

1974

The foremost theatrical production on campus at that time was the Waa-Mu Show, a musical variety show founded in 1929 by undergraduate Joe Miller, who continued to produce and direct the show after becoming Northwestern's dean of special events and director of student affairs. Waa-Mu, an acronym for the Women's Athletic Association and the Men's Union, two campus organizations that collaborated to present the first show, proved groundbreaking for its time and contributed to Northwestern's world-class theater and performance reputation. The show was ostensibly written and performed by students; however, Miller's forty-year control deeply impacted their original work.

As Lazar recalled,

> By my junior year I had seen one or two Waa-Mu shows. I have a lot of respect for the work that went into these shows, and the kids who were in them had great talent, so I will not describe here my rather strong reaction to these shows other than to say I was disappointed. I had seen the wealth of great creative talent at NU—in the theater and dance productions, in the dorms where talented singers and songwriters like the late and very talented Michele Marsh played. So much talent, yet it seemed Waa-Mu had put a stranglehold on the students to produce a sanitized, *Leave It to Beaver* "doo-wa" show that had nothing to do with the scope of the students' real talent or the fact that we were in the middle of a cultural revolution, and antiseptic-looking kids doing squeaky-clean sketches [that were] forty years outdated did not cut it.
>
> We needed another show. We needed Mee-Ow.

Lazar went to a meeting of the Associated Student Government (ASG) at the brand-new Norris University Center, which was essentially the student union, though it wasn't named as such. At the time, this naming decision was considered another example of the lack of trust between administration and students, likely due to the multiple instances of protestors occupying student unions on other campuses.

Lazar pitched his idea and asked for recognition of a new organization that would produce a show created entirely by student writers, directors, performers, and producers. The show would feature all forms of original creative expression, including—but not limited to—music, dance, singing, acting, comedy, and poetry.

The ASG officers asked about Lazar's staff, producer, director, and other practical information. He hadn't thought that far ahead, and failed to receive approval.

Pondering his next steps, Lazar thought of sophomore Paul Warshauer, a theater major with ambitions to write and direct, who had convinced the School of Speech to allow him to become Northwestern's first interdepartmental studies major. He served as the secretary and treasurer of House Three at the Foster-Walker Complex, a new campus residence center that offered ample space for community events, and he arranged for students to attend concerts, plays, and dinner events. He also produced Madame D's Coffee House, a showcase for student talent such as Michele Marsh singing and Lazar reading poetry and playing guitar. This coffeehouse production was, in effect, a precursor of the Mee-Ow Show.

"Paul's maturity as an organizer and producer—a guy who could *get things done*—was extraordinary," Lazar recalled. "He was a born Barnum and Bailey entrepreneur. When Paul said, 'Hey, we're gonna do this and this and this and this and we're gonna get it done in two days,' you were mesmerized. You believed him."

Lazar approached Warshauer and explained his idea. "You're the best producer I know," he said. "If anyone can do this, you can!"

Warshauer agreed to consider the possibility, and by the time they met again, he had embraced the role of cofounder. Lazar had named the show "MeeOw" to parody Waa-Mu and reference the Wildcat mascot. Warshauer added a hyphen to more closely parallel Waa-Mu.

They set a date for spring 1974 for the first Mee-Ow Show.

The First Meeting

Lazar and Warshauer decided to tread lightly, because Waa-Mu had a reputation for being ruthless toward any competition. Nevertheless, Lazar paid for a quarter-page ad in the October 8, 1973, edition of the student-run campus newspaper, the *Daily Northwestern*. It read "Had Enough of Waa-Mu?"

As Warshauer said at the time, "So much for trying to play nice."

They placed a second ad a week later, urging "All Those Creatively Inclined" to attend an informational meeting at Norris on October 17. It was surprisingly well attended.

Some students from Waa-Mu, having heard about the attempt to create a new show, attended to protest, arguing that the two shows would compete. Warshauer and Lazar explained how the shows would be different: the Mee-Ow authors and composers would have input into the final performance, while "Waa-Mu never afforded that privilege to any of their contributors." The Waa-Mu folks objected to this characterization but were overruled. Lazar made the case that all playwrights, musicians, writers, performers, and lyricists deserve respect, explaining his experiences of Off-Broadway theater and summarizing with the phrase, "Every man is an artist." Slowly, the crowd coalesced around the idea that Mee-Ow was not so much an anti-Waa-Mu show as it was an alternative to the status quo.

Warshauer asked if anyone had material to discuss. Several students spoke about current political events, such as Watergate and the Vietnam War. Others spoke about trends in contemporary music, film, and theater, including rock operas such as *Hair* and *Tommy*. And a few introduced ideas of a more absurdist nature. All ideas were treated with respect and enthusiasm.

Rick Kotrba recalls performing "a few snippets primarily of bits I had written for WNUR [the campus radio station], wanting to demonstrate that I could do a variety of voices and characters. The only one I still recall specifically was 'Jimmy Stewart for Blue Moon Chewing Tobacco.'"

Martin (Marty) Pasko had an idea for a sketch that had been rejected by Waa-Mu and asked if Mee-Ow would consider it: a game-show parody called "Let's Make a Wake," which Warshauer recalled as "morbidly funny." It was the first sketch approved for the show.

"At the first Mee-Ow meeting," Malcolm MacDonald recalled, "I was visited by the Muse. I quickly scribbled out an idea that hit me for a blackout sketch that was an update of the classic James Thurber bit about confusing the container for the thing contained, and I submitted it on the spot."

Official Recognition

When Lazar and Warshauer returned to the ASG in November to request recognition and funding as an official student organization, they learned that they needed a written constitution. As Warshauer recalled,

The first ad for the new Mee-Ow Show

HAD ENOUGH OF

WAA-MU?

Tired of Someone else running your show?

--Introducing--

The MEE-OW Show

Help Create N.U.'s only creative show.

For info. call:

JOSH LAZAR 475-1979

PAUL WARSHAUER 869-9726

> About fifteen of us gathered at Norris because we had to file the paperwork *that night*, or we would not be recognized for the 1973–1974 school year. No constitution, no Mee-Ow Show.
>
> I dragged in my manual Smith Corona typewriter and typed the constitution. I know we were under a deadline because the language is sloppy. Josh was busy studying for his finals. If he had seen the terrible job I had done, he would have torn up the document and started over.
>
> The group dictated some phrases that sound like the spirit of Mee-Ow now, fifty years later, but the rest was a hodgepodge. Still, we got it done at 6:45 p.m. I showed up at 7:00 and was told we needed *two* copies. The business office upstairs was closed, but somehow a door was open, and I used their copier. We returned in time, a vote occurred, and the Mee-Ow Show was officially recognized.

Radding's surrealist illustration for the program back cover, 1974

The new Mee-Ow Show was given an office and a locker in Norris and $500 in seed money. Warshauer told Lazar that they would need a lot more and proceeded to raise funds from other student groups, including a $500 donation from Orgy of the Arts.

Behind the Scenes

In the fall of 1973, Warshauer and Lazar interviewed potential directors, finally deciding on senior Jeff Wilson based on a paper he had written about original student productions that shared their vision of a student-created show. Wilson wrote a formal "Mee-Ow Manifesto" that included this statement of purpose:

> There is a need at Northwestern University for an independent forum of original works and talents. There is, and always will be, a need to allow artists of all sorts (performers, writers, composers, dancers, and musicians) the freedom that is due to them as artists.

That's when it dawned on Warshauer that the Mee-Ow Show was a bigger project than he had ever expected.

Meetings were already happening. Students were submitting material and volunteering to help. Warshauer printed stationery and helped art student Joe Radding screen-print T-shirts in the basement craft room. Radding also produced graphics and illustrations for posters and asked to be listed in the program as "Surrealist-in-Residence."

Warshauer and Lazar met with John Duffek, director of the Norris Center, and his assistant Sid Miller to discuss performing the show in the McCormick Auditorium. The auditorium was designed to be a lecture hall, not a performing arts space, but as Norris was a new building, there were not many scheduled events. The dates for the first show were formalized as April 12, 13, and 14, with a week of exclusive use beforehand for setup and rehearsal. In addition, when the space was dark, Mee-Ow could hold dance rehearsals and band practice. Music director George Lisle was ecstatic since he wanted as much time in the space as possible. His vision had grown from a single band into a thirteen-piece orchestra, with musical numbers requiring written arrangements. Several Waa-Mu student musicians worked as Mee-Ow arrangers, but under aliases so as not to upset Dean Miller.

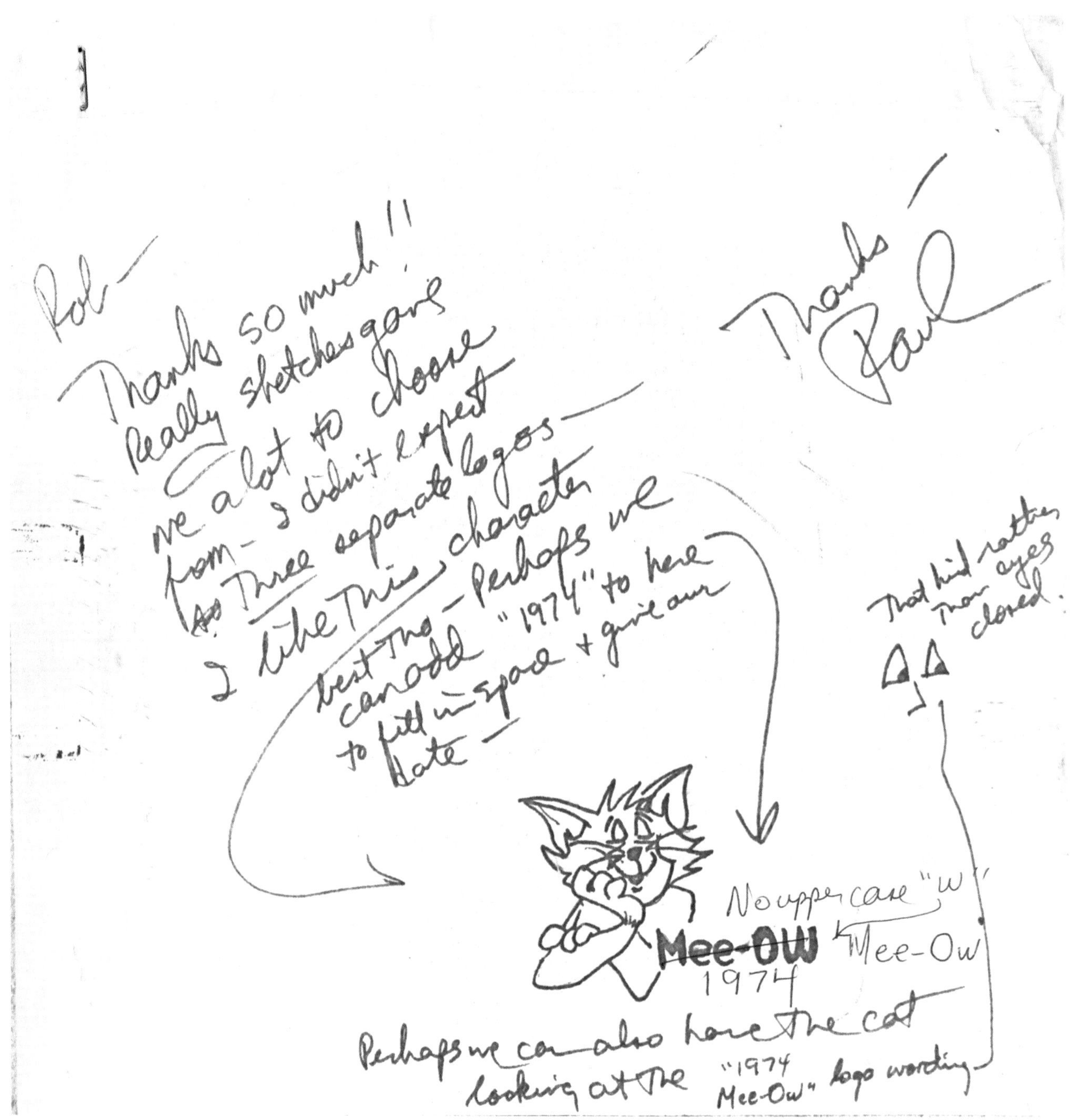

The first year's logo concept from Rob Maciunas with notes by Warshauer

Technical director and set designer Chris Rusch undertook the daunting tasks of designing and building a large set for the McCormick stage, and drew up plans for the platforms for the orchestra. The Mee-Ow Show would be the first real production in the lecture hall auditorium, so Warshauer asked senior Roy Lamberton to inspect the facility. Lamberton brought a few lighting students along, including Walter Olden, Mark Mongold, and Peter Rudoy, who asked, "No dimmers?" There was a dimmer board in the booth, but it had not been connected, and there was not nearly enough voltage to power the necessary lighting.

With no faculty advisor or clear regulations for student organizations, Warshauer assumed that as the producer of Mee-Ow he had the authority to issue purchase orders for equipment, supplies, and services, and he formally requested the rewiring of McCormick Auditorium "for additional amperage." The university would later send him a bill for $1,700, an expenditure which became the core of public controversy.

Developing the Show

During the fall and winter quarters, scripts were written on typewriters, duplicates were copied at Norris, and countless spiral notebooks and legal pads were filled with notes, cast selections, and sketch ideas.

A significant conflict arose between two different philosophies: Would the show honor its initial premise that authors' material would be respected by being performed as written, or would the director and performers be able to revise the material throughout the rehearsal process? The problems that arose from this disagreement were certainly exacerbated by the lack of show development time. But the lack of communication, as well as miscommunication, between the principals was a major contributing factor. In addition to technical difficulties, one reported incident occurred when Warshauer, having seen a rewritten sketch being performed by Bill Nuss and Dusty Kay, yelled, "What the hell was that? Those lines weren't in the script!" Nuss turned his back to Warshauer and replied, "I don't have to talk to you. If you have got any complaints, tell them to the director." Kay added muffled obscenities through a paper bag he was wearing over his head as part of his costume for the sketch. When Rick Kotrba, the author of the sketch, complained to Nuss, Nuss again replied, "I only talk to the director. Don't waste your breath."

Warshauer recalled a late night typing the first running list of songs, comedy routines, poems, and dance numbers on the same manual typewriter he'd used to write the Mee-Ow constitution. The show as proposed would run four and a half hours and would feature funny or absurdist comedy sketches, dance numbers, political satire, serious poetry, and folk songs. Wilson concluded that a unifying theme was necessary to bring these disparate elements together and created a storyline of traveling through time, hence the somewhat prophetic title of the first Mee-Ow Show: *Just in Time.*

Cast member and writer Rick Kotrba recalled:

> It was like joining a family—a cult, really—whose guru was Jeff Wilson, who was going to direct this show in a way that made us feel like we were a profound part of the still-dawning age of Aquarius. I found him reminiscent of Victor Garber in the 1973 film musical *Godspell*, traipsing around with his disciples. He was encouraging and appreciative of anything you did. One of his affectations was to manage to be convulsed with laughter without having any sound coming out. He led us in lots of improvisational games and also physical exercises. This was a lot of fun. I had never done improv before! Now, oddly, I don't think a single comedy bit in the show was born out of those games, but they caused us to bond. What did emerge, however, was the "connecting narrative" of the show involving a group of time travelers. I was not one of them, so I didn't pay much attention to that aspect of the show.

Wilson decided that the show would be narrated by a time-traveling doctor, similar to Doctor Who but without the regeneration capability, and the material was divided in a way that fit this new storyline. The first draft looked like this:

Opening: *Daydream through Time*

Scene 1. The Central Characters Meet Dr. Strong: *Searle Hall, Campus Capers, Waiting for . . . , The Congressman*

Scene 2. Time Machine Explanation: *To Make You Smile, The Baby Song, It Just Seems Funny, The Janitor*

Scene 3. Time Travel: *A Night at the Watergate, They'd Be Nothing without You, Inspector Mallomar, Photograph under a Frame, R = One Minus Cosine Theta*

Scene 4. The Experiment Breaks Down: *Shadows, Dream*

Scene 5. Performances by the Centrals: *Intermission Switch, Happiness Is a Full Tank of Gas, Dude's Boogie*

Scene 6. The Expedition: *Two Voices, Fat Rats, Monster Smash, Ma Bell*

Scene 7. Conclusion of the Experiment: *The Pier*

Scene 8: Art as Art, Conflict Resolution: *Or Perhaps It Will Rain, Little Old Mary's Dead, I'm Too Good for You, Schlepardy, A Dance by Debbie Gabor*

Scene 9. Denouement: *I Am a Clown, All My Songs, Knowing You*

Finale: *Somedays and Maybes*

Still, no one knew exactly what the hell would happen.

The show's structure remained in flux. By opening night, the order of some sketches and musical numbers had changed, and a couple of sketches and songs were replaced with others. "Inspector Mallomar," "Photograph under a Frame," "Happiness Is a Full Tank of Gas," and "Two Voices" were gone. Pasko's sketch, "Let's Make a Wake," the first accepted for the show and subsequently dropped, was once again in, as was the song "Feeling the Best That I've Known." "Fat Rats" and "Dude's Boogie" were moved to the first act.

On Wednesday nights, a core group of Mee-Ow friends, including Warshauer, Peter Lucas, Chris Rusch, and Joe Radding, would meet at the Big Pickle restaurant near campus. These informal meetings served as a much-needed bolster to the morale of the group. Each, in turn, explained their reasons for participating in Mee-Ow. Always the promoter, Warshauer continued to cheerlead the idea of a student-created show. He was outwardly positive and upbeat, but the stress was showing. Lucas, a pre-med biology major, was an avid audiophile, and appreciated the opportunity to engineer the show's sound as a much-needed break from his intense studies. Rusch, the theater design student, also appreciated supervising design and tech, rather than simply working on others' projects. Radding explained that he enthusiastically supported the original rebellious conception of the Mee-Ow Show as an alternative to the status quo, and that the juxtaposition of many seemingly incongruous elements proposed for the show was in keeping with a surrealist philosophy.

The Show Highlights

The room was packed. As the audience walked in they heard what Kotrba described as "a surreal audiotape." They were excited, but uncertain about what to expect.

With no curtain to be drawn, the attendees looked at the simple, modular stage setting. Rusch had designed the stage sets as a collection of movable platforms of varying sizes and heights, all painted the same brown. The backdrop was a large cloth the full height of the stage that served as a projection screen.

While the audience waited, they looked over the program. The front cover featured the first Mee-Ow Show cat logo, designed by Rob Maciunas. Radding's surreal illustration of a humanoid cat with elements of dance, music, film, art, and time travel appeared on the back. A cast of forty-one performers was credited as "The Company," with a board, staff, and crew of thirty-four, as well as a thirteen-piece orchestra, seven arrangers, and five accompanists.

Kotrba grabbed the audience's attention with his one-man preshow. Accompanied by an onstage reel-to-reel tape player playing music and sketches about cats, he ran up and down

1974

the aisles amusing the audience by reacting to the sounds. Some attendees considered this the funniest part of the night.

The show opened with the evocative ballad "Daydream through Time," written by Steve Humphrey. As performed by the orchestra, this opening number set an upbeat mood, but with an element of mystery.

Next, the audience met Dr. Strong, played by Ron Ensel in a white lab coat, and his companions, to whom he explained that he had invented a time machine with which they all could explore the wonders of the world.

An old industrial control panel with lighted buttons and switches, built into a modular set piece that could be moved on- and offstage as needed, served as the center of the time machine. The entirety of the rest of the stage was, in effect, the inside of the time machine, or "time ship," with the different times and places created by projections and changes in lighting color, placement, and shape.

Act 1 included "Fat Rats" by Bob Chimbel, about how the squirrels on Northwestern's campus were more prosperous than other squirrels, in keeping with the wealthy backgrounds of many alumni; "R = One Minus Cosine Theta," a love song for math nerds by Dan Guss that was to include a six-foot laser hologram and a dance-break duel with slide rules; the Pasko-written sketch "Let's Make a Wake," featuring Kotrba as ghoulish game-show host Mozzy Leum; and writers Doug Day and Phil Rosenberg's send-up of the Marx Brothers that parodied the Nixon administration's Watergate scandal, titled "A Night at the Watergate." President Nixon resigned later that year, so the sketch was timely and popular.

Music director Lisle wrote a tour de force jazz piece for the full orchestra called "Dude's Boogie" that brought the house down at every performance.

Lisle arranged the tune "To Make You Smile" by Guss to use as the entr'acte. Jim Page wrote and delivered some serious poetry, and Lazar sang "Little Old Mary's Dead."

The second act also included the sketch "Schlepardy" by Kotrba, featuring Nuss as a game-show host and Kay as a mafioso in witness protection wearing a paper bag over his head.

The show concluded with the song "Somedays and Maybes," written by Chimbel, which summarized the theme of the show.

The cast took a bow together. There were no curtain calls.

Opening night lasted three hours.

The cast performing "Somedays and Maybes" during the first year's finale

Reviews

Just in Time played to sold-out audiences and garnered decidedly mixed reviews. In a piece titled "Mee-Ow, Good Idea But Schmaltzy, Trite Production," in the April 16 edition of the *Daily Northwestern*, Steve Siegel wrote,

> It wouldn't be especially difficult to pan the Mee-Ow show, entitled "Just in Time," which was presented here last weekend. Shows of its type are easy to blast.
>
> But somehow, in this case, it seems useless to just say the songs were schmaltzy, the comedy often trite and the whole thing rather camp. It's true. But that's not the point.
>
> Mee-Ow began as a rebellion against the banality and complacency of Northwestern's only student-produced show, Waa-Mu. Furthermore, certain students felt—with justification—that this show had become less than "student produced."
>
> The idea of a free-form revue is to give students with talent a chance to create and perform. This implies some amateurism and less than perfect professional cohesiveness.
>
> The major reason for doing an original student musical-comedy revue ought to be for fun. It shouldn't have to be a large-scale artistic endeavor. The people who produce it should have as good a time as those who watch it.
>
> From that point of view, Mee-Ow is a success. Not a howling success, but judging from the response of those present at the Saturday evening performance (during the performance—not their comments afterwards) the show worked. . . . Mee-Ow does prove that students can do something new and on their own initiative, which is a very hopeful sign. If nothing else, the show had a more than generous supply of spirit and on this campus that's a valuable commodity.

That last sentiment was perhaps best described by Wilson in a letter that he sent to every member of the cast and crew:

> I value the friendships and experiences of this year's show more than any I've ever worked on. I learned a great deal about working with people—both within and without the organization, and got some good ideas about making dreams come true. I hope some of the things we learned about commitment and communication can continue and grow throughout the creation of future Mee-Ows, and will hopefully lead to the establishment of an art form worthy of the title.

Ken Elliott as Groucho and Rick Kotrba as Nixon in "A Night at the Watergate" (*left*); Warshauer watching auditions in Norris University Center (*right*)

Clockwise from top left: Dance rehearsal in Scott Hall; set construction on stage; musical rehearsal in Scott Hall; musical rehearsal in Scott Hall; dress rehearsal in McCormick Auditorium

1974

After the Show

Mee-Ow presented two events to raise money to cover its outstanding debt of $1,700 for rewiring McCormick Auditorium. The first was called a "Beer-haus"—a coffeehouse, but with beer—called *Folks at Home,* which featured live music performances in Willard Hall and raised a small sum. The second was the dinner theater production *Don't Drink the Water,* a joint presentation of Garden Party Productions and the Mee-Ow Show in the Louis Room at Norris. A quarter-page ad in the *Daily Northwestern* read, "Woody Allen and Chicken Tetrazzini for Under $5!" The show ultimately lost money, ironically due to the cost of rewiring the Louis Room for theatrical purposes.

This additional electrical work order, along with the $1,700 it cost to rewire McCormick Auditorium for the first Mee-Ow Show, raised questions at the ASG about who was supervising Mee-Ow's books, and Warshauer, Lazar, and Kay were eventually charged by the University Hearing and Appeals System with "Overspending on a Student Show." Lazar and Kay agreed to a conciliation, but the ASG was unable to reconcile differences with Warshauer. Though his friends testified on his behalf (one even made buttons that said "Free the Warshauer $1700"), it was still a difficult time for Warshauer, who withdrew from Northwestern in February 1975 after resigning from Mee-Ow the previous fall.

In an open letter in the *Daily Northwestern* on October 31, 1974, he wrote:

> I dared to dream about an ideal and will never regret it! I will never regret taking a huge chance with a show that had very little promise from the very beginning. But we shared our dream and at the end nearly 90 other people became directly involved with our show. More important than this final product were the concepts and spirit generated by the show. Even though we represented a "radical" theater faction, no one save for illness or serious academic or scheduling problems resigned before that final curtain went up to three full houses last April. Even though we had all the cards stacked against us, an apathetic theater people clique, and uncompleted script, un-orchestrated music and some minor technical problems, the show went on because people took a chance, worked hard, and they dared to dream.
>
> I encourage many people to stay, or get involved, in Mee-Ow. It is theoretically the best possible show to work on as performers, writers, composers, or musicians. I only hope and pray that those people running the show this year will never lose sight of Mee-Ow's original concept, a concept that I have tried to observe: To work directly and openly with all student artists.

Free
The
Warshauer
$1700

Warshauer at one of the hearings

STATEMENT OF PURPOSE

The concept of the Mee-Ow Show is to present student designed art in many forms of artistic expression. Our desire is to work closely with all staff to afford the best possible presentation. In so working, especially with writers and musicians, we are conscious of the fact that artistic compromises can be made, thus, Mee-Ow appears as an artistic group effort.

Our creed then, runs along with the thoughts of Henry Miller who said, "Everyman is an artist," a concept often lost in the world of the theatre. We therefore respect the artistic freedom of all members involved in the show.

Mee-Ow began in October as a seed, and has grown and blossomed into a show of larger proportions than we ever imagined. The show, regardless of its tangible appearance, has been a dream for a great number of artists whose work you shall see today. A dream that would allow them to work and perform in an atmosphere of co-operation, where cast, musicians, staff and crew have all worked together towards the final creation of many new, and different forms.

PAUL WARSHAUER AND JOSH LAZAR
Creators and Producers

At this point in time, one must wonder what to say, in one paragraph, that will adequately grasp the toil, anguish, joy and love that was and is Mee-Ow 1974. The production itself is living proof of the creativity and effort that brought the show from conception to fruition in only half a year.

The formation of Mee-Ow as an entirely student organization has been an incredible learning experience—filled with excitement, frustrations, friendships, "production problems," boundless enthusiasm, and much more. The innumerable sleepless nights and the energy-packed days of rehearsal and preparation have served immensely to bring all of us together into a close, happy family.

The opportunities for cooperation, commitment, and involvement have shown everyone the results possible when fully exercising our individual and group potential. Despite the countless revisions, adjustments, sacrifices, and improvements that have been made during the development of the production, a powerful story has grown and flourished, incorporating separate elements of all forms (dramatic literature, humor, music, choreography, poetry, artistic innovations, cinema, and technical excellence).

Mee-Ow 1974 tells the story of one man's attempts to discover the motivating forces of today's world. I invite you to join in this quest, relax, and let your imagination run wild.

J.W.

From the first Mee-Ow Show program

The Arts Alliance

In April 1974, after the conclusion of the Mee-Ow Show, Warshauer had the idea to merge all student performing-arts organizations together to form an alliance that would share a common calendar, funding, marketing, and promotions. He called the meeting with a handful of groups, including the Dolphin Show, the Gilbert and Sullivan Guild, Garden Party Productions, Orgy of the Arts, and the NU Dance Company. They quickly drafted a constitution and filed with the ASG to be a student organization.

The first formal board meeting of the Northwestern University Arts Alliance was held in September 1974 in Warshauer's apartment. The groups all agreed to maintain their own identities and logos, but no one was sure how finances would be managed. Warshauer proposed a giant pot of money generated by all the shows, with each show being able to draw out what it needed per production. In that way, there would always be money coming in and going out at different times of the year. All in attendance agreed.

The Arts Alliance is now the oldest student-run arts group at Northwestern University and has grown to become one of the largest student arts organizations in the country. Its annual season consists of special events throughout the year and three mainstage productions, including the Mee-Ow Show.

2 Survival and Stumble

1975–1983

Following the mixed reviews and financial problems of the first show, no one was certain that Mee-Ow would continue. The next several years were a time of trial and error, experimenting with different formats and finding what was true to Mee-Ow. This came with its fair share of disagreements, primarily about the direction of the show. Should they continue with the original concept of "all creators welcome," including dance, poetry, and music? Or should they stick to comedy?

Long story short: comedy prevailed.

Music and improv found their home as well.

During these years, Mee-Ow persevered through all sorts of growing pains and controversies. It also became a professional launching pad for cast and crew members who went on to The Second City, *Saturday Night Live*, and other entertainment careers.

Facing page: Mark Lancaster and Laura Matalon from the 1982 cast

1975

MEE-OW YEAR TWO

What Did You Expect?

Friday, February 28, at 8 p.m.; Saturday and Sunday, March 1–2, at 8 p.m., McCormick Auditorium

Dusty Kay and Bill Nuss took the reins as codirectors and coproducers, initially thinking they should "burn it all down and start over."

"We didn't, for two reasons," Nuss said. "One: we liked the title 'Mee-Ow' because it played off of Waa-Mu and the Northwestern cat. And two: Curtis Katz's logo."

Katz was a cast member and also a cartoonist. "He came to us with a drawing of a cat that had been beat to shit, that was on a crutch, and with a bandage and stars over his head," Nuss continued. "So, we decided, OK, let's keep Mee-Ow."

Kay and Nuss agreed that the 1975 show would be edgier and more contemporary than the previous year, and that they would take it in an entirely comedic direction. "I was invited to be in the cast and to make sure that we included the most outstanding content possible, with the title of comedy coordinator," Rick Kotrba recalled. "Maybe the laughs that they received during my 1974 sketch 'Schlepardy' gave Nuss and Dusty faith in my ability to pass judgment on what material to include. It was also useful to have a third person in the hierarchy who could serve as a tie-breaker if there was a conflict over some creative detail concerning the show. The third leg in a stool is pretty important."

They held their first organizational meeting on October 23, which "writers, composers, performers, and techies must attend!" Soon after came open auditions, where aspirants would tell jokes and participate in improv games. Kathy Kirshenbaum recalls singing "This Is My Country" very loudly and intentionally off-key. Scott Harlan Rothburd, a freshman in the theater department who had auditioned unsuccessfully for Waa-Mu, joined the cast of Mee-Ow and wrote for the show. Since the very beginning of the Mee-Ow Show, writers were in the cast, and the cast wrote the show.

In addition to the returning coproducers and codirectors Bill Nuss and Dusty Kay, who also performed, the final cast of returning performers

THIS YEAR IN HISTORY

Margaret Thatcher elected leader of UK Conservative Party • Vietnam War ends • Suez Canal reopens • Unemployment 9% • US recession ends • Dow Jones year-end close 852 • Average new car $4,950 • 1 gallon gas $0.57 • *Jaws*, *The Rocky Horror Picture Show*, *Monty Python and the Holy Grail*, *Tommy*, *The Stepford Wives* • Paul Simon, *Still Crazy After All These Years*; Bruce Springsteen, *Born to Run*; Fleetwood Mac, *Fleetwood Mac*

1975

included comedy coordinator Rick Kotrba, Wendy Gajewski, and Wendy Taucher. New cast members were Carol Appleby, Mike Bonner, Eloise Jane Coopersmith, Betsy Fink, Thomas Fitzgerald, David Garrett, Neal Gold, Roy Alan Hine, Michelle Holmes, Laurie Karon, Curtis Katz, Kathy Kirshenbaum, Kitty Knecht, Charlie Lucci, Jeff Lupetin, Jane McClary, Brad Mott, Lisa Nesselson, Karen Alison Pepper, Keith Reddin, and Scott Rothburd.

In what became an enduring practice, everyone pitched possible titles. Kotrba suggested "What Did You Expect?," and there was "an immediate roar of consensus that embraced it."

Challenges

Money was the biggest challenge. "Nuss and Dusty came to me with the request to help Mee-Ow stay alive," said Ira Deutchman, chairman of the Activities and Organizations Board, Northwestern's student-run entertainment programming board. "They made the case that if they had the support of an organization like A&O, they could make a go of it." Deutchman set conditions on funding Mee-Ow, specifically that the budget would not be controlled by its directors. Consequently, the 1975 Mee-Ow Show was presented by A&O, and Deutchman was listed as the executive producer.

There is a difference!

We are dedicated to:

- creating and presenting various kinds of high entertainment to the Northwestern community.
- presenting a fantastic show in the spring of original student material, written, composed, produced and directed by Northwestern students.
- entertaining and enlightning the current N.U. student body, faculty and friends.
- And most importantly--we are sincerely dedicated towards working directly and openly with all student "artists", be they writers, composers, performers or technical theatre people.

Our Show Board for 1975

DIRECTOR........David Wohl
PRODUCER........Dusty Kay
MUSICAL DIRECTOR........Bill Hinden
COMEDY COORDINATOR........Rick Kotrba
CHORAL DIRECTOR........Kip Snyder
ASST. MUSIC DIRECTOR and CONDUCTOR........George Lisle
Co-TECHNICAL DIRECTOR and SET DESIGNER........Chris Rusch
Co-TECHNICAL DIRECTOR and LIGHTING DESIGNER........Mark Mongold
COSTUME CONSULTANT........Karen Wheeler
ARTIST IN RESIDENCE........Joseph Radding

PRESIDENT OF MEE-OW ORGANIZATION
Paul Warshauer
SPECIAL EVENTS MANAGER
Wendy Nadler

IMPORTANT ORGANIZATIONAL MEETING

Discussion of concepts and themes for '75 show

WED.-OCT. 23-7 PM - NORRIS 2G

— ALL MATERIAL FOR THE SHOW IS DUE NOV. 15 —

Announcement that appeared in the *Daily Northwestern*

There was also the ongoing technical challenge of lighting. Union electricians had installed theater lighting with a type of plug that, while in accordance with code, was incompatible with standard rented lighting used in theaters. Mark Mongold recalled that before every show in McCormick Auditorium, he and other lighting techs would spend hours in the rafters replacing and rewiring the nonstandard plugs with theater-appropriate plugs. Then, after the show, they would spend hours reversing the process so that the fire marshal wouldn't discover the substitution and shut down further productions.

MEE-OW NOW!
CL Kat 75
TONIGHT, TOMORROW, AND SUNDAY
8:00 p.m. in McCormick Aud.
Tickets STILL available
at the Norris Info Desk for only $2.00
Aren't you just a little bit curious?

Every theatrical production has its challenges during rehearsal. Kotrba recalled a particularly difficult night where Kay, visibly frustrated, said there would not be a Mee-Ow Show and stormed out of the room:

> What happened next is one of the proudest moments of my life. As the cast members started putting on their coats, I told everybody to stop and advocated that we were, in fact, going to do the show even if it was sans Dusty, and so we resumed the rehearsal. An hour later he walked in the room and sheepishly offered a profuse apology, saying that if he'd returned and there was nobody there, it really would have been the end of Mee-Ow. So, I hope you can see why I have always thought of myself as the guy who saved the Mee-Ow Show.

The Show Highlights

McCormick Auditorium in the Norris Center was packed, with people standing in the back and sitting on the floor. Nuss recalled that Dr. Leslie Hinderyckx, chair of the theater department, and theater professor Robert Schneiderman had to sit in the aisles because no more tickets were available.

The program for *What Did You Expect?* included a statement from the directors:

> This show is not the work of the same tired faces you've seen gracing Northwestern stages over and over again. And there's a reason for that. They all quit.
>
> In all, 15 people, mostly MEE-OW Executive Board members, have quit the show since October. They range from actors to the original director. Their reasons range from the material was too dirty, to they were having trouble with their girlfriend. In short, loyalty and commitment have not been MEE-OW '75's strongpoint.
>
> We've gone through hell to put together this show. Because of production problems, because of the stupidity with which MEE-OW '74 was run, MEE-OW '75 had lost the full support of student government

and University funding. It seemed like everybody in the world tried to stop the show from coming off. How close they came, they'll never fully realize.

But now, all excuses are bullshit. MEE-OW '75 will stand on its own. You either like it or you don't. We think it's a statement on only one thing. What is contemporary entertainment.

The program went on to credit twenty-six performers, an orchestra of eleven, and a staff of dozens. It also included a note about the creation and content of the show, which became the model for Mee-Ow going forward:

> The comedy portion of this year's MEE-OW SHOW was developed predominantly through improvisation. The material you see tonight represents the cast's ability to function as an ensemble. In short, it is their show.

The night opened with "What Did You Expect?," a musical number by Karen Alison Pepper, whose lyrics ended with a surprising payoff: "What . . . did . . . you . . . ex—" *Blackout.*

Act 1 included a three-part sketch about Batman and Robin starring Keith Reddin and Brad Mott; a song about Linda Lovelace by Bob Chimbel; and "Oz Patrol," featuring Rick Kotrba as police sergeant Joe Friday from *Dragnet* arriving in Munchkinland to investigate a murder. Curtis Katz played the Munchkin, Jane McClary played Glinda, Jeff Lupetin played Detective Bill Gannon, Betsy Fink played Dorothy, and Mike Bonner was the Scarecrow. The deadpan, monotone Friday asked Glinda, "Are you a good witch or a bad witch?" She replied, "You'll never know, copper!"

The first act ended with a sketch called "Noodles for Bic Butane," featuring Dusty Kay as a stoner named Noodles who endorsed the reliability of Bic Butane lighters (act 2 included "Noodles at Burger King," where he recommends the restaurant for when you get the munchies). It was later performed on *The Phil Donahue Show* and taped for a national showing at WGN-TV, after which Nuss contacted Bic's US headquarters and discovered that, contrary to his expectations, they loved the sketch. They even sent him a box of lighters.

A highlight of the night was Nuss and Kay's "Who's on First?" Styled after the famous Abbott and Costello baseball bit, their version was a conversation about the names of rock bands, including the Who, and later appeared on the TV show *Eight Is Enough.* They had originally written it for the 1974 Waa-Mu Show, where it had been heavily edited and rewritten, or in their words, "butchered." In a note in the 1975 Mee-Ow program, they wrote, "We feel that the greatest comment we can make on the Waa-Mu system is to present the material again as it was intended to be performed."

Reviews

What Did You Expect? sold out all three performances, and Kay recalls a "thumbs up" from Les Hinderyckx in the hallway outside McCormick Auditorium after the show.

In his review in the *Daily Northwestern*, Steve Siegel wrote:

> In a sense, it was as though there were two shows going on alternately on the same stage. One that was generally funny, crazy, wry and satirical and another that was schmaltzy . . . cliched, and actually embarrassing to sit through. . . . I can only point out that there was something good going on part of the time. The audience knew it and could appreciate it, simply and without any reservation. Now, it's just important to understand what it was and consider it.

Codirectors Bill Nuss and Dusty Kay

1976

MEE-OW YEAR THREE

THE ARTS ALLIANCE AND A&O BOARD

Bill Nuss and Mike Baron

Executive Producers

Proudly Present

The MEE-OW SHOW 1976

"SPIRIT, MY ASS"

WITH

Peter Bales	Betsy Fink
Alice Tell	Jeff Lupetin
Stew Figa	Kyle Heffner

KEITH REDDIN

Produced By Bruce Martz and Dusty Kay

Directed By Dusty Kay

Spirit, My Ass

Thursday through Sunday, March 4–7, at 8 p.m., McCormick Auditorium

Planning for the 1976 Mee-Ow Show began in the fall of 1975, with Dusty Kay directing on his own since Bill Nuss was doing an independent study in the Virgin Islands. Upon his return to campus for winter quarter, however, Nuss assumed the role of executive producer, along with A&O chair Mike Baron.

Every fall the Waa-Mu Show performed highlights from their recent show during new student week, which eventually became known as "Wildcat Welcome." In the fall of 1975, the Mee-Ow Show also performed.

The selected sketch featured Betsy Fink being chased by Curtis Katz, who portrayed a flasher wearing black shoes, socks, and a trench coat over underwear. Brad Mott played the head of NU security Wayne Luttrell being interviewed by a *Daily Northwestern* reporter and oblivious to Fink, who repeatedly blew on a rape whistle, the use of which had been heavily promoted by campus security in response to assaults on campus. The sketch ended as a whistle finally caught his attention, except the whistle didn't belong to Fink. It belonged to the Sandwich Man.

Developing the Show

The final cast of the 1976 Mee-Ow Show included director Dusty Kay, executive producer Bill Nuss, Peter Bales, Stew Figa, Betsy Fink, Kyle T. Heffner, Jeff Lupetin, Keith Reddin, and Alice Tell.

The original cast had been much larger.

Kay took his responsibility to build on the success of the previous year very seriously. He organized the cast into groups to develop sketches through improvisation, but during the rehearsal process he worried that some of them were "stalled," not "gelling." Nuss recalls Kay trying to encourage them, but after another rehearsal went by with groups returning without anything that Kay considered usable, he reportedly fired several people.

THIS YEAR IN HISTORY

US Bicentennial • First Concorde passenger flights • First space shuttle, the *Enterprise* • Dow Jones year-end close 1005 • Average new car $5,416 • 1 gallon gas $0.59 • *Taxi Driver*, *Rocky*, *All the President's Men*, *Network*, *Carrie*, *Silent Movie* • Stevie Wonder, *Songs in the Key of Life*; Ramones, *Ramones*; Eagles, *Hotel California*

1976

In a *Daily Northwestern* article on March 3, 1976, the day before the first performance, Richard Eisenberg wrote, "Until Feb. 19, the show had twelve cast members, who all wrote and performed the materials. But come the first performance, March 4, Mee-Ow will have an ensemble of seven performers. What happened to the other five Mee-Ow members, including one of the two original comedy coordinators?"

Kay replied, "No comment. It just didn't work out. Their material is no longer in the show."

One unnamed "fired" performer is quoted in the article saying, "It's all still mystic to me. Dusty asked four of us to leave, and the fifth left because of the other four. The decision was entirely Dusty's, and it came as a complete surprise to all of us."

Of the remaining seven performers, five were men. "The cast is predominantly males on purpose," the article continues, "because Kay says he wanted to use the 'basic formula' used in the Chicago comedy troupe Second City."

Reddin had vivid memories:

> I remember very strongly that Dusty [said] it was just too much. Too many voices, too many people. Not that he was dictatorial or suppressing other people's ideas, but I think he wanted a more coherent show. I do remember there was a feeling of let's not get too slick, let's not get too organized, let's keep it raw. And I

The Sandwich Man

The Sandwich Man was the pseudonym of William "Bill" Froehlig. Long before the advent of vending machines in dorms, the Sandwich Man, accompanied by his dog, made the rounds of campus housing pulling a wooden cart full of homemade sandwiches for sale. When he arrived at a residence hall or fraternity house, he whistled a distinctive three-note pattern.

Several Mee-Ow Shows have included sketches referencing the Sandwich Man, who was more of an entrepreneur than was commonly understood. Cast member Mark Gunnion of the 1983 Mee-Ow Show explained:

> After I graduated, trying to gather travel money to get out of Evanston, I worked for [the Sandwich Man] that summer. And what he had besides the truck on campus, is he delivered these handmade sandwiches to every 7-Eleven in the Chicagoland area. I was one of three van drivers, my two best friends were the other two van drivers. We each had three routes. We worked six days a week and went twice a week to a third of the 7-Elevens in Chicago. We had to count which [sandwiches] were there and replace them. And he also supplied all the Slurpees for those [stores] because he came up with exotic flavors. He would mix two of them and call it Papaya Punch or something. So he had this giant vat that my two friends often had to climb into and scrub like once a month. And he sold the giant pressurized tanks. His operation was somewhere on the west side of Evanston.

Jon Freedman wrote and directed a 1981 documentary about the Sandwich Man that aired on Chicago's WTTW television series *Image Union*. Froehlig retired in 1988 and passed away in 2018.

1976

The 1976 cast: Peter Bales, Jeff Lupetin, Keith Reddin, Stew Figa, Kyle Heffner, and Betsy Fink

do remember that there was some pushback with some of the other people and Dusty early on saying, "What is our tone? How are we going forward? How are we doing sketches, who does what sketches? How do we bring the sketches in? How are they developed? Who has the final say?" I was one of those people who thought, I'm just going to keep my head down and do the comedy and not get involved in politics. But sadly, I do remember that as it went on, there was a real battle for the spirit and the structure and the shape of it. I remember Dusty was saying, "Well, we can't do as much, we can't have as many people. We really need to focus it. It should be a tighter show. It should be a show that's more accessible to people." He was taking the reins, and [it was perceived as a] kind of power play, and that rubbed a lot of people the wrong way.

Others enjoyed the rehearsal process. It was fun, Heffner recalled, "I mean, it was a genre that I was really comfortable in. And, you know, I was [thinking] I found my tribe. I was in some really good company with hysterical people. And we all just really fed off of each other and put the show together. [We used] the system where we would just do sketches and improvise, and it was all recorded on a little cassette tape machine and then pieced together."

The year 1976 was the United States bicentennial, and this celebration dominated the media. That year's Waa-Mu Show was named *That's the Spirit!* Consequently, despite an intentional move away from referencing the Waa-Mu Show each year, when the suggestion was made to title the Mee-Ow Show *Spirit, My Ass*, the choice was approved unanimously.

1976

The Show Highlights

The 1976 Mee-Ow Show was sponsored by Garden Party Productions and the A&O Board. The show omitted musical numbers that were not specifically parody.

One sketch, called "The Philosophy OD," centered on an emergency help line, similar to a suicide prevention line but for people who were "overdosing" on philosophy. Heffner explained, "I was taking Intro to Contemporary Philosophy, so I was studying Hume and all the rest of those contemporary philosophers. I wouldn't say I was a writer, I wasn't sitting there banging out the words with them. But when we started improvising, [because] I'm in the middle of this class I was pretty good with the lingo at that point. So I was able to improvise [about philosophy] and that's how that [sketch] came about."

FROM THE DIRECTOR...

Seven weeks ago, this show did not exist. Through improvisation, we have developed what you will see here tonight. This form of theatre offers the actor the unique opportunity of not only playing a character, but of creating it as well. In many ways, these cast members are the most complete performers you will see on this campus, participating both in a primary art and an interpretive art simultaneously.

Improvisation, however, is not merely an exercise for the actor. Its primary goal is entertainment for the audience. This entertainment is born out of identification of self in a familiar situation—or the exaggerated extension of self in an absurd situation. Whatever the cause, the result is the veiwer's irresistable impulse to enjoy.

That's the spirit of the Mee-Ow Show. "Spirit, My Ass" should not be construed as a statement of American society. Rather, it is a statement about the people and lifestyles found in that society. During its presentation, we hope you, the audience, see yourselves as the gently comic figures on which this show is based. For if we all have one common spirit, it is not the ability to laugh at ourselves, but the ability to want to.

Dusty

Dusty

From the 1976 show program

1977

MEE-OW YEAR FOUR

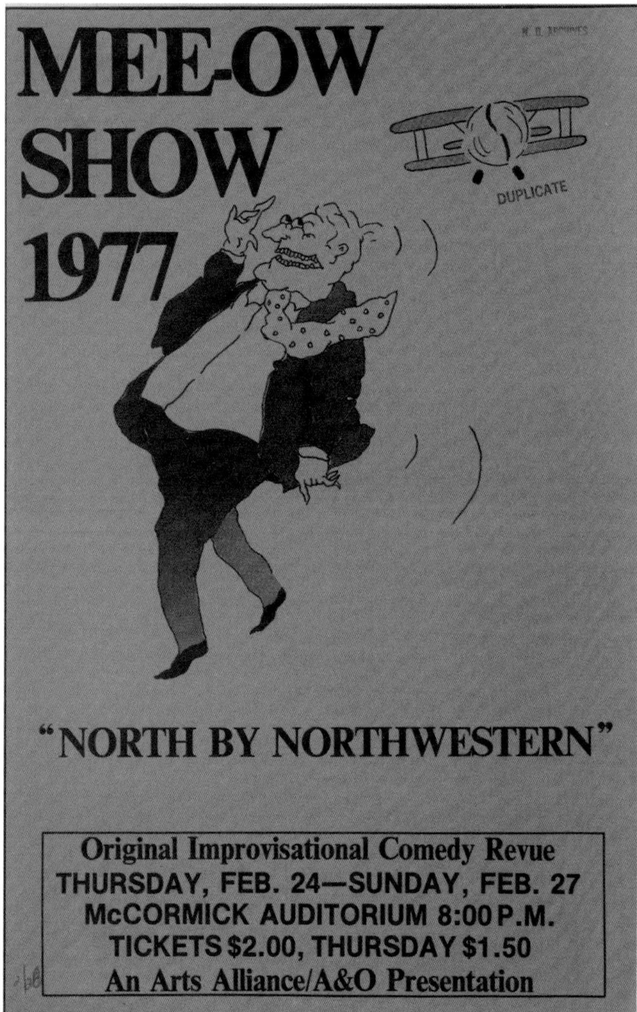

North by Northwestern

Thursday through Sunday, February 24–27, at 8 p.m., McCormick Auditorium

The 1977 Mee-Ow Show was the first to have none of the cast members who had been in the first show in 1974. It also represented a change in mood from the "edgier and more contemporary" shows, as Bill Nuss called them, to something that has been variously described as a "hippie sensibility" and a John Belushi style of physical, rambunctious, almost anarchic humor. Also, a short film was added to the performances, along with improv games informed by audience suggestions.

Casting the Show

An ongoing challenge for Mee-Ow and other student-produced and -directed shows at the time was the casting resolution of Waa-Mu Show director Tom Roland, who succeeded longtime director Joe Miller. Essentially, this policy meant that students who auditioned for officially sanctioned University Theatre productions as well as other shows would be effectively blacklisted from University Theatre shows if they accepted a role in another production.

In a letter in the *Daily Northwestern* (October 26, 1976), Philip A. Kraus, the student director of the Gilbert and Sullivan Guild, expressed frustration with Roland's policy that "U.T. productions come first," rather than "a theater student's own personal development of his craft." In the same issue, Arts Alliance cochairman Stew Figa wrote, "An actor has the inherent right to decide whether or not a role is valuable for him, a waste of time, or, perhaps, even harmful."

Students had to choose. Would they commit to only audition for and perform in official University Theatre productions? Or would they choose to perform in Mee-Ow?

Due to resistance from the students, and likely also due to the participation of talented students Dana Olsen and Allison Burnett in both Waa-Mu and Mee-Ow, the casting resolution was soon dropped, or at least ignored.

The December 3, 1976, call for auditions in the *Daily Northwestern* first mentioned the title of the

THIS YEAR IN HISTORY

Jimmy Carter inaugurated • Panama Canal Treaty signed • NYC blackout • *Roots* on TV • Elvis Presley dies • Dow Jones year-end close 831 • Average new car $5,813 • 1 gallon gas $0.62 • *Star Wars*, *Close Encounters of the Third Kind*, *Annie Hall*, *Pumping Iron*, *Saturday Night Fever* • Fleetwood Mac, *Rumours*; Billy Joel, *The Stranger*; The Clash, *The Clash*; The Sex Pistols, *Never Mind the Bollocks, Here's the Sex Pistols*

1977

1977 show as "North by Northwestern," which had already been chosen by the returning cast, director, and producer. Auditions consisted mostly of improv games, although some people presented prepared material.

Kyle T. Heffner, a returning cast member, remembered newcomer Dana Olsen from high school speech competitions: "I thought he was the funniest guy I'd ever seen. I still remember some of his jokes and his original comedy. And then [my] sophomore year, [Dana] came through my dorm, Willard, with a high school senior tour group. And I saw him and I was like, 'Dana, Dana! Are you thinking about NU?' And he said, 'Yeah.' I said, 'Come here, man. There's so much opportunity. And there's a thing called the Mee-Ow Show that you have to do.' "

Olsen continued the story:

> So flash forward a year, and I'm there [at Northwestern] and I don't know if I had it in my mind, I don't even know if I remembered that he told me the words "Mee-Ow," but I saw an ad in the *Daily Northwestern* about open auditions for Mee-Ow. And the guys that I was living with were mixing up screwdrivers on that particular afternoon. So I drank a couple of screwdrivers to work up my courage. And I went over to the auditions and I'm sure I bumped into Kyle. It was on a Friday afternoon, which was kind of an odd thing. And there were a pile of people there. So they threw me into an improvisation. I don't even know if they gave us a premise, to be honest with you. All I remember is the first thing that I did at the audition, they put me with a freshman girl who was not funny, and so I was just doing whatever I could out of self-preservation to try to get a laugh out of Bales and the assistant director or whoever else was there watching it. All I recall is that very first one. But I remember that I got some laughs. So I left there thinking I did OK, and then I got the callback for Saturday and that was an all-day, arduous callback. I remember working with Kyle Heffner. We did the usual improv games. Then they started throwing premises at us, and they threw some musical premises at us. And then I worked with Tom Virtue. I remember that was a long day on Saturday and I was cast. I might have been the only freshman in that show.

Allison Burnett was also a freshman. He had been cast in the first big University Theatre production he auditioned for that fall, and he was the only first-year student with a speaking role. So in winter quarter when he auditioned both for a play and for the Mee-Ow Show, he was disappointed not to be cast in either. As Burnett tells it,

> I was absolutely gutted. I remember walking up to that sheet on the wall and just feeling utterly humiliated and I couldn't fathom why. It took about maybe two or three weeks before word got to me that they had screwed up, and that the director, [Peter] Bales, of Mee-Ow, and the director of this play had each thought that the other one was claiming me because I was in dispute, because there was a good part for me in the play and I could have been like the juvenile in Mee-Ow. That made me feel a little bit better, but it still kind of sucked. Then maybe another week went by and somebody had to drop out of Mee-Ow. So I came in as a substitution a little bit into the process. They had already been rehearsing for a few weeks. Material had started to generate. Tom Virtue was already shining like the resident genius. Jeff Lupetin and Betsy Fink were just wonderful, and they were the heart and soul, they were like the den parents. They were already committed to each other in a loving relationship that's

> lasted to this day. But it cast a nice spell over the show because they were very generous of spirit. Jeff is very inclusive. And it's pretty easy to feel like an outsider when you're a freshman and everyone knows everyone.

The final cast of the 1977 Mee-Ow Show included returning performers Peter Bales, who also directed, Betsy Fink, Kyle T. Heffner, and Jeff Lupetin. New cast members were Allison Burnett, Cindy Milstein, Dana Olsen, Suzie Plaksin, and Tom Virtue. Janie Fried was also cast but did not perform.

The Show Highlights

The show began with the "North by Northwestern Waltz," written and performed by pianist Jim May. The other song credited in the program was "I Like to Sing" by Jeff Lupetin and Jim May, in which the cast sang about a rival production, in an implied reference to the Waa-Mu Show.

Highlights included Tom Virtue as a weatherman who delivered the forecast in multiple accents that matched the area of the country he was pointing to. The final punch line was "In Idaho, there was no weather." Virtue also gave his impersonation of George C. Scott in the movie *Patton* and was featured in a moving scene at the end of the first act. As Allison Burnett explained,

> It was an old man talking to the grave of his dead wife, Beatrice. Clearly he's eighty [years old] and they've been together their whole lives and she's dead. He walks out kind of hunched over and he's talking to his wife and talking to the grave. All he's doing is sharing the little newsy things that happened in his life, like having spaghetti at the senior thing. And it's just heartbreakingly beautiful. It's like a Norman Rockwell kind of thing because you're laughing, but people are crying. It's crazy how beautiful it was. He's a nineteen-year-old kid doing this old man voice. And it wasn't like this sort of typical vaudeville, burlesque kind of crappy old man because he channeled this old man that he had known when he was a kid. So it really elevated the show to a very high level. I'd love to see Tom do it now. Now that he's getting closer to the real age.

There was a sketch about dating done in the style of the *Goofus and Gallant* comic from the kids' magazine *Highlights for Children*, with Burnett as the "good" date and Heffner as the "bad" date. Burnett said, "I opened the car door and took the girl's jacket, and Kyle [Heffner] was practically humping this girl's leg."

Director Heffner recalled that "in '77 we had a short film, a mock horror film, by Allison Burnett." It was the first time since the original show in 1974 that Mee-Ow made an effort at a multimedia presentation.

Reviews

In his February 25 review in the *Daily Northwestern*, Michael Kaplan wrote, "Nearly a fifth of the show revolves around audience participation, allowing the cast to do on-the-spot improvisations. For the nine cast members, this is both the challenge and the pleasure involved in working in Mee-Ow."

Michael Bennet wrote a few days later that "if the 1977 Mee-Ow Show had left out its on-the-spot improvisation and kept to the material cast members had worked with for the past few weeks, the result would have been a much tighter comedy revue." While he praised the individual performers, especially Tom Virtue and Suzie Plaksin, he concluded his review with, "Maybe next year the company will stress the scripted improv and leave out the rest."

Bennet's opinion has been stated by others and is one of the major philosophical differences about improvisation over the many years of the show. Some Mee-Ow alums prefer scripted sketches that began as improv and were refined through multiple iterations. Others prefer the occasional brilliance that often occurs during onstage improv. Audiences appreciate both, as was made clear by letters to the *Daily Northwestern* that praised the show and took issue with the review.

Olsen said that although previous cast members Brad Mott and Keith Reddin were not in this cast, "on opening night they came backstage and sought me out in particular to tell me they liked what I did, which meant the world to me as a freshman in my first time on stage."

Mee-ow Show

CAST

Peter Bales, Allison Burnett, Betsy Fink, Kyle Hefner, Jeff Lupetin, Cindy Milstein, Dana Olsen, Suzie Plaksin, Tom Virtue, Jim May on piano.

EXECUTIVE BOARD

Producer	Bill "Killer" Flanagan
Director	Peter Bales
Lighting	Paul Zucker
	Ken Belkhof
Settings	Paul Zucker
	Cindy Milstein
Associate Producer	Melanie Barker
Assistant Director	Rachel Lederman
Publicity	Mark Ganshirt
Costumes/Props	Anne Greenberg
Scripting	Robert Mendel
Choreography	Bridget McDonough
Mime Consultant "The Hands"	Rand Whipple
Technical Director	Paul Zucker
Stage manager	Sherry Krsticevic
Stage Crew	Anne Greenberg
	Randy Oppenheimer
	Charles Talbert
House Manager	William Springer
Executive Producers	Michael Baron
	Stewart Figa

1978

MEE-OW YEAR FIVE

In Search of the Ungnome

Thursday through Saturday, February 16–18, at 8 p.m., McCormick Auditorium

The only returning performers were Kyle T. Heffner, who also directed, and Dana Olsen. New cast members included Paul Barrosse, Jerry Franklin, Shelly Goldstein, Ken Marks, Jane Muller, Rush Pearson, Tina Rosenberg, and Bill Wronski, with Larry Schanker playing the piano and Dave Silberger as stage manager.

Shelly Goldstein recalled Rush Pearson's audition:

> This was like seeing the unveiling of the *Mona Lisa* for the first time, or seeing Vesuvius erupt right before it buries the city. There was nothing like it. There will never be anything like it again. How he auditioned became a famous character of his called Red Snaps. He sat in a chair and a gorgeous, beautiful, magnificent, thick, viscous bungee cord of saliva came out of one side of his mouth and it would just dance to within millimeters of the floor. And then he would zip it back, and up and down it would go, like lysergic acid on a yo-yo. It was unbelievable. And that was basically what he did, just this saliva going up and down and up and down. And I'm watching this and I'm thinking, I'm not sure what they're looking for from me, you know? It was staggering.

Developing the Show

One suggestion was to name the show *A Norris Line*, after the popular 1975 Broadway musical *A Chorus Line*. The Arts Alliance wanted to name it *Ate at My Wake* in response to that year's Waa-Mu Show, *Wake Me at Eight*. According to stage manager Dave Silberger, Heffner said, "Are we going to sell out while we're still in college?" and chose the name *In Search of the Ungnome*, after a popular weekly television series called *In Search of . . .* and the book *Gnomes* by Wil Huygen and Rien Poortvliet.

While improv games were still part of rehearsals, Heffner decided to eliminate them from performances to focus entirely on sketches.

THIS YEAR IN HISTORY
Camp David Accords signed • Jonestown suicides • First test-tube baby born • Dow Jones year-end close 805 • Average new car $6,379 • 1 gallon gas $0.63 • *Superman*, *Grease*, *Animal House* • Blondie, *Parallel Lines*; The Cars, *The Cars*; Van Halen, *Van Halen*

1978

Olsen recalled that the shows were "scripted from the beginning to the end":

> I thought [it] was an improvement because they were tighter and we were able to work on our writing chops and we learned pace and running order and we edited ourselves and we were disciplined. . . . We would tape the rehearsals and try to edit and transcribe the stuff that sounded promising from those recordings. Paul and Rush were very dedicated scripters. The two of them would go back to Rush's place after rehearsal and sit up until 2:00, 3:00 in the morning, writing songs, snippets, and transcribing and scripting. Periodically, I would join them. But for the most part, it was just a matter of revisiting premises that we liked, that we felt worked, over and over again until it began to take shape and then we would script them. But it was rare that anything was born originally as a script.

Larry, the Piano Guy, Joins the Cast

Because they were emulating the format of Second City, Heffner wanted to find a pianist who could add ambiance and heighten sketches like longtime Second City music director Fred Kaz. Orgy of the Arts president Robert Brooks Mendel remembers hearing Larry Schanker play the piano in Norris rehearsal room 1B and inviting him on the spot to become part of Mee-Ow. Schanker recalled:

> I came in as a music major. I was a piano guy, but I always felt a little bit of a square peg in a round hole in the whole classical music vein. I was always looking for something different. I was interested in theater. I was a jazz guy and I did an ad hoc major in commercial music. So I was really looking for some different directions. Somehow I bumped into one of these guys and talked about piano, and they invited me to come to a rehearsal and check it out with them. Then they saw that I could be a part of it with them and basically improvise and play anything they wanted me to. I remember going to the Norris Center and rehearsing with these wild guys. And here's Rush [Pearson], who was able to run at what looked like full speed and just slammed himself into a brick wall, like in a cartoon. They were really so much fun and so funny to hang out with. I just gravitated towards it right away. And they were thrilled to have someone who could improvise, and be a strong part of what they're doing, and help them write the tunes, or turn the tunes they were writing into real tunes. And boy, we had an awful lot of fun every year with Mee-Ow. . . . I would be hanging out at rehearsal. It was very organic and I was learning as I go. I could tell you all the things that influenced [me] later in my life that I wouldn't have known how to do without the Mee-Ow Show.

Schanker described his process as "either providing a bed of sound underneath that gives a rhythm to the sketch they're doing, or it could be a sound effect. For example, if a candle lights, you've got a [plays sound on piano]. Or if someone's climbing or someone's running or someone's relaxing or it's some sort of fashion show, you got a little fashion show music [plays piano]. I learned how to provide this. So who knows how many sound effects and moods I learned to do for these guys. And it probably fed what they were doing too and helped them along."

Schanker also contributed to the show's musical numbers:

There were songs, a bunch of them throughout each of the shows, where they would have an idea for a song, and I would help them flesh it out. They probably would be playing a guitar. I remember there was always an opening song and a closing song. Then as we got closer to showtime, there was always music in between. They would have a spotlight moment for me to play something. So I got started with what I later called the "kitchen-sink overture." Basically I'd throw in a whole bunch of stuff. It would be something a little classical and then some ragtime and then some familiar jazz and then back to Mozart. I kind of knew how to play the audience. I remember one of these overtures, I ended with that famous part of [the Derek and the Dominos song] "Layla" [plays "Layla" on piano]. We're college kids, and we want that group to be rocking out. So I always made sure that element was there for them.

The Show Highlights

The McCormick Auditorium was sold out for every performance. Heffner recalled, "When [we] got McCormick rocking it was fantastic. Fantastic. And I watched the audiences build from '76. We had good crowds, but by the time we got to *In Search of the Ungnome*, it was standing room only. It was rockin'. It was just riotous. It was wonderful to watch that build."

In the program, he included "A Gnote from the Director":

> Tonight, when you see a character you recognize, smile. When you see the character is your friend, snicker. When you see the character is yourself, guffaw.

The show began with "Theme," by Rush Pearson and Paul Barrosse. Olsen recalled:

> I went back to my high school in Park Ridge and borrowed eight cheerleader sweaters,

In their cheerleader sweaters: (*back row*) Jerry Franklin, Dana Olsen, Bill Wronski, Ken Marks, Rush Pearson, and Paul Barrosse; (*front row*) Jane Muller, Shelly Goldstein, and Tina Rosenberg

1978

> and there's a picture of it I'm sure you'll see in the archives. And our opening number was like this "Up with People" thing. We had these red-and-white-striped cheerleader sweaters. In retrospect, they should have been purple and white, but my high school colors were red and white, so that's what we ended up with. Larry comes out and plays the overture and then he goes into this theme song for the opener that we did in the house. Lights came up and we were in back standing on that riser behind the back row in McCormick. And the first song was "We're going to make it, after all" like [the theme song of] *The Mary Tyler Moore Show*. Then we all ran down through the aisles, up on the stage, and we were shaking hands and saying, "God bless you!" and "Up with People"–type stuff. That was the opener of '78.

A highlight for Goldstein was "a great sketch from this show. I don't think I was in it at all, even as an extra, but it was hilarious and it was Shakespearean Western stuff, which was a combination of Shakespearean dialogue and the trope of every cliché of every Western. I remember Rush because there was a little *Gunsmoke* thing here. He was Festus [speaking in character voice]: 'Sheriff!' And it was just hilarious and smart and funny. It was a funny Shakespeare sketch and it was a funny Western sketch."

Schanker remembered writing a shoe-store opera, where "it was just turning a mundane thing, like someone shopping for shoes, into an opera. And of course the salesman falls in love with the feet of a beautiful woman and it goes on from there."

Reviews

In his review in the *Daily Northwestern*, R. C. Pride wrote:

> For a college revue, this year's Mee-Ow show exceeds expectations. And, when compared to the pitiable lack of good comedy elsewhere, especially on Saturday Night Live and other television shows, "In Search of the Ungnome" shines even brighter. The cast is funny, particularly audience favorite Rush Pearson, who dives into a number of manic parts with great zeal. His borscht-belt History Prof is very right. Bill Wronski is good in his bits, takeoff of Italian stereotypes, silent comedy, but is best doing Shakespeare, especially playing a wimpy Shakespeare good guy facing a showdown with bad guy Paul Barrosse.

Heffner summed it up like this: "So, yeah, I knew something was going on when my professors started showing up in the audience. There were professors there and I was like, oh wow, OK, I see what's going on now."

Launching a Career

An ad in the *Daily Northwestern* announced a performance of *Broadside—Women's Comedy*, on Friday, May 25, 1978. Shelly Goldstein (Mee-Ow '78) was asked to take over the show, which was an alternative to the male-dominated Mee-Ow Show. Other members of the gender-balanced cast included Ira Glass, Gary Kroeger, and Tina Rosenberg (Mee-Ow '78).

Goldstein's work in Mee-Ow and Broadside eventually led to her being hired by television and film producer, writer, and director Garry Marshall.

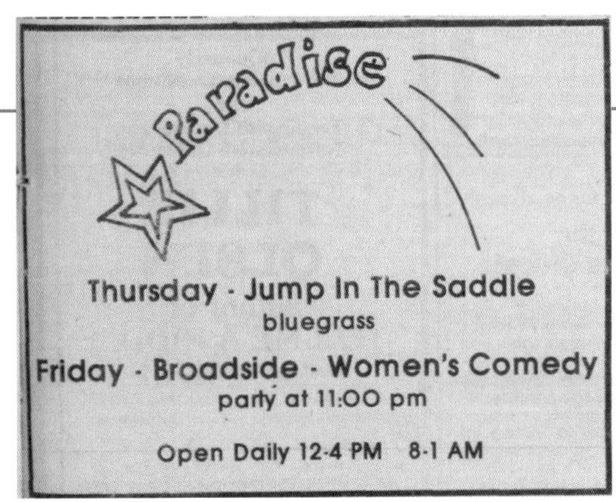

Paradise
Thursday · Jump In The Saddle
bluegrass
Friday · Broadside · Women's Comedy
party at 11:00 pm
Open Daily 12-4 PM 8-1 AM

1979

MEE-OW YEAR SIX

But Is It Art?

Thursday through Sunday, February 15–18, at 8 p.m., McCormick Auditorium

Continuing the tradition begun at the end of the 1976 show, outgoing director Kyle T. Heffner and producer Melanie Barker named the 1979 Mee-Ow Show codirectors: Dana Olsen and Meryl Friedman (the previous year's assistant director).

Returning performers included Olsen, Paul Barrosse, Rush Pearson, and Larry Schanker on piano. Dave Silberger returned as stage manager. New cast members were Bill Aiken, Winnie Freedman, John Goodrich, Barb Guarino, and Althea Haropulos.

The Audition Process

Winnie Freedman had a lengthy history of improv before coming to Northwestern. She was in the Waa-Mu Show, eventually serving as cochair, and knew Olsen, who was in both Waa-Mu and Mee-Ow. According to Freedman, Olsen walked up to her and said, "So, Winnie, did you ever think about auditioning for Mee-Ow?" She replied, "Well . . . I don't know." Dana said, "Well, then, think about it," and walked away. She auditioned and was cast.

Goodrich recalled discovering the Mee-Ow Show:

> I was extremely in love with doing improv comedy, and at that point in time, there was a comedy explosion of sorts, thanks principally to *Saturday Night Live*. It just kind of dominated the pop culture of the comic zeitgeist of the time. So I went to NU and got there as a kid from Kansas. We're all a little fish in a big pond when we get there. I was trying to double major in theater and in radio, television, [and] film. The dean wouldn't let me, but I spent my first part of my freshman year hanging around a lot of theater folk and they're like, "Oh, you've got to see the Mee-Ow highlights. You like improv? You've got to see the highlights." So I went to see the highlights of the previous year's show, *In Search of the Ungnome*, and it just blew my mind. I just watched these guys

THIS YEAR IN HISTORY

Three Mile Island nuclear reactor accident • Panama Canal Treaty takes effect • Iranian students storm US embassy, take hostages • Dow Jones year-end close 839 • Average new car $6,847 • 1 gallon gas $0.86 • *Kramer vs. Kramer*, *Apocalypse Now*, *Alien*, *The Jerk* • The Clash, *London Calling*; Pink Floyd, *The Wall*; Talking Heads, *Fear of Music*; Fleetwood Mac, *Tusk*

1979

> up there doing this outrageous, energetic comedy. And I was like, "This is exactly what I want to do."

It was a "very heady time," said Goodrich, for a "wet-behind-the-ears frosh":

> When you're a kid, before you get beaten down by society and academic pressures and a looming adulthood . . . at that point in time, it's like I can do anything. You know, the world's my oyster. I had no clue. And that's probably what got me the show. I didn't have any hesitation. I didn't have any doubt. I just remember going in to do the auditions, which at that point in time is improv, exercise-based sketch comedy. So [we ran through] a whole bunch of a variety of improv exercises. There was some real basic stuff back in that era. Improv, of course, has gone a long ways, evolved considerably since then. I was lucky enough to make it through the audition and the callback, [which] as a freshman blew my mind. I remember that I had a ball. And then, of course, if you're having fun, if you're doing a sketch, even if you're doing really weak comedy, if you're doing patsy, cheesy comedy, if you're having fun, the audience is going to be with you regardless. You've won them over by at least 50 percent just by the fact they're watching you have fun. And that was it. I was just having fun.

Developing the Show

While the previous year had only two returning cast members, this year had a strong returning cast whose Mee-Ow institutional memory proved to be a key element. The group settled into a mostly stable process of sketches being developed through improv and then reworked and refined.

"There was this sense of comedy being a radical revolutionary thing, potentially counterculture," Goodrich remembered. "[*Saturday Night Live*] still had that energy, Aykroyd, Murray, kind of just insouciant, totally off-the-wall comedy. And that energy was just intoxicating. It was wonderful. And we told ourselves that we had enough satirical elements, that we were like, you know, offering commentary on society and everything instead of just providing clowning antics."

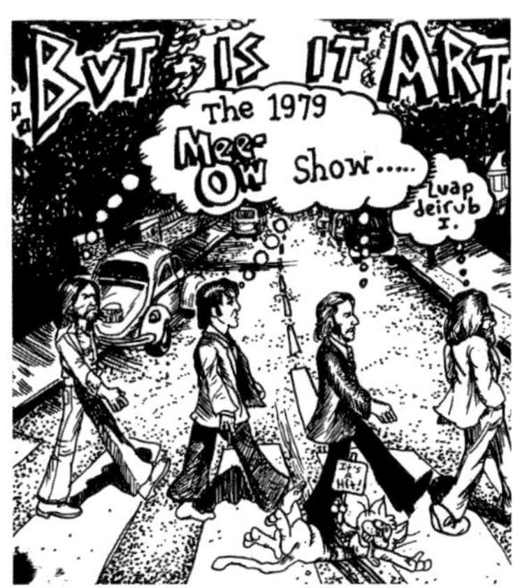

Illustrations by John Goodrich

1979

Goodrich recalled the group's rehearsal process:

> We'd go into rehearsal and we'd run a variety of improv exercises. When an idea really gelled, when it really went somewhere, we'd go, "OK, hey, let's come back to that." Then that night or the next night's rehearsal, we'd say, "You guys, this thing you guys were doing with the carpool bit. Try that again." And so we just keep working it, and adding to it, and trimming it down until we get to the point where the person taking notes would start scripting it. And that's the way it ended up working out for years. For the first few weeks we'd do all sorts of straight improv exercises and nonsense like that. And sometimes we'd go out and leave the rehearsal room and wander campus and just try nutty stuff out.

For Olsen, a specific moment from rehearsal stood out:

> I think it was the funniest night we ever had at rehearsal. We had a standing rule where one rehearsal per show, everybody had to come baked or drunk. It was in the '79 show and John Goodrich was a freshman. He and Rush Pearson were doing a scene—I don't even remember what it was—but it got physical and Rush somehow ended up with his hand in John's shirt pocket and pulled it, ripped the shirt pocket open. Then there was a pause. And John reached over and grabbed Rush's shirt pocket and pulled it down and ripped it open. And they began this spontaneous choreography, and it was like a Laurel and Hardy sketch, where they tore the shirts off each other's bodies, piece by piece, in shreds. And we were all watching it. And it was the funniest goddamn thing I saw in four years. They were so tolerant of each other doing it, and just for the sake of the sketch. It was hilarious. And there is no way that we could re-create that for the show. At the end, John was just holding this pile of rags going, "Oh man. That was my favorite shirt."

The Show Highlights

In addition to the usual campus- and Evanston-specific references, many of the sketches were parodies of movies and television, including one where the horror movie *Halloween* was set on Valentine's Day. Other sketches pushed the boundaries of taste, such as Helen Keller playing in traffic and the last of the Flying Wallendas, a trapeze troupe who suffered notable tragedies during performances. Being a show of its time, there was some drug humor, such as a kid going into the Hoos Drugs (the closest drugstore to campus) to buy medical cannabis for glaucoma.

One particularly touching sketch featured Freedman and Bill Aiken as octogenarians singing "You don't warm my milk up" to the tune of "You Don't Bring Me Flowers," a duet with Barbra Streisand and Neil Diamond.

One sketch that remained virtually unchanged from its initial improv version featured Barrosse and Goodrich as country boys talking about going to the A&W drive-in restaurant; their conversation gradually became a sophisticated discussion of esoteric foreign films and animation.

Schanker remembered several sketches:

> I remember a fashion show [sketch] of different types [of people at Northwestern] that might have been kind of a recurring bit. They were just so good at pinpointing stereotypes, whether it was the theater major with the brown shoulder bag or a young sorority girl, and I remember the line was, "Oh, she's not worried. She doesn't have to declare her wardrobe until next year."
>
> Then there was Rush's Godzilla. He did a wonderful Godzilla. And they had this hat that was called "Le Hat." And at different points in the show different people would have on "Le Hat." And finally the lights went up and the payoff was it was Godzilla again, and he put on the hat and it was back to the fashion show music for Godzilla.
>
> Some of the sketches were really sweet. I remember Winnie Freedman was the young kid who was kind of around while the friends were having a sleepover. And it just ended really sweetly because they took her under their wing.

Reviews

In his *Daily Northwestern* review on February 16, Charlie Suisman wrote:

> It seems to me that the Mee-Ow Show, which opened last night at McCormick Auditorium, is the perfect college show . . . because it asks only that we allow them to bestow a grand, good time on us. No other pretensions, no other demands. But does it deliver? Yes, a good deal of the time it does. . . . Much of the physical humor could stand some prudent editing and there is a noticeable lack of, shall we say, humor that appeals to anything above the belly . . . Still, many of the short blackouts are little gems, especially Winifred Freedman's dramatic re-interpretation of some chilling moments from *West Side Story*.

Suisman also noted the contributions of pianist Larry Schanker, whom many considered an integral member of the cast: "Much credit should go to Larry Schanker, whose musical accompaniment is witty and whose solos are more than pleasing. I particularly enjoyed the prologue medley and the serviceable opening number."

In conclusion, wrote Suisman, "I'm not sure Mee-Ow is for everybody so I can't recommend it without reservation. If you can overlook some of the tasteless material, then by all means go."

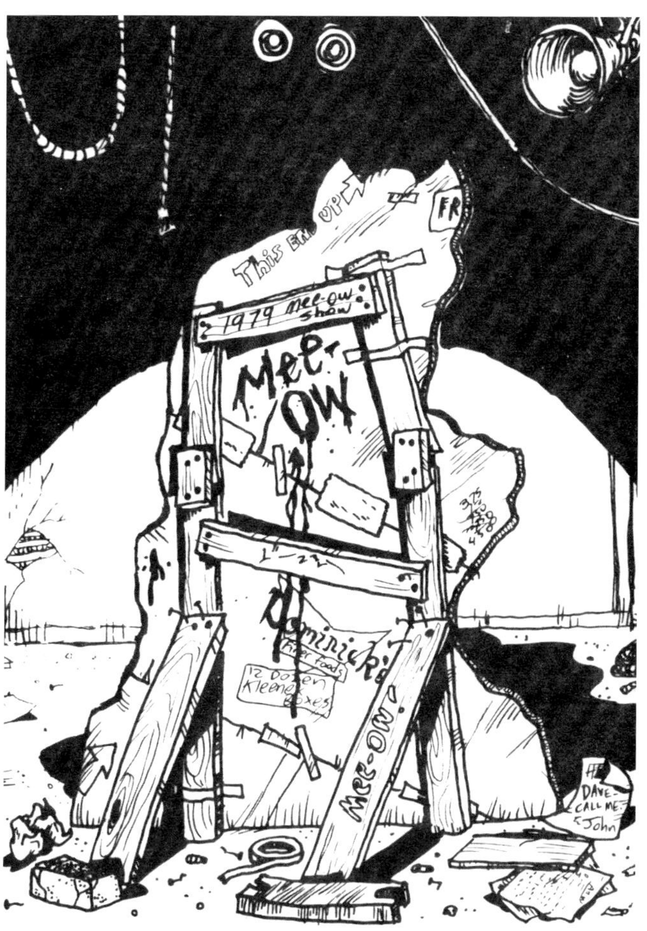

Laughtrack, Attack Theatre, and the Start of the Practical Theatre Company

In 1979 an Evanston-based comedy group called Laughtrack was created by Northwestern alumni Gary Kroeger, Jeff Lupetin (Mee-Ow '75, '76, '77), Bill Wronski (Mee-Ow '78), Victoria Zielinski, and manager Bridget McDonough (Mee-Ow '77, '78). The group performed on campus and at venues in Chicago.

In the spring of 1979, four Northwestern students began their own theater company. Paul Barrosse (Mee-Ow '78, '79, '80) was joined by Brad Hall, Robert Mendel, and Angela Murphy to form Attack Theatre, dedicated to the production of new and rarely seen plays.

Attack Theatre's first production, *Clowns*, was staged on April 11, 1979, in Shanley Hall. A play about two improvisational comedians, it was written and performed by Paul Barrosse and Brad Hall. Their next production, *Subnormal*, included Mee-Ow Show cast member Rush Pearson.

Attack Theatre's first season concluded with two one-act plays performed at the National College of Education. *Playgrounds* was written by Brad Hall. *On the Fritzz* was written by Grace McKeaney and Lewis Black, and starred Laura Innes.

In October 1979, after determining that their name had aggressive and potentially negative implications, they renamed themselves the Practical Theatre Company.

1980

MEE-OW YEAR SEVEN

Ten Against the Empire

Thursday through Sunday, February 7–10, at 8 p.m., McCormick Auditorium

Held over: Thursday through Sunday, February 14–17, at 8 p.m., McCormick Auditorium

Returning cast members included Dana Olsen, who again directed, Paul Barrosse, John Goodrich, Rush Pearson, and Larry Schanker on piano. Dave Silberger returned as coproducer.

New cast members were Julia Louis-Dreyfus, Rod McLachlan, Mike Markowitz, Ken Marks, and Judy Pruitt. "What I can tell you about Julia Louis-Dreyfus's audition," Olsen recalled, "is she walked in, and in thirty seconds I knew I was going to cast her. I thought, 'Oh, my God, this is the best female comedian I've seen in four years.' She was *amazing*. She came in fully loaded, man. She was funny. She had balls. She did characters. She did accents. She was *great*. And so she was like family right away."

Developing the Show

The movie *Star Wars* had been released in 1977, and the sequel *The Empire Strikes Back* was due to premiere in May 1980. Olsen recalled:

> We used to go around and around and around about titling the show. The whole *Star Wars* thing gave us an easy thing to anchor the rebellion on. So we ended up calling [it] *Ten Against the Empire.* Again, it was the idea of the Mee-Ow Show rebelling, the comedy rebellion. We actually published a series of six-panel cartoons in the *Daily Northwestern* tracking "The Adventures of the Ten." We each gave ourselves a cartoon avatar, and John Goodrich, who was also a cast member and [later] directed two shows, drew these cartoon strips leading up to the show as a marketing tool.

Several rules were established by Olsen for that year's show: "Commit to the bit, no meta, yes and, don't negate, no toy toy (i.e., no toilet humor)."

According to Silberger, on the first night of rehearsal, Louis-Dreyfus was the first cast member to show up. When she asked, "What is

THIS YEAR IN HISTORY

"Miracle on Ice" • Mount St. Helens erupts • Iran-Iraq War begins • CNN begins • Post-it notes first sold • John Lennon killed • FBI Abscam investigation implicates members of Congress • Dow Jones year-end close 964 • Average new car $7,574 • 1 gallon gas $1.19 • *The Empire Strikes Back*, *9 to 5*, *Airplane!*, *The Blues Brothers* • AC/DC, *Back in Black*; Talking Heads, *Remain in Light*; Bruce Springsteen, *The River*

this thing?" Silberger replied, "Kid, you're in for the ride of your life."

Olsen remembered that Louis-Dreyfus and Markowitz went off to work on a sketch. "I don't know if it was Rush or Paul who tried to join in and started imprinting his own point of view. Julia booted him out. I mean, you know, she stood right up."

One cast member recalled that during the development and rehearsal of a sketch in which Louis-Dreyfus played the cheerleader girlfriend of Rod McLachlan, Paul Barrosse ignored her and only spoke to Rod. At one point she punched Paul in the arm in frustration and said, "Hey! I'm here too!" Upon being asked to confirm this story, Louis-Dreyfus said, "I will confirm it with this caveat. I don't specifically remember it, but it sounds like something I would have done."

A few people recalled a tradition of "fucked-up rehearsal night once per year" that involved the consumption of intoxicants before, during, and after rehearsal. However, no one was certain when this tradition began, or when it ended.

The Show Highlights

Schanker was again considered an integral part of the cast for his mastery of musical genres, his timing, and the quality of his performances.

The musical number that opened the show was performed by the entire cast. Louis-Dreyfus recalled the "unbelievably" funny opening number:

> *Shoulder to shoulder*
> *Elbow to knee*
> *Zipped down your fly*
> *When you're in company*
> *We are the vanguard*
> *We'll show them how.*
> *Mee-Ow, Mee-Ow.*

Olsen remembered a particular sketch titled "Brad's Dick":

> Julia did [a] sketch with Ken Marks where it was like a split screen on the stage. And she and Ken were boyfriend and girlfriend. And she was sort of like flirting with him and teasing him and trying to turn him on. And then Rush Pearson was curled up in a ball on the other side of the stage with the spotlight on him. And, you know, it wasn't like tracking what exactly he had to do with what was going on with the two of them. And eventually, as she got Ken sort of hotter and hotter, Rush uncurled himself and became rigid, and it became evident that he was playing Ken's penis. And that was really fun to watch the audience as they became aware of what was going on, because it was so *not* evident at the beginning.

Another sketch parodied a movie-review show, with Marks and Olsen playing Chicago film critics Gene Siskel and Roger Ebert. They showed film clips shot specifically for the show, and discussed and rated them. One of the films featured Louis-Dreyfus and Pruitt in a "Bergmanesque two-shot" speaking beginning language learner phrases such as "My pen is on the table and this is the pen of my aunt," in French and pidgin French. Another film clip featured Markowitz as Marlon Brando from *Apocalypse Now*, which was released in 1979.

"We did a musical commercial about venereal disease called the VD Song," Olsen recalled:

> It was sort of a '60s kind of a bouncy [singing] "Oh, baby, you know, you can please me, but don't disease me." That kind of thing. It was a public service announcement, but it was a musical one. It was all about "Making sure you practice safe sex, and don't get venereal disease!" So we're singing. We're like

1980

> the Modernaires and we're singing the song. I think Paul [Barrosse] was the narrator. He's like, "You know, venereal disease affects one out of ten people and blah, blah, blah, blah. So you've got to go to your doctor and get checked out and make sure you're clean." And so the girl says to the guy, "Have you been to the doctor?" And he goes, "No," and he shakes his head. And so she turns him down and she walks away. So the end line is they split up, they decide not to have sex because someone hasn't been to the doctor. And Paul's line is "Too bad, baby. It would have been fun fucking you!" And to this day, I'm arguing with Paul, that was a step too far. When my parents came to see the show, that was the only thing that my father objected to. He said, "Why did you have to say that?" And at the time we were like, "Well, the whole point is we have to offend somebody at some point." We were always arguing about how many F-bombs we were going to put into the show. Paul and I would go at each other for hours about where to put our strategic F-bombs in the show. And so I'd like to pull a couple of those back.

Schanker remembered a sketch that "was basically people talking at a party like New Yorkers":

> But it was such a wonderful rub of New Yorkers, of which I was one. And it was really hysterical what they kept coming up with. Someone said, "Woody Allen," and everyone went, "Woody Allen! Woody Allen! Woody Allen! Woody Allen!" That was such a New York thing. "Oh, did you see the Chicago production of *A Chorus Line*?" And Rod McLachlan said [disdainfully], "Ah. I'll never go see another Chicago production again. Don't ruin my evening." It was really such great fun, because all of us at Northwestern had bumped into real die-hard kind of private-school New Yorkers.

The 1980 cast: (*top photo*) Markowitz, Goodrich, Olsen, Pruitt, Barrosse (*in tree*), Marks, Louis-Dreyfus, McLachlan, Pearson; (*bottom photo*) Marks, Goodrich, Louis-Dreyfus, Pruitt, Markowitz, McLachlan, Pearson, Barrosse, Olsen

1980

Reviews

In his February 15 review in the *Daily Northwestern,* Sean Enright praised the show:

> "Ten Against the Empire," the 1980 MeeOw Show, has been held over at McCormick Auditorium due to enormous popular acclaim that led to sold-out houses during its run last weekend. This popularity is well warranted: the Mee-Ow show is a collection of forty-odd comedy skits and songs, which at their worst are still entertaining, and at their best approach hysteria. . . . As an ensemble, the performers work well together, with complete confidence and amazing fluidity. . . . "Ten Against the Empire" makes for an evening of first-class comedy. Tickets are on sale at the Norris box office—you'd better hurry because demand is great.

One letter to the *Daily Northwestern* found fault with the number of women in the cast and the roles they played. Katherine S. Guess wrote,

> I am incensed by the Mee-Ow show's portrayal of women in "Ten Against the Empire." Why, out of a cast of ten, were there only two women? Why are women not considered funny except when they're the butt of sex jokes?
>
> . . . Women have been portrayed as being devious and duplicitous since time immemorial. The image of the scatterbrained woman, flaunting herself to inflame a man's senses and deny him, and not understanding what the hell she's doing seems unreal and naive to me.
>
> The show seems to reveal college students' inability to conceptualize male-female roles outside a narrow range of mutually exploitative situations.
>
> These portrayals of women as victims and objects of male disgust and loathing have got to go.

The Practical Theatre Company Takes Flight

During the spring of their senior year of 1979, Paul Barrosse and Brad Hall, with two other Northwestern students, started Attack Theatre in a space in Evanston.

In the fall of 1979 they changed the name of the company to the Practical Theatre Company and moved into Evanston's Noyes Cultural Arts Center. There, Barrosse was in a production directed by Rush Pearson called *Bag o' Fun* (which was a title Rush had suggested for Mee-Ow every year). By the fall of 1980, Practical Theatre had moved into a space on Howard Street, the dividing line between Evanston and Chicago.

They invited Peter van Wagner to join and put together a rock musical, the story of Riffmaster and the Rockme Foundation. The Practical Theatre house band included Peter van Wagner (as Riffmaster), Rush Pearson (vocals, bass, guitar), Paul Barrosse (vocals and guitar), Brad Hall (vocals and guitar), Steve Rashid (vocals, keyboards, harmonica, horns), Larry Schanker (piano), and Ronny Crawford on drums. They performed all original material.

Del Close, renowned actor, improv coach, and cofounder of ImprovOlympic, advised Practical Theatre. Productions included *The Adventures of Citizen Stumpick*, *Nightfall*, *Scubba Hey*, *The Brothers Bubba*, and *Thrills & Glory.*

Well-known director Sheldon Patinkin introduced the members of Practical Theatre to Second City founder Bernard Sahlins, who invited them to perform in a nearby space. One longstanding theory is that Second City was tired of losing talent to *Saturday Night Live*, whose producers would come to Chicago to look for cast members and writers. Second City could direct *SNL* people to go to the Practical Theatre space to look for talent, keeping their own cast intact. The credibility of this version is supported by the events of 1982, when *SNL* producer Dick Ebersol hired Paul Barrosse, Julia Louis-Dreyfus, Brad Hall, and Gary Kroeger as writers and performers. Rush Pearson was away performing with the Sturdy Beggars in the Mud Show at Renaissance festivals.

1981

MEE-OW YEAR EIGHT

Candy from Strangers

Thursday through Sunday, February 26–March 1, at 8 p.m., plus 11 p.m. show on February 28, McCormick Auditorium

Friday, March 6, at 8 p.m., and Saturday, March 7, at 8 and 11 p.m., McCormick Auditorium

The returning cast members included Ken Marks, who also directed, John Goodrich, Julia Louis-Dreyfus, Rod McLachlan, Mike Markowitz, and Larry Schanker as music director. Dave Silberger returned as producer. The new cast members were Bekka Eaton, Mark Lancaster, Bill Lopatto, and Sandy Snyder.

This year, for the first time, the Mee-Ow Show was performed on two consecutive weekends, most likely in response to the previous year's show being held over an extra weekend.

The Show Highlights

The show began with a silent film by Goodrich. Then, as in previous years, the cast joined in singing the original theme song.

One sketch featured Louis-Dreyfus and Markowitz as seated airline passengers. He speaks only English. She speaks only French. He begins teaching her incorrect English phrases that she naively accepts as accurate. Eventually, they are joined by Rod McLachlan, who speaks to Louis-Dreyfus in English, and she replies with one of the incorrect phrases she learned from Markowitz. The humorous punch line is that McLachlan replies to her with another of the incorrect English phrases that Markowitz taught Louis-Dreyfus.

Louis-Dreyfus was featured in a solo sketch portraying three different personalities of Mary Tyler Moore from *The Dick Van Dyke Show*, *The Mary Tyler Moore Show*, and the movie *Ordinary People*. The student reviewer described this as "done with biting wit" and "almost a show unto itself."

Reviews

In his *Daily Northwestern* review on March 6, 1981, Fred Monyak wrote:

> During its relatively brief history, the Mee-Ow Show has established something of a tradition at Northwestern. It isn't difficult

THIS YEAR IN HISTORY

First space shuttle mission • Sandra Day O'Connor appointed to SCOTUS • DeLorean DMC-12 debuts • Iran releases American hostages • Reagan fires striking air traffic controllers • First IBM PC using MS-DOS • Dow Jones year-end close 875 • Average new car $8,910 • 1 gallon gas $1.31 • *Raiders of the Lost Ark*, *On Golden Pond*, *For Your Eyes Only*, *Time Bandits*, *Porky's* • Rush, *Moving Pictures*; The Cure, *Faith*; The Police, *Ghost in the Machine*; The Rolling Stones, *Tattoo You*

1981

to see why. This collection of zany, irreverent comedy sketches is cut from the same mold of quick-witted lunacy that kindled the phenomenal success of *Saturday Night Live*, *Second City*, and the movie *Animal House*. For better or worse, Mee-Ow's humor is "in."

As a part of this comic trend, Mee-Ow blatantly seems to parody everything it can possibly think of in satirical, often scornful, no-holds-barred fashion. The humor consists mostly of broad, slam-bang skits that are either hit or miss (there's little middle ground with this kind of humor). As it happens, the 1981 show, entitled "Candy from Strangers," nails roughly half the laughs it aims for.

But even the duds—and there are more than a couple—don't tax our patience since they're never very long. We're always aware of a fresh, completely different skit waiting in the wings. By providing a seemingly endless supply of comic sketches—interjected by songs and improvisation—Mee-Ow never bogs itself down. It is a fast, often funny outflow of what's been glibly termed "college humor."

Things don't begin so well, however. As the lights go down, the audience is subjected to a murky, too-long silent film that methodically introduces each cast member as he or she performs some ludicrous acts of inanity. The laughs are few, if non-existent. As Ken Marks, the director, should know, Mee-Ow's brand of humor plays far weaker on the screen—especially without words—than it does on the stage. Why lose your audience before an actor even steps on stage?

Especially when you're blessed with such talented comic actors as John Goodrich, Julia Louis-Dreyfus, Mike Markowitz and Rod McLachlan—the bright spots of a cast of nine that, once it gets going, can trigger plenty of laughs. Still, there's enough wit here to fill a good part of the evening. As the cast charges through skits in rapid-fire succession, they parody such diverse things as American Express Card commercials, foreign-speaking TA's, the Bank 24 machine, the Space Invaders electronic game, nuclear waste and Freudian dreams. There's a noticeable lack of skits about campus affairs, although the ones that are (defective Bank-24 machine, late-night dorm security) are among the funniest in the show.

Probably the best display of comic technique is delivered by Louis-Dreyfus' depiction of the three personalities of Mary Tyler Moore—the one in *The Dick Van Dyke Show*, the one in *The Mary Tyler Moore Show*, and the one in the recent film *Ordinary People*. It's all done with biting wit, and it's almost a show unto itself.

Louis-Dreyfus is also in top form as she affects a French accent in a skit in which she plays a naive airline passenger duped by a prankish American passenger (Mike Markowitz).

The foundation of the evening, though, is Goodrich, who supplies the hyperbolic energy that carries the show through most of the evening. This comic has been convulsing Mee-Ow audiences for three years now, and he isn't about to let us down. Watch him as he crashes into an imaginary dormitory lobby as a barbarian who stops at nothing to get upstairs (he has no key card). Or as the father of a girl who dreams of the two of them galloping through a forest of phallic symbols. Goodrich also shines in the group's improvisational routine.

The only thing, in fact, that weighs the show down is the absence of the kind of truly inspiring material that can have an audience in stitches. Well, maybe we can't have everything. Mee-Ow never explodes with hilarity, but it does offer an ample share of laughs.

1981

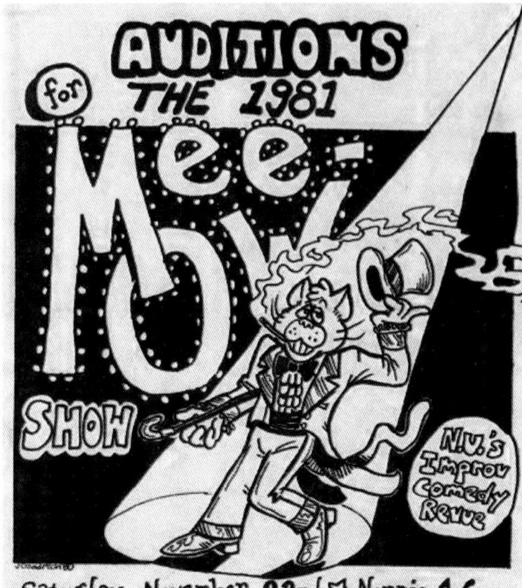

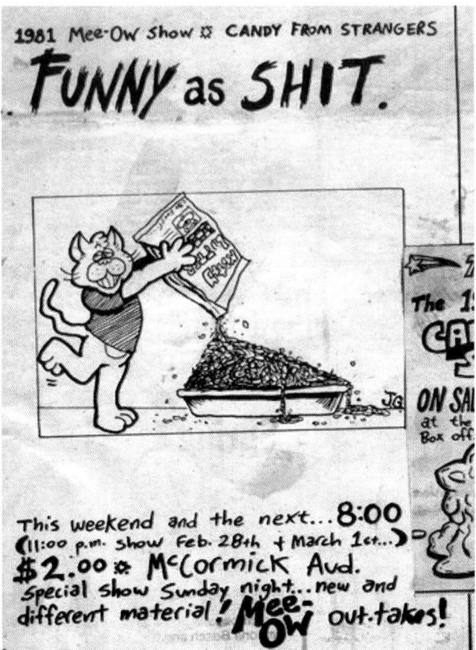

Mee-Ow in sweet delight

Now that you've survived the first week of waking up before noon and rushing to classes that seem harder and harder each day, you deserve a treat. And nothing does it better than a taste of "Candy from Strangers," the 1981 Mee-Ow show. The cast of the Mee-Ow show will present highlights from last year's production in McCormick Auditorium tonight at 7:30 and 9:30. And for an added sweetner, admission is free.

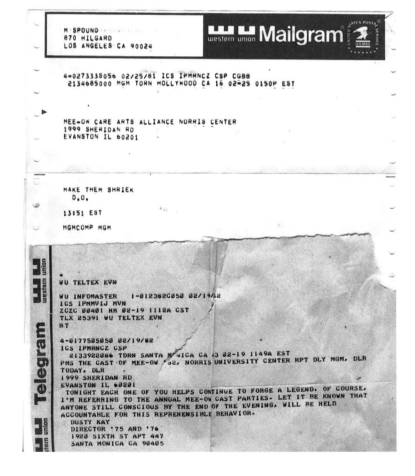

western union Mailgram

M SPOUND
870 HILGARD
LOS ANGELES CA 90024

4-027333S056 02/25/81 ICS IPMRNCZ CSP CGBB
2134685000 MGM TDRN HOLLYWOOD CA 16 02-25 0150P EST

MEE-OW CARE ARTS ALLIANCE NORRIS CENTER
1999 SHERIDAN RD
EVANSTON IL 60201

MAKE THEM SHRIEK
D.O.

13:51 EST

MGMCOMP MGM

western union Telegram

WU TELTEX EVN

WU INFOMASTER 1-012382C050 02/19/82
ICS IPMMVIJ MVN
ZCZC 00401 HH 02-19 1112A CST
TLX 25391 WU TELTEX EVN
BT

4-017750S050 02/19/82
ICS IPMRNCZ CSP
2133922086 TDRN SANTA M NICA CA 3 02-19 1149A EST
PMS THE CAST OF MEE-OW '82, NORRIS UNIVERSITY CENTER RPT DLY MGM, DLR
TODAY, DLR
1999 SHERIDAN RD
EVANSTON IL 60201
TONIGHT EACH ONE OF YOU HELPS CONTINUE TO FORGE A LEGEND. OF COURSE, I'M REFERRING TO THE ANNUAL MEE-OW CAST PARTIES. LET IT BE KNOWN THAT ANYONE STILL CONSCIOUS BY THE END OF THE EVENING, WILL BE HELD ACCOUNTABLE FOR THIS REPREHENSIBLE BEHAVIOR.
DUSTY KAY
DIRECTOR '75 AND '76
1920 SIXTH ST APT 447
SANTA MONICA CA 90405

Memorabilia from
Candy from Strangers

CANDY FROM STRANGERS

(1) Oh, mama, did we do so wrong
Went and grew up while we been gone
I dreamed about your mom last night
But it was clean
You know what I mean
Ain't no reason to get uptight
(1) Geez, the mother was surrounded by light
She yelled pretty loud, really gove us a fright
I felt as though we had done something wrong
and fell out of bed
Her voice ringin' in my head
She started singin' that same worn out song
She said, son. . . .
(2) DODODODO DODODODO DODODODODODO DODODODODODO DODODODODODODO
(3) Don't read those silly naughty books – All. Boys
Don't cross the street alone
Don't play with Mary Alice
when theres no one else at home
(4) Don't play in daddy's liquor stash – Girls
Don't go out after dark
Don't leave your little brother lying
tied up in the park
Don't terrorize the cat – All.
Wipe your feet on the welcome mat
DODODODO DODODODO DODODODODODODODO DODODODODODODODO DODODODODO
(3) Don't ask me how I got here
Lying sprawled out on the floor
Whos that knocking
What s that knocking
Strangers at the door?
(5) Candy from strangers
Candy from strangers
Candy from strangers
Candy from strangers
Candy from strangers
No need for fear –

~~whoa whoa whoa hwoa~~
nummy nummy nums – Julia
guarenteded to rot your gums – Mark
look out ma, here it comes – Ken
beats carrying 'round some guns – Bek.

Spoken w/ rhythm

hamboone

Candy from strangers

Original lyrics for the opening theme

1982

MEE-OW YEAR NINE

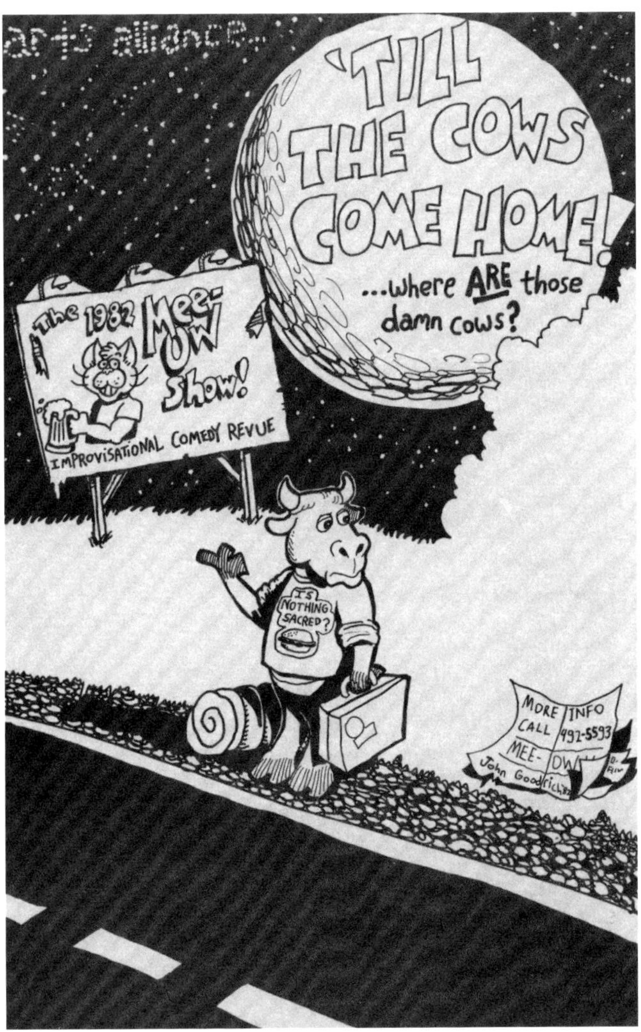

'Till the Cows Come Home . . . Where ARE Those Damn Cows?

Friday and Saturday, Feb 19–20, at 8 p.m., McCormick Auditorium

Thursday through Sunday, Feb. 25–28, at 8 p.m., McCormick Auditorium

As in previous years, the cast of the 1981 Mee-Ow Show performed highlights of the show during the annual new student week activities. Future cast member John Cameron Mitchell recalled:

> There was a blackout sketch where Julia [Louis-Dreyfus] is with a couple of stoners and one of them is like, "God you know, when I was little I used to think there were one hundred people in the world and they would just change clothes and come around the bend and be different people. There were only one hundred people in the whole world." And then Brad Hall looks at the other guy and goes, "She knows." And then people come out of the wall and that's a blackout. So I was like, OK, yeah, I want to be part of this.

Although neither Brad Hall nor Gary Kroeger had been in Mee-Ow, they were invited to participate in the highlights show since the majority of the previous cast had graduated.

The returning cast included John Goodrich, who directed, and Mark Lancaster. The previous year's assistant director Tricia Galin returned as producer. New cast members were Steve Beavers, Rob Chaskin, Chris Hueben, Laura Matalon, Sarah Partridge, and Susan Wapner.

"We were like a fraternity in that period of time," Goodrich recalled:

> I used the term "fraternity," although there were women involved too. But it really was a fraternity and Mee-Ow was such a *thing*. It was all year long. We'd be hanging out and doing other things together, other projects together. There were a lot of other little fundraising comedy revue shows or highlight shows or other theatrical projects I ended up working on. Paul directed *Threepenny Opera*,

THIS YEAR IN HISTORY

AT&T breakup mandated • Argentina invades Falkland Islands • *Late Night with David Letterman* premieres • Poisoned Tylenol kills 7 in Chicago • Vietnam Veterans Memorial dedicated in Washington, DC • Dow Jones year-end close 1047 • Average new car $9,903 • 1 gallon gas $1.22 • *E.T. the Extra-Terrestrial, Tootsie, Star Trek II: The Wrath of Khan, Poltergeist* • Michael Jackson, *Thriller*; Prince, *1999*; Roxy Music, *Avalon*; Duran Duran, *Rio*

1982

and Rush Pearson and Julia Louis-Dreyfus and I were in that. We'd work together all year long and had this sense of community. We'd hang out together, we'd work together on different projects. Dana Olsen, who directed '79 and '80 and was a four-year man, and I collaborated on a comic strip in the *Daily Northwestern* for a couple of years. I actually dropped out of school briefly. I thought that I was not getting anywhere academically and I needed to take some time to clear my head and I was going to travel. And about the time they were having Mee-Ow auditions, I got an itch. I was like, "I can't leave Mee-Ow." So I actually reenrolled, got back into school just to do Mee-Ow.

Julia Moving On

Although she was again cast in the 1982 Mee-Ow Show and performed in the fall highlights show, Louis-Dreyfus left school at the beginning of her junior year for a career opportunity. In the November 4, 1981, *Daily Northwestern*, Ruth Podems wrote:

> Last Friday, Dreyfus attended a preliminary audition at the Second City Nightclub in Chicago. She returned for the call-back Monday afternoon, was cast in the company on the spot, memorized her script within a few hours, and performed that same night. . . . This past summer Dreyfus performed [with] The Practical Theatre on Howard Street in "Scubba Hey!," an improvisational comedy show. Some of the people from Second City, who knew she was in the show, came to see it. "It was probably a help in getting cast," Dreyfus said.

The Show Highlights

In an article in the February 26, 1982, *Daily Northwestern*, Fred Monyak describes the opening of the show:

> Just before the 1982 Mee-Ow Show begins, the audience gets a peek back to the recent past. As the lights go down, a spotlight focuses on a quintet of oddlooking, tuxedoed musicians. The mere sight of the lead singer, Rush Pearson, with his long blond hair, wire-rimmed sunglasses and deadpan stare, breaks the audience into laughter. Then Pearson and his rockabilly band perform a medley of commercial jingles—from Budweiser to Brown's Chicken—although they sing their lyrics to the tunes of 1950s rock music. Perfectly attuned to his material, Pearson's antics are nearly enough to bring the house down. . . .
>
> Early on, Goodrich and Rob Chaskin are a pair of neglectful kitchen-workers who call in a pint-sized archaeologist (Chris Hueben) to excavate their dish-filled sink and find the long-lost drain. The project quickly becomes a life-threatening mission that kindles eruptions—both literally and comically.
>
> Another skit parodies a fetish with avant-garde poetry. As Chaskin, Susan Wapner, Steve Beavers and Laura Matalon take turns reciting their ludicrous attempts at eloquence, Matalon's accidental expletive—"Oh, I stubbed my toe!"—earns the most praise.
>
> Mee-Ow also takes a timely swipe at military slogans: Mark Lancaster is all ironic double-talk as he describes the Marines—"It's not just a job, it's an adventure"—and adds the additional prerequisites of being poor, black, uneducated and criminal.

1982

One of the show's most inventive skits closes Act I: The cast dances and sings the score from *A Chorus Line* while inserting their own satirical lyrics about Norris Center. Leave it to them to make comic hay out of Szabo burgers, Mini-Courses and the Browsing Library.

Even more ingenious are a depiction of a Monopoly board come to life and a hilarious vignette that transports *I Love Lucy* to Russia—ending up with a simultaneous parody of Chekhov and American television.

At the start of Act II, the band gives us another dynamic medley, this time featuring music of Chuck Berry, Alice Cooper, Steely Dan, The Beach Boys and the NU alma mater—always injecting their own bizarre comic twists.

Monyak also noted that the show included a film but did not feature any improvisation during the performance he attended.

Reviews

In his review in the *Daily Northwestern*, Fred Monyak wrote:

> Pearson, who graduated two years ago, may well have been the supreme comedian in MeeOw's nine-year history. As he wins us over before the actual show even starts, we begin to wonder how in the world this year's performers can match the talents of their own former great.
>
> Happily, the worry proves needless. Right after Pearson and Co. complete their medley, the 1982 performers take over and—rest assured—they don't disappoint.
>
> Like its predecessors, this year's show, entitled "Till the Cows Come Home," consists of short vignettes built around a wide assortment of topics. The cast of eight—five men and three women—are asked to play everything from lizards and WCTU ladies to

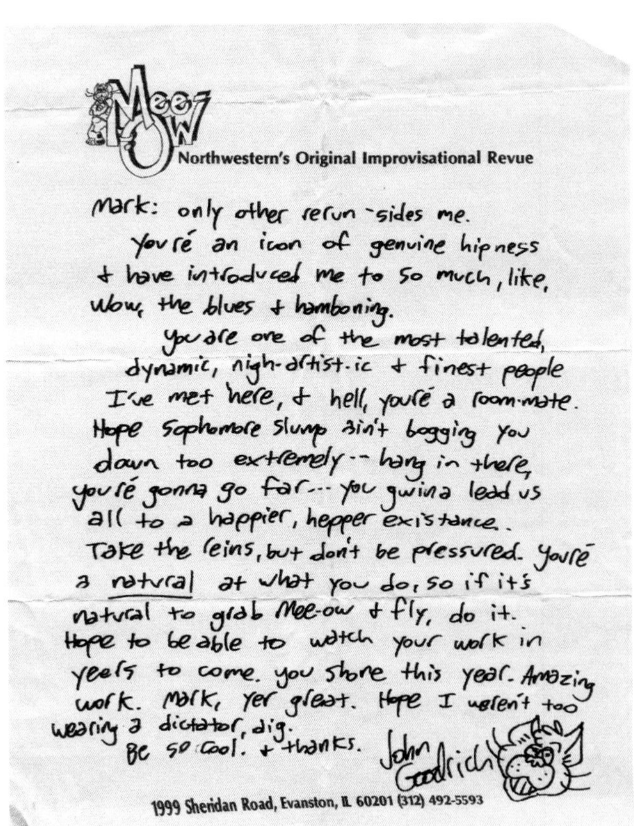

MeeOw
Northwestern's Original Improvisational Revue

Mark: only other rerun 'sides me.
You're an icon of genuine hipness
+ have introduced me to so much, like,
wow, the blues + hamboning.
you are one of the most talented,
dynamic, nigh-artist-ic + finest people
I've met here, + hell, you're a room-mate.
Hope sophomore slump ain't bogging you
down too extremely -- hang in there,
you're gonna go far... you gwina lead us
all to a happier, hepper existance.
Take the reins, but don't be pressured. You're
a natural at what you do, so if it's
natural to grab Mee-ow + fly, do it.
Hope to be able to watch your work in
years to come. You shone this year. Amazing
work. Mark, yer great. Hope I weren't too
wearing a dictator, dig.
Be so cool. + thanks. John Goodrich

1999 Sheridan Road, Evanston, IL 60201 (312) 492-5593

Note to Mark Lancaster from director John Goodrich, and Goodrich's illustration from the program

Bazooka Joe and Robert Young. Fortunately, the scattered dud scenes are few and don't spoil the evening's fun.

More often, the cast has a grand time showing off their versatile comic gifts. This production not only far surpasses last year's largely uneven show, but it creates echoes of laughter in the most intelligent way possible: by satirizing the hypocrisies of contemporary society, rather than by reaching easily for cheap, unearned jokes.

Certainly credit has to go to John Goodrich, the show's director and only four-year performer. With his crisp delivery and boundless imagination, Goodrich cuts a perfect path to comic abandon and the others faithfully follow suit. The evening moves with lightning-quick occasions when the jokes don't register.

All along Goodrich keeps the movement flowing, and he never directs too much attention to himself. While the director is superb when using his high-charged physicality for such roles as gallant dragonslayer, a nervous man's conscience and the Evanston wind, he allows plenty of room for the equally impressive Hueben, Lancaster and Chaskin.

The evening isn't without its lapses . . . Yet it usually doesn't matter. Both the cast and Pearson's farcical band are on hand throughout, and they're both a consistent source of fun.

Perhaps that's the show's secret recipe: Even as we're able to savor one of NU's former giants of comedy, the 1982 performers are at work creating vintage memories of their very own.

Black Folks Theatre and Out Da Box

In 1971, having noticed a lack of real opportunities for Black performers in existing theater groups at Northwestern, School of Speech student Eileen Cherry created Black Folks Theatre as a group under the umbrella of the Northwestern Black student organization For Members Only. Dr. Eileen Cherry-Chandler is now an associate professor emeritus of theater and film at Bowling Green State University.

Ads in several issues of the *Daily Northwestern* announced the group's first production.

In 1984 Black Folks Theatre was renamed the African American Theater Ensemble (AATE). During the 1980s, one of the productions of the AATE was Out Da Box, an original sketch-comedy show that became a yearly tradition in its own right.

Black theatre

Black Folks Theater, a newly formed black graduate and undergraduate theater group, will present its first major production this weekend.

The group will perform "The Black Portrait,", a collection of three one-act plays written by black playwrights, in the Speech School Auditorium at 8 p.m. tomorrow and Saturday. Tickets are $1 and are available at Scott Hall.

The plays are "The Suicide", by Carol Freeman, "Sister Son ji" by Sonia Sanchez, and "We Own the Night" by Jimmy Garrett.

The Life-Death Situation, a black jazz combo will provide musical accompaniment for the plays.

Black Folks Theater is the theatrical group of For Members Only, Northwestern's black student organization.

"'TIL THE COWS COME HOME"

Hey Diddle Diddle
The Cat and the fiddle
The cow jumped over the moon
Now that he's gone
The party goes on
and he won't be back till the 10th of June

In India they praise 'em
In Iowa they raise 'em
McDonald's justs slays 'em
But we're (beat, beat)
    we're waitin' (beat, beat)
    we're waitin' till the cows come home.

(pick up tempo)

We're gonna sing till the cows come home
We're gonna laugh till the cows come home
We're gonna dance till the cows come home
We're gonna sing, laugh dance and drop our pants
till the cow-ow-ows come ho-ome.

The butcher likes to freeze 'em
The bulls they like to please 'em
The farmer likes to squeeze 'em
But we're (beat, beat)
    We're waitin' (beat, beat)
    We're waitin' till the cows come home.

We're gonna romp till the cows come home
We're gonna stomp till the cows come home
We're gonna joke till the cows come home
We're gonna romp, stomp, joke and maybe smoke (hand over mouth)
Till the cow-ow-ows come ho-ome.

(KEY CHANGE)

We're gonna party till the cows come home
We're gonna party till the cows come home
We're gonna party till the cows come home
We're gonna P till the cows come
    A till the cows come
    R till the cows come
    T till the cows come
    Y till the cows come
Party till the cows come home!

(The next verse is sung in Chinese.)

(Scat your ass off--------- Where are those damn cows?
-----Mee-ow)

Original typewritten script for the theme song sketch

1982

Cast members giving hot chocolate and blankets to passersby on campus, January 1982; shown here, Mark Lancaster (Mee-Ow '81, '82, '83)

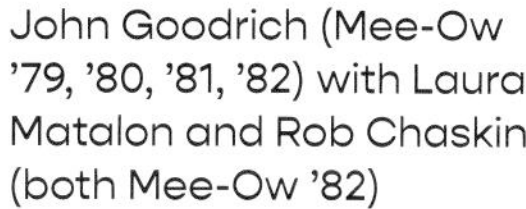

John Goodrich (Mee-Ow '79, '80, '81, '82) with Laura Matalon and Rob Chaskin (both Mee-Ow '82)

Cast members performing the musical sketch "A Norris Line," with a hand-painted rendition of Monet's *Houses of Parliament, Sunset* as a backdrop

1983

MEE-OW YEAR TEN

Wake Up, Yo Tinheads

Thursday through Saturday, Feb 24–26, at 8 p.m., McCormick Auditorium

The 1983 Mee-Ow Show is the *Rashomon* of the history of Mee-Ow. People recall it differently. Some attendees found it funny, while others remember it as providing a more challenging experience than audiences were accustomed to.

Certainly it is not as simple as the "it sucked" lore that has unfortunately and unfairly arisen about the show over the decades. Different is not necessarily bad, and experimentation and boundary pushing were absolutely consistent with the raison d'être of Mee-Ow.

Marking a change in the improv-based sketch-comedy structure first initiated by Dusty Kay and Bill Nuss, the 1983 show did not include improv games or a film. While these and other decisions altered the structure that had evolved over the previous decade, the rebellious tradition that the directors and cast of the 1983 Mee-Ow Show were upholding was significant. They were willing to experiment with the form and substance of the show. Such experimentation is risky, requiring courage and commitment; the results are never predictable when audience expectations are redirected, confounded, or subverted.

The only returning performers were Chris Hueben and Mark Lancaster, who also codirected. New cast members were Taylor Abbott, Mark Gunnion, Tami Hinz, Sue Klein, Ellen Kohrman, and Michael Simon.

"I remember the audition well," Gunnion recalled:

> Forty or fifty people in a large classroom, and they were having us do various exercises. I didn't have any comedy training or specific improv training. I had nothing to lose, so I figured the only way I was going to stand out was to be big. I was going to try to be extreme. And I was also going to try to subvert the directions, like try to add something, twist every suggestion. There was a mime exercise. And [Chris, the director] said, "OK, you're in a hall of mirrors now." So the people I'm with are miming it up [with the mirrors].

THIS YEAR IN HISTORY

US invades Grenada • IRA Christmas bombing outside Harrods • First mobile phones available for purchase • ARPANET begins creating the internet • *M*A*S*H* final episode • Cabbage Patch doll craze • Dow Jones year-end close 1259 • Average new car $10,607 • 1 gallon gas $1.16 • *Return of the Jedi*, *Octopussy*, *Flashdance*, *WarGames* • R.E.M., *Murmur*; Violent Femmes, *Violent Femmes*; The Police, *Synchronicity*; U2, *War*; David Bowie, *Let's Dance*

1983

And I [mimed pulling] out a hammer and smashed the mirrors down and started stepping through and hurting my feet and stuff like that. I took my shirt off and threw it down on the ground so this girl who was in the scene with me could stand on it and I could drag her across. So that's what I was doing. I was trying to be visual. [Then] they said I had a bow and arrow, and so I did this little thing [mimes shooting the arrow] and carried out the scene. I later heard that it was right then that I got cast because I had technically done that well, I had shot this arrow, but then I watched it and watched it land. . . . Mee-Ow started out as a protest show and then it became established enough that it was on the verge of slipping into becoming [just] another little thing you could tell the freshmen about. There was a little feeling of Reagan in the air and stuff like that. So I wanted to echo back to the provocative, rebel band kind of thing, trying to recapture that counterculture feeling a little bit.

The Show

As in previous years, the show began with an opening song built around the title; in this case, "Wake Up, Yo Tinheads," sung to the tune of "Roll Out the Barrel."

This was followed by "The Sandwich Man of the Opera," featuring an organist playing Bach's Toccata and Fugue in D Minor and revealing the secret of the Sandwich Man's food as similar to that of *Sweeney Todd: The Demon Barber of Fleet Street*. Although he had been the subject of sketches before, Bill Froehlig (the actual Sandwich Man) did not appreciate this interpretation.

Gunnion described the sketch titled "Deconstructions" as "very weird, very abstract." It began with a couple talking in bed and ends with a quote from the Dr. Seuss book *Hop on Pop*. Then someone yells "Cut!" and the scene is revealed to be a play. Then it's revealed to be a motion-picture set making a movie about a play about Dr. Seuss. Then it took another step back, revealing a news reporter talking about the making of the movie. The scene kept opening up until, at the

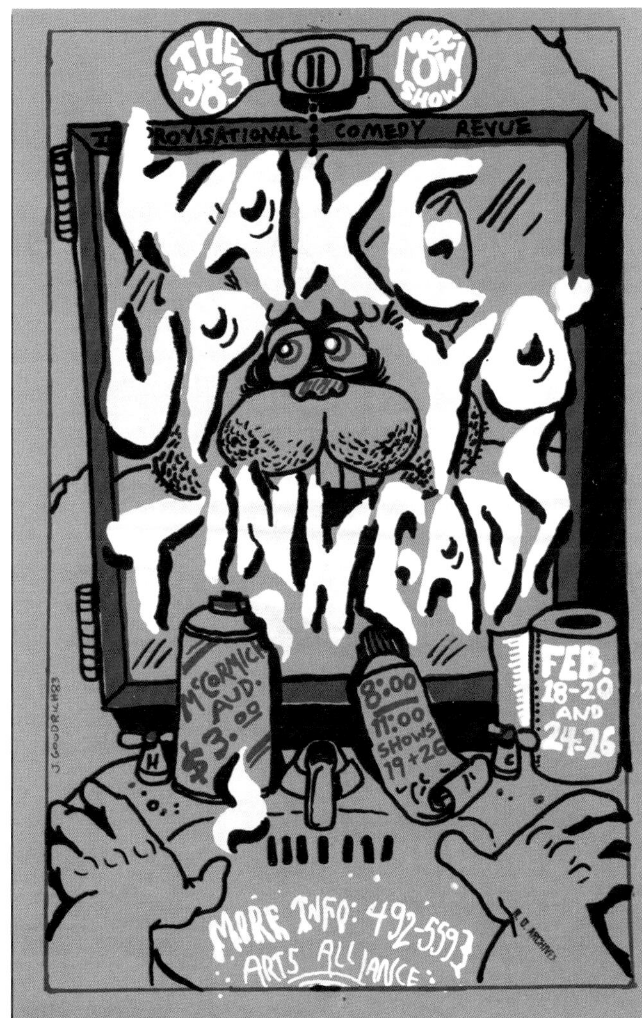

Poster for the 1983 show

end, a band of armed terrorists came out from the wings, held everyone on stage hostage, and announced that the audience was "ordered to leave the room to go out and talk to their parents and smoke a clove cigarette and be back here in fifteen minutes or we'll kill 'em all." Lights out, intermission.

Some perceived the reaction of audience members as confusion, remembering that some people did not return for the second act.

Others who were present recall no one leaving, and standing-room-only crowds for the performances.

Other sketches included a parody of Ronald Reagan; Hueben as a southern man trying to convince his relatives that marrying a mermaid should give him access to his inheritance; Lancaster as an avant-garde poet who says a lot about nothing; Lancaster and Hueben as cocaine users in a frenzy after massive consumption; and Kohrman as former Olympic gymnast Cathy Rigby in a commercial for the fictional product "Menopads," with the slogan "For those of you who can't do it like you used to but want to feel like you can."

There was no band. Music director Steve Huffines played the piano, intentionally off-key.

Reviews

The creators of this year's show clearly intended to be thought-provoking, and while many appreciated their approach to comedy, it seems that the show was not universally well received. While staff members recalled sold-out shows, others recalled that ticket sales declined throughout the run of the show, and that for the first time in many years, the Mee-Ow Show lost money.

Laura Koss noted in her February 25, 1983, review for the *Daily Northwestern* that there were a couple of energetic and entertaining sketches, but also commented on the limited participation of the entire cast. It seemed to her that it was primarily a two-man show, rather than a true balanced ensemble. She concluded, "Although showcasing only a few, 'MeeOw' leaves out some trite conventions and adds life of its own, providing fresh, new blood to this year's show."

Future cast member Dermot Mulroney recalled, "I can tell you from an audience member of the

KELLY SHEEHAN

The 1983 cast: (*back row*) Abbott, Gunnion, Kohrman, Simon; (*middle, top to bottom*) Hinz, Klein, Lancaster; (*right, foreground*) Hueben

’83 show, it was not a popular show among my group.”

In retrospect, people have suggested that the 1983 show was the result of an evolution of the counterculture of the ’70s that had become too anarchistic, nihilistic, or aggressive. Others contend that the reinvention of form, or at least of tone, was in keeping with the rebellious philosophy of the first Mee-Ow Show.

The 1983 show did not underestimate the literacy or intelligence of the audience. And opinions about the quality, humor, and entertainment value of the show differ wildly. The directors and cast may have misunderstood how much the ambitious, hardworking student audience wanted and needed the escape of silliness in their entertainment, rather than another intellectually challenging experience.

When asked, “Would it be correct to say that the ’83 Mee-Ow Show was intentionally challenging the comfort of the audience?” Lancaster replied:

> An honest response will be yes, because that’s what we wanted, but we also did not intend to alienate in any way other than Brechtian. But I believe people laughed from start to finish and it had nothing on the surface of it that was like, “Step in here if you dare, conservative, upright people.” If we were outrageous, then the Bangles [American pop band] were outrageous. I’m sure I would have rather been seen like Public Image Ltd [English post-punk band] or the Clash [English punk and post-punk band], but I think we were kind of like the Fabulous Thunderbirds [American blues-rock/Texas-rock band].

Describing the approach as Brechtian explains some of the audiences’ mixed reactions to the show. German dramatist-director Bertolt Brecht included reminders of the artificiality of theatrical performance in order to intentionally distance the audience from emotional involvement in his plays. Such an intention toward alienation was in contrast to the Mee-Ow Show’s usual approach of evoking laughter, thoughtfulness, and even the occasional tear from their audiences.

Certainly, the 1983 Mee-Ow Show was a turning point, as its reception and aftermath solidified the show’s purpose and direction for the future.

1983

KELLY SHEEHAN

The 1983 cast: Kohrman, Simon, Hinz, Gunnion, Klein, Lancaster, Hueben, and Abbott

ALEX GARCIA

3 Recovery and Success

1984–1990

With a change of leadership and stellar casts, Mee-Ow continued to hone its form, delivering its unique combination of social satire, political commentary, and madcap zaniness to sold-out audiences, all while honoring its original mission of providing a space for student expression and student response to the world around them.

Additionally, Mee-Ow cast members moved beyond the Shanley and McCormick stages, performing at twenty-four-hour improv marathons, Mayfests, and high schools and fraternities. They even crossed the pond for the Edinburgh Festival Fringe, where their appearances contributed to the creation of the successful improv television show *Whose Line Is It Anyway?* in Britain and the United States.

By the Mee-Ow Show's tenth anniversary, what had started as a rebellion had become an institution.

Facing page: Ana Gasteyer, Jessica Hughes, and Jill Cargerman in the 1988 Mee-Ow Show, *Mee-Ow Tse-Tung*

1984

MEE-OW YEAR ELEVEN

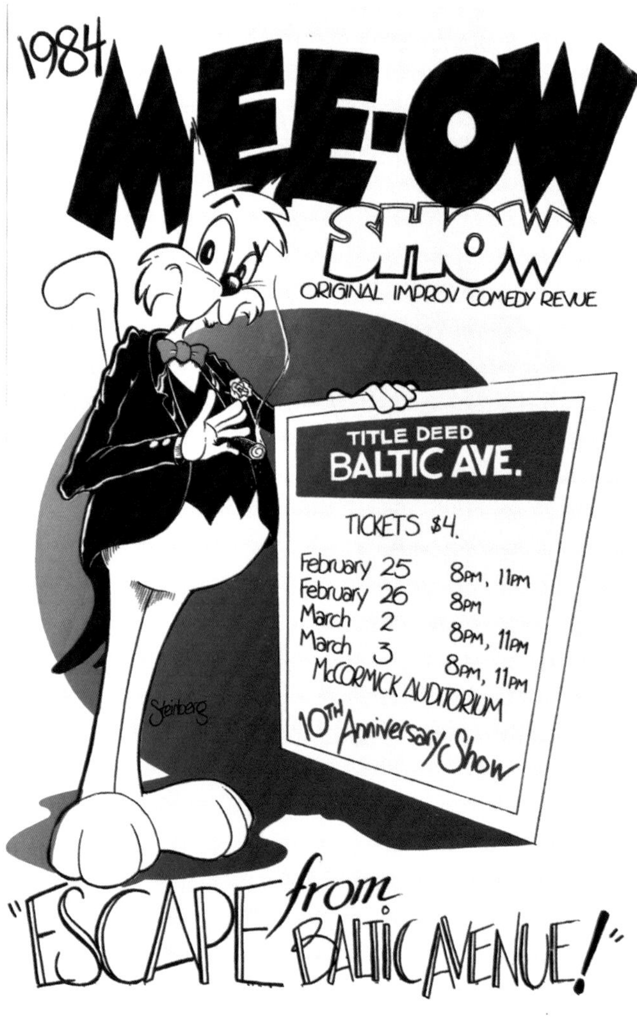

Escape from Baltic Avenue

Previews: Saturday, February 11, at 8 and 11 p.m., Shanley Pavilion

Mainstage: Saturday, February 25, at 8 and 11 p.m.; Sunday, February 26, at 8 p.m.; Friday and Saturday, March 2–3, at 8 and 11 p.m., McCormick Auditorium

For the first time since the inception of the Mee-Ow Show, there were no returning cast members. This was due to several factors, including the appointment of a new director and producer by the Arts Alliance Board.

Following the financial problems of the 1974 show, the Arts Alliance Board took its fiduciary responsibilities seriously. At some point after its formation in fall 1974, the Arts Alliance gained the authority to name directors and producers of the shows in their member groups.

Reportedy the Arts Alliance Board was disappointed in the critical reception and financial results of the 1983 show. As had occasionally been the practice dating back to at least 1976, the Arts Alliance placed announcements in the *Daily Northwestern* in mid-May asking for petitions from students who wanted to direct and produce the 1984 Mee-Ow Show.

Less than two weeks later, the Arts Alliance Board named board member senior Eric Gilliland as the director and junior Mark Brogger as the producer. Perhaps in solidarity with their director, Mark Lancaster, or for other reasons, the remaining cast of the 1983 show (except for Mark Gunnion and Chris Hueben, who had graduated) chose not to audition for the 1984 show. Lancaster was a senior and could have auditioned to be in the cast, but chose not to. Gilliland has since said that he absolutely would have cast Lancaster, who had several years of improv experience.

Gilliland was reluctant to take on the role of director, admitting that he didn't know how to do improv. The board told him to learn. He had wanted to direct a stage version of the popular 1961 comedy album *Stan Freberg Presents the United States of America, Vol. 1*, but instead, he threw himself into this new Mee-Ow assignment.

THIS YEAR IN HISTORY

Indira Gandhi assassinated • Super Bowl Orwellian "1984" Apple Macintosh commercial • Band Aid "Do They Know It's Christmas" fundraiser • 1984 LA Summer Olympics • Pesticide leak in Bhopal kills 3,500+ in India • Dow Jones year-end close 1212 • Average new car $11,374 • 1 gallon gas $1.13 • *Beverly Hills Cop*, *Ghostbusters*, *Indiana Jones and the Temple of Doom*, *Gremlins*, *The Karate Kid*, *Footloose* • Prince, *Purple Rain*; The Smiths, *The Smiths*; Bruce Springsteen, *Born in the U.S.A.*; Talking Heads, *Stop Making Sense*; Cocteau Twins, *Treasure*

He recalled:

> I spent that summer going downtown to improv shows and watching and learning. I had a friend who was in an improv group and I just watched her and watched her and watched her and learned really simple games. Then there was a letter-writing campaign from the old Mee-Owers to the president [of the university] saying, "Hey, why is Eric Gilliland directing this? Why isn't Mark Lancaster directing it? Because the legacy of Mee-Ow must continue through its forbearers." [I thought] "Oh fuck, I stepped in it." Obviously, nothing happened, but there were letters written that were really anti me.

Because Gilliland had written for Waa-Mu, some students considered him a die-hard Waa-Mu guy and thought his appointment represented a takeover of the once-upstart Mee-Ow Show. This perception was understandable but unwarranted, since prior to Mee-Ow, Waa-Mu had been the primary venue for aspiring writers on campus, and even Kay and Nuss had submitted material to Waa-Mu.

The final cast included Gilliland, Karen Cooper, Jesse Dabson, Kelley Hughes, Richard Kaplan, Wendi Messing, John Cameron Mitchell, Dermot Mulroney, Richard Radutzky, and Romy Rosemont.

Developing the Show

The entire cast brainstormed ideas for the title. Regarding the final choice, Gilliland recalled:

> *Escape from Baltic Avenue* was a play [on the idea] that the show before us was like Baltic Avenue, the lowest-priced property in the Monopoly game, and we were escaping from it. . . . We did a month of just basic improv games, because none of us had done it before. I got to use all of these games I learned and we didn't write anything down. It was all out of improv. We started with really easy games, then more advanced scene making. We had a long rehearsal process and we were aces.
>
> We just drilled these games and built the trust. And everyone was really super funny. We were in the trenches together. We didn't know what we were doing, so I pretended to know. I knew a little more than they did, but not much. But I'm a pretty good organizer or leader and I'm not a dick and I have fun. I had a really good time. Then I would say, "OK, break up into groups and do a scene that takes place at a French restaurant." And they go off and they do a little thing, and you might talk about a little bit, and talk about what works. Then we do that constantly, finding what would work. Nothing was written down, ever. Mark Brogger, the producer, and I would choose which sketches were working, which ones were not. We must have done a hundred different [sketches] to come down to the fifteen we did. Mark Brogger was very responsible for helping the show a lot.

Rosemont said that the cast got a specific direction from Gilliland. "He basically said, do not swear onstage unless you are going to get a huge laugh from that. Don't be gross just to be gross."

"Eric innately knew Mee-Ow needed a redo," Mulroney recalled. "Classic TV comedy really was probably the strongest influence for Eric. Marx Brothers and classic cinema comedy too. He was a student of it then and obviously now he's a master teacher of it."

The Shanley Preview Shows

One weekend of preview shows took place in January in Shanley Hall and served as an opportunity for the cast to gauge audience reactions and refine the sketches. Richard Kaplan's instrumental music trio, the Undecideds, played for these Shanley shows.

This was the first year that the Mee-Ow Show performed for the public in Shanley Hall, which had recently been renovated and renamed Shanley Pavilion. In an article in the *Daily Northwestern* (February 10, 1984), "New Shanley Hosts Mee-ow," Martha Ross wrote:

> Almost more than Norris, the newly refurbished Shanley Hall (or Shanley Pavilion as it's known in more polite circles) has proven to be one of the more versatile structures on campus.
>
> Originally built as a naval training facility for radio operators during World War II, it has served as a classroom for the post-war influx of students, a mess hall for commuters, a pre-Norris campus bookstore and Amazingrace, an early '70s coffee house that served lunches of lentil soup and evenings of folk music.
>
> Recently, however, Shanley had deteriorated into a storage dump for assorted junk and pieces of an old piano. Norris authorized the building's renovation this summer for "Food and Fiction," a dinner show presented by the Theater and Interpretation Department.
>
> "They cleaned it out, patched up the carpet, gave it a fresh coat of paint, built a new stage and even put flower boxes outside," said Bill Graef, Norris asst. operations manager. They also snazzed "Hall" to "Pavilion," retaining the "Shanley" in honor of English Prof. Jay Lyndon Shanley.

Mulroney recalled that "what Eric and this new regime brought in [as an audience] was the fraternity boys. The place was packed with suddenly a whole different audience instead of esoteric hippie style. You know, loosey-goosey, comedy theater people. Suddenly Shanley Hall had people lining up outside in the night, drinking in the freezing cold and trying to get in to see the second show of Mee-Ow. So it caused its own sensation, and a different culture began to come out of that show that continued."

The McCormick Show Highlights

This year's show included more of the improv games that had proven popular with audiences. The mix of content was about one-third improv and two-thirds sketches.

Mitchell said that they knew they were under a microscope because of the reception of the previous year and the success of Practical Theatre. Consequently, *Escape from Baltic Avenue* featured less '70s-style "stoner" humor and more pure, nonpolitical parody and schtick, giving the audience what they wanted.

The opening musical number was written by band leader Fran Banich (now Banish), consisting of a medley of old TV show themes and setting the mood for the fun of the show.

The title-themed Baltic Avenue sketch was a trip through the game Monopoly as if it were a trip through hell like Dante's *Inferno*. Kaplan and Gilliland were a version of Dante being guided through hell by the ancient Roman poet Virgil. The entire cast was in the sketch, including Mitchell as an old crone-like character.

Radutzky played Phil Donahue in a sketch based on *The Phil Donahue Show*, a popular talk show that had become nationally syndicated in 1970 and relocated to Chicago in 1974. The guest of the show was a baby played by Rosemont, who didn't speak but only uttered "KAAH" in what was described as a sound similar to a cat throwing up a hairball. The other guests on the show interpreted Baby KAAH's words. The punch line was when KAAH spoke in real words about being delivered by C-section.

Baby KAAH returned later in the show with Radutzky playing a psychiatrist who interpreted the "profound" meaning of KAAH's utterances. Radutzky handed Baby KAAH a piece of paper and asked her to draw something. She stuck out her tongue through the paper.

The "Dueling Comedians" game-show sketch featured Kaplan and Mulroney, with Radutzky as the moderator and game-show host. After the comedians told a joke, Radutzky asked the audience to choose the winner of that round.

Kelley Hughes played a therapist with patient Mitchell as a troubled London punk schoolboy that he described as "a Johnny Rotten" type of character. At first he was very hostile toward her. Hughes "had a handbag with [odd] things like lampposts coming out of it, and I was startled." She turned out to be his old nanny, Mary Poppins, and he eventually ended up crying while she held him. After he left, she changed character with the next patient, becoming who the patient needed her to be. Mitchell recalled the sketch as being "very cute."

Reviews

The show was very well received by audiences. Shows were sold out, and there was sufficient demand to warrant performance of a highlights show at the end of the year.

Gilliland recalled that on opening night at McCormick Auditorium, Mark Lancaster, the previous year's director, "came over and shook my hand and said, 'That was really fucking great. Congratulations.'"

In retrospect, it is possible, perhaps even likely, that the success of the 1984 show under the direction of Gilliland saved the Mee-Ow Show from being discontinued.

The Mee-Ow Show Cast: Putting the improv back into improvisational.

KELLY SHEEHAN

Daily Northwestern, February 24, 1984

1985

MEE-OW YEAR TWELVE

Local an' Aesthetic

Previews: Friday and Saturday, February 8–9, at 8 and 11 p.m., Shanley Pavilion

Mainstage: Fridays and Saturdays, February 22–23 and March 1–2, at 8 and 11 p.m., McCormick Auditorium

Returning to the tradition of the outgoing director and producer naming the next year's director, Eric Gilliland and producer Mark Brogger named Romy Rosemont as the director of the 1985 Mee-Ow Show. She was the first female director in the history of the Mee-Ow Show.

The returning performers included Rosemont, Richard Kaplan, Dermot Mulroney, and Richard Radutzky. Brogger returned as producer. Fran Banich's band played again. New cast members were Beth Bash, Craig Bierko, Allyson Rice, and Karen Schiff.

Developing the Show

As in previous years, the entire cast brainstormed possible names for the show. Mulroney remembered those times as "some of the funnest nights. I never, not once, had a good idea for a title. So then it was just like an early version of one of those reality shows like *Survivor* or something, where you ally yourself with the person who has a title that might be OK because you just really don't like the other title."

This year's title was a clever double entendre, meaning both "local and aesthetic(ally pleasing)" and "a local anesthetic" (to dull the pain in a specific location, rather than a general anesthetic that would put you to sleep).

The Show Highlights

Eric Gilliland had graduated the previous year, and the 1985 cast flew him in to see their show. Gilliland got onstage and did improv with them.

The mix was close to fifty-fifty improv games and comedy sketches, a change from the previous year's one-third improv and two-thirds sketches, and there was once again musical improv in which audience members would suggest topics that the cast would ad-lib song lyrics about.

THIS YEAR IN HISTORY

Live Aid concerts for famine relief • New Coke debacle • Greenpeace ship *Rainbow Warrior* sunk by France • Michael Jordan named NBA Rookie of the Year • Dow Jones year-end close 1547 • Average new car $11,838 • 1 gallon gas $1.12 • *Back to the Future*, *The Color Purple*, *The Goonies* • Dire Straits, *Brothers in Arms*; Tears for Fears, *Songs from the Big Chair*; The Cure, *The Head on the Door*

1985

Fran Banich's band played between sketches and during intermission. Their selections included popular hit songs and recognizable TV theme songs, a practice that has continued.

Sketches included Rosemont reprising her baby character KAAH, who could only make the sound "KAAH," like a cat throwing up a hairball (the audience made the same sound along with her); "The Hall of Has-Beens," similar to the animatronic Disney Hall of Presidents but instead populated with once-famous celebrities; and "The Bored Room," which Bierko recalled like this: "Richard Kaplan and I came up with a thing called 'bored room.' It was just lights up—and I think we took a whole minute—and I think we got laughs at just [stares silently] two guys who had nothing to say. And then I think the first line was something like, 'Is there any seltzer left or crackers?' And all, it was a 'bored' meeting. That was the punch line. But it worked. It was just basically *Waiting for Godot* if it were a sketch in Mee-Ow."

In a five-minute solo sketch, Bierko portrayed a "very unpleasant British guy, a performance artist named Plack" who was supposed to answer questions from the audience but instead would condescendingly insult the questioner. He recalled:

> I would just look at what they're wearing, where their accent is from, and I never addressed the question. I just attacked them. Looking back, I think about the arrogance. . . .

HUH UNHOH . . . IS THIS MIKE WORKING? WHAT? OH, IT IS . . . OKAY THEN, I'D LIKE TO THANK EVERYONE FOR STOPPING BY THE PREVIEWS OF THE 1985 MEE-OW SHOW. HOPE YOU ENJOY THE GALA PRODUCTION WE HAVE IN STORE FOR YOU TONIGHT. THE DANCING GIRLS, THE DAZZLING COSTUMES, THE STROBE, PYROTECHNICS LIKE YOU WOULDN'T BELIEVE — YOU PEOPLE ARE CERTAINLY IN FOR A TREAT !! SO JUST SIT BACK, TAKE A LONG PULL ON THAT CIGERETTE IN YOUR TIGHT LITTLE FIST AND LET THE SEARING GUITARS OF THE UNDECIDED LULL YOU SOMEWHERE OVER THE RAINBOW ! THANKS FOR THE BUCK.

PRODUCED BY--- MARK BROGGER
DIRECTED BY---- ROMY ROSEMONT

CAST

BETH BASH	RICHARD RADUTZKY
CRAIG BIERKO	ROMY ROSEMONT
RICHARD KAPLAN	KAREN SCHIFF
DERMOT MULRONEY	ALLYSON RICE

STAFF

STUART FELDMAN	ROBERT RAMSEY
GRACE KAHNG	SUE PETSCHE
BARRY GRIBBON	MARY JANE HERMAN
DAN GUYETTE	DAN FISHER
TODD GRINNELL	KENNY CHODOCK
LARRY WELZEN	CATHY HAMMOND
JOE SZADOWSKI	JAMIE GOLDMAN
LIZ KRUEGER	DEBBIE DECKER

LORI COZEN

The interior of the 1985 program, including a note from director Romy Rosemont

> I love the idea of playing with tone, starting with something silly that becomes [serious]—what would be the paradigm? Like if you could actually get the cast of *Gilligan's Island* and then have a hurricane come in and it's devastating. That's what I wanted the [*Gilligan's Island*] reunion to be when I was a kid. And I didn't understand it. I thought they were going to do a TV movie. I thought it would have been really cool. And I bet all of those actors could have done it if it were dark and they were fucking depressed. . . . That would have been really fascinating.

The "Selling of Mrs. Goodkind's Deli" sketch exemplified this changing of tone, and included the entire cast, with Schiff playing the owner, Mrs. Goodkind. Bierko remembered that Radutzky played the heavy:

> He was coming in to buy this local deli and it was just like *Cheers* [the TV sitcom]. We had characters sitting there. Richard Radutzky and I were two old Jewish men. This guy comes in and he's brokered a deal to buy the deli and he goes, "I need you all out." He's just playing the vicious heavy. We were not playing it for laughs. As soon as he walked out, there was this moment of silence. People were thinking, "Where are we going to go?" And then it became a musical. We sang this song I wrote with the guy who did the music. I remember bits and pieces of it.
>
> *Don't sell the place,*
> *Mrs. Goodkind.*
> *It will only make you cry.*
> *This boy can carve a lunchmeat angel*
> *And give them wings*
> *Of rye!*

Colbert and the No Fun Mud Piranhas

In November 1984, sophomore Chris Pfaff and transfer student Stephen Colbert auditioned for Mee-Ow but were not selected. The following summer, Pfaff and Colbert were both working in the collections department of the Northwestern University Library. Pfaff asked Colbert to join a Northwestern team for "the Harold," a new style of long-form improv created and produced by improv pioneers Del Close and Charna Halpern, who had founded ImprovOlympic (now iO Theater) in Chicago in 1981.

Halpern was developing university improv teams based on the Harold, with two already established at the University of Chicago and Yale. Pfaff was on an ImprovOlympic team, and Halpern asked him to create a Northwestern team.

Colbert recruited his then girlfriend, Ayun Halliday, and Trey Nichols, and Pfaff recruited Larry Buhl, Marc Goldsmith, and Jessica Hughes.

Halpern named the Northwestern team "Green Eggs and Hamlet." But Pfaff remembered how the final name of the team was chosen: "Colbert and I had a colleague at the library—a woman named Jean Dixon (yes, like the then-popular psychic)—who had recounted a nightmare of her young child, in which the boy found himself trying to traverse a mud puddle which was stocked with piranhas who hated laughter. We thought this 'No Fun Mud Piranhas' story was so hilarious that we should use it for the name of our troupe since no one else would come close to anything remotely similar."

Halpern coached the No Fun Mud Piranhas in October and November of 1985, and the team competed with Yale and U of C in a Thanksgiving Week '85 tournament.

In the November 22, 1985, *Chicago Tribune* preview article titled "To Win This Game, Hit Crowd with a Schtick," reporter Ron Grossman explained the competition in sports terms, accompanied by a photo of Close in a striped referee jersey posing between the NU team and the U of C team, the "Avant-Garfields."

Pfaff left the No Fun Mud Piranhas to join the Mee-Ow cast for the 1986 show. David Schwimmer joined the group after not being cast in the Mee-Ow Show.

Sometime later, the No Fun Mud Piranhas became inactive. The group was revived in 2012 by Medill senior and Mee-Ow cast member Matthew Hays and Weinberg senior Tim White as an audition-free, cost-free, drop-in group for students interested in learning improv.

A parody of the TV game show *To Tell the Truth* centered around the libel suit by former US Army Chief of Staff General William Westmoreland against CBS News. The format featured three contestants, two of whom were impostors, and panelists had to determine which one actually committed libel. This sketch presumed that the audience was aware of the $120 million suit brought against the television network for its documentary that asserted Westmoreland had manipulated intelligence about enemy strength in Vietnam to give the impression of progress. On February 18, 1985, only days before the trial was to go to the jury, Westmoreland agreed to dismiss the case.

Reviews

In the *Daily Northwestern*, Thomas A. Troppe wrote:

> Romy Rosemont, who directed "Local an' Aesthetic," placed a high emphasis on improvisation, probably more than ever before in Mee-Ow's 11-year history. Out of 19 comedy sketches in the "Local an' Aesthetic" show, no less than nine required some audience participation.
>
> As a result, the cast established themselves as quick-witted, intelligent performers and involved the audience in the performance. The other 10 skits were delightfully intelligent. They dealt largely with the "Aesthetic" the title promises. Subjects ranged from Greek tragedy and modern art to professional wrestling and TV game shows. The one "Local" piece jabbed humor at the McDonalds restaurant being built in Evanston.
>
> The band that played during intermission and between skits deserves mentioning. Though they're listed only as "the band" in the program, they kept the show going with great music and theme songs from old TV shows.
>
> But the whole cast performed well. In general, the men seemed to outshine the women a bit, but no individual carried the show.

Cast member Allyson Rice in a "bag lady" sketch she wrote with Romy Rosemont

The Loss of a Cast Member

Dermot Mulroney recalled the untimely loss of fellow castmate Beth Bash:

She died right at the end of college and our group experience now plays in that context. So if I'm somewhat traumatized about the 1985 show . . . you know, those were the events that ensued shortly thereafter. It was the end of my senior year and we had been boyfriend and girlfriend. You can touch on that in your book. I've never discussed it anywhere, not out of protecting my experience or her family, it has just simply never come up. I've since supported suicide prevention in every way I could. Every class in every college, somebody didn't make it through. Beth Bash, bless her, was an incredible cast member, an incredible musical comedian. With perfect pitch and dancing and tap dancing and super skills. A super energetic and risk-taking comedian.

1986

MEE-OW YEAR THIRTEEN

Oedipuss 'n Boots

Previews: Friday, February 7, at 8 p.m.; Saturday, February 8, at 8 and 11 p.m., Shanley Pavilion

Mainstage: Fridays and Saturdays, February 21–22 and February 28–March 1, at 8 and 11 p.m., McCormick Auditorium

Liz Kruger had been the stage manager of the 1985 Mee-Ow Show. As she recalled,

> I joined Arts Alliance and I really wanted to be the producer of the Mee-Ow Show. I had to submit for it and they gave it to me, and then I had to pick a director. [One] person who wanted to direct, who subsequently became a friend, was a guy named Adam Grant, who was friends with all the people from the prior year: Bierko, Karen Schiff, Allyson Rice, and that whole group. Adam basically said to me, "If you pick me, you get all the people from the legacy, and if you don't pick me, none of these other people are going to be in the show," which made me feel like I'm not going to be bullied into picking somebody. But Dan [Patterson] just had that kind of Monty Python sort of sense of humor that I really responded to. Dan's aesthetic was similar to mine also because we do have a sentimental streak in us. And Adam was more into the intellectual side of things. I really thought that Dan Patterson was a genius. It turned out I wasn't wrong about that. I wasn't afraid to start fresh. I saw something in Dan Patterson, I saw a vision, and I felt like I'm going to take a flier on this guy. And we were great partners together. We cast a whole new group, and they put on a great show. The women in particular are still really close today.

In what was an exception over the years, Patterson did not perform as a member of the cast. John Lehr recalled that Patterson was in grad school, "so he was already thinking about 'What am I going to do after I get out of grad school?' So, yeah, he was looking at it from a whole different angle than we were. We [the cast] were just, you know, doing drugs and drinking and having fun. And [Dan] was thinking about his career.

THIS YEAR IN HISTORY

Chernobyl nuclear disaster • Space shuttle *Challenger* disaster • *The Oprah Winfrey Show* debuts nationally • Hands Across America • *The Phantom of the Opera* premieres in London • Iran-Contra Affair • Dow Jones year-end close 1896 • Average new car $12,650 • 1 gallon gas $0.86 • *Top Gun*, *Crocodile Dundee*, *Platoon*, *Back to School*, *Aliens*, *Ferris Bueller's Day Off* • Paul Simon, *Graceland*; Beastie Boys, *Licensed to Ill*; Madonna, *True Blue*; Run-D.M.C., *Raising Hell*

1986

And basically, he turned the Mee-Ow Show into *Whose Line Is It Anyway?* And I think he would agree with that."

For the second time since the inception of the Mee-Ow Show, there were no returning cast members. This was due to a combination of factors, including a new director who had not been in the previous show, several cast members graduating, and a few cast members deciding not to continue.

The final cast included Mollie Allen, Dave Clapper, Jon Craven, Andy Hirsch, Lisa Houle, Jessica Hughes, John Lehr, Barry Levin, Catherine Newman, and Chris Pfaff.

The Show Highlights

Of the title sketch, Patterson said:

> I'd gone back to England and I'd gone to see an amateur group do a play [*Puss in Boots*]. It was on a very bouncy, noisy stage and they were all wearing clomping shoes and they were clomping around the stage and you couldn't hear the dialogue. I started convulsing with laughter. So in Mee-Ow, they did a scene from *Oedipus Rex*, but whenever anyone is talking, everyone else is moving, so you can never hear anyone because they're all clomping around. It was a very silly sketch we called "Oedipuss in Boots." So we were able to combine the cat imagery and also this ridiculous thing of people clomping around in heavy footwear so you couldn't hear any of the speech.

The creation of one sketch depicting four sportscasters in a car demonstrated that improvisers are always paying attention and can draw source material from any situation. Pfaff recollected its origin:

> The group of us—including Dan and his brother, me, Dave Clapper, Barry Levin, and Mollie Allen—were sitting in a round booth at The Bar, when [the waitress], a fellow R/TV/F student, took our order. She rattled off six different kinds of cheese for Dan's brother's burger, and he—a Londoner—shook his head and said, "Ah—somethin' 'bout America."
>
> Dave, Barry, Mollie, and I picked up on the "over-the-top American" vibe that Dan's brother was feeling, and started joking around about John Madden, whose "Boom!" commentary on NFL telecasts was a big thing, and the next thing you know, we started riffing on sportscasters having a conversation during a meal. "Pass the salt, Mollie!" said Barry, and I chimed in with, "Oh, Mollie has really upped her salt passing this season!" and Dave added something about, "The lineup of ketchup and condiment bottles is no match for Mollie's salt passing!" and we just kept it up.
>
> Dan did not really know John Madden, but I did a Madden telestrator bit showing how Mollie's pass had perfect rotation, and he was fascinated. We kept this up the whole meal. It was one of those amazing Mee-Ow moments where the riffs just kept adding to the hilarity. Of course, Barry—the REAL sports fan and would-be commentator in the group—was able to keep the thread moving quickly. He and I would later joke about rehearsing in Shanley Pavilion, à la Pauley Pavilion at UCLA, when we started preparing for the previews, in January; "Ah, it's a donnybrook at THE PAVILION!"
>
> After our spirited meal at The Bar, Dan took this whole idea of sportscasters staying in character through mundane everyday

1986

moments and transitioned it to the "Sportscasters in a Car" speeding-ticket scene, which had some great sight gags. John Lehr was added to the sketch, and his bit with the window sound effects was just hysterical. The skycam view, Madden telestrator, and Dave Clapper as traffic cop/referee were all riffs that we had done in The Bar and somehow Dan brought them into focus in the sketch.

I really think if we had hung out more at The Bar after rehearsals—or on off-days—we would have dreamed up at least a dozen other skits. That night at The Bar, Dan's brother, unbeknownst to him at the time, was our "audience" for some improv magic.

Based on an idea by Patterson, one sketch featured the entire cast of ten and was called "Ten Little Indians," in reference to the novel by Agatha Christie. This sketch depicted kids at a party all suggesting party games, and whoever suggested the game then died playing that game. "These kids who were about seven were going, 'I got a game, I got a game!'" Patterson remembered. "They played the game, and then one of them is dead and then they carry on. Taste-wise, I'm not sure I would do that now."

Additional sketches included "The Justice League of Toledo," featuring useless superheroes; Barry Levin auditioning henchmen for Batman villains; and an improv game that was about *The Wizard of Oz*. With her petite stature and dark hair, Lisa Houle resembled Dorothy, so of course, the character of Dorothy was played by Levin.

About the conclusion of the show, Liz Kruger recalled that she and Patterson "allowed the comedy to have an arc in the show. It did end on that kind of [sentimental] sketch, about what [would have happened] if Dave Clapper

The Edinburgh Festival Fringe Trip

Director Dan Patterson arranged for Mee-Ow to perform at the Edinburgh Festival Fringe in Scotland. Established in 1947, the Fringe is now the world's largest performance arts festival, so named because it was "on the fringe" of the more mainstream Edinburgh International Festival of Music and Drama.

To raise money for their August 1986 trip to Scotland, the cast performed at high schools, for alumni, and at other venues. As reported in *Dialogue*, the magazine of the School of Speech, "Dean Roy V. Wood pledged financial support from the School of Speech, and other funds came from Northwestern trustees, alumni, and local contributors." In addition, the cast performed at the first Mee-Ow-athon, a ten-hour improvisation event.

By the time of the Fringe, Patterson had already been hired by the BBC. So he brought BBC executives to a Mee-Ow performance and pitched the idea of an improv radio and TV series. This became the popular show *Whose Line Is It Anyway?*, which Patterson said was the runner-up title for the 1986 Mee-Ow Show.

In addition to performing with Mee-Ow in Edinburgh, Hirsch, Hughes, and Levin also performed in two plays with a New York City acting company, including the play *Moonchildren*, in which Levin played the lead role. They rehearsed the plays for a month in London before meeting the rest of the Mee-Ow Show cast in Edinburgh.

Reviewing Mee-Ow's Edinburgh performance in the newspaper *The Scotsman*, Hayden Murphy wrote:

> This is an American "great fun show" that manages, for once, to justify the hype. At the YWCA the cast of ten were slick movers, quick thinkers, and even on the night of the fireworks produced a cracking good show, which was only vaguely late. They are an attractive lot. They begin in the format of *Fame* which has begat so many bad shows on the Fringe over the years. Then they start plundering the audience for "participators." . . . Unlike other groups their guests were treated well. They were not mocked and they were gently involved. If late at night you want a humorous encouraging start to the next day I recommend this show.

hadn't been alive. [The sketch quickly replayed the show, showing] all the terrible shit that would have happened to every actor during the show and how everybody would have died in the show and in a funny way, because Dave wasn't there."

Poster for the Mee-Ow Show's Edinburgh Festival Fringe performances

1987

MEE-OW YEAR FOURTEEN

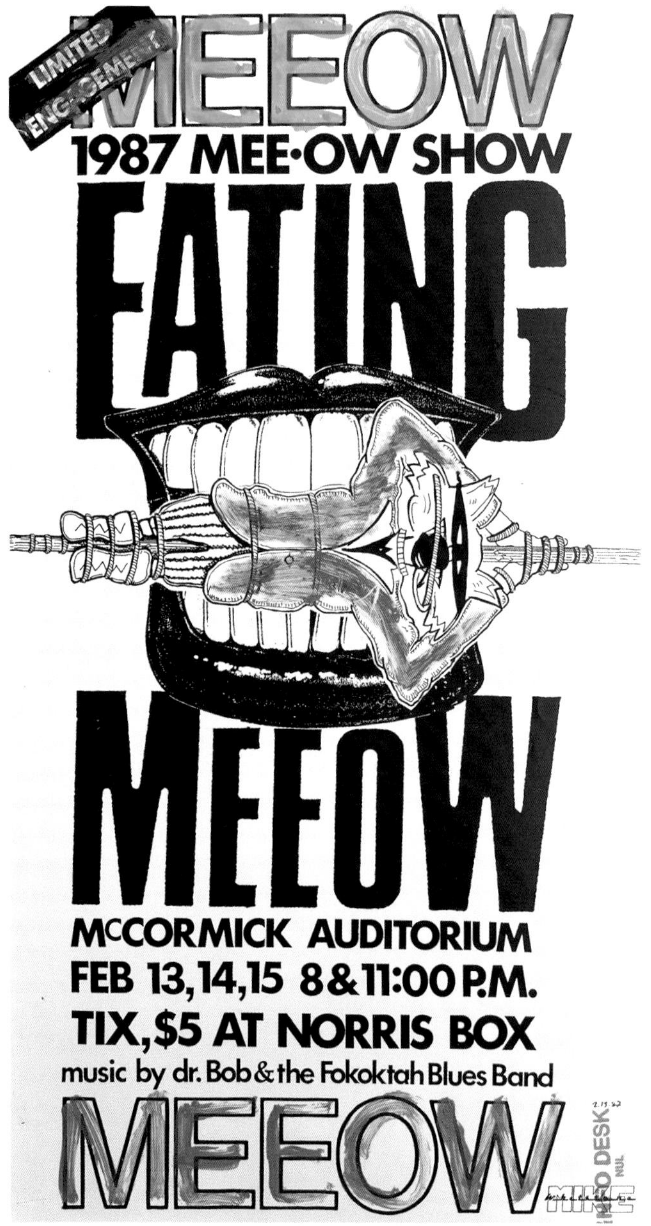

Eating Mee-Ow

Previews: Friday and Saturday, January 30–31, at 8 and 11 p.m., Shanley Pavilion

Mainstage: Friday through Sunday, February 13–15, at 8 and 11 p.m., McCormick Auditorium

Previous year cast member Jon Craven was chosen to direct but did not perform in the 1987 show. He remembered the casting process:

> I wanted to focus a little bit more on the improv aspect, and create opportunities for more organic, drawn-out improvisational situations. So that was kind of the impetus behind the change that I made. We had a cast of ten or eleven the year that Dan [Patterson] directed it. Looking back, it all feels like kind of a big mess. Socially for me, this was my very, very worst nightmare. I had a nervous breakdown the night I posted the final callbacks and then the cast. I literally had a nervous breakdown that morning, I woke up and I could not walk. My back went out. It was like an emotional [response]. I couldn't get out of bed for three days. I was mortified because I think I was such a people pleaser. But I also had this idea for what [Mee-Ow] should be, and I thought it should be smaller. I wanted to use some of the people from the previous year, but not all of them. All of my college roommates auditioned and none of them got in, and not all the people from the previous year got in. But, you know, it's funny. Almost forty years later, looking back, I realize it really had a big impact on people's lives. I wasn't able to go to each one of the people I didn't bring back and say why I like these [other] people for the show and not you. I knew when I didn't cast David Schwimmer that it was a big deal because David was so at ease onstage and so funny. Comedy and light drama, everything came so easily to him. I knew David pretty well and I knew him to be one of the most talented people overall in the school. But I just didn't feel like he would fit as well in an ensemble, and hilariously now, I like to tell people that I'm the guy who didn't cast David Schwimmer.

THIS YEAR IN HISTORY

First *The Simpsons* shorts premiere • Ronald Reagan's "Tear Down This Wall" speech • US stock market crash, 22.6% drop • Dow Jones year-end close 1939 • Average new car $13,383 • 1 gallon gas $0.90 • *Fatal Attraction*; *Good Morning, Vietnam*; *The Untouchables*; *Lethal Weapon* • U2, *The Joshua Tree*; Guns N' Roses, *Appetite for Destruction*; Michael Jackson, *Bad*; R.E.M., *Document*; Depeche Mode, *Music for the Masses*; INXS, *Kick*

1987

Returning cast members included Mollie Allen, Lisa Houle, John Lehr, and Catherine Newman. Jessica Hughes was an associate producer. New cast members included Robert "Bo" Blackburn, Marc Goldsmith, Melanie Hoopes, and Jerry Saslow.

The Show Highlights

Goldsmith recalled, "I had these very typical '80s pair of MC Hammer pants that were blue with black flowers on them, and they became my lucky pants and people always [were saying], 'You can't wear those pants every show.' I'm like, 'I wash them, but they're my lucky pants. They're going to bring us luck.' And sure enough, I believe I wore them at every show, including Edinburgh. And I don't think we ever had a bad show. So I mean, I attribute it to the pants."

Sketches included an escort service run by the philosophy, French, and theater departments; then President Reagan as senile and easily distracted; and actors having a very deep conversation while putting on makeup before a show. That scene ended when the audience realized that they were the members of KISS and had been having a conversation that was incongruous with the image of the band.

In the *Daily Northwestern*, Nicole Craig wrote, "Another skit, paws-down the most inspired in the show, depicts the parts of an answering machine gossiping about their owner, conspiring against her callers and doctoring her messages. Not only is the scene hysterical, but it captures wonderfully the fear many of us have—or, perhaps, should have—of every encroaching technology."

Lookingglass Theatre Company

David Schwimmer cofounded Lookingglass Theatre Company with fellow Northwestern students Eva Barr, David Catlin, Thom Cox, Lawrence DiStasi, Joy Gregory, David Kersnar, and Andy White. The company's first production, *Through the Lookingglass*, was produced at the Great Room in Jones Residential College on the Northwestern University campus.

Schwimmer, an actor, comedian, producer, and director, is also known for costarring on the long-running television series *Friends*.

As reported in the July 30, 1987, *Daily Northwestern*, Mee-Ow Show director Craven helped Lookingglass make their first trip to the Fringe in Edinburgh. They performed *Alice in Wonderland*, "an experimental improvisation based on the interpretation of Lewis Kiles' [*sic*] text . . . Although the play is scripted, the rehearsal process has been largely improvisational," said Schwimmer, the play's director.

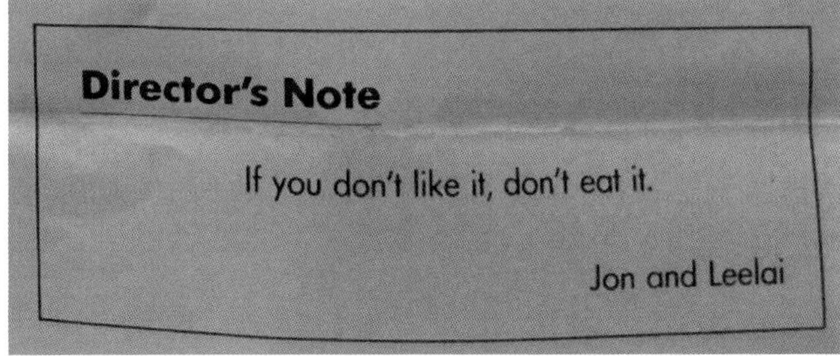

Director's Note

If you don't like it, don't eat it.

Jon and Leelai

Program note from director Jon Craven and associate director Leelai Demoz

1987

Reviews

In the February 13 *Daily Northwestern*, Nicole Craig wrote:

> Good improv is a fine art, almost indigenous to this city, and this year's Mee-Ow Show, "Eating Mee-Ow" (think hard, it'll come), admirably upholds Chicago's reputation. The simple truth is that this knock-'em-over-with-energy-and-talent cast . . . makes a most difficult job look incredibly easy. "Eating Mee-Ow" is structured beautifully to showcase the cast and the medium.
>
> Along the way, the audience often has to perform some mental gymnastics itself. At its best, improv is fertile ground for spontaneous, creative, and sometimes wild humor, and "Eating Meow" delivers just that. Basically, it's prrrty close to prrrfect.

The Fringe: Return Trip

The Mee-Ow Show performances at the Edinburgh Festival Fringe were well received. Based on the success of the previous year, the '87 show was given a more central venue and an earlier start time. They performed at the Bedlam Theatre with special guests the Rhythm Dogs blues band.

Jon Craven and John Lehr also "did some busking in Edinburgh, and made a ton of money," recalled Lehr. "I juggled. I'm a good juggler. I made like £1,500 all in the last week. And I took it and met my girlfriend in London and we blew it all. It was fantastic."

Dillo Day Alumni Performance

The Mee-Ow Show, scheduled to perform again at the Edinburgh Festival Fringe in August 1987, needed to raise funds for their trip. In addition to another twenty-four-hour improv marathon in Shanley, performances at Mayfest on May 25, and performances at high schools and fraternities, the cast performed at an alumni event.

This alumni performance coincided with Dillo Day, an annual all-day music festival on the Lakefill area of campus. Originally called Armadillo Day, the event was founded during the 1972–73 school year by two Medill journalism students from Texas and is now the largest student-run music festival in the country.

Of this performance, John Lehr recalled:

When we all had our wits about us, we did certain [corporate] gigs, and we went over great. [But] I remember we had to do a gig for the alumni association that we got paid for, but it was on Armadillo Day. Armadillo Day is raging outside and the alumni association is having a dinner and drinks kind of thing. [The alumni] were all in suits and stuff. It was in McCormick [Auditorium]. And Dillo Day is going on outside. And we were the entertainment at the end of their evening. And it just couldn't have gone worse. This was the '87 cast and everybody was tripping on mushrooms. And I remember Jon Craven, the director, saying, "OK, you guys, try . . ." he didn't even try to say don't do any drugs on Armadillo, he just said, ". . . try to do the drugs early in the day." And so we all showed up, I mean, we were all out of our minds. And one cast member, nobody could find her. And I remember they kind of wheeled her in like a, I don't know, she was like a mental patient. She had no shoes on. She was filthy. And they said they found her out on the rocks just staring out at the lake. It was just a train wreck. They're like, "What's wrong with them?" We had people wandering offstage and I know it was crazy. It was a terrible show, I'm sure, because, I mean, it's difficult to focus and listen to your player when you're on hallucinogenics, it turns out. It was insane.

1987

MEE-OW
SHANLEY HALL
JAN. 30&31
1987
8&11p.m.
MAW
PREVIEWS
$2 (N.U.&21 I.D. REQ. FOR 11 PM SHOW)
music by dr. Bob & the Fokoktah Blues Band

1988

MEE-OW YEAR FIFTEEN

MEE-OW
TSE-TUNG
an improvisational comedy show
Feb 19-20 26-27
8PM and 11PM
$5.00 with N.U. I.D.
tickets at Norris Box Office
An Arts Alliance Production
McCORMICK
AUDITORIUM

Mee-Ow Tse-Tung

Previews: Friday and Saturday, February 5–6, at 8 and 11 p.m., Shanley Pavilion

Mainstage: Fridays and Saturdays, February 19–20 and 26–27, at 8 and 11 p.m., McCormick Auditorium

Jessica Hughes ('86 cast member and '87 associate producer) directed and performed in the show. The returning cast members were John Lehr and Jerry Saslow, and new cast members included Betsy Braham, Jill Cargerman, Tim Ereneta, Stu Feldman, and Ana Gasteyer.

The Show Highlights

The content of these sold-out shows was somewhat more improv than sketches, with musical segues between. Some of the audience's suggestions for improvs were "Head wounds!" "Earwax!" and "People without knees!"

Sketches included satires of an untalented folk-singing duo, the Miss America pageant, and the Bible, and parodies of academics, sexual anomalies, off-campus living, Greek life, and television, among other subjects.

As in many years, the sketches dealing with undergraduate life resonated with the audience. In the February 26, 1988, *Daily Northwestern*, Cotten Seiler noted, "During a skit depicting the horrors of apartment life, the guy behind me kept shouting 'Yeah!' in excited agreement. These sketches play off our familiarity with the trials and tribulations of campus life—they show us our own ridiculous selves."

Reviews

In another *Daily Northwestern* article, Darren Cahr confessed that he was surprised. He wrote:

> Friends had been telling me for nearly two years that the annual Northwestern *Mee-ow Show* was an absolutely hysterical night out, and I'd be a fool to miss it. Not trusting my friends, and even more suspicious of any production completely conceived of and performed by students, I missed it last year. This year, recognizing some names on the cast list, I broke down and saw the previews.

THIS YEAR IN HISTORY

Soviet Army begins withdrawal from Afghanistan • Iraq launches poison gas attack on Kurds • Terrorist bombing of Pan Am jet, Lockerbie, Scotland • Stephen Hawking, *A Brief History of Time* • Dow Jones year-end close 2169 • Average new car $13,933 • 1 gallon gas $0.90 • *Rain Man*, *Who Framed Roger Rabbit*, *Die Hard* • Public Enemy, *It Takes a Nation of Millions to Hold Us Back*; N.W.A., *Straight Outta Compton*; Leonard Cohen, *I'm Your Man*; The Traveling Wilburys, *The Traveling Wilburys Vol. 1*; U2, *Rattle and Hum*

Quite frankly, it was great. The entire cast (including Stu Feldman, Jerry Saslow, Betsy Braham, Jill Cargerman, Ana Gasteyer and director Jessica Hughes), in spite of a somewhat unimaginative audience, proved to be a talented and resourceful bunch, and they put on one hell of a show.

For those unfamiliar with the *Mee-Ow Show*, it's somewhat reminiscent of a *Second City* show: about half prewritten skits and half improvisation. The skits showed a deal of creative energy, with cast members showing they would do anything for a laugh. They brilliantly spoofed a folk-singing duo (something like what Simon and Garfunkel would have been like if they had no talent whatsoever), the Miss America Pageant, the Bible and far too many other things to mention in a single review.

However, it's the cast's improvisational skills which are most impressive. Improv is never easy, which is what explains the poor improv shows one can see almost anywhere. But the *Mee-Ow* cast, especially John Lehr and Tim Ereneta, pulled off quite an impressive show of quick thinking and imaginative acting. Some of the "games" they played were truly remarkable. Even the band, playing brief segues from skit to skit, is quite amazing—inviting comparisons to Paul Shaffer's on *Late Night* (even if the lounge singer who opened the show epitomized the concept of sleazy). All in all, *Mee-Ow* proved to me that a student-run production really can be fun.

The *Mee-Ow Show* . . . [is] a genuinely funny way to spend the evening, as well as an entertaining alternative to studying your calculus.

In the February 26, 1988, *Daily Northwestern*, Cotten Seiler wrote:

> The art of improv is alive and well at NU.
>
> This year's Mee-Ow Show, *Mee-Ow Tse Tung* (a much better title than last year's *Eating Mee-Ow*) lives up to Northwestern's long-standing tradition of quality improvisational comedy. What sets the improv form, and the show itself, apart from the traditional comic revue is the demand that the players be spontaneously funny, regardless of the material. As a result of grueling rehearsals and an obvious onstage rapport, the cast of *Mee-Ow Tse Tung* are able to pull this off with style.
>
> Yeah, but is it funny? Yes, it's very funny—and very clever. The cast—Ana Gasteyer, Stu Feldman, Jill Cargerman, Tim Ereneta, John Lehr, Betsy Braham, Jerry Saslow, and director Jessica Hughes—all turn in excellent individual performances such as Gasteyer's irresistible Iris and John Lehr's confused Charlene—despite the wealth of talent, all the players work wonderfully as a tight-knit comedy team.
>
> The only possible problem with this year's Mee-Ow Show is its length. Friday's show was a full three-hour experience (subsequent performances have reportedly been streamlined to a less exhausting length). Nevertheless, it moves at a nice, professional pace, thanks in no small part to the Mee-Ow band, which plays the upbeat segue tunes between each sketch. They're tight enough to invite comparisons to Paul Shaffer's Late Night band—you'll hear thirty seconds of a lot of great songs. All this for five bucks.

1989

MEE-OW YEAR SIXTEEN

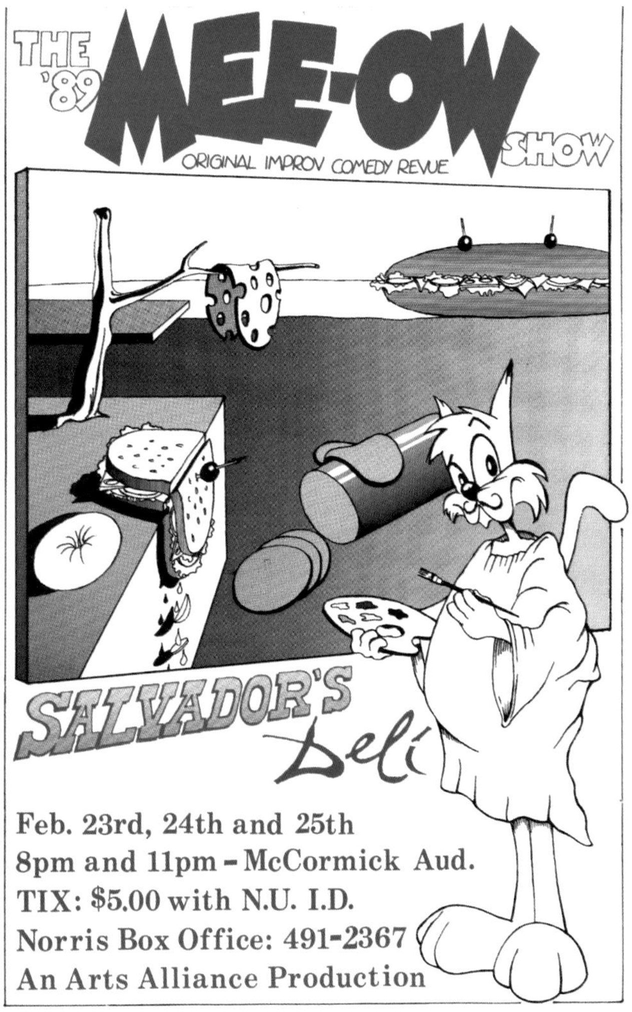

Salvador's Deli

Previews: Friday and Saturday, February 10–11, at 8 and 11 p.m., Shanley Pavilion

Mainstage: Thursday through Saturday, February 23–25, at 8 and 11 p.m., McCormick Auditorium.

Tim Ereneta (1988 cast member) returned to direct but did not perform. The returning cast members were 1987 cast member Bo Blackburn and 1988 cast members Jill Cargerman and Ana Gasteyer. New cast members included Mary Jackman, Eric Letzinger, J.P. Manoux, Philip Pawelczyk, and Spencer Shapiro.

In the Thursday, February 23, 1989, *Daily Northwestern*, a letter complained about a Mee-Ow Show sketch:

> I was sincerely disappointed to see the cast of the 1989 Mee-Ow show exploit the recent "Roommate Key Throwing" incident in their previews last weekend. It disturbed me to be surrounded by people who were laughing at an event which I found simply unfunny. While I am not personally acquainted with the two women involved in the key-throwing, I can appreciate and have a great respect for any individual's privacy. I like a funny sketch as much as the next guy, but I hope the cast will display more maturity in their McCormick shows this weekend.

In a clarification published on February 24, the *Daily Northwestern* pointed out that the author of the letter, J.P. Manoux, was actually *in* the sketch he wrote to complain about, and that his letter was a publicity effort.

A scathing editorial by Rich Scannel appeared in the *Daily Northwestern* on March 1, taking Manoux to task for his effort:

> So The Daily got hoodwinked.
>
> Chalk one up for those crazy folks who write those crazy shows. What cards!
>
> When a lie—no matter how seemingly innocuous or funny it might be—appears in any publication, it dilutes the credibility of that publication. It hurts a vehicle that strives 100 percent of the time to tell the truth and play fair with all comers.

1989

THIS YEAR IN HISTORY

Tiananmen Square protests • Berlin Wall comes down • *Exxon Valdez* oil spill • Nintendo Game Boy first released • First postwar elections in Poland • Velvet Revolution in Czechoslovakia • Tim Berners-Lee proposes World Wide Web • Dow Jones year-end close 2753 • Average new car $14,372 • 1 gallon gas $1.00 • *Indiana Jones and the Last Crusade*; *Batman*; *Honey, I Shrunk the Kids*; *Field of Dreams* • Nirvana, *Bleach*; Nine Inch Nails, *Pretty Hate Machine*; Lou Reed, *New York*; Madonna, *Like a Prayer*; Janet Jackson, *Rhythm Nation 1814*

> The policy of this newspaper is to publish whatever letters it gets, within the confines of its small page. The author is checked to see if he is who he says he is. If it checks out, the letter usually is printed verbatim. An unspoken trust, or good-faith agreement, is struck between folks who want to write letters and the editors who publish them.
>
> You have something, anything, to say, and The Daily gives you a place to say it. No strings attached. Just sign your name and include your phone number.
>
> All we ask is that you be honest with us.
>
> And most folks are. This fellow wasn't.
>
> Fault in this instance can be spread around. A night editor at The Daily knew about the association, but didn't say anything about it, for instance. Others involved with the show knew in advance that this person was going to do this.
>
> But the fact remains that someone intentionally misrepresented himself and his product to save the cost of an advertisement and, perhaps, to make The Daily look bad.
>
> Yes, I am a bit thin-skinned when it comes to this sort of thing. And whether I like it or not, some clown out there is sooner or later going to pull the same thing again.
>
> But I hope he thinks about it before he does it.
>
> Unless, that is, he doesn't mind being branded a liar in public when found out.

Following this, yet another letter complained about Scannel's column, stating that it was "excessive" and "reminiscent of a certain Hawthorne novel."

The Show Highlights

In a preview article in the February 10 *Daily Northwestern*, Wendy Hover wrote, "This year's Mee-Ow show will rely more on improvisational audience-participation games than scripted skits." She quoted cast member Ana Gasteyer as saying, "There's more of an emphasis on actual skills of improvisation. We really trust each other on stage."

J.P. Manoux recalled, "I'll never forget watching the brilliant John Lehr and Jerry Saslow improvise together. As seniors, they were also socially welcoming to an enthusiastic freshman who had not yet earned his comedy stripes. Those guys lit my path."

Ana Gasteyer and Jill Cargerman wrote a sketch called "C.O.O.T.I.E.S.," which parodied the ubiquitous and hyperbolic cautionary public service commercials about sexually transmitted diseases, in particular HIV and AIDS, by relating them to the imaginary contagion of childhood.

Free Delivery, a blues fusion band, played at intermission and between sketches.

Handmade collage poster for the 1989 Mee-Ow Show, featuring cast photos: (*clockwise from top*) Gasteyer, Manoux, Blackburn, Pawelczyk, Letsinger, Cargerman, Shapiro, and Jackman

1989

C.O.O.T.I.E.S.

CHARACTERS: Announcer, boy, girl, mom, dad, other kids.

Boy and girl playing at opposite ends of the playground with other kids. Suddenly they break away, running backwards into each other, fall to ground.

Other kids: Gasp!

Girl: You hit me!

Boy: Uh, uh...you hit me...

Both: ...we touched.

Other kids: You've got Cooties!!!

(all exit)

Announcer: What is Cooties? Cotties is an acronymn standing for Coincidental Or Overt Touching Infecting Either Sex . Although there is no known cure for Cooties, the U.S. Public Health and Education Services are researching to find a cure. Perhaps no other illness of our time has been so dominated by ignorance and misinformation.

(cut to boy and mom stage left)

Mom: Eric, Honey...what's the matter?(goes to hug him)

Boy: Don't touch me , Mom! I'm contagious...

(cut to girl and Dad, stage right)

Girl: Dad, something happened to me at school today...

Dad: Do you need to talk?

Girl: I feel so dirty...

(cut back)

Eric: You see, I was just playing in the playground...

(cut)

Girl:...I wasn't careful, Dad.

(cut)

Boy: ...and we fell down...

(cut)

Girl; ,,,and we touched...

(split focus)

Both: I've got Cooties!

Announcer; How is Cooties transmitted? Cooties is transmitted only through kissing or gum chewing with a memberof the opposite

-2-

there is no evidence that cooties can be transmitted through casual contact, or through the air.

Boy: I should have watched where I was going.

(cut)

Girl: It's all my fault, Dad.

(split)

Both: I guess I just didn't think it could happen to me.

Announcer: Who's at risk? Only a small percentage have or will have Cooties. Nearly all reported cases of cooties have occurred among boys and girls ages 6 to 10, who have not begun the journey into puberty.

Mom: The clinic called...you're okay.

Dad: And even if you did have it...I'd still love you.

Announcer: So seperate the facts from fiction concerning Cooties, For more information, call toll-free 1-900-COO-TIES. Educate your friends and family.

END

Script for the sketch "C.O.O.T.I.E.S." by Jill Cargerman and Ana Gasteyer

More Mee-Ow Show Alums Join Second City

In the May 23, 1989, *Daily Northwestern*, H. Hollister Bundy wrote about two Mee-Ow Show alums who were accepted into Second City:

John Lehr and Jerry Saslow, 1988 School of Speech graduates, recently were accepted into Chicago's famed Second City comedy troupe following an open audition in April.

Saslow and Lehr signed a contract Sunday after being chosen from 200 applicants for eight places in the show.

Speech senior Tim Ereneta, 1989 director and a Mee-Ow show veteran, praised both graduates. "Their styles were very different from most people, but they were extremely talented," Ereneta said. "Both had a sense of humor that is difficult to pinpoint. . . . I suppose that you could say that John and Jerry were masters of physical comedy, like John Belushi. They both had a sense of outrageousness about them."

After graduation, Lehr worked with Saslow over the summer as comic relief during the filming of the movie "Major League" at County Stadium in Milwaukee. Saslow and Lehr entertained the movie crowd between scenes and told the audience about upcoming scenes in the movie.

1990

MEE-OW YEAR SEVENTEEN

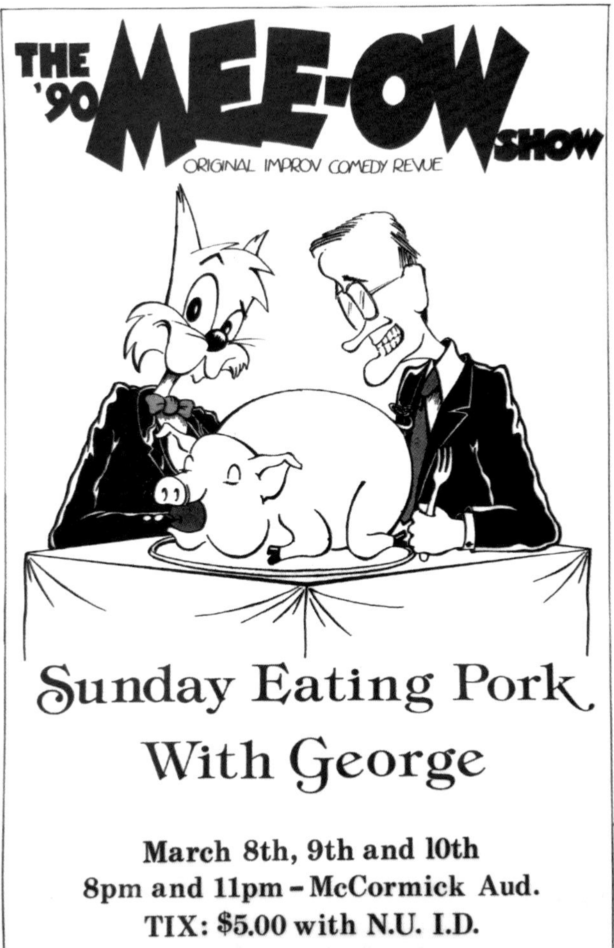

Sunday Eating Pork with George

Previews: Friday and Saturday, February 9–10, at 8 and 11 p.m., Shanley Pavilion

Mainstage: Thursday through Saturday, March 8–10, at 8 and 11 p.m., McCormick Auditorium

Previous year cast member Jill Cargerman returned to direct but did not perform. The returning cast members were J.P. Manoux, Philip Pawelczyk, and Spencer Shapiro. New cast members included Jason DeSanto, Kate Fry, Lillian Hubscher, Greg Rice, and Jon "Pep" Rosenfeld.

Manoux said that "this year's Mee-Ow Show cast, chosen in October for the February show, became very comfortable working as a unit." He continued, "It's an incredible blast knowing these people. You get to know them so intimately by the time of the show weekend, you just want to keep going."

The name of the show was a parody of the title of the 1985 Pulitzer Prize–winning musical *Sunday in the Park with George*, about the creation of the popular pointillist painting *A Sunday on La Grande Jatte* by Georges Seurat in the collection of the Art Institute of Chicago. DeSanto described the show poster as "a caricature of [President] George H. W. Bush eating ham." President Bush's favorite snack was known to be pork rinds, and he once famously declared, "I do not like broccoli. And I haven't liked it since I was a little kid and my mother made me eat it. And I'm president of the United States and I'm not going to eat any more broccoli!"

The Show Highlights

As in previous years, there were preview shows at Shanley Pavilion, followed a month later by the mainstage show at McCormick Auditorium. An advertisement in the *Daily Northwestern* asked people to "bring those wacky props" to the McCormick show. The props were used in a "prop tag" improv game.

The shows were an equal mix of sketches and improv games, with the band playing interstitial music between sketches and games, and at intermission.

Most of the sketches in the Shanley preview show made it into the mainstage McCormick

THIS YEAR IN HISTORY

Hubble space telescope launched • Nelson Mandela released from prison • Ozone layer hole worsens • Dow Jones year-end close 2634 • Average new car $15,045 • 1 gallon gas $1.15 • *Ghost*, *Home Alone*, *Pretty Woman*, *Dances with Wolves*, *Total Recall* • Depeche Mode, *Violator*; Public Enemy, *Fear of a Black Planet*

1990

show, although given the venue and the audience, "the 11 o'clock Saturday shows were pretty rowdy," recalled DeSanto. "It was much more intimate . . . To call it a cabaret style is kind of highfalutin'. But yeah, it was a little more anarchic."

One of the sketches was about President Bush and his opponent in the 1988 presidential campaign, Democratic governor Michael Dukakis, who was now specializing in back rubs for President Bush. "This was a J.P. Manoux special," said DeSanto. "He was way ahead of his time, and absolutely lampooning 'We Didn't Start the Fire' by Billy Joel, which had just come out."

Sketches included a *Star Trek* parody by Pep Rosenfeld; a parody of the Spike Lee movie *Do the Right Thing* but with privileged Northwestern students going into Gigio's, a neighborhood pizza place in Evanston that served New York–style pizza; and a *Jeopardy* parody by Greg Rice featuring DeSanto, Philip Pawelczyk, and J.P. Manoux as contestants. The categories were intentionally absurd, Pawelczyk recalled, "the most intricate, bizarre palindromes."

At times, the creative processes of writing and improvisation can result in eerily accurate predictions. DeSanto recalled a particularly prescient sketch:

> The strangest is the Donald Trump and Ivana Trump group marriage counseling sketch. Pep [Rosenfeld] played Donald Trump. [Philip Pawelczyk played Ivana.] In retrospect, maybe that was the most political thing we did without knowing that it was political. It was like an encounter group, sort of like one of those old *Saturday Night Live* sketches with John Belushi and Laraine Newman, in that style. So we're thirty years, two wives, and one presidency later. That's the sketch that still would have the most legs.

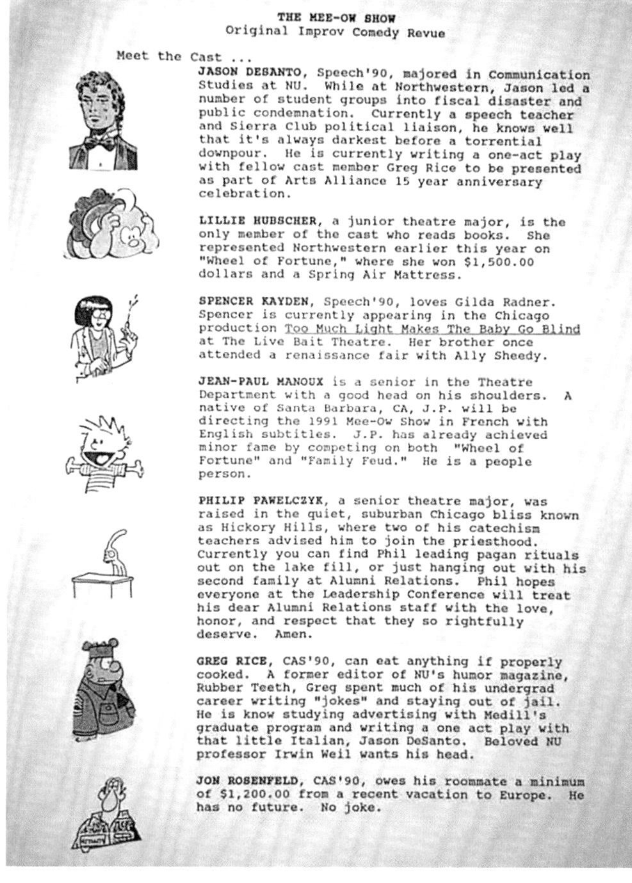

THE MEE-OW SHOW
Original Improv Comedy Revue

Meet the Cast ...

JASON DESANTO, Speech'90, majored in Communication Studies at NU. While at Northwestern, Jason led a number of student groups into fiscal disaster and public condemnation. Currently a speech teacher and Sierra Club political liaison, he knows well that it's always darkest before a torrential downpour. He is currently writing a one-act play with fellow cast member Greg Rice to be presented as part of Arts Alliance 15 year anniversary celebration.

LILLIE HUBSCHER, a junior theatre major, is the only member of the cast who reads books. She represented Northwestern earlier this year on "Wheel of Fortune," where she won $1,500.00 dollars and a Spring Air Mattress.

SPENCER KAYDEN, Speech'90, loves Gilda Radner. Spencer is currently appearing in the Chicago production Too Much Light Makes The Baby Go Blind at The Live Bait Theatre. Her brother once attended a renaissance fair with Ally Sheedy.

JEAN-PAUL MANOUX is a senior in the Theatre Department with a good head on his shoulders. A native of Santa Barbara, CA, J.P. will be directing the 1991 Mee-Ow Show in French with English subtitles. J.P. has already achieved minor fame by competing on both "Wheel of Fortune" and "Family Feud." He is a people person.

PHILIP PAWELCZYK, a senior theatre major, was raised in the quiet, suburban Chicago bliss known as Hickory Hills, where two of his catechism teachers advised him to join the priesthood. Currently you can find Phil leading pagan rituals out on the lake fill, or just hanging out with his second family at Alumni Relations. Phil hopes everyone at the Leadership Conference will treat his dear Alumni Relations staff with the love, honor, and respect that they so rightfully deserve. Amen.

GREG RICE, CAS'90, can eat anything if properly cooked. A former editor of NU's humor magazine, Rubber Teeth, Greg spent much of his undergrad career writing "jokes" and staying out of jail. He is know studying advertising with Medill's graduate program and writing a one act play with that little Italian, Jason DeSanto. Beloved NU professor Irwin Weil wants his head.

JON ROSENFELD, CAS'90, owes his roommate a minimum of $1,200.00 from a recent vacation to Europe. He has no future. No joke.

The 1990 cast: J.P. Manoux, Jon "Pep" Rosenfeld, Lillian Hubscher, Greg Rice, Kate Fry, Phil Pawelczyk, Spencer Shapiro, and Jason DeSanto

JESSICA KINGERY

4 New Groups Emerge

1991–2001

Coming into its twentieth year, Mee-Ow settled on a smaller cast and continued its sold-out runs of student-developed shows. Now viewed as the elite institution of campus comedy rock stars, Mee-Ow was inspiring other students to create new improv groups on campus for the same reason that the first Mee-Ow Show started: there were more comedy creators than opportunities to perform.

These included the improv comedy group Your Imaginary Friends, the long-form improv specialists the Titanic Players, and the multicultural sketch and improv comedy group Out Da Box.

Meanwhile, Mee-Ow alums formed teams at ImprovOlympic, were invited to showcase at the HBO Aspen Comedy Festival, and performed as "The Shanley Seven" in Los Angeles.

Facing page, the 2000 cast: Heather Campbell, Luke Hatton, producer Karyn Meltz, Ryan Harrison, Kristen Schaal, Scott Speiser, Lauren Flans, Matt McKenna, and Jess Lacher

1991

MEE-OW YEAR EIGHTEEN

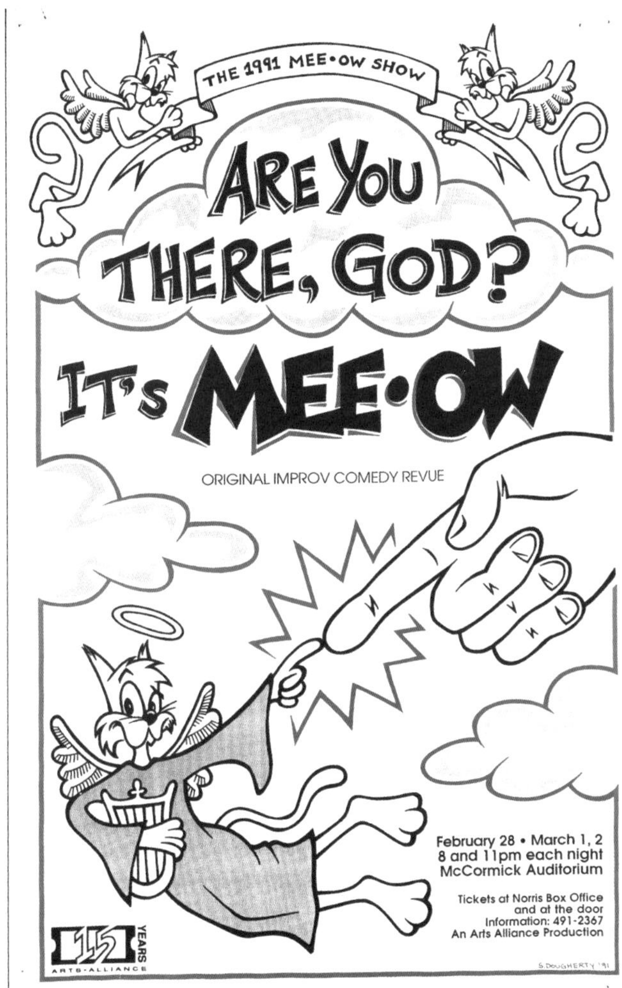

Lawrence of Your Labia

Friday and Saturday, February 8–9, at 8 and 11 p.m., Shanley Pavilion

Are You There, God? It's Mee-Ow

Thursday through Saturday, February 28–March 2, at 8 and 11 p.m., McCormick Auditorium

J.P. Manoux returned to direct, and Lillian Hubscher returned as the stage manager. New cast members included Lesley Bevan, George Brant, Daniele Gaither, Rachel Hamilton, Mark Kretzmann, Bruce McCoy, Jon Mozes, and Kirsten Nelson.

For the first time, the Shanley show had its own title, different from that of the mainstage show in McCormick. Previously, the Shanley show was referred to simply as the Mee-Ow Show "preview."

"We never tried to mean too much with our titles," Manoux wrote. "Always liked simple puns that were a little provocative. *Lawrence of Your Labia* comes to mind. That came from a sketch the women in our cast wrote, in which they played the clueless, all-male executive board of a company that manufactures feminine hygiene products."

This title elicited a few negative reactions, including some posters advertising the show being covered with stickers reading "This Promotes Women Hating." In the Letters column of the *Daily Northwestern* (February 8), Jennifer Quinn wrote, "I will not be going to this year's show and hope that others will not go until the Mee-Ow troupe changes the title of its show and apologizes for the (one would hope) unintended sexism."

In the same Letters column, Manoux expressed his disappointment at the stickering of posters and attempted to clarify the situation: "The . . . stickering and (I suspect) removal of many of our advertising posters demonstrates a hasty passing of judgment based on a gross misunderstanding. This weekend's performances have evolved from, if anything, a feminist perspective. I ask that those who question our title and our position regarding it SEE THE SHOW and then decide."

THIS YEAR IN HISTORY

Operation Desert Shield • Operation Desert Storm • Former Soviet territories declare independence • Jeffrey Dahmer arrested • Dow Jones year-end close 3169 • Average new car $15,473 • 1 gallon gas $1.14 • *The Silence of the Lambs*, *JFK*, *The Addams Family* • Nirvana, *Nevermind*; Pearl Jam, *Ten*; U2, *Achtung Baby*; A Tribe Called Quest, *The Low End Theory*; Red Hot Chili Peppers, *Blood Sugar Sex Magik*; R.E.M., *Out of Time*

This was followed by a letter from music director Matt Heaton, who also defended the show: "The women involved in the Mee-Ow Show (who make up more than half of the cast and staff) are not offended by these posters, neither are any of the other people to whom I have spoken."

On February 8, the day of the opening night performance in Shanley, in his column in the *Daily Northwestern* titled "Only the Spineless Resort to Vandalism," editor in chief Stephan Benzkofer wrote:

> Vandalism is gutless. There is no question in this matter. In a society where open comment about public issues is welcomed, not restricted or penalized, vandalism is nothing but a crime.
>
> There is no question of whether these people are expressing their First Amendment right to free speech. That right is reserved to the people with the backbone to stand behind their words or actions.
>
> This goes for people spray-painting "no blood for oil" on a concrete wall, this includes people painting "End Apartheid" on the sidewalks and this includes people putting stickers on Mee-Ow Show signs advertising the previews to the upcoming show titled "Lawrence of Your Labia."
>
> I don't care if you find this offensive. Anonymous stickers get you nowhere. It does not lead to discussion of the issue and it does not lead to better understanding between the parties involved.
>
> And although I am a white male (though not dumpy), this does not preclude me from understanding the issue at hand. Some of the stickers read, "This is offensive to women." It is offensive to some men too. I was offended when I first read the posters and I wondered what the group had in mind.
>
> I would have been more offended if I didn't think of two things:
>
> - Considering the people involved with Mee-Ow, including a large number of women, something else was up.
> - This poster is about a comedy improv, which leads one to logically believe that a little satire is in play here.
>
> So we now have an unsigned, gutless, thoughtless protest of something the "protesters" probably would agree with upon further investigation. But from the looks of the stickers, which look to be mass produced professionally, not a lot of thought was put into them in the first place. This group or person just had them made for just this circumstance—something they found offensive.
>
> How refreshing these stickers would have been if a name or group or phone number had been added. That would have been a true, courageous statement. As it is, I feel like we should wait by the phone to hear some voice take responsibility. Sort of reminds you of the way they have to wait for a terrorist group to call in after a bombing.
>
> But maybe these people will surprise me and give me a call.
>
> Then again, maybe not.

While it was appropriate for the editor in chief to criticize vandalism, Benzkofer's statement about the First Amendment was not accurate. The Supreme Court has protected anonymity in speech and association in several decisions.

Following the Shanley show, once the audience realized that the sketch was parodying the patriarchy, not supporting it, the controversy disappeared.

1991

The Show Highlights

Remembering the charged opening moments of the Shanley show, Kirsten Nelson said, "The Shanley shows were more electric because of that intimate setting and the fear of dying in Shanley [because of the building's state of disrepair]. So our cue, we always knew, was when [the band] started playing 'Shaft.' And we're like, there it is. There it is. That simpatico that we had with our house band. It was 'Sanford and Son' [the TV show's theme song] that led into 'Shaft'—those two iconic themes. Those guys [in the band] set the feeling, they set the vibe, they set the energy for our audience to bring us out. And it was electric."

Of the titular opening sketch, Nelson recalled that the women in the cast played the male executives of a company that manufactured feminine hygiene products:

> Razors, wax strips, depilatory creams. It's important because we're playing these clueless male executives, the patriarchy. It was important for the women to play these roles. [There was a] moment when you brought something up like, "Oh, what about a nice depilatory cream?" And you know, the women in the audience were screaming like, you don't understand what you men do to us! And that knowledge and that shared experience, that's what we were talking about. Taking the patriarchy and turning it on its head. And that's where *Lawrence of Your Labia* came from. That was the name of the company. And [the sketch] was filled with wonderful pauses that would just hang there and laughter would ensue about what these clueless men thought women needed. And that beauty was coming from them. They were offering [women] these wonderful products to help them become beautiful.

The opening number of the mainstage show *Are You There, God? It's Mee-Ow* dealt with the 1990–1991 Gulf War. As Nelson recalled,

> In comedy you can't ignore what's going on in our world. We were suddenly [fighting] Iraq, and [President] Bush had said our troops are going over there. We had a couple of Northwestern kids sign up. I remember it was a big deal. They're like, "I'm going in the army. I'm going to fight for my country." And we're like, "What? What's happening?" And it was this unstable time with politics and world events suddenly hitting down on us as college students where we were in this beautiful atmosphere of just being protected. We were in our bubble. But at the same time, the bubble was kind of bending inward to us. Will it pop? Because we now knew students who were leaving school to go enlist. So we knew that we had to address the Gulf War. We knew that we had to. How do you do it in a funny way? You know, because it's hurting, but comedy soothes and it releases. So . . . if Mee-Ow was invented as a reaction to Waa-Mu, we did

Your Imaginary Friends

The first mention of another improv comedy group, called "Your Imaginary Friends," was the announcement of a performance at the Prism Gallery in Evanston on November 2, 1990. Future Mee-Ow cast member Jason Winer (Mee-Ow '94) recalled that the group was started by Michael "Tall Mike" Elyanow, who went on to teach screenwriting at Columbia College Chicago. Winer unofficially audited courses taught by Elyanow at Northwestern. When Winer joined the group, he suggested calling it "Imaginary Friends," but that name was already taken, so the group became "Your Imaginary Friends."

An April 19, 1991, article in the *Daily Northwestern* reported on the ongoing performances. Members of the group included Winer and fellow future 1993 and 1994 Mee-Ow Show cast member Amanda Weier.

Short-lived but popular, the group was mentioned as being on "indefinite hiatus" in a *Daily Northwestern* article about comedy and improv on campus dated January 13, 1993.

the "Waa-MU.S.O." Our entire opening for the mainstage show was a USO type of show [singing to the tune of "Please Mr. Postman" by the Marvelettes]: "Stop. Hold on. Wait a minute, Mr. Saddam. / Kuw-ay, ay, ay, ait, Mr. Saddam," and our band did it all. Our band played it live with us [singing]: "Oh Mr. Sa-ddam. Can't you see? / Kuwait deserves its liberty-ee." So we did that one. We did "Saddam You're Rockin' the Boat" [singing to the tune of "Sit Down, You're Rockin' the Boat" from the Broadway musical *Guys and Dolls*]: "And the people all said, / Saddam, Saddam, you're rockin' the boat." Three of the gals were holding up their hijabs [singing to the tune of "I Cain't Say No" from the Broadway musical *Oklahoma!*]: "I'm just a girl who can't go out." Then I did "refineries" to "memories" from *Cats* [singing]: "Refineries. All aglow in the moonlight. / Don't you worry. It's all right. / We still have Texaco." And we wrote and performed all of that. Everybody got solos. Everybody had to dance. It was brilliant. It was so good. And that's what started the show. It hit you right from the top.

Nelson wrote the sketch "The Gods Must Be Crazy 8s," depicting the Greek gods playing poker. The title of the sketch combined the title of a popular movie, *The Gods Must Be Crazy*, with the name of the card game Crazy Eights, in a structure known as a phrasal overlap portmanteau.

A recurring musical sketch called "Vanilla Ice Capades" parodied "Ice Ice Baby," the Vanilla Ice song that was frequently played on the radio. The audience was excited each time they heard the opening of the song (which Vanilla Ice had plagiarized from Queen and David Bowie) repeated. As Nelson recalled, "I was Andrew Dice Clay singing about being a misogynist and being an asshole, singing 'I'm Andrew Dice, Dice, Baby.' Later Mark and Bruce went into 'Heist, Heist, Baby.' For the final one, George Brant was Jesus singing 'Christ, Christ, Baby.' That played really well around Easter."

Despite the poster-stickering campaign and complaints about the preview title, the show was well attended and well received. There were no further complaints.

The 1991 cast: Lesley Bevan, Daniele Gaither, Rachel Hamilton, Kirsten Nelson, George Brant, Jon Mozes, Bruce McCoy, and Mark Kretzmann

1992

MEE-OW YEAR NINETEEN

THE 1992 MEE•OW SHOW
It's a Wonderful
LIFE SENTENCE
WANTED
NEW
February 27, 28 & 29
an Arts Alliance Production

Dental Damn Yankees

Friday and Saturday, February 7–8, at 8 and 11 p.m., Shanley Pavilion

It's a Wonderful Life Sentence

Thursday through Saturday, February 27–29, at 8 and 11 p.m., McCormick Auditorium

Lillian Hubscher (1990 cast member and 1991 stage manager) returned to direct but did not perform. The returning cast members were Lesley Bevan, Daniele Gaither, Mark Kretzmann, and Bruce McCoy. New cast members included Scott Duff, Anne Eggleston, Chris Grady, and Jean Villepique.

As in previous years, the cast brainstormed names and came to an agreement. However, rather than puns based on "Mee-Ow," this year's titles were both types of phrasal overlap portmanteau. The first show combined the name of the prophylactic "dental dam" with the title of the 1955 stage musical and 1958 movie musical *Damn Yankees.* The second show combined the title of the 1946 movie *It's a Wonderful Life* with the phrase "life sentence."

"Students Grit Their Teeth over Dental Dam Posters" was the headline of a January 30, 1992, article in the *Daily Northwestern.* Anna Giuliani wrote, "Puzzled students scratched their heads in bewilderment as they read the words, 'It's 10:00—Have You Hugged Your Dental Dam Today?'" The posters on campus were part of a

NOTE

As my days barrel along towards June, I try to prepare for my inevitable propulsion into the Real World. While hearing discouraging reports about life on the outside, I have found solace in chuckles and the eight bearers of this priceless gift of humor. Whether dealing with "larger issues" or just being silly, this bunch takes creativity and comedy to its limits, politically correct limits of course. So if you find yourself laughng at things you'd rather not write home about, go ahead. I'll be the one beside you in the dark, chuckling. Maybe it will be a wonderful life sentence after all. — Lillian Hubscher, Director

THIS YEAR IN HISTORY

Chicago Loop flood • Cartoon Network launches • Mall of America opens • Euro Disney grand opening • Dow Jones year-end close 3301 • Average new car $16,334 • 1 gallon gas $1.13 • *Basic Instinct, Batman Returns, A Few Good Men, Wayne's World* • R.E.M., *Automatic for the People*; Rage Against the Machine, *Rage Against the Machine*; Alice in Chains, *Dirt*; Dr. Dre, *The Chronic*; Stone Temple Pilots, *Core*

teaser campaign for the Mee-Ow Show. Some students laughed, while others found this "gross."

The Show Highlights

Sketches included a press conference with the new president, Dan Quayle, following the unexpected death of President George H. W. Bush. A reporter asks President Quayle, "Why are you so stupid?" The press laughs, nudges each other with elbows, and high-fives. Another reporter calls to Quayle, who looks over at the reporter. "Ha! Monkeys always look," says the reporter. Quayle mutters, "Awww," with hurt feelings.

Reviews

In the February 7, 1992, *Daily Northwestern*, Cynthia Wang previewed the Shanley show, "Dental Damn Yankees":

> Things will be bigger, more slick at McCormick Auditorium, but for the sake of the previews, [producer Darren] Turbow still wants the show to turn out spectacular. "The atmosphere is completely different here," says Turbow of Shanley. "It's more like a comedy club, a night club. Personally, I like it here better—more interaction with the audience."

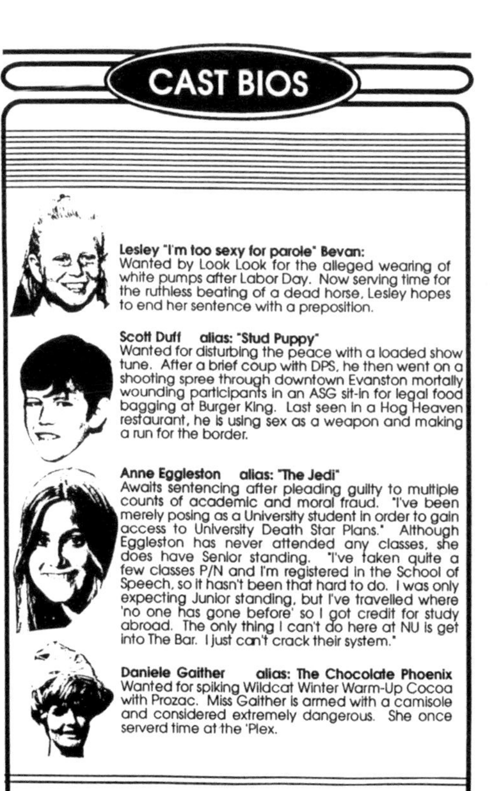

CAST BIOS

Lesley "I'm too sexy for parole" Bevan:
Wanted by Look Look for the alleged wearing of white pumps after Labor Day. Now serving time for the ruthless beating of a dead horse, Lesley hopes to end her sentence with a preposition.

Scott Duff alias: "Stud Puppy"
Wanted for disturbing the peace with a loaded show tune. After a brief coup with DPS, he then went on a shooting spree through downtown Evanston mortally wounding participants in an ASG sit-in for legal food bagging at Burger King. Last seen in a Hog Heaven restaurant, he is using sex as a weapon and making a run for the border.

Anne Eggleston alias: "The Jedi"
Awaits sentencing after pleading guilty to multiple counts of academic and moral fraud. "I've been merely posing as a University student in order to gain access to University Death Star Plans." Although Eggleston has never attended any classes, she does have Senior standing. "I've taken quite a few classes P/N and I'm registered in the School of Speech, so it hasn't been that hard to do. I was only expecting Junior standing, but I've travelled where 'no one has gone before' so I got credit for study abroad. The only thing I can't do here at NU is get into The Bar. I just can't crack their system."

Daniele Gaither alias: The Chocolate Phoenix
Wanted for spiking Wildcat Winter Warm-Up Cocoa with Prozac. Miss Gaither is armed with a camisole and considered extremely dangerous. She once serverd time at the 'Plex.

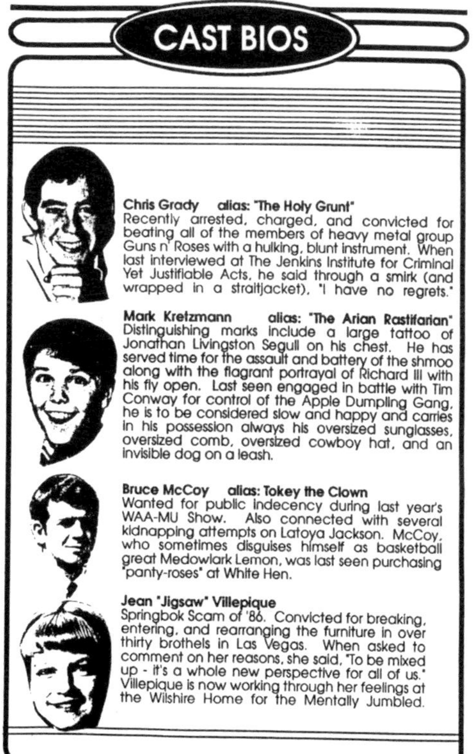

CAST BIOS

Chris Grady alias: "The Holy Grunt"
Recently arrested, charged, and convicted for beating all of the members of heavy metal group Guns n' Roses with a hulking, blunt instrument. When last interviewed at The Jenkins Institute for Criminal Yet Justifiable Acts, he said through a smirk (and wrapped in a straitjacket), "I have no regrets."

Mark Kretzmann alias: "The Arian Rastifarian"
Distinguishing marks include a large tattoo of Jonathan Livingston Segull on his chest. He has served time for the assault and battery of the shmoo along with the flagrant portrayal of Richard III with his fly open. Last seen engaged in battle with Tim Conway for control of the Apple Dumpling Gang, he is to be considered slow and happy and carries in his possession always his oversized sunglasses, oversized comb, oversized cowboy hat, and an invisible dog on a leash.

Bruce McCoy alias: Tokey the Clown
Wanted for public indecency during last year's WAA-MU Show. Also connected with several kidnapping attempts on Latoya Jackson. McCoy, who sometimes disguises himself as basketball great Medowlark Lemon, was last seen purchasing "panty-roses" at White Hen.

Jean "Jigsaw" Villepique
Springbok Scam of '86. Convicted for breaking, entering, and rearranging the furniture in over thirty brothels in Las Vegas. When asked to comment on her reasons, she said, "To be mixed up - it's a whole new perspective for all of us." Villepique is now working through her feelings at the Wilshire Home for the Mentally Jumbled.

Cast member bios illustrated with photos of actors from the TV series *The Brady Bunch*

1993

MEE-OW YEAR TWENTY

an Arts Alliance production
THE mee-ow SHOW
The Tao of mee-ow
FEB 25
at 8
&
FEB 26-27
at 8 & 11
at the MCCORMICK THEATRE
stu. $5(cheap)
fac. $7
oth. $9(ouch!)

When I Think about You, I Touch Mee-Ow

Friday and Saturday, February 5–6, at 8 and 11 p.m., Shanley Pavilion

The Tao of Mee-Ow

Thursday through Saturday, February 25–27, at 8 and 11 p.m., McCormick Auditorium

This year was another exception to the usual tradition of choosing the director from the cast of the previous year. Paul Vaillancourt was a graduate student working toward his MA in theater. He had been in an improv group as an undergrad, studied and performed at Second City, was taking classes at ImprovOlympic, and described himself as "obviously just drunk in love with improv. Northwestern was, in a lot of ways, my day job. I was really there to study improv. So getting the chance to put everything I knew into action was the best."

While Vaillancourt was not in the cast of the previous Mee-Ow Show, he thought that the previous year's director, Lillian Hubscher, who had suggested that he apply to direct, had also recommended him to the board.

He insisted that the show would be "clean," eschewing "blue humor" and instead focusing on an approach known as "heightening the scene," in which performers add information to build upon what was previously created and make the events in the sketch have greater consequences for the characters.

In addition to directing, Vaillancourt also performed. The only returning cast member was Jean Villepique. New cast members included Colby Beserra, Anjali Bhimani, Ed Herbstman, Abby Kohn, Ethan Sandler, Deborah Stern, Amanda Weier, Dan Weiss, and Adrian Wenner. Brad Bruskotter was the producer.

Sandler recalled that the "pack of dudes were like puppies, but Jean was there to call them on their sexism and [say] that dick jokes were not OK."

1993

THIS YEAR IN HISTORY

Bill Clinton inaugurated • Branch Davidian siege in Waco • Nelson Mandela, F. W. de Klerk awarded Nobel Peace Prize • World Trade Center bombed • Dow Jones year-end close 3754 • Average new car $16,829 • 1 gallon gas $1.11 • *Jurassic Park*, *Mrs. Doubtfire*, *The Fugitive*, *Philadelphia* • The Smashing Pumpkins, *Siamese Dream*; Nirvana, *In Utero*; Pearl Jam, *Vs.*; Liz Phair, *Exile in Guyville*; Snoop Dogg, *Doggystyle*

Developing the Show

Some cast members brought rough ideas for sketches that were developed through improv. For others, improv led to ideas that were then developed.

Under Vaillancourt's direction to heighten the scenes, there were more Viola Spolin games and more scene work at rehearsals.

A three-hour-long rehearsal was spent entirely on brainstorming the name of the show. In the end, Vaillancourt selected *The Tao of Mee-Ow*. As Ed Herbstman recalls,

> Paul was very into East-West philosophy and mysticism. He has a yin-yang symbol tattooed on maybe his wrist or somewhere. And he was very into the Tao. And *The Tao of Physics* [*The Tao of Physics: An Exploration of the Parallels between Modern Physics and Eastern Mysticism*, a best-selling 1975 book by physicist Fritjof Capra] was a book he wanted us to all read. And I did, and I loved it. It was great.
>
> In 1992 the Tao, or Taoism, was like a new, popular, exciting, strange thing. I really wanted to figure out something like a super-clever turn of phrase. And I think we settled on Tao. I think we spent a full three-hour rehearsal at a chalkboard writing titles. I mean, truly, 80 percent of Mee-Ow is trying to come up with the title. At a certain point you are exhausted, and you give in and you stop fighting and you end up with "Tao of Mee-Ow," which I thought was curiously unclever, but I truly didn't care at that point. I was beaten down. I voted against it.

Viola Spolin

Viola Spolin (1906–1994) was an actor, educator, director, author, and the creator of Improvisational Theater Games, a system of actor training that uses games to teach the formal rules of theater.

Spolin's son Paul Sills cofounded The Second City in Chicago in 1959, and Spolin became the company's director of workshops. Her book *Improvisation for the Theater*, published in 1963 by Northwestern University Press, significantly affected American theater by changing the way acting is taught.

By MICHAEL J. GRAVEN/Daily Staff Photographer

In the limelight

Speech sophomore Ethan Sandler makes his point during a "directory assistance auditions" skit Friday night. The performance was part of the 1993 Mee-Ow Show, held this weekend at Norris University Center's McCormick Auditorium.

1993

The Show Highlights

The Tao of Mee-Ow was mostly sketches, with three or four improv games and interstitial music from the three-piece band that occasionally accompanied sketches.

The opening sketch was based on the name of the show. Anjali Bhimani described the scene: "The entire cast were monks in a monastery whose focus was all about improv, and the head monk was Paul Vaillancourt. Paul spoke about the Tao of Improv being about 'Yes, and . . .' Then Ed Herbstman played a contrary monk. Ed got up and said, 'No, no, no, no, nooo!' And he just basically broke all the rules of improv, immediately diving for the blue humor and making the audience laugh."

One running sketch referenced a then-current promotional campaign by the relatively new submarine-sandwich chain Jimmy John's. Their slogan was "Freaky Fast," and the new location in Evanston would deliver to dorms. Jimmy John's also started delivering condoms to college campuses with their subs (a campaign that ended by 1995). This sketch featured Sandler and Kohn as a couple in a dorm. In the first scene, Sandler orders Jimmy John's, and, faking surprise, he "casually" notices the included condom. The second scene is postcoital, and Sandler asks, "Should we get more subs?"

Another sketch depicted a couple sitting back-to-back, watching television and talking on their phones. The implication was that they were in different places, but the end of the sketch revealed that they were in the same location, foreshadowing the social isolation of increasing screen use.

Another sketch was mostly silent, featuring a couple depicted in three stages of their relationship: meeting, dating, and breaking up. A street mime played by Wenner falls in love with a woman played by Bhimani. After they start living together, she grows increasingly frustrated, then can't stand it, and they break up. He's in an empty apartment, then he's in a bar. She walks into the bar and says the first spoken line of the sketch, "I'll have what he's having." They get back together.

Herbstman recalled a sketch that featured the women cast members:

> Jean and Amanda and Abby and Debbie Stern did a scene where the four of them are walking down the street, each in their own world. Then they see each other and go, "Oh my God!" And they have this high-pitched gibberish back and forth that goes on for quite a while. And then three of them leave. And then Colby walks in, "What was that all about?" Jean turns to him and says, "Well, Debbie's got a thing with her boyfriend. And I've got a new job. Amanda thinks that she's not going to get a good grade on the test." So it was a play on how women communicate. Translating the high-pitched gibberish into "dude."

In one touching sketch, Herbstman and Wenner play a father and son on a canoe trip. The father is focused on talking about "back in my day." Meanwhile the son brought a fax machine and computer aboard the canoe. Eventually, the son throws it all overboard, and the father and son connect.

Reviews

The Tao of Mee-Ow played just before spring break, so there appears to have been no review in the *Daily Northwestern*. However, in the January 13, 1993, issue there was a two-page article about student comedy at Northwestern, including the Mee-Ow Show. Heather Brewer wrote:

> For 19 years, this 10-member student production has captivated audiences with its improv sketches and games, providing a springboard for young comedians like Julia Louis-Dreyfus to jump into the limelight.
>
> Members of this year's cast are preparing to make that jump themselves. Director Paul Vaillancourt, a second-year graduate student in theater, says improv "forces you to get beyond yourself." He hopes to turn comedy into a career by writing scripts and one day working on Saturday Night Live.
>
> "I would like to do improv my whole life," he says. "It's a great process for creating."

1993

In addition to participating in the Mee-Ow Show, some of the cast take advantage of Chicago's comedy scene by taking classes at local clubs like Second City to improve their skills. Ed Herbstman, a Speech sophomore and a two-year [*sic*] member of the troupe, says his classes have taught him the sacred "Yes, and . . ." rule of improvisation, which means an actor must always heighten what the others on stage have already done.

"You're there to make your partner look good," said Herbstman, who once sprained his wrist stage diving as part of a punk rock sketch.

The group does shows during New Student Week and during fraternity Rush. Its major productions, however, are in winter when it presents its show at McCormick Auditorium and goes on tour during spring break. This year, Mee-Ow travels to Los Angeles.

This performance schedule, which is almost as fast-paced as a scene from the show, gives the cast a real taste of the theater. "We put the show together completely on [our] own," said Mee-Ow cast member Amanda Weier, a Speech junior. "I got a lot of professional experience."

But the fast pace of improv can take its toll, says Mee-Ow producer Brad Bruskotter, who warns of a "burn-out effect."

In spite of the intensity of improvisational acting, Herbstman plans to turn his improv experience at NU into a career.

"Of course it's emotionally draining," Bruskotter, a CAS senior, said, "but no matter what your passion is, it's going to drain you."

As a further step in preparing its cast for a life of comedy, the Mee-Ow Show recently joined forces with NSTV's "Stinky's Pub," NU's live sketch comedy show. According to Herbstman, the new "Stinky's Pub," which will be on the air this spring, combines Mee-Ow improv with "Stinky's" scripted comedy.

1994

MEE-OW YEAR TWENTY-ONE

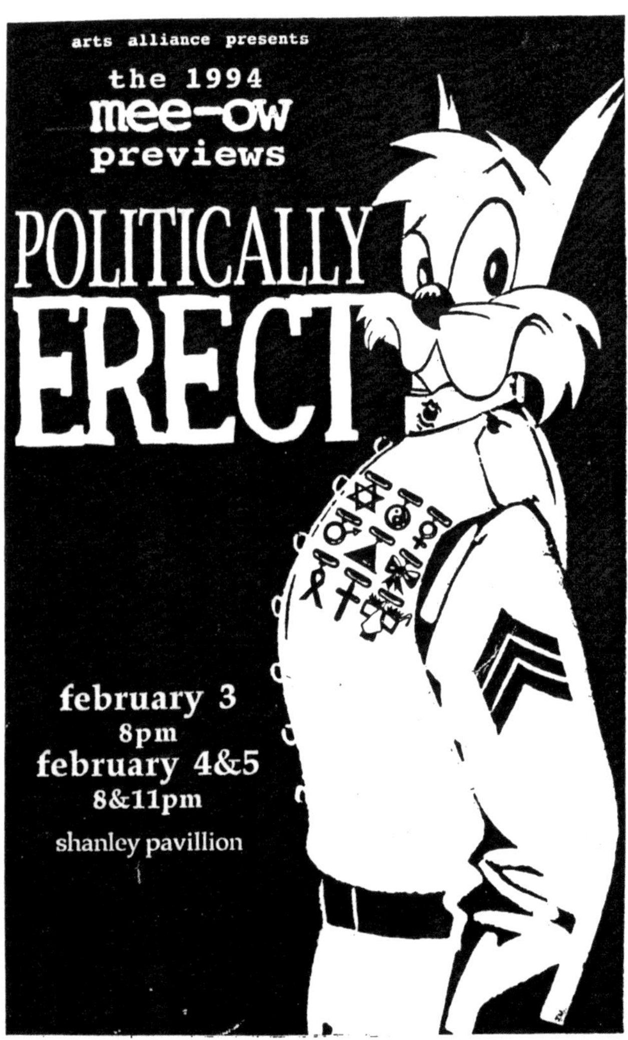

arts alliance presents
the 1994
mee-ow
previews
POLITICALLY
ERECT
february 3
8pm
february 4&5
8&11pm
shanley pavillion

Politically Erect

Thursday, February 3, at 8 p.m.; Friday and Saturday, February 4–5, at 8 and 11 p.m., Shanley Pavilion

Teach Mee-Ow to Love Again

Friday and Saturday, February 25–26, at 8 and 11 p.m., McCormick Auditorium

Returning cast member Ed Herbstman directed and performed. Other returning cast members included Ethan Sandler, Jean Villepique, Amanda Weier, and Adrian Wenner. New cast members included Jill Alexander, Louise Lamson, Dan Weiss, and Jason Winer.

Having begun as an obscure progressive phrase, "politically correct" had seen a spike in usage in the early 1990s when it was adopted as a pejorative by conservatives objecting to what they perceived as progressive curriculum and teaching in secondary and higher education. In response, comedian Bill Maher created the television talk show *Politically Incorrect* in 1993. The title *Politically Erect* was a response to, and parody of, this issue in popular culture.

Winer recalled that one of the first rehearsals for *Teach Mee-Ow to Love Again* involved the cast playing the improv game "Word at a Time" while lying on their backs in an upstairs room at Norris Center with the lights turned out.

This year marked the introduction of the long-form Harold improv into rehearsals by director Herbstman. The Harold structure introduces characters and themes that then reappear to connect with other scenes. The Charna Halpern and Del Close book *Truth in Comedy*, which included a description of the Harold, was published in 1994. Herbstman had been studying with Del Close in Chicago before starting at Northwestern.

At first, Herbstman was only going to direct, not perform. But as cast member Winer put it, "It was like, dude, you're the best improviser of all of us. You're going to perform." In later years, this common dilemma of the director being one of the best, most experienced performers was solved through the appointment of codirectors,

THIS YEAR IN HISTORY
Nelson Mandela elected president of South Africa • Olympic skater Nancy Kerrigan attacked • Channel Tunnel opens • Dow Jones year-end close 3834 • Average new car $17,803 • 1 gallon gas $1.11 • *The Lion King*, *Forrest Gump*, *The Mask*, *Dumb and Dumber* • Weezer, *Weezer*; Nas, *Illmatic*; Soundgarden, *Superunknown*; Green Day, *Dookie*; The Notorious B.I.G., *Ready to Die*

which ultimately became the normal practice for the Mee-Ow Show.

The Show Highlights

For the first time this year, every cast member sang a short solo accompanied by the house band. For example, Winer sang the Elvis Costello song "Mystery Dance."

Herbstman recalled the musical number that opened the Shanley show:

> We did a big musical number because that year the story of the year was the "don't ask, don't tell" policy. And one of the professors at Northwestern, Charles Moskos, was the author of that policy. He was a bigwig in sociology and a revered professor, but people had mixed feelings about "don't ask, don't tell," to say the least. So we did a musical number that started out with a bunch of real macho bros coming back from weekend leave to their bunks at the army base, talking about their sexual exploits with all the women that they had sex with, [saying], "Twelve women. I was fucking all weekend. And I fucked with my dick," and all of this stuff. Then you would freeze-frame on one of them and they would be like a deer in headlights and they would say, "I'm gay!" And then they'd say the truth: "This week I had sex with two men who blah, blah, blah." Then they'd get snapped back into their bro thing where they were pretending. Then finally one of them just cracked and couldn't handle it anymore and went into this [singing]: "Don't ask, don't tell. My life's a living hell." Gradually all of them would chime in, and it turns out they were all gay and hiding it and would sing the song together. We felt pretty proud of ourselves for addressing it, but it also was an easy target.

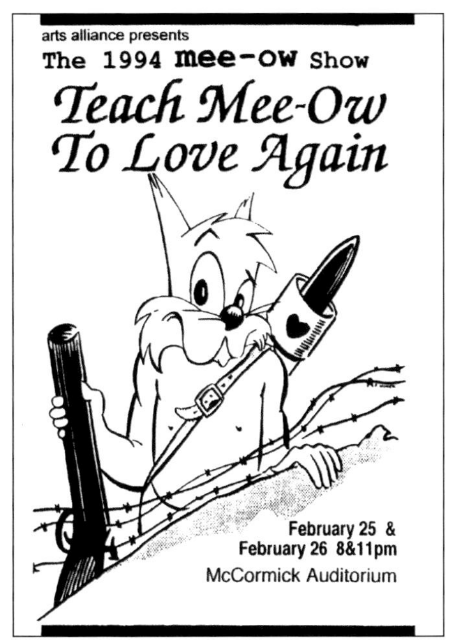

arts alliance presents
The 1994 mee-ow Show
Teach Mee-Ow To Love Again
February 25 &
February 26 8&11pm
McCormick Auditorium

There were no women in this opening number, which according to Winer was a source of some resentment among the women in the cast. The opening of the McCormick show included them, possibly in reaction to the Shanley show.

The song was cowritten by Dan Weiss, who also wrote another song about a man who was "a politician, but he's not politically motivated. He just wants to sleep with everybody's wife. It's basically skewering two-faced politicians who say one thing but really are in it for personal power."

Also This Year

In an article in the *Daily Northwestern* (April 29, 1994), Mandy Stadtmiller wrote about the challenges facing the Waa-Mu Show as it tried to present more up-to-date and relevant material. Stadtmiller noted, "With 'Lost and Found,' Waa-Mu tries to regroup for the '90s—but it's not quite there yet."

1994

1994 cast members Jill Alexander, Jean Villepique, Amanda Weier, and Louise Lamson

Mee-Ow Alums Working Together

Following the Mee-Ow Show, Ethan Sandler, Adrian Wenner, and Jason Winer were in a production of *Hamlet*. Winer was Hamlet, Sandler was the ghost of Hamlet's father, and Wenner was Horatio.

After graduation, Ed Herbstman, Dan Weiss, Adrian Wenner, and Jason Winer moved to Chicago, where they joined Paul Vaillancourt and formed a team at Impro-vOlympic, studying with Del Close. Eventually several of them moved to Los Angeles, where they began doing improvised movie sketches, a concept that was started by the Family improv group.

This group of Mee-Ow alums performed at the 1999 HBO Aspen Comedy Festival. At the time, it was "the Super Bowl of comedy," said Winer. He recalled:

> For an act, an emerging standup, or a sketch group—or in our case, an improv group—to get invited to showcase at Aspen was "The Thing." And it was out of that that we got signed by CAA and it was there that we did our full, long-form improvised movie that had been coached by Del and that we performed to a packed ballroom of TV and film executives, as well as luminaries. Steve Martin was in the room. I recall Martin Short was in the room. And it went on and on, in terms of who was there to see us improvise a movie. And we killed that night, it went great.

The group was signed by Creative Artists Agency (CAA) to generate show ideas. One of the shows they created was initially titled "Sue Your Ex." This eventually became the semi-scripted TV game show *The Blame Game*, which ran for four seasons on MTV. Winer described the show as "very racy," and "ahead of its time."

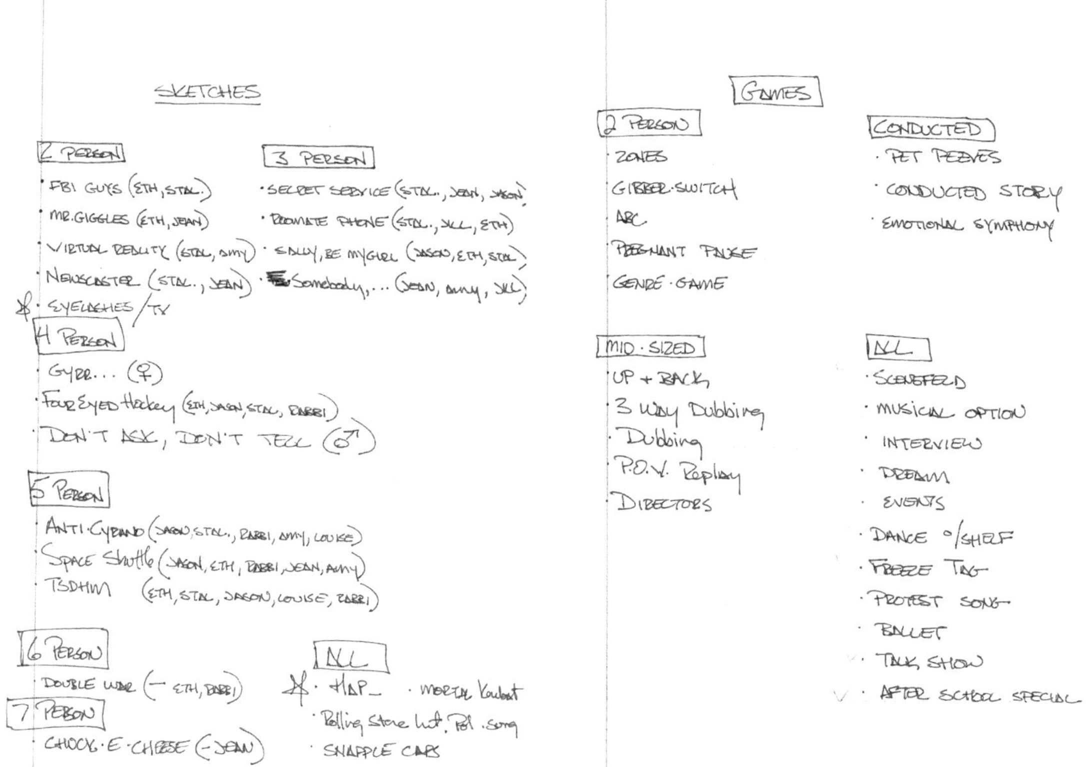

SKETCHES

2 PERSON
- FBI GUYS (ETH, STAL.)
- MR. GIGGLES (ETH, JEAN)
- VIRTUAL REALITY (STAL, AMY)
- NEWSCASTER (STAL., JEAN)
- EYELASHES / TV

3 PERSON
- SECRET SERVICE (STAL., JEAN, JASON)
- PROMATE PHONE (STAL., JILL, ETH)
- SALLY, BE MY GIRL (JASON, ETH, STAL)
- Somebody, ... (JEAN, amy, JILL)

4 PERSON
- GYRR... (♀)
- Four Eyed Hockey (ETH, JASON, STAL, RABBI)
- DON'T ASK, DON'T TELL (♂)

5 PERSON
- ANTI-CYBAND (JASON, STAL., RABBI, AMY, LOUISE)
- Space Shuttle (JASON, ETH, RABBI, JEAN, AMY)
- TSDHM (ETH, STAL, JASON, LOUISE, RABBI)

6 PERSON
- DOUBLE WAR (– ETH, RABBI)

7 PERSON
- CHUCK-E-CHEESE (– JEAN)

ALL
- HAP_
- MORTAL Kombat
- Rolling Stone list, Pol. song
- SNAPPLE CAPS

GAMES

2 PERSON
- ZONES
- GIBBER-SWITCH
- ABC
- PREGNANT PAUSE
- GENRE-GAME

CONDUCTED
- PET PEEVES
- CONDUCTED STORY
- EMOTIONAL SYMPHONY

MID-SIZED
- UP + BACK
- 3 Way Dubbing
- Dubbing
- P.O.V. Replay
- DIRECTORS

ALL
- SCENEFELD
- MUSICAL OPTION
- INTERVIEW
- DREAM
- EVENTS
- DANCE O/SHELF
- FREEZE TAG
- PROTEST SONG
- BALLET
- TALK SHOW
- AFTER SCHOOL SPECIAL

1994 cast members Jason Winer, Adrian Wenner, Ethan Sandler, and Dan Weiss

1995

MEE-OW YEAR TWENTY-TWO

Pope Fiction

Thursday, February 2, at 8 p.m.; Friday and Saturday, February 3–4, at 8 and 11 p.m., Shanley Pavilion

For Whom the Bell Curves

Thursday, February 23, at 8 p.m.; Friday and Saturday, February 24–25, at 8 and 11 p.m., McCormick Auditorium

Ed Herbstman, the previous year's director, decided to focus only on performing, and returning cast members Jean Villepique and Adrian Wenner were appointed codirectors. This allowed each codirector to perform while the other directed, which eventually became the normal practice for the Mee-Ow Show.

Other returning cast members included Jill Alexander, Louise Lamson, and Dan Weiss. New cast members included Rob Janas and Liv Oslund.

Regarding the names of the 1995 shows, *Pope Fiction* and *For Whom the Bell Curves*, Herbstman said, "The pope was in the news and [the movie] *Pulp Fiction* was a big deal." Also in the news: the controversial book *The Bell Curve*, first published in 1994. Members of the cast had either read it or were aware of its fallacious contentions that intelligence was related to race. Herbstman said he "thought it was astonishingly backward and racist when we read the book. And we had a big reaction to it. So we thought we were really cool, kind of snarky cultural critics by saying be careful for whom the bell curves. It just might curve for you."

The title of the show alludes to John Donne's 1624 poem, which also became known to many as the title of a novel by Ernest Hemingway: "Therefore, send not to know / For whom the bell tolls, / It tolls for thee." The message, therefore, was that if racial discrimination is used to falsely justify discrimination against one group of people, it can be used against anyone. Also contained within the message of the show's title was the idea in German Lutheran pastor Martin Niemöller's 1946 statement beginning, "First they came for the socialists, and I did not speak out . . ."

1995

THIS YEAR IN HISTORY

Oklahoma City bombing • eBay founded • Tokyo nerve gas attack • JavaScript invented • Dow Jones year-end close 5117 • Average new car $17,897 • 1 gallon gas $1.15 • *Die Hard with a Vengeance*, *Toy Story*, *Apollo 13*, *Se7en*, *Waterworld*, *Jumanji* • The Smashing Pumpkins, *Mellon Collie and the Infinite Sadness*; Alanis Morissette, *Jagged Little Pill*; Foo Fighters, *Foo Fighters*; No Doubt, *Tragic Kingdom*

The Show Highlights

This year continued the practice begun the previous year where each cast member sang a brief solo of their favorite song. Herbstman recalled, "I did 'I'm So Tired' by the Beatles because I had just gotten out of the hospital with mono."

He also remembered a sketch called "Blockbuster": "Louise Lamson and Adrian Wenner were on a first date. Every line of dialogue was the title of a movie. And it was brilliant. They were at a Blockbuster on their first date trying to pick out a movie. They had a reason to say movie titles, but the movie titles communicated what they wanted to really say to each other. It was very clever, very, very complicated, because you really have to memorize them. Yes. In fact, I remember Louise pitched it to me the year I directed, and I [thought it was] too complicated."

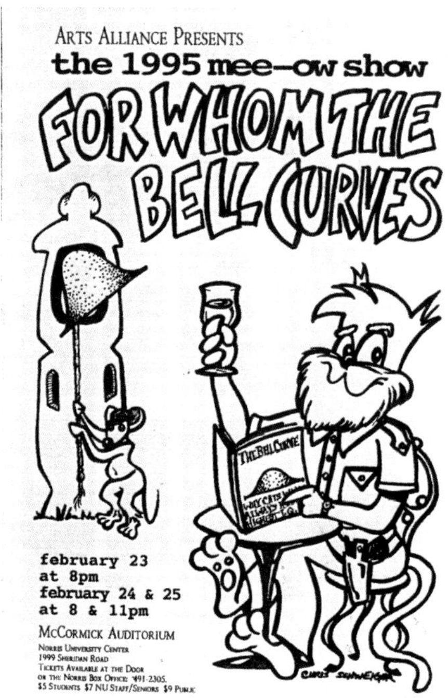

The Titanic Players

Mike Abdelsayed started the Titanic Players in the fall of 1994 after twenty-four unsuccessful auditions at Northwestern, including an audition for Mee-Ow. Per their website:

> The Titanic Players are one of the most successful college improv organizations in the country. In 2007, and again in 2009, we took home the 1st place trophy in the National College Improv Tournament prevailing over a field of over 100 teams. We are the only organization to win multiple tournaments, to open for MadTV, to perform live on WNUR radio, and to perform as a team on the iO schedule. We perform all types of improv but specialize in long form, where we improvise entire pieces from a single suggestion. We are educated and supported by One Group Mind, the first ever developing Improvisers Guild, and perform regularly at their venue in Chicago, The Comedy Clubhouse.

The cast also improvised movie trailers. "So we would shout 'Close up!'" said Herbstman, "and the person would stand closer downstage. And pull back to reveal a sheriff, and you'd walk backwards slowly and then have a gun at your side. We did that sort of thing."

The McCormick show's first act opened with a review of history told through rap. The second act opening was a song about O.J. Simpson, whose murder trial was receiving ubiquitous media coverage.

1995

The 1995 cast: Adrian Wenner, Ed Herbstman, Jean Villepique, Liv Oslund, Jill Alexander, Dan Weiss, Louise Lamson, and Rob Janas

The 1995 cast, Take 2: Oslund, Alexander, Weiss, Wenner, Herbstman, Villepique, Lamson, and Janas

1995

Directors' Notes

The Mee-Ow tradition at Northwestern is an important part of student life. It gives us the opportunity to laugh at what bothers, confuses or angers us. It is an inspiration not to take anyone or anything too seriously. If you're not sure whether or not to laugh or be offended--laugh. We waste too much time looking for the bad.

--Jean

Twelve years ago I saw something resembling tonight's show for the first time. It shook me. I needed to do it. I'd like to thank anyone who has encouraged/helped me to become a better improviser/writer/actor...You know who you are. I can only hope that I transfer some of my passion for this art form to this cast, crew and audience. Or at least to a ten year old.

--Adrian

Random Mee-Ow Quotes

"This is not a show about cats!" -Stephanie March

"Who *are* you?" -Cary Brothers

"I'm going to get some candy." -Rob Janas

"Doughnuts. Juice." -Apphia and Kristin during Load In

"Hi. I'm here to assistant produce your ass." -Melissa to Cary

"Let's fry alley cats at the Rock. That'll get 'em in McCormick." -Adrian

"Wait, I don't get it.....I'm NOT five years old!" -Matt Sherman

"I love how we use hinges for shit like this." -Matt Gilmore

"American art is very representational." -Chickpea

"Will you grow old with me and produce Saturday Night Live when I'm rich and famous?" -Adrian to Sas

"That's *my* boyfriend!" -Jean to Sas

"Riddlin. It's medication they give to hyperactive children." -Jean to Rob

The 1995 Mee-Ow Show Motto:

We didn't do it!!!!!!

Attempted humor from the program

1996

MEE-OW YEAR TWENTY-THREE

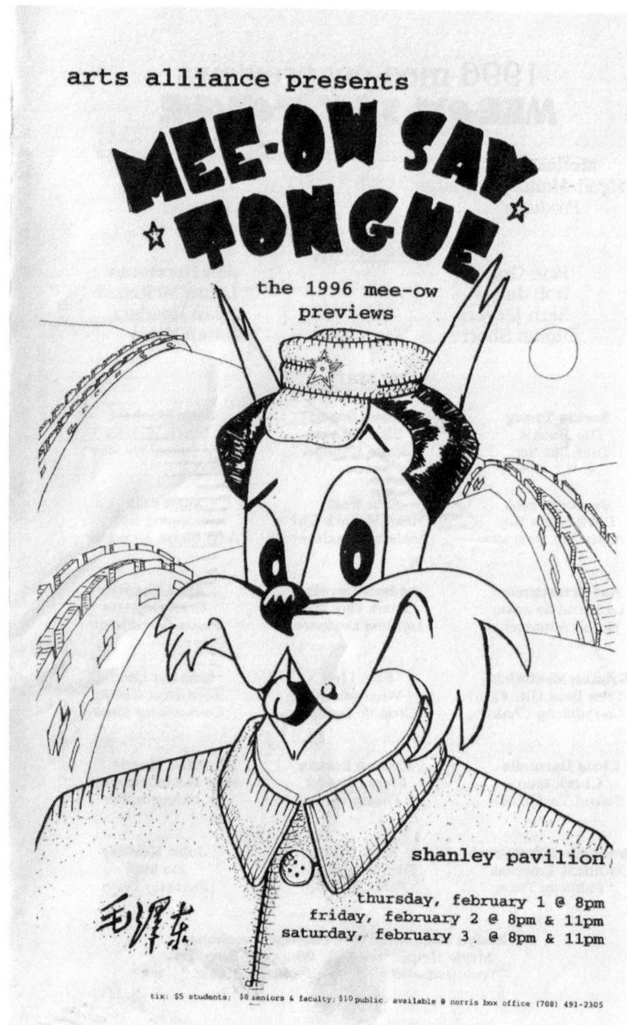

Mee-Ow Say Tongue

Thursday, February 1, at 8 p.m.; Friday and Saturday, Feb 2–3, at 8 and 11 p.m., Shanley Pavilion

It's a Wonderful Lie

Thursday, February 22, at 8 p.m.; Friday and Saturday, February 23–24, at 8 and 11 p.m., McCormick Auditorium

Future cast member Josh Meyers recalled his brother Seth auditioning:

> I was a theater major and so I was always auditioning for shows. Seth and I shared a job where we would tutor a couple of high school kids somewhere on the North Shore. I couldn't tell you where exactly, but we would trade off. Seth would do two days a week, I would do two days a week. Then there was a week when he asked if I could do the whole week because he was busy. I was like, sure. I forget what we were getting paid, like maybe twenty bucks an hour. And it was two hours each time you go up. So that's big money. And I did a full week of tutoring. Then I was like, "What were you doing this week?" And he's like, "Oh, I auditioned for this comedy show." I was like, "Well, why wouldn't you have said you were auditioning for this comedy show? Maybe I would have auditioned for this comedy show." He's like, "Well, you didn't know about it, so sorry." [laughs]

Returning cast member Jill Alexander directed and performed. Rob Janas also returned. New cast members were Peter Grosz, Jen Horstman, Laura McKenzie, Seth Meyers, Ryan Raddatz, Robin Shorr, and Sarah Yorra.

Consistent with the practice of previous years, the names of the shows came first, and then the opening sketches were developed. Seth Meyers remembered that "*Mee-Ow Say Tongue* was just because it was a stupid pun and it made for a really good poster of just the Mee-Ow cat and the famous Warhol poster. And *It's a Wonderful Lie* maybe because there were some cinema-related sketches. But there wasn't a lot of logic to

THIS YEAR IN HISTORY

Centennial Olympic Park bombing • Dolly the sheep born • Mad cow disease outbreak • Mars *Pathfinder* launch • Dow Jones year-end close 6448 • Average new car $18,523 • 1 gallon gas $1.23 • *Independence Day*, *Twister*, *Mission: Impossible*, *Jerry Maguire* • Weezer, *Pinkerton*; Beck, *Odelay*; Outkast, *ATLiens*; Jay-Z, *Reasonable Doubt*

1996

it. I think more than anything else, it was trying to have a name that was catchy that other people would think was smart. The shows were mostly reverse engineered."

The Show Highlights

In the *Daily Northwestern* (February 21, 1996), Stephen Tiszenkel wrote about the upcoming McCormick show, quoting Heather Landy, the Mee-Ow publicity director, as saying, "There's only one returning actor from last year. That makes a big difference. The show really has a different flavor. I think the cast is a lot more sarcastic, and all of them play off each other pretty well."

Cast member Ryan Raddatz recalled, "We would use the Shanley shows to try out different sketches, with the idea being we'd pick the best sketches from Shanley to put into the more polished McCormick shows. The McCormick shows were fun, but I recall the Shanley shows having a chaotic, unpredictable energy that made them special. The audience would sneak in drinks, so it was basically a big party, especially the 11 p.m. shows."

Of the live rock band that played between the games and sketches, Raddatz said, "They were awesome. At some point in the show, each cast member would join the band and sing thirty seconds of a rock song they'd chosen. This was mainly so the rest of the cast could do a quick costume change, but it was such a blast to see my friends getting to be thirty-second rock stars. I think in my first year I sang 'Youth Gone Wild' by Skid Row, and it was right after a sketch where I was dressed as a giant game piece from the board game Sorry. It was ridiculous and fun."

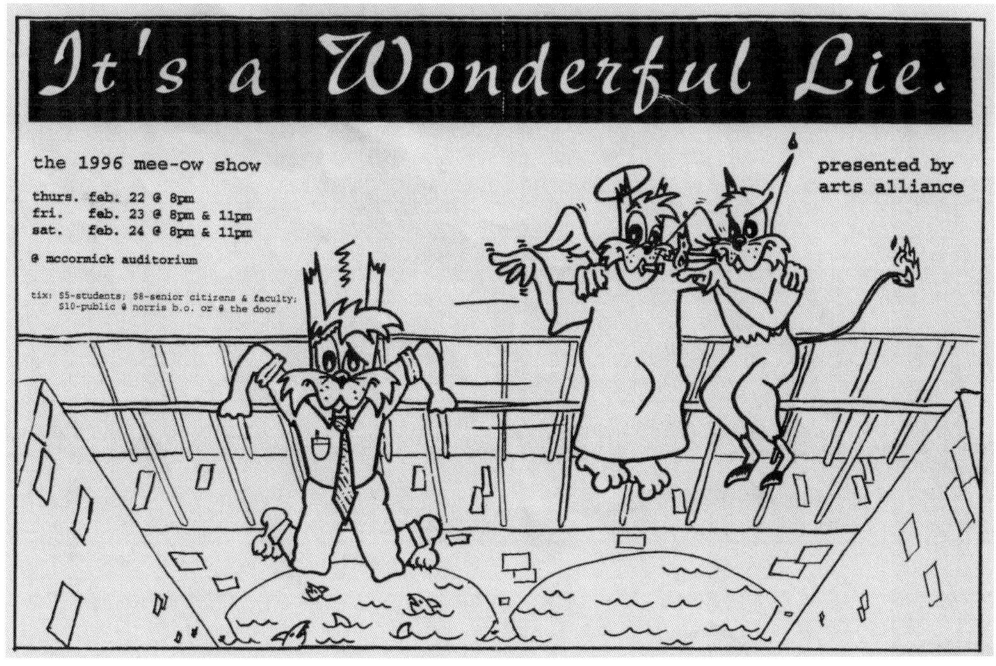

Raddatz also remembered the group's backstage warm-ups, which "were just silly improv games, but they always served to bring us together, regardless of what was going on in our lives or what personal conflicts were going on within the group. There was almost a meditative quality to the warm-ups as we'd invest in these ridiculous games and prepare to be one 'group mind' onstage together."

Robin Shorr recalled that "Seth Meyers wrote some killer sketches. He was a drunk Luke Skywalker in a Star Wars sketch that always did so well. He also wrote a sketch called 'Jumanji' that came out of an improv I did with Rob Janas. Disney had just bought ABC, and we sang a song about how Disney was taking control of the world."

Seth Meyers also recalled the Star Wars sketch, among others: "We wrote a sketch about the Star Wars characters late in life, things not going as well. This is before they rebooted all the Star Wars. We were ahead of the curve there. God, I can remember costumes now. We did a gender-swapped James Bond—Jane Bond—again ahead of the curve. [And a sketch] called "Gramm" about a roadie with a British rock band. But it was a grandmother. That was really good."

In an article in the April 3, 1996, *Daily Northwestern,* Tamara Ikenberg reported on the Mee-Ow Show's spring break West Coast trip. Featured in the story was a photo of the cast with the venerable actor Ernest Borgnine.

MEE-OW AND NORTHWESTERN FOOTBALL:
TOGETHER A WINNING TEAM

1996 MEE-OW SHOW
THIS WEEKEND!

ARTS
ALLIANCE

Big Ten co-champions with Mee-Ow cast members: (*clockwise from nine o'clock*) Jen Horstman, offensive lineman Brian Kardos, Sarah Yorra, Robin Shorr, punter Paul Burton, Laura McKenzie, kicker Sam Valenzisi, Ryan Raddatz, Peter Grosz, Rob Janas, running back Darnell Autry, and Seth Meyers. (Special thanks to Steve Schnur.)

The cast meeting Hollywood veteran Ernest Borgnine during their West Coast spring break trip: (*front, seated*) Horstman, Janas, Borgnine, Meyers, Alexander, and producer Melissa Meloro; (*back*) Janas, McKenzie, Yorra, assistant director Jeremy Fleck, and tour director Saskia Young

The 1996 cast: (*back row*) Alexander, Meyers, McKenzie, Yorra, Horstman, Grosz; (*front row*) Raddatz, Shorr, Janas

1997

MEE-OW YEAR TWENTY-FOUR

Apocalypse Mee-Ow

Thursday, January 30, at 8 p.m.; Friday and Saturday, January 31–February 1, at 8 and 11 p.m., Shanley Pavilion

The Mee-Owtsiders

Thursday, February 20, at 8 p.m.; Friday and Saturday, February 21–22, at 8 and 11 p.m., McCormick Auditorium

Returning cast member and director Jill Alexander again directed and performed. The other returning cast members were Ryan Raddatz and Robin Shorr. New cast members included Liz Cackowski, Heather Campbell, Josh Meyers, Jamey Roberts, and David Terry.

Both show titles this year were parodies of well-known movies, *Apocalypse Now* and *The Outsiders.* Cast member Josh Meyers recalled:

> It sounds so crazy to me now, but we rehearsed six days a week . . . three hours a night. And then maybe one of the days it was four. Then on my days off, I would take a train into the city and take a class at Second City. So I was like seven days a week, at least three hours a day, working on improv. So you would sense we've got a show coming up and let's start bringing in sketches and everybody who gets an idea, write stuff up, and then you just put it on its feet.

The Show Highlights

Meyers recalled the shows being about "half and half" sketches and improv games, and "while we were setting up scenes or changing things over, everyone in the cast would have a song that they would get to do and the band would play and we would pick the song." He sang "Sexual Healing," by Marvin Gaye, and he noted, "We weren't like the Rolling Stones, but [for the audience] it was like, 'We saw the Rolling Stones in like a two-hundred-person venue!' That's what Shanley felt like. You're right up against the audience, and they were right with you."

1997

THIS YEAR IN HISTORY

Steve Jobs returns to Apple • China regains control of Hong Kong • Heaven's Gate cult members found dead • Princess Diana dies • Stock markets crash • Dow Jones year-end close 7908 • Average new car $19,190 • 1 gallon of gas $1.23 • *Titanic*, *Men in Black*, *The Fifth Element*, *The Full Monty* • Radiohead, *OK Computer*; Foo Fighters, *The Colour and the Shape*; Daft Punk, *Homework*

One sketch was an infomercial for the Lazy-Christ chair, a parody of La-Z-Boy recliners. Meyers had very long hair for a role in the musical *Hair*, and in the sketch he portrayed Jesus. Raddatz played Ed Begley Jr., as a celebrity announcer/endorser. "It was like a beanbag chair with a sort of a cross behind it," Meyers recalled. "I'm sure people would really get their knickers in a twist about it at this point. But it was just a way that [since] Christ had to be up on this cross, why be uncomfortable?"

Apocalypse Mee-Ow also included a sketch about a woman in a fraternity where the men never realized she was female, and one about a man who was breastfed until age seven.

Reviews

In a review in the January 31, 1997, *Daily Northwestern*, Patrizia Pensa wrote:

> In its 23rd year running, this year's show focuses on social commentary about organized religion and life in the '90s. "The theme is how strange the '90s are, how crazy everything has gotten," Heather Campbell said. "We can't help but write about it because it's part of our everyday lives."
>
> The focus on religion developed when the cast of diverse religious backgrounds began planning sketches. Performers began to debate issues involving religion, and resolved their arguments with jokes. "When you get eight people together in a room, a lot of latent tendencies come out," said director and cast member Jill Alexander, a Speech senior. "We have one Jew, one adamant Christian, and a lot of people in between."

THE ARTS ALLIANCE
PRESENTS...
THE
MEE-OWTSIDERS
THE 1997 MEE-OW SHOW

MCCORMICK AUDITORIUM

SHOW TIMES:
THURSDAY FEBRUARY 20TH @ 8:00 PM
FRIDAY FEBRUARY 21ST @ 8:00 PM AND 11:00 PM
SATURDAY FEBRUARY 22ND @ 8:00 PM AND 11:00 PM

1998

MEE-OW YEAR TWENTY-FIVE

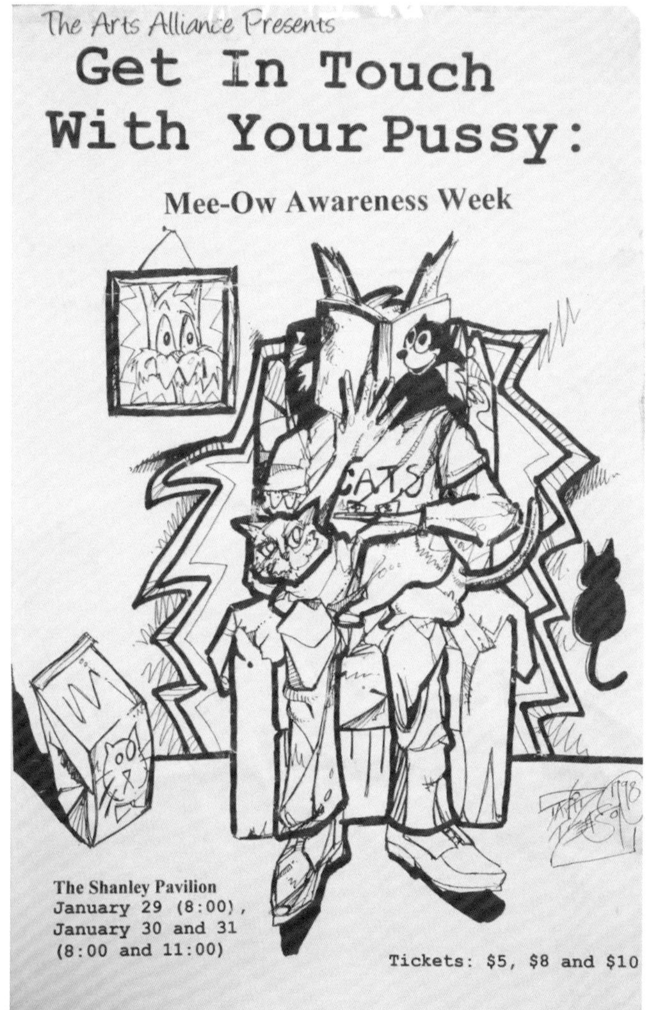

The Arts Alliance Presents
Get In Touch With Your Pussy:
Mee-Ow Awareness Week
CATS
The Shanley Pavilion
January 29 (8:00),
January 30 and 31
(8:00 and 11:00)
Tickets: $5, $8 and $10

Get in Touch with Your Pussy

Thursday, January 29, at 8 p.m.; Friday and Saturday, January 30–31, at 8 and 11 p.m., Shanley Pavilion

Hell No, Mee-Ow Show!

Thursday, February 19, at 8 p.m.; Friday and Saturday, February 20–21, at 8 and 11 p.m., McCormick Auditorium

Returning cast member Ryan Raddatz directed but did not perform. The other returning cast members were Liz Cackowski, Heather Campbell, Josh Meyers, Jamey Roberts, and Robin Shorr. New cast members included Luke Hatton, Justin Spitzer, and David Terry.

Mee-Ow ran an awareness campaign to promote their preview shows, posting attention-getting messages on the walls at the Norris University Center that said, "Get in touch with your pussy," "1 out of 5 cats is gay," "There are no cats on the Board of Trustees," "Cats are five times more likely to be sexually harassed in the workplace," and "Mee-Ow demands its own major."

In the article "Pussy Galore" in the *Daily Northwestern* (January 30, 1998), Patrizia Pensa wrote, "Members of the Mee-Ow Show have been campaigning for greater awareness of the problems cats face, but Northwestern students have been interpreting 'Get In Touch With Your Pussy Mee-Ow Awareness' in the wrong way."

When Raddatz was asked by Pensa about the meaning of the show's theme, he replied, "It's about Mee-Ow awareness. I don't understand why people are interpreting it in another way. We're just demanding that the campus be aware of us. We may be a minority on campus, but that doesn't mean we can't get awareness."

Raddatz described the response to the campaign as "nothing but positive. When people heard 'Get in Touch with Your Pussy,' I've seen them weep and say it's about time. We've heard cheers. Our particular choice of the word 'pussy' is in relation to the pussy cat. It's better than saying 'cat,' and if you say 'pussy cat,' it's too much. If you say 'pussy,' it cuts right through."

THIS YEAR IN HISTORY

Google founded • FDA approves Viagra • Northern Ireland Good Friday agreement • President Clinton affair denial, then admission • Dow Jones year-end close 9181 • Average new car $20,242 • 1 gallon gas $1.06 • *Armageddon, Saving Private Ryan, There's Something About Mary, Mulan, Shakespeare in Love* • Outkast, *Aquemini*; Lauryn Hill, *The Miseducation of Lauryn Hill*; Madonna, *Ray of Light*

1998

An article by Jeremy Mullman in the February 18, 1998, *Daily Northwestern* reported on "a sunrise poster rampage at Norris University Center," where Raddatz, identifying himself as "General Fun," led a group of ten people, including members of the cast and staff, dressed in military fatigues, wearing dark sunglasses and face paint, and carrying two-by-fours cut into "tommy guns." Raddatz detailed the action:

> 7:00 A.M. Two of the Mee-Ow guys are now crossing guards, duck walking across the driveway, wooden artillery resting vertically upon their right shoulders. A latecomer, also decked out for the occasion, is ordered to "drop and give me 20," which he does, receiving a *Full Metal Jacket* style reprimand the whole time. As the troops distribute rations of donuts and coffee—which they share with the wartime press and the growing . . . Canadian contingent—Raddatz is now delivering a pep talk from atop a covered garbage can, a 6′5″ Ross Perot act-alike waving a tommy gun frantically, preaching of how crucial victory in the "poster wars" is.
>
> 7:30 A.M. Mee-Ow has long since packed tight around the front doors, pushing the other groups to the periphery of the mass. Some of the lesser-numbered groups are down on all fours, frantically taping their signs together for efficiency. "We're totally screwed," a member of one of the later organizations concedes, looking over at the militant Mee-Ow group. "Last week, we were them, only without guns."

The same year, Mee-Ow ran a second unusual promotional campaign for their mainstage show. This time they urged students to protest comedy and boycott Mee-Ow, which set up the opening musical sketch of the mainstage show.

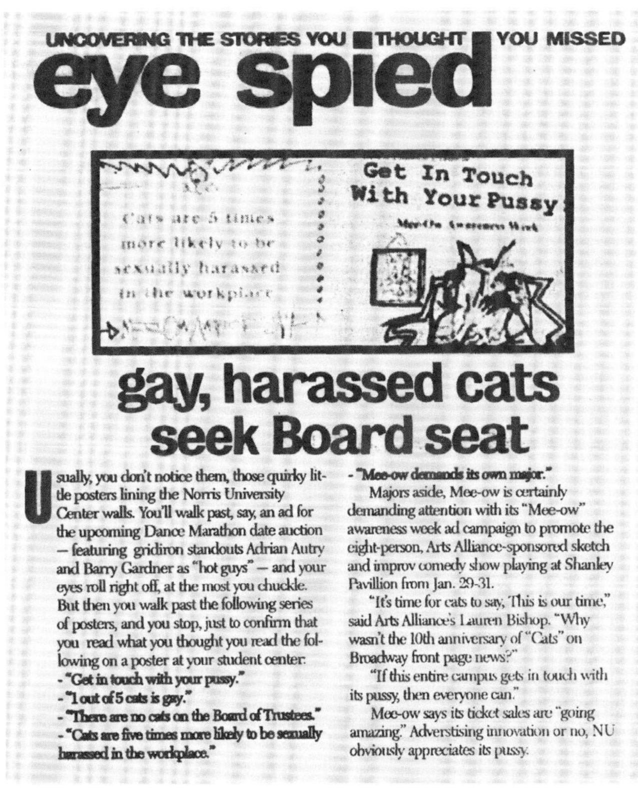

UNCOVERING THE STORIES YOU ■ THOUGHT ■ YOU MISSED

eye spied

Cats are 5 times
more likely to be
sexually harassed
in the workplace
Get In Touch
With Your Pussy

gay, harassed cats seek Board seat

Usually, you don't notice them, those quirky little posters lining the Norris University Center walls. You'll walk past, say, an ad for the upcoming Dance Marathon date auction — featuring gridiron standouts Adrian Autry and Barry Gardner as "hot guys" — and your eyes roll right off, at the most you chuckle. But then you walk past the following series of posters, and you stop, just to confirm that you read what you thought you read the following on a poster at your student center:

- "Get in touch with your pussy."
- "1 out of 5 cats is gay."
- "There are no cats on the Board of Trustees."
- "Cats are five times more likely to be sexually harassed in the workplace."
- "Mee-ow demands its own major."

Majors aside, Mee-ow is certainly demanding attention with its "Mee-ow" awareness week ad campaign to promote the eight-person, Arts Alliance-sponsored sketch and improv comedy show playing at Shanley Pavillion from Jan. 29-31.

"It's time for cats to say, This is our time," said Arts Alliance's Lauren Bishop. "Why wasn't the 10th anniversary of "Cats" on Broadway front page news?"

"If this entire campus gets in touch with its pussy, then everyone can."

Mee-ow says its ticket sales are "going amazing." Adverstising innovation or no, NU obviously appreciates its pussy.

The Show Highlights

Heather Campbell recalled:

> The whole publicity run leading up to it was handing out flyers around campus and being like, we're protesting the Mee-Ow Show, and like basically not saying we were from the Mee-Ow Show, but [saying,] "We're showing up at the auditorium. We're shutting down the show. It's offensive," et cetera. And then when the lights came up, there was nobody onstage. And we ran in from the back shouting, "We did it! We shut down the Mee-Ow Show!" And we were a rival group who hated

comedy and were like, "These are serious times!" And then immediately launched into a song about how much we hated comedy. And then Josh Meyers stepped forward and said, "No, this is wrong. We love comedy and we should embrace it. And people are here to enjoy the show." And on the final night of the show the woman who had just been crowned Miss America (Kate Shindle, Theater, '99) from Northwestern was in the second row of the house. So Josh sang, and he improvised some line about how Miss America was coming there for comedy and brought her up onstage, I think, or maybe just a spotlight shined on her.

Luke Hatton wrote the "Boardgame Models" sketch. According to Meyers, "covers of board games always used to [show] families playing together, and [the sketch] was looking back at the lives of these people who had become famous for being board game models. They were being brought out of obscurity to relive their glory days."

Justin Spitzer recalled that sketch as the one where he always got the most laughs:

> The photographer (played by Luke) would say "OK, now it's a group of people playing Clue, in 3 . . . 2 . . . 1 . . . go!", and we would strike a pose. Everyone did different poses for each [different game], except my character, who could never think of anything to do except the same hammy pose each time—standing in the center with my hands above my head and a big goofy smile, and Luke would act like I had somehow nailed it once again. Now that I think about it, it was basically a version of the *SNL* "More Cowbell" sketch, although this was two years before that aired. It always killed.

arts alliance presents
Hell No,
Mee-Ow
Show

1998

Spitzer also remembered a "whole, big choreographed song-and-dance routine" the group would break into "when an audience member suggested something dumb and gross and juvenile, basically mocking them. But after a show went by where we didn't get any juvenile suggestions, we started putting a plant in the audience, just in the event that happened again. They'd wait until the show was almost over, and if we hadn't gotten an opportunity to do the song, we'd call on them and they'd pitch something purposely stupid. It's the only time we ever used a plant."

Campbell recalls that the song was written by Josh Meyers and that it was called "The Poop Song":

> It was a song when [we asked the audience for a suggestion], "Hey, can we have any object?" and somebody would shout "Dildo!" and we'd be like "Ugh." Then we'd immediately break into this song. And I remember the end of the song was, "Because you had to be the big clown. You get to wear the poop crown. It's poop!" And you'd put this filthy crown on their head in the audience and be like, "This is the guy.! He did the thing!" And then you'd go back to the show. Every night somebody would yell "Dildo!" and that has continued to almost every show that I have ever asked for a suggestion in my life. The problem is objectively, it's a funny structure, like the word itself is funny. Like if it was "plate" it wouldn't be something to shout, but it's got a sort of musicality to it that makes it as funny as the object.

Director's Note

Whenever I'm watching a serious play, I get this strange urge to jump out of my seat, leap on stage, and dance around like a crazy monkey-child. I always wonder what would happen in the audience, and if the actors would even react to the presence of a monkey-child in their midst, or just keep on going with their lines.

I think that's what the Mee-Ow Show has been about for 25 years--it's one big disruption that's exciting to watch because you never know what that monkey-child will do next.

We're all dancing monkey-children in our own way. Welcome to the convention.

Ryan

Producer's Note

Leave it to Ryan to write something profound about monkeys, but that's why we love him. That's why I love Mee-Ow. I love that months of hard work and dedication of the cast and staff come together to form experiences that can never be forgotten, friendships that can never be equaled, and a room full of laughter. And Mee-Ow has been doing this for 25 years. It's all about having fun in life and sharing those moments with the people close to you.

I hope you're laughing at us.

Libby

1999

MEE-OW YEAR TWENTY-SIX
(The Twenty-Fifth Anniversary Show)

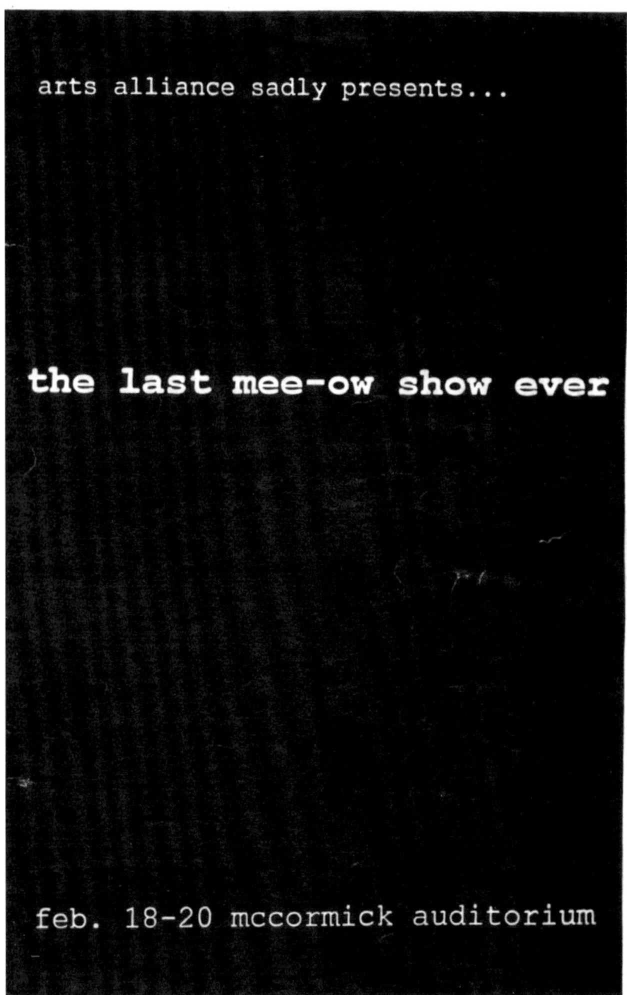

arts alliance sadly presents...
the last mee-ow show ever
feb. 18-20 mccormick auditorium

That Was Then, This Is Mee-Ow

Thursday, January 28, at 8 p.m.; Friday and Saturday, January 29–30, at 8 and 11 p.m., Shanley Pavilion

The Last Mee-Ow Show Ever

Thursday, February 18, at 8 p.m.; Friday and Saturday, February 19–20, at 8 and 11 p.m., McCormick Auditorium

Returning cast members Liz Cackowski and Jamey Roberts codirected and performed. The other returning cast members were Heather Campbell and Luke Hatton. New cast members included Dave Asher, Kristen Schaal, Michael Sinclair, and Scott Speiser.

The eight of them began improvising and brainstorming during the 1998 fall quarter, shortly after the cast was set, which thereafter became the normal practice.

The name of the mainstage show, *The Last Mee-Ow Show Ever*, referred to the widespread "end of the world" myths, rumors, and stories about the computer millennium bug causing an impending apocalypse at midnight on December 31, 1999. If the world had ended, then this would indeed have been the last Mee-Ow Show ever.

The Show Highlights

Heather Campbell remembered a sketch written by Jamey Roberts called "Late Reaction Family," where "every line was reacting to the wrong line, and it was confounding. Like Dad saying, 'Pass me the peas.' And then somebody else saying, 'How was your day today?' Then somebody else being like, 'I don't have the peas,' and then somebody else being like, 'It was fine. Why are you asking?' But two other lines had happened before those responses. Oh, it was so hard to memorize."

Scott Speiser recalled that his father, who had never seen him perform in anything, wanted to come to Northwestern to see him in something:

> I told him about this Mee-Ow show he's never seen and never heard of, and probably

THIS YEAR IN HISTORY

Y2K "millennium bug" • Columbine High School shootings • Euro currency launched • Dow Jones year-end close 11,497 • Average new car $20,697 • 1 gallon gas $1.17 • *The Phantom Menace*, *The Sixth Sense*, *The Matrix*, *The Mummy*, *The Spy Who Shagged Me* • Red Hot Chili Peppers, *Californication*; Nine Inch Nails, *The Fragile*; Rage Against the Machine, *The Battle of Los Angeles*; Blink-182, *Enema of the State*; Eminem, *The Slim Shady LP*

didn't know anything about it. I don't think I'd seen him in years. And this is always where I was nervous. He was there, but I told him, "Look, I'm not going to have much time to hang out with you because this is the one weekend of the McCormick show. Like it's a busy freakin' week." And he never told me this, but I know that what he was expecting was something like an elementary school production of *Our Town* or some play, and that his son was going to be, like, the third tree from the left. And he wanted to support me, but he was going to have to be really nice about it afterwards. "You were a lovely tree." Like that. So he walks into this theater and it's packed. I had reserved him seats. Well, a few weeks before that, he was in LA with a friend, and they went to see *The Tonight Show* and on *The Tonight Show* was Miss America Kate Shindle, who was a year older than me at Northwestern, maybe two years older. And he walks in and sits down and sitting behind him is Miss America. And he recognized her because a few weeks ago he saw her on the set of Jay Leno. And so he's like, whoa. Then he sees this show. Which was awesome, it was just flat-out fucking awesome, and he saw his son, one of eight people up there, and I remember being a little nervous because he was there. But I remember the times I saw him. I just couldn't believe the smile on his face. And he was truly, utterly blown away. I think that was the moment where he was like, OK, I guess I can, maybe I should, support my son in this artistic creative life. But that's my boy up there.

Mee-Ow alums at the 25th anniversary: John Goodrich, Dana Olsen, Dave Silberger, Steve Jarvis, Tricia Galin, Ed Herbstman, Paul Warshauer, Jean Villepique, Libby Minarik, J.P. Manoux, Ryan Raddatz, Robert Mendel, and Mark Lancaster

1999

Mee-Ow Show cofounders Josh Lazar and Paul Warshauer attending the 25th anniversary show

The 1999 cast: Scott Speiser, Kristen Schaal, Jamey Roberts, Liz Cackowski, Michael Sinclair, Dave Asher, Luke Hatton, and Heather Campbell

Waa-Mu Copies Mee-Ow

In a February 24, 1999, article in the *Daily Northwestern*, John Balz wrote:

It's been said that imitation is the sincerest form of flattery. So after being spoofed for years by Mee-ow, Waa-Mu saw its chance with last week's Mee-ow show posters.

The improvisational comedy group ran a publicity campaign based around the slogan "The Last Mee-ow Show Ever," so Waa-Mu countered with, "The Last Waa-Mu Show Ever": Same typeface, same font size, same black background.

Waa-Mu co-chair Kate Strohbehn said the joke was done in good fun.

A group of Waa-Mu organizers loved Mee-ow's teaser posters and last weekend's show and thought the posters would be a great hoax, she said.

"They spoof us all the time, so we thought, 'Hey let's get 'em,'" Strohbehn said.

Most Mee-ow performers took the joke in stride, taking it more as a compliment than an insult. But Mee-ow producer Jaime Morgenstern said she was a bit shocked when she saw the posters for the first time Tuesday.

"I had no idea that they were capable of copying our publicity," Morgenstern said.

Flattery or copying aside, the most important thing to remember is that this joke won't work for your history paper.

THE ARTS ALLIANCE PRESENTS
THE 1999 MEE-OW SHOW
PREVIEWS
THAT WAS THEN
THIS IS
MEE-OW
PREMIERING ON THE
SHANLEY
CHANNEL
THURS, JAN 28 AT 8:00
FRI, JAN 29 AT 8:00 & 11:00
SAT, JAN 30 AT 8:00 & 11:00
STUDENTS $5.00
FACULTY $8.00
GENERAL ADMISSION $10.00
TIX ARE AVAILABLE AT THE NORRIS BOX OFFICE AND AT THE DOOR
FEATURING THE KATMANS!

1999

2000

MEE-OW YEAR TWENTY-SEVEN

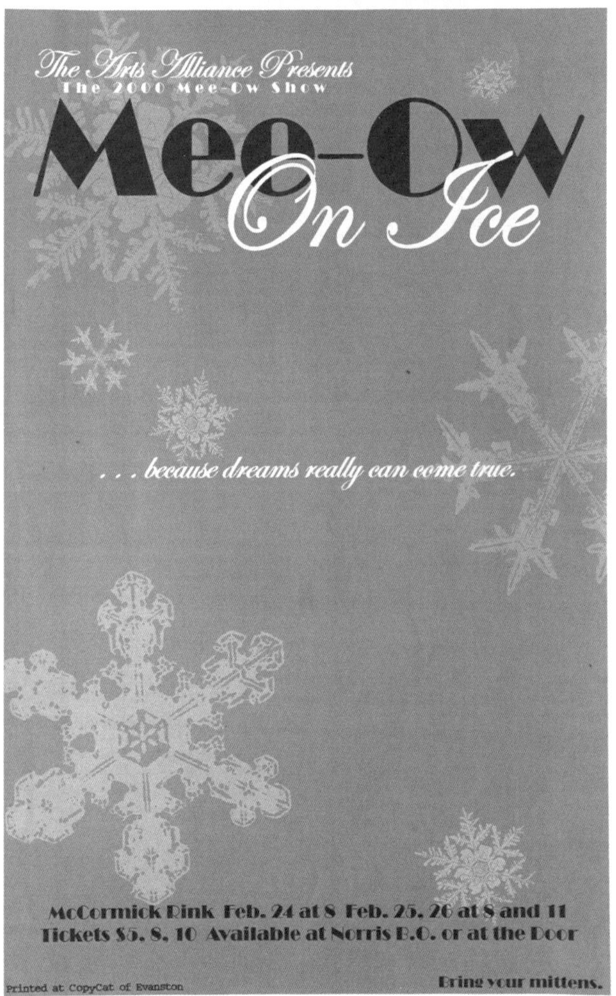

Don't Tread on Mee-Ow

Thursday, February 3, at 8 p.m.; Friday and Saturday, February 4–5, at 8 and 11 p.m., Shanley Pavilion

Mee-Ow on Ice

Thursday, February 24, at 8 p.m.; Friday and Saturday, February 25–26, at 8 and 11 p.m., McCormick Auditorium

Returning cast member Luke Hatton directed and performed. The other returning cast members were Heather Campbell, Kristen Schaal, and Scott Speiser. New cast members included Lauren Flans, Ryan Harrison, Jess Lacher, and Matt McKenna.

Harrison recalled:

> I auditioned with Matt [McKenna] and I must have been in the callbacks with Jess [Lacher] because we were the three that were ultimately cast that year because there were five seniors. I remember Matt being a natural. I remember him just killing it. I actually remember him coming into a scene and they said, "You're a pilot." And he came in and said [speaking drunkenly], "Don't go to Three Dog Ale. Like, there's something wrong with the vodka." And it was just like an opening line that was more sophisticated than my ability to improvise at that time. Oh, you just got cast as a pilot, but he's coming in drunk. It's like a good choice. I remember him being very good. . . . Mostly I remember being nervous and excited and really wanting to be in the show. I was not confident that I would necessarily make it.

The title of the preview show was a parody of the motto on the Revolutionary War–era Gadsden Flag, "Don't Tread on Me" (and presciently predated the revival of this motto by the small-government, anti-tax, conservative "Astroturf" Tea Party movement of 2009). As Lauren Flans recalled, "The big controversy that year was that they were allegedly thinking they were going to tear down Shanley. So our opening song was about how we shouldn't let them tear down Shanley, how we had to save Shanley. Like, we were

THIS YEAR IN HISTORY

Supreme Court ends Florida vote recount, giving presidency to George W. Bush • Vermont legalizes same-sex civil unions • Dow Jones year-end close 10,788 • Average new car $21,430 • 1 gallon gas $1.51 • *Gladiator*, *Cast Away*, *How the Grinch Stole Christmas* • Radiohead, *Kid A*; Coldplay, *Parachutes*; Eminem, *The Marshall Mathers LP*; Outkast, *Stankonia*; The White Stripes, *De Stijl*

2000

going to tie ourselves to the posts outside. And the bulldozer is going to come, and the chorus [sung in response to the bulldozer] is 'Shanley wouldn't tear *you* down.' It was sort of the subtitle of the show. I'm shocked that Shanley is still there."

The title of the mainstage show was based on the popularity of touring ice-skating shows, such as *Ice Follies* and *Holiday on Ice*. In 1995 the name of the popular show *Walt Disney's World on Ice* was changed to simply *Disney on Ice*.

In a preview article in the *Daily Northwestern* (February 24, 2000), Jaimie Webb wrote that *Mee-Ow on Ice* was really going to be performed on ice:

> "I think (people) don't believe us, so when they see us, they're going to be in awe," Speech senior Scott Speiser said. "I think people are going to love it. How many shows at NU have you seen on ice?"
>
> To accomplish this mini-feat, they plan to lay water-based ice on the stage at McCormick Auditorium and drop the temperature to keep the ice frozen, co-producer Heather Campbell said.
>
> To learn how to ice skate on stage, the cast took lessons from a Russian figure skating coach named Katchkov, whom they contacted through the Slavic languages and literature department, co-producer Karyn Meltz said.
>
> "When I called, he was great, but he was a little leery working with amateurs," said Meltz, a Weinberg junior.
>
> However, he soon became comfortable with the group.
>
> "He was a tough Russian guy," Speech freshman Matt McKenna said. "He has nicknames for me, like 'Little Big Bear.' He would call me when I was not getting the moves. He would start ranting."
>
> But he wasn't all bite, said Jess Lacher, a Speech sophomore.
>
> "Once you got to know him, he was one of the sweetest human beings I've ever met," she said. "You have to get past the gruff exterior."
>
> After working with Katchkov, the group practiced downtown.
>
> "We tried running through some of the sketches on Skate on State and it was, like, wipeout," Lauren Flans, a Speech senior, said.
>
> For Lacher, the skating allowed her to relive part of her childhood.
>
> "I (skated) seriously, but I kind of stopped when I got to high school. When this whole thing came along and we put it on ice, it was a happy coincidence. It's been a fun experience to skate again."
>
> The eight-member cast wrote all the sketches, including one about Edgar Allan Poe and another about an atypical high school show choir.
>
> "I take inspiration from Saturday morning cartoons," said Campbell, who is also NYOU's cartoonist. "I really like superheroes."
>
> "A lot of it comes from watching the absurdity of this campus," she added.

2000

The Show Highlights

Mee-Ow on Ice began with a musical number based on the title of the show. "We rented a fog machine," Campbell recalled. "When you came into McCormick, the stage was completely fogged over the entire time. And we came out on ice skates—full blades, full ice skates—and did the entire opening number with ice skates on, like metal-clunking ice skates. But there was no ice under the fog. It was just a visual effect."

Speiser elaborated: "We put tape on [the skates] so they weren't destroying the wood [of the stage]. But we did the whole thing, including dance numbers, wearing ice skates. But obviously they're not sliding. There's no ice. So we're just super uncomfortable, super awkwardly, like barely able to stand up [singing]: 'It's Mee-Ow on ice!' and we're on these skates. It was awesome."

At intermission, Mike Sherman rode out on a tricycle disguised to look like a Zamboni, the machine that smooths the ice for an ice show or hockey game. He is credited in the program as the Zamboni driver.

One sketch was written by the "pirate-obsessed" Matt McKenna, as Flans remembered him, although McKenna contended he was not. Campbell recalled that "it was a sitcom called *R Mateys*, like roommates, and it was about how a pirate and a feminist lesbian were roommates in New York City. It was like the most obtusely sexist, misogynist pirate, and a Sylvia Plath–reading militant feminist."

Harrison remembers the pirate referring to a treasure called "the clit ring of Coronado."

A sketch called "Graduation Day" was written and performed by Harrison wearing a cap and gown and delivering a dry, clichéd high school valedictorian speech. As Campbell recalled, "It was just like, [speaking in monotone] 'A lot of you have asked us how we got here. And I reply to that with, "How did anyone get anywhere?" ' It was just like a plain valedictorian [speech], and it killed every single time he did it. It felt at the time like a masterpiece because on paper, there were no jokes at all. And when he would do it, it would be laughter for every line because they were so devoid of meaning."

Commenting on a Controversy

Since its beginning, the Mee-Ow Show commented on current events and controversial issues in the country, and especially on campus. In 2000, a campus controversy that began in 1977 and received national attention was finally parodied in a sketch.

Shortly after receiving tenure, Arthur R. Butz, an associate professor of engineering, self-published a Holocaust denial book. This was uncovered by the *Daily Northwestern*, leading to students and faculty expressing their outrage. Then in 1997, as public use of the internet began to increase dramatically, Butz posted his views online, using the university's servers.

Butz stated that he kept his personal opinions out of the classroom, and although denouncing his views, the university supported academic freedom. So despite complaints by faculty and students, Butz remains on the faculty today.

Flans described a sketch written by McKenna:

> Matt was [a professor] leading a discussion section, and he just kept denying everything that the students were saying, making him look like a buffoon. No matter what a student said, Matt would be like, "Well, Ernest Hemingway didn't write *The Old Man and the Sea*." And a student would say, "This is the book." And he'd be like, "No, he didn't write it." It was that kind of a bit. Then at one point he put a sheet over his head and said, "I'm invisible, I'm not here." And the students are like, "We can see you. You have a sheet over your head." He said, "Never happened." Everybody got [the point of the sketch] because this was huge news when I was at school.

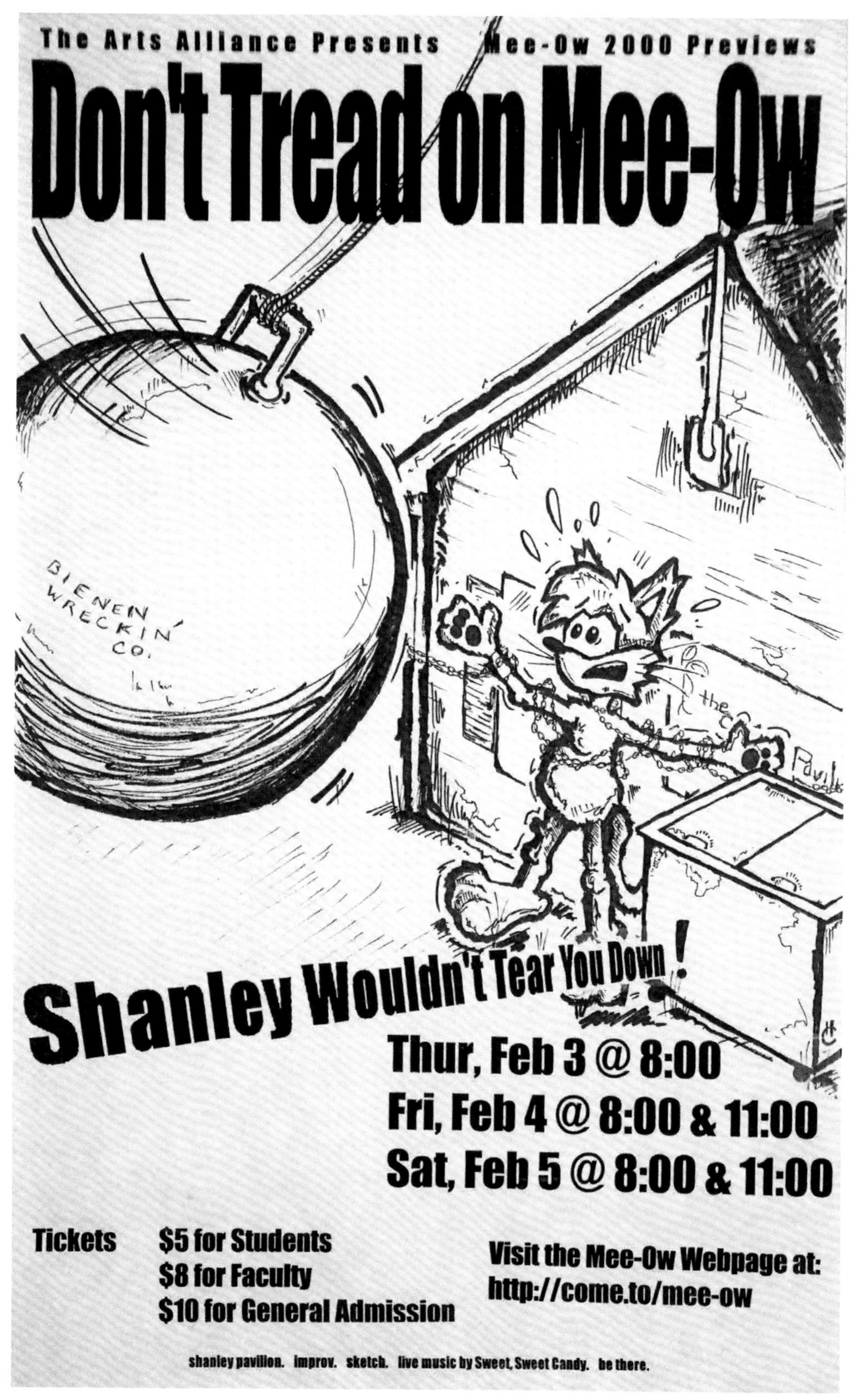
The Arts Alliance Presents Mee-Ow 2000 Previews
Don't Tread on Mee-Ow
BIENEN WRECKIN' CO.
Shanley Wouldn't Tear You Down!
Thur, Feb 3 @ 8:00
Fri, Feb 4 @ 8:00 & 11:00
Sat, Feb 5 @ 8:00 & 11:00
Tickets $5 for Students
$8 for Faculty
$10 for General Admission
Visit the Mee-Ow Webpage at:
http://come.to/mee-ow
shanley pavilion. improv. sketch. live music by Sweet, Sweet Candy. be there.

2000

Kristen Schaal wrote a sketch called "Cartwheels and Somersaults" that Flans described as "very Kristen Schaal":

> There was no dialogue. There was some underscoring. First Ryan Harrison would come out on stage and he would execute like a perfect cartwheel and then he'd bow. Then Jess Lacher would come out on stage and she would do a not as good cartwheel, but it was fine. And then Kristen would come onstage and do like a really fucked-up cartwheel. It was not a good cartwheel. Harrison would come back onstage and do a perfectly executed somersault and like that. And then Jess would come and do a very mediocre somersault. At the end of the sketch was a slow fade on Kristen trying to do a somersault, but she couldn't get all the way over and it was just a really slow fade as she was onstage, rolling off. And it was just very weird. It did get a pretty good reaction.

For the sketch called "Tuna Cologne," Flans recalled that "there was elevator-type music playing in the background, and Heather doing a voiceover: 'And now, tuna cologne.' Luke Hatton opened a can of tuna and he's smelling it. And people are losing it in the audience. People are just screaming, 'No!' And then at the end of the sketch he just colognes his face. And then it's a blackout. People just couldn't handle a guy putting tuna fish on his face."

Ryan Harrison wrote a sketch called "Discussion Section." As Flans described it,

> We were students critiquing *Citizen Kane*. The teacher was like, "OK, so what did we all think of it?" And it was just students being like, "Yeah, I didn't get why it was in black and white. Like we have color." Then Matt McKenna as Orson Welles would be like, "Well, I was making a point." And the student would be like, "Yeah, that didn't really come across." So it was basically students being pretentious and shitty to really famous people. It was dead on. Then the callback to it later was Scott [as Jonas Salk] sitting there and the teacher was like, "And so does anybody have any questions for Jonas Salk, who was so kind to come here today?" And a student was like, 'Yeah. I mean, I like that you cured polio, but . . ." And then, the "out" of the sketch was Matt as Orson Welles still in the class, saying, "Yeah. [Shakes head.] I didn't like that." And that was the end. I still, to this day, will say that to myself. I'll be like, "Yeah. I don't like that."

At both shows each cast member sang a thirty-second excerpt of a song, accompanied by the band. During her freshman year, Flans had made a promise to her best friend, Mike, who played the harmonica, telling him, "If I ever get into the Mee-Ow Show, I will pick a song with harmonica in it so that you can play harmonica on the song." And then, she explained, "It took me four fucking years, but senior year . . . I finally got in and I was keeping my promise. I was like, 'You realize you have to be at all the shows? You're committing?' So I sang 'Last Dance with Mary Jane,' [*sic*] by Tom Petty, which has that great harmonica solo. And he was there."

Out Da Box

As reported in the February 10, 2000, *Daily Northwestern*, in 1998, "the AATE board withdrew 'Out 'da Box' from its yearly programming because the play had become too 'raunchy.' 'Out 'da Box' returned last winter as a purer version of its former self."

On February 10, 2000, a new, original Out Da Box sketch-comedy show, codirected by Robin Thede and Andre Gaines, opened at Shanley Pavilion. This grew into the only ongoing multicultural comedy group at Northwestern.

ODB generally has a smaller fall show and a larger spring show in Shanley Pavilion with lights, props, and a set. They also perform other small gigs and pop-up shows throughout the year.

Out Da Box alumni include Robin Thede, comedian, actor, and creator of *A Black Lady Sketch Show*, and screenwriter and producer Mara Brock Akil.

At the various performances, Harrison sang "Ziggy Stardust," by David Bowie. Speiser sang "Under Pressure," by Queen and David Bowie; "Iris," by the Goo Goo Dolls; and "Don't You (Forget About Me)," by Simple Minds. He recalled that the previous year "Liz Cackowski had the most incredible skill. She was never in the [same key as the band], but in whatever key she was singing in, she was accurate. For someone that can sing and has a bit of a music understanding, I can't fathom it. It's impossible."

The Shanley Seven

Several of the graduating Mee-Ow Show cast members from 2000 moved to LA. In the absence of a comedy theater, they rented a space and performed as "The Shanley Seven." As Heather Campbell recalled, "We did the same style show, where it was improv, sketch, and a live band singing cover songs, because it was a format that we knew worked. And it was a great way to get the cast in front of agents, managers, and everything else. It was the baggage I carried to Los Angeles when I moved here right out of college." The Shanley Seven included Campbell, Lauren Flans, Ryan Raddatz, Kristen Schaal, and Scott Speiser.

Cast lets the cat out of the bag, onto ice

'Mee-Ow On Ice' skates by with figure-skating coach, cartoon-inspired sketches

by Jamie Webb
j-webb@nwu.edu

The cast of Mee-Ow is used to people not taking them seriously. But this weekend's Mee-Ow Show, "Mee-Ow on Ice," is really being performed on ice.

"I think (people) don't believe us, so when they see us, they're going to be in awe," Speech senior Scott Speiser said. "I think people are going to love it. How many shows at NU have you seen on ice?"

To accomplish this mini-feat, they plan to lay water-based ice on the stage at McCormick Auditorium and drop the temperature to keep the ice frozen, co-producer Heather Campbell said.

To learn how to ice skate on stage, the cast took lessons from a Russian figure-skating coach named Katchkov, whom they contacted through the Slavic languages and literature department, co-producer Karyn Meltz said.

"When I called, he was great, but he was a little leery working with amateurs," said Meltz, a Weinberg junior.

However, he soon became comfortable with the group.

"He was a tough Russian guy," Speech freshman Matt McKenna said. "He has nicknames for me, like 'Little Big Bear.' He would call me when I was not getting the moves. He would start ranting."

But he wasn't all bite, said Jess Lacher, a Speech sophomore.

"Once you got to know him, he was one of the sweetest human beings I've ever met," she said. "You have to get past the gruff exterior."

After working with Katchkov, the group practiced downtown.

"We tried running through some of the sketches on Skate on State and it was, like, wipeout," Lauren Flans, a Speech senior, said.

For Lacher, the skating allowed her to relive part of her childhood.

"I (skated) seriously, but I kind of stopped when I got to high school," Lacher said. "When this whole thing came along and we put it on ice, it was a happy coincidence. It's been a fun experience to skate again."

Mee-Ow, which is in its 27th year, began as a parody of Waa-Mu. But as Mee-Ow evolved, it became more about sketch comedy and improv, Campbell said.

But that doesn't mean the rivalry between the shows has completely abated, Speiser said.

This year's show consists of comedy sketches, improv and a few choreographed dance numbers with a band.

The eight-member cast wrote all the sketches, including one about Edgar Allen Poe and another about an atypical high school show choir.

"I take inspiration from Saturday morning cartoons," said Campbell, who is also NYOU's cartoonist. "I really like superheroes."

"A lot of it comes from watching the absurdity of this campus," she added.

The cast has been together since October, so they have become good friends.

"We're tighter than the cast of 'Friends,'" Flans said.

Their friendship makes it easier to attend the daily rehearsals, Speiser said.

"I'm excited to be at rehearsal every night," he said. "It's work, but we're having a good time."

"Mee-Ow on Ice" runs tonight at 8 p.m. and Friday and Saturday at 8 p.m. and 11 p.m. Tickets are $5 for students.

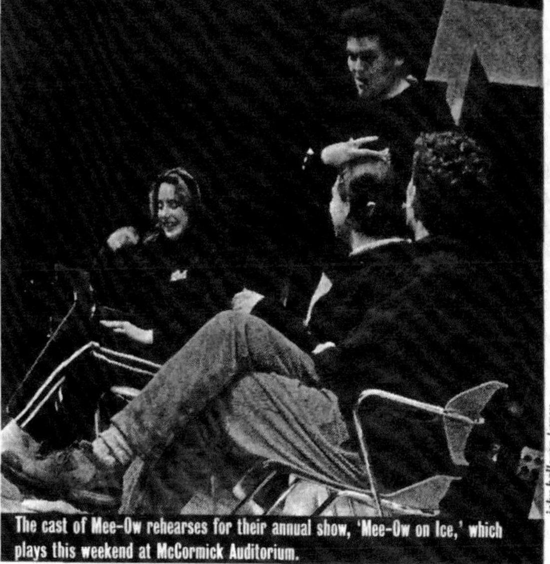

The cast of Mee-Ow rehearses for their annual show, 'Mee-Ow on Ice,' which plays this weekend at McCormick Auditorium.

The *Daily Northwestern* preview article in which the entire cast convincingly maintains that the show actually will be performed on ice

2001

MEE-OW YEAR TWENTY-EIGHT

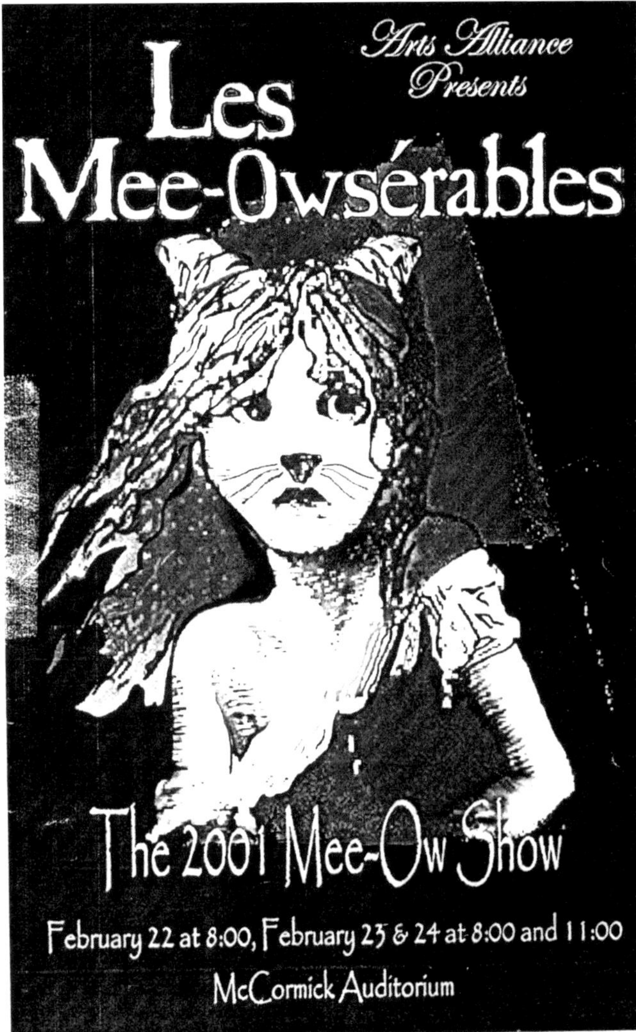

Sesamee-ow Street

Thursday, January 25, at 8 p.m.; Friday and Saturday, January 26–27, at 8 and 11 p.m., Shanley Pavilion

Les Mee-Owsérables

Thursday, February 22, at 8 p.m.; Friday and Saturday, February 23–24, at 8 and 11 p.m., McCormick Auditorium

Returning cast members Ryan Harrison and Matt McKenna codirected and performed. The other returning cast member was Jess Lacher. New cast members included Drew Callander, Laura Grey, Dan Mahoney, Martha Marion, and Lee Overtree.

Sesamee-ow Street was an obvious play on *Sesame Street*, which was familiar to the cast and audience, who had all grown up watching the children's TV show. Having had a successful run in France and London, the musical *Les Misérables* premiered on Broadway on March 12, 1987. The musical was very popular and well known to the cast and audiences.

Harrison remembered the origin of a shared joke: "One thing in Mee-Ow which also exists in other groups I've been in is that a lot of the bad ideas get remembered and [repeated] in the group. [This] was one of those. Schaal had one that was about cake. That was a year before me, but it was still a joke by the time I was there. Whenever anyone would see a cake, someone would scream, 'Cake!' I guess she was having a bad nightmare of the time she baked a bad cake. For the professional comedian the misses are almost funnier than the hits.

Kristen Schaal not only confirmed the cake story but said that whenever she sees anyone from the cast, they still scream, "Cake!"

The Show Highlights

The Shanley preview shows opened with a seven-minute musical number, with dialogue. According to Mahoney, this comprised "weird riffs on *Sesame Street* characters." Harrison recalled that Lee Overtree played "Groper," a parody of Grover, and Matt McKenna played "the Scone Banshee," a parody of the Cookie Monster.

THIS YEAR IN HISTORY

iTunes released • George W. Bush inaugurated • Dale Earnhardt killed in Daytona 500 • 9/11 • Operation Enduring Freedom, Afghanistan • Dow Jones year-end close 10,022 • Average new car $21,439 • 1 gallon gas $1.46 • *Harry Potter and the Sorcerer's Stone*; *The Lord of the Rings: The Fellowship of the Ring*; *Monsters, Inc.*; *Shrek*; *The Mummy Returns* • Radiohead, *Amnesiac*; The White Stripes, *White Blood Cells*; System of a Down, *Toxicity*; Jay-Z, *The Blueprint*; Gorillaz, *Gorillaz*

Of the Shanley show, Marion said:

> That was the first Shanley show I did. And I remember because that show was the raucous show. The Shanley show was the crazy show. The McCormick show was still crazy, but like the proper mainstage show. It's midnight in that place. If it rained a little bit, it's flooded. The Shanley show was where you felt, "Oh, this feels like a lineage of comedy, of the edgy, exciting, radical comedy that I always wanted to be a part of." Ever since I've become a fan of comedy, like that's what that show felt like always, which was the best feeling in the world.

Harrison recalled a sketch that was "kind of a lark":

> We came out and it looked like it was going to be an improv, and we asked people, "Can we get a nongeographical location? Can we get a thing? OK, can we get an object? OK, and can we get a relationship? OK, mother-daughter. OK. And we just kept going on and did maybe like twelve of them. The acting game was trying to [convey that] we do need all these things. And then at the end the lights would go down and when they'd come back up—I guess the first thing we asked for was an object and it would be a clock, for instance—and then when the lights would come back up [it] would just be Drew Callander onstage. And he'd say, "So there I was fucking this clock." And the lights would go down again. Yeah, probably not the most fun thing for the audience, but we found it very amusing.

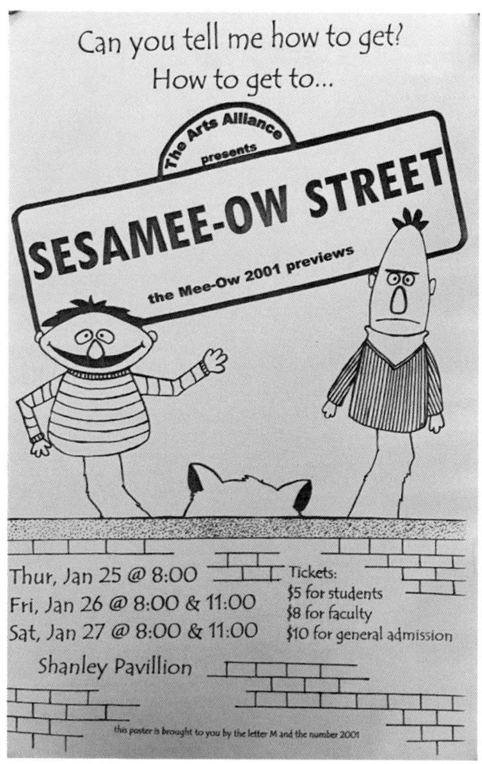

Can you tell me how to get?
How to get to...
The Arts Alliance
presents
SESAMEE-OW STREET
the Mee-Ow 2001 previews
Thur, Jan 25 @ 8:00
Fri, Jan 26 @ 8:00 & 11:00
Sat, Jan 27 @ 8:00 & 11:00
Shanley Pavillion
Tickets:
$5 for students
$8 for faculty
$10 for general admission
this poster is brought to you by the letter M and the number 2001

The mainstage shows opened with a musical number that included new lyrics to the tune of "Do You Hear the People Sing?" from *Les Misérables*. As in the scene from the musical, the cast was waving large flags. They wore simple costume elements that evoked the French revolutionary era. As the people became more and more miserable, the lyrics were about the fight for their right to laugh. The cast sang and danced, including Mahoney, whom McKenna described as having "an amazing, big baritone."

Martha Marion remembered a particular moment in an improv game from the show:

> Each year that I was [at Northwestern] had a pretty big political moment. So in 2000, that was the election that George Bush won via the Supreme Court. And so that spring of 2001, we had the McCormick show not far after the inauguration. And there was an improv between God and the devil. I played God and Lee Overtree played the devil and we were bickering about something, and he

[referred to] an unnamed bad person. And I just turned to him and said, "Well, now he's the president. Are you happy?" And the whole audience gave a standing ovation in the middle of this improv.

Lacher recalled a sketch about a fictional "buddy cop TV show" called "Nun and Bear!" Harrison described it: "The theme song was [singing] 'Nun and Bear! Bear and Nun! Nun and Bear! Nun and Bear!' And it was like just two people, one's a nun and one's a bear. It's a promo for a TV show, and the nun and bear never even talk. It's just about how awarded the show is. And then you'd sing the theme song again and then more things about the show, more awards about the show."

Harrison also recalled a McCormick show sketch called "Quarters" that he performed with Lacher:

> It was a silent sketch, a blackout. I was her uncle and she'd be sitting in a chair and I'd go up and I'd [gesture that I] see something in her ear, and I'd pull it out and I'd show, "Oh, it's a quarter. You had a quarter in there." And then I'd look at her other ear. I'm like, "Oh, look, another quarter. Amazing." And she was like a young girl, amazed. And I'd be like, "Oh, what's in your mouth? Oh, look, another quarter." There'd be a pause and then she would start to cough and then she would throw up like thousands of coins, which she had been holding in her arms. They weren't actually in her mouth. But we loved that one.

Again this year each cast member performed an excerpt of a popular song, accompanied by the band. Marion, who recalled singing "a lot of power ballads," sang Meatloaf's "I'd Do Anything for Love." Overtree sang "Paint It Black" by the Rolling Stones. As Marion recalls, "I think he put his own lyrics to it at some point and just kept saying other things that he wanted to paint black."

Reviews

In a preview article in the *Daily Northwestern* (February 22, 2001), Kris Kitto wrote:

> Those crazy Mee-Ow kids are at it again . . . I stop by the performance space early in the week hoping to get a taste of the atmosphere in which this weekend's shows will take place. The lights are dim. The stage has a flimsy, pitiful facade flapping around on it . . . As I walk down the aisle, I see the cast, warming up for rehearsal by tossing around an all-too-lifelike chocolate-colored dildo. And they are not ashamed.
>
> When one of the cast members hears that I'll be interviewing him, he asks, "Can I talk into the dildo?" I respond, "Actually, I'd prefer not to touch the dildo, but I can put my tape recorder right up next to it, if you'd like." I make a vain attempt to maintain a certain air of pseudo-professionalism.
>
> Thus begins the 28th season of the traditionally gut-busting Mee-Ow Show.
>
> The theme of this year's staging spoofs Andrew Lloyd Webber's most popular musical, "Les Miserables." In line with this epic motif, the cast takes a revolutionary spin on its improvisational comedy format.
>
> "We're fightin' for our right to laugh," explains Speech junior Matt McKenna, a cast member and the show's director.
>
> The most exciting weapon they'll be using while in combat?
>
> "There'll be cannons," he reveals.
>
> While one may think that their humor is ready to fire at will, surprisingly, MeeOw people do have serious sides. Both McKenna and producer and cast member Jess Lacher, a Speech junior, stress the collaborative efforts of the group.
>
> Whereas, in years past, cast members worked on sketches individually and then brought their developed ideas back to the group, this year they generated many skit ideas as a team.
>
> "This year is much more ensemble based," McKenna says.
>
> The group got to test these shared ideas in its preview show, which, this year, ran from Jan. 25 to Jan. 27 in Shanley Pavilion. The preview served as a testing ground for the sketches that will appear in this weekend's performances.

While the cast uses some of the same material in the feature show as it does in its previews, Lacher explains that this weekend's show has an entirely different feel to it.

"This is the next level because it's bigger and a different environment. When we perform here I feel like it's a little bit more formal."

Whether they perform in Shanley, McCormick or at a dorm munchies, though, Mee-Ow cast members live by one rule: Play at the top of one's intelligence.

The players are used to hearing stock suggestions from the audience, so they try to pick out the more unique ideas for their improv games.

"It's very easy to resort to dicks and vaginas for humor, but there's nowhere really to go with that," McKenna says. "It's like what Groucho Marx said: 'If you have to be dirty to be funny, you're not really funny.'"

This campus theater group's best asset, then, is its versatility. Sure, maybe the set is no more than a couple of pieces of balsa wood staple-
gunned together, but Mee-Ow performers don't need much more to accompany their antics.

"You could put us down in just about any place with just about any degree of set, audience, lighting and costumes, and we would still be able to put on a really great show," Lacher says. "The eight of us have gotten really accustomed to performing as a group so that the space matters a lot less than the people we're performing with."

Audience members should come to performances prepared to enjoy intelligent wit at its best.

Heed one warning, though. Beware the chocolate dildo.

On the prowl again

Mee-Ow Show creator and original cast member return to old haunts as this year's Mee-Ow cast takes the stage

BY RANI GUPTA
The Daily Northwestern

As a Northwestern student 27 years ago, Paul Warshauer created a performance group to challenge the well-attended Waa-Mu show.

This weekend Warshauer returned to campus to see how that vision has grown into a legacy of laughter for NU students.

Mocking Waa-Mu's name, Warshauer named his student-run show, featuring comedy, dance and music, "Mee-Ow" after the school's feline mascot.

This year's performance, called "Les Mee-Owserables," runs through Saturday at McCormick Auditorium.

In 1974, the show included many types of media, including songs, dance, skits, satire and even an attempt at laser holography.

However, by its third show, Mee-Ow had evolved into its present, comedy-centered form, said Rick Kotrba, a member of the original cast who lives in the Chicago area.

The two original cast members said they initially had hoped to attract some Waa-Mu members, but a negative ad in THE DAILY alienated Waa-Mu members and marked the beginning of a rivalry between the two groups.

"We never tried to nurture the adversarial atmosphere," Warshauer said. "But we knew it was inevitable. I think some people were jealous that it was a free-form show."

Although the directors had to cut some acts, Warshauer said that the debut Mee-Ow Show "tried to give everybody a shot."

"Everybody felt that they got their two cents," he said.

Warshauer said Mee-Ow appealed to students who might not get involved in traditional productions.

"These were off-beat, talented people," he said. "They were irreverent, clever, satiric and creative."

JASPER CHEN/THE DAILY NORTHWESTERN

Paul Warshauer, left, and Rick Kotrba, members of the first Mee-Ow Show, play on the set of Mee-Ow's upcoming show, "Les Mee-Owserables."

But Kotrba said, "They were not always the best-looking kids."

"I don't know," Warshauer countered. "We had some pretty people."

Despite long hours of preparation, the first show was beset with difficulties.

"It was ghastly long and it was pretentious," Warshauer said.

Because Norris University Center was new in 1974, Mee-Ow had to pay to wire lighting in McCormick for its debut, an expense that put the group $1,700 over its budget.

The debut's title, "Just in Time," referred both to its time-traveling theme and the feeling that the group just barely put the show together, Kotrba said.

"Some of the professors thought it was the blind leading the blind," Warshauer said. "But we pulled it off."

"Sketch comedy is what really appeals to college-age kids. They don't want that Waa-Mu stuff – that's for old people."

PAUL WARSHAUER,
Mee-Ow founder

"We did?" Kotrba said.

Warshauer said that the real legacy of the show was not the show itself, but the group of people involved.

"The process of bringing all the people together far outweighed the schmaltzy production we ended up with," Warshauer said.

Some past members of Mee-Ow have gone on to prominent careers in comedy, including Julia Louis-Dreyfus, former "Seinfeld" co-star, Brad Hall, a former "Saturday Night Live" regular and Gary Kroeger, former host of the "Newlywed Game."

Kotrba worked in comedy for five years after graduating from NU while Warshauer took up writing and directing for theater.

The two have seen a handful of shows since leaving NU, most recently in 1999, when they celebrated Mee-Ow's 25th anniversary.

Warshauer said he is "delighted" with Mee-Ow's evolution into improv and sketch comedy.

"Sketch comedy is what really appeals to college-age kids," he said. "They don't want that Waa-Mu stuff – that's for old people."

The pair said they are looking forward to seeing Saturday's Mee-Ow performance, although they said deserved preferential treatment as the show's creators.

"People really should call us and say they can fly us up at their expense," Warshauer joked. "First class, of course."

5 The Formula

2002–2010

In the wake of the political and cultural events of the early aughts, including the September 11 attacks, the US invasion of Iraq, the devastation of Hurricane Katrina, and the inauguration of Barack Obama, the Mee-Ow Show sharpened its political satire, tackling contemporary issues with humor, ferocity, and the rebellious spirit that had been its founding principle. Some sketches landed, others did not; but as it entered the digital age, Mee-Ow remained a place for students to react—and respond—to the world around them.

The cast continued to experiment with the structure of the show, arriving at the enduring formula of one-third sketch, one-third improv, and one-third rock and roll. As in previous decades, cast and crew members went on to successful careers in the entertainment industry.

Facing page, from the 2007 cast: (*clockwise from the top center*) Nick Kanellis, Carly Ciarrocchi, Adam Welton, Jessica Lowe, Matt Sheelen, Jack Novak, and (*center*) Chris Hejl

2002

MEE-OW YEAR TWENTY-NINE

the 2002
mee-ow
previews
Seven
Minutes
in
Heaven
presented by the arts alliance
shanley pavillion
tickets: $5 for students
thur, jan 24 @ 8:00
fri, jan 25 @ 8:00 & 11:00
sat, jan 26 @ 8:00 & 11:00
improv. sketch comedy. spin the bottle.
Copies Provided by QUARTET COPIES

Seven Minutes in Heaven

Thursday, January 24, at 8 p.m.; Friday and Saturday, January 25–26, at 8 and 11 p.m., Shanley Pavilion

Mee-Owd to Be an American

Thursday, February 21, at 8 p.m.; Friday and Saturday, February 22–23, at 8 and 11 p.m., McCormick Auditorium

Returning cast members Laura Grey and Dan Mahoney codirected and performed. The other returning cast members included Ryan Harrison, Jess Lacher, Martha Marion, and Lee Overtree. New cast members included Kate Mulligan and Frank Smith.

The title of the Shanley show, *Seven Minutes in Heaven*, referred to a teenage party game where two people are selected by some method, such as spin the bottle, to go into a closet and do whatever they like for seven minutes. The general assumption is that the participants will kiss or engage in sexual activity, although some do nothing and just wait for the time to expire.

Mee-Owd to Be an American referenced the refrain, "I'm proud to be an American," from the 1984 song "God Bless the USA" by country singer Lee Greenwood, which enjoyed renewed popularity and radio ubiquity in the aftermath of the terrorist attacks on September 11, 2001. Cast members remember this year as the most explicitly political show they had ever done.

The Show Highlights

Mee-Owd to Be an American opened with a big musical number set to the tune of the Greenwood song, complete with a waving American flag. As Ryan Harrison recalled, "All of us did short monologues about what America means to us. Those shows had just a very different energy, and it was like we just had a lot more political material because everything changed so drastically."

Harrison described an improv game of freeze tag at the Shanley show:

> We were told before that there were going to be some kids from a Christian high school

THIS YEAR IN HISTORY

George W. Bush's "Axis of Evil" speech • Salt Lake City Winter Olympics • Jimmy Carter awarded Nobel Peace Prize • Euro enters circulation • Department of Homeland Security established • Dow Jones year-end close 8342 • Average new car $21,866 • 1 gallon gas $1.36 • *The Lord of the Rings: The Two Towers*, *Harry Potter and the Chamber of Secrets*, *Spider-Man* • Coldplay, *A Rush of Blood to the Head*; Beck, *Sea Change*; Bruce Springsteen, *The Rising*; Audioslave, *Audioslave*

2002

> [in the audience]. Our producer asked us to maybe go easy on any sort of Christian stuff. So we all did, except for Dan Mahoney. There were three of us onstage and we were all making some sort of gesture and he came to the first person and as a priest he said, "I see you have the body of Christ." Already we're thinking, *Dan, why are you doing the Christian stuff?* Then he goes to the next person, "And you, of course, have the blood of Christ." And then he comes up to me, and my gesture is like this [hand making a gripping gesture], and we're looking at each other in the eyes and I'm just telling him with my eyes, *Don't do it!* And of course, he's like, "And you, of course, have the cock of Christ." So yeah. Dan's a very funny improviser. Certainly within guardrails, but he'll never not do the thing.

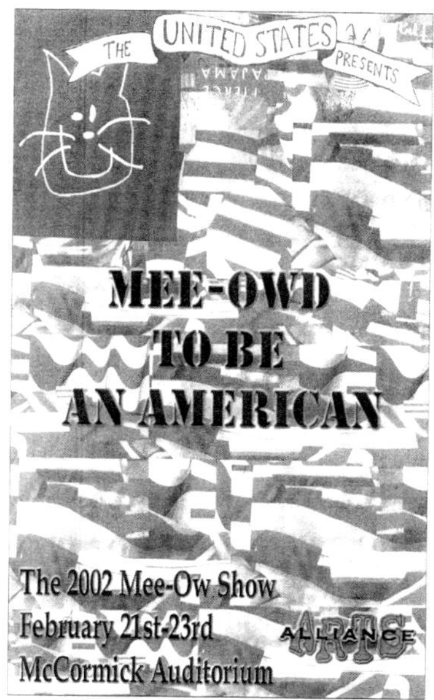

Also at the Shanley show, each cast member performed a monologue about themselves as children. As Harrison recalled, "Jess Lacher and I realized that we had both won for our writing speeches for the DARE program in fifth grade. And we each got to read our speeches, about why people should stay off drugs, in front of our auditoriums in fifth grade and we actually found them and we reread them."

One sketch Harrison remembered eventually led to a professional partnership:

> I tell the story with my writing partner, Frank Smith. We did the show together senior year. It was a eulogy for a guy named Bruce, who is kind of an unlikable guy. It's basically a few people from his office have shown up for his funeral and the priest says, "If anyone would like to say some words, now would be the time," and no one gets up. And so this one guy from the office, who I play, gets up and is trying to say nice things about Bruce, but it's hard. And so the parishioners were all standing in front of me, and [Frank] always had a very hard time not laughing for that one. When I was looking for people to write with after school, I always remembered that Frank and I really shared that we thought that shit was really funny, even if other people were unmoved by it.

Overtree and Harrison played old-time comedians in a sketch. As Harrison recalled,

> It was called "Ryan and Lee." We played under our own names and it was like [singing], "Ryan and Lee, Ryan and Lee, specializing in co-me-dy." And we just did schlocky jokes and tried to land them. But then it came out that one of us was screwing the other one's wife and it sort of breaks down. [It ended with] either I punched him or he punched me because the song goes [singing], "Ryan and Lee, a punch and a pow. How about hearing some comedy now?" And then it's just like big borscht belt kind of physicalized comedy.

2003

MEE-OW YEAR THIRTY

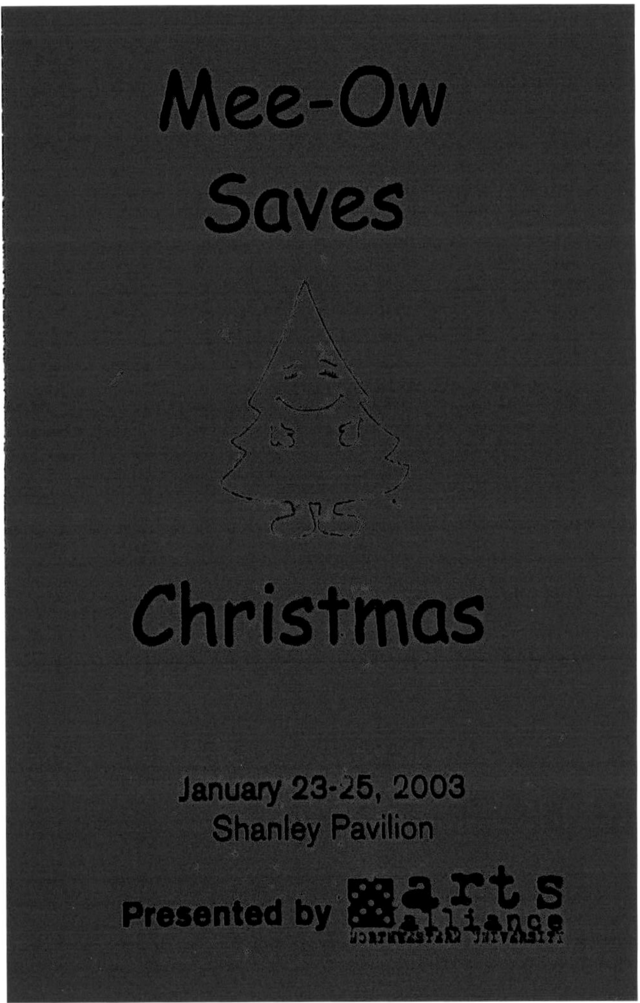

Mee-Ow
Saves
Christmas
January 23-25, 2003
Shanley Pavilion
Presented by arts alliance

Mee-Ow Saves Christmas

Thursday, January 23, at 8 p.m.; Friday and Saturday, January 24–25, at 8 and 11 p.m., Shanley Pavilion

There's a Bear in the Theater!

Thursday, February 27, at 8 p.m.; Friday and Saturday, February 28–March 1, at 8 and 11 p.m., McCormick Auditorium

The only returning cast members, Martha Marion and Kate Mulligan, codirected and performed. New cast members included Chris Gorbos, Briggs Hatton, Jason Kessler, Alex Marlin, Bridget Moloney, and Dan Sinclair.

Bridget Moloney recalled her audition:

> I was so nervous and excited before my callback. I also had a head cold and I accidentally took real Sudafed. So I was awake all night. And then I went to the callback and [we had to do] ten characters for ten seconds each. I remember feeling like I was pretty good, and halfway through someone [looking for a different meeting] walked in the room and they [interrupted, asking,] "Oh sorry. Is this . . . ?" Then we restarted it, but I saved it and I did a good job. . . . I got a phone call from Martha and [producer] Dory Weiss saying come to Martha's apartment at midnight that night. I didn't realize that meant I had gotten in. I had someone drive me from [a meeting at] Vertigo Productions, which was the student-written theater group where I was a board member, because our meeting was over at like ten thirty or something. I was skulking around and Martha was like, "Come in! Congrats, you're in Mee-Ow!"

She called the *Mee-Ow Saves Christmas* show "a conceptual ouroboros":

> We were like, "Let's do a show about how you do a show to save a holiday." It was very silly. Other pitches that year were "Hats Are for People," and "Things Are Everywhere." I remember that because I still say "things are everywhere" all the time. We were getting very absurd. The idea was Christmas is going

THIS YEAR IN HISTORY

US invades Iraq • Human Genome Project completed • Space shuttle *Columbia* disaster • Dow Jones year-end close 10,454 • Average new car $21,664 • 1 gallon gas $1.59 • *The Lord of the Rings: The Return of the King*, *Finding Nemo* • The White Stripes, *Elephant*; Radiohead, *Hail to the Thief*; Death Cab for Cutie, *Transatlanticism*; Jay-Z, *The Black Album*

> to be canceled unless we put on a good enough show to save it. We had Christmas lights that we put up in Shanley and then there was no holiday material, if memory serves [laughs]. There was an opening number in which we talked about saving Christmas, but that was it. We weren't really worried about being on theme.

Martha Marion recalled what the mainstage show title *There's a Bear in the Theater!* meant, and its execution during the show:

> This is the spring of 2003. This is the invasion of Iraq. And we've all pretty much spent the whole year protesting to absolutely no avail. Shock and awe. It's going to happen. It's going to happen. I was a senior at this point. This was a directly political move, but we wanted to absurdify it. We were all in college and in 2000, the election got stolen. So the bloom is off the rose a little bit. But then in 2002, we all just had 9/11. We know that Iraq had nothing to do with this. We saw this lie, this idea that if you tell a lie enough times, people believe it. And we were like, but we were just there! It just happened. This is like two seconds ago. We were all there. What's happening? And to see that like this march to war and just have people be like, oh, they want to go to war, so they're going to go to war, and it doesn't matter what we do. We marched and marched and marched and we saw how the media was, for the most part, playing along with it. It was the absurdity of that political reality. *There's a Bear in the Theater!* essentially was our stab at how the media can make people hysterical out of nowhere for no reason. And it can be absurd. You say it on TV and people will believe it. . . . To me [the show] was about the absurdity of there [being] no threat, but then the government just decides there is and they say it enough times on TV and everyone is going to believe it. I remember feeling like I needed this show to have some relevance to what was going on. And I felt like that did feel meaningful. We had the show literally a couple of weeks before the invasion. It was heavy on people's minds.

The sketches, Moloney said, sometimes came out of improv, but often somebody would have an idea for something:

> Then they bring in a written sketch and we'd read it and then we'd stage it and then be like, "That's funny." And then you keep working on it or not. Then we would have a day a couple of weeks before the show, where we'd put them all up on a board and vote for which ones would get in. We'd try to always have at least two because they change every night, every show. So they'd rotate. The really good ones would be in every show or at least one show, the eight o'clock or the eleven o'clock.

The 2003 cast: Bridget Moloney, Martha Marion, Chris Gorbos, Briggs Hatton, Jason Kessler, Kate Mulligan, Alex Marlin, and Dan Sinclair

The Show Highlights

Marion recalled a disturbing sketch, "Monster in a Box," in the Shanley show, preceded and followed by an improv game to change up the mood. It was written by Dan Sinclair, whom Marion described as one of "the darkest, driest wits I have ever met."

> He wrote a sketch called "Monster in a Box." It was just dark as hell. It's this giant jack-in-the-box and I played an adorable little girl who goes over [to it]. It's a big box and she's just very innocent. She starts doing the thing [makes a motion turning the crank] and you kind of know what's going to happen. And she goes [replicating the tune of "Pop Goes the Weasel"]. And then this very scary monster, truly terrifying monster, played by Dan, pops out and she just starts screaming. And the rest of the sketch is her just having an actual horrified reaction where she's crying and like no one's coming to help her. And the monster is just like, "Oh, this is getting too real." And it was one of those ones where it's funny. And then the audience is like, "Oh, God, this is still happening." And then it just keeps happening until it's funny again. The monster doesn't know what to do now. It can't really help it. Like no one can really help. So he's like, "I'm supposed to be done." And she's just like heart palpitations and I can't breathe, weeping. Eventually the monster just [shrinks back into the box] like, "I'm so sorry. I'm sorry. I can't." And I'm like, "Dan, this is dark as hell." Basically the direction was just keep doing it until it's funny again. That's when it stops. I really like the sketches that have the moment that you're not expecting realism, then something is like ultra realism. It's very funny to me. I think we put it in the middle of the show so you can lead everybody out of that forest, like back to some place to end on a triumphant note.

Moloney recalled the sketch somewhat differently, thinking she played the friend of the little girl who was played by Marion. She remembered being grabbed by the monster and taken back into the box, which provoked Marion's crying because her friend was gone. "We crouched in the box and after we started dating, we made out."

Marion recalled that the McCormick show kept being interrupted by newscasters talking about this bear in the theater: "It's very dangerous. You should all be very afraid. Who are you going to believe? Me or your lying eyes? There's clearly no bear in the theater, but by the end of the show, we will gin up enough hysteria that you will definitely believe in the threat. So that was our way of using comedy to express our political opinion and our despair to some degree."

Producer Dory Weiss recalled renting the bear costume. "We had caution tape [and signs saying], 'There's a bear,' 'Careful,' and bear paws [prints]."

Marion recalled two feminist sketches "that were grotesqueries that were intended to put a finer point on what people did not seem to have a problem with." The first sketch, from 2003, was a parody of *Girls Gone Wild* called "Girls Gone Completely Crazy":

> And it was the guy [waving] the beads and being like, "Whoo-hoo!" but then it was just like really tragic portrayals of mental illness. And then the guys with the beads were sort of like, "Oh, I shouldn't be cheering at this," But then the announcers were still like [in hype announcer voice], "Whoa! Check out this!" And then it turns to a woman in real distress. So [the audience] is watching the male characters figure it out, because the announcer was still telling them this is sexy and great, but you could see the male characters being like, "This doesn't feel sexy like I'm told. What should I do now? I feel kind of bad about the situation." So just watching them wrestle in their own minds with what they're being told something is and how they should look at it and how it feels inside.
>
> Another sketch [from 2002] was a band we created called the Wet Holes, which was a female punk band that only sang punk versions of extraordinarily misogynistic songs. We didn't change any of the words, the misogyny. But in this punk-like, very grotesque, just putting it in your face, these are the actual lyrics of these songs. I think either Laura Grey or Jess Lacher came up with the name the Wet Holes, but [the band] was Laura, myself, and Kate Mulligan.

Continuing a tradition, each member of the cast sang a ninety-second-long excerpt of a song of their choice. During the Shanley show, Sinclair sang "The Electric Slide," by Marcia Griffiths and Bunny Wailer. During the McCormick show, Moloney sang "Tainted Love," by Soft Cell; Kessler sang "Kiss from a Rose," by Seal; and Sinclair sang "Jenny from the Block," by Jennifer Lopez. As Weiss recalled, "Martha Marion did a version of 'Come to My Window' by Melissa Etheridge, which still is what I hear in my head when I think of that song, because it was so iconic. And Kate Mulligan did a version of the 'America the Beautiful' song and she made a joke about [every line of the song] starting with [the word] 'For.' It was more of a recitation and it was just brilliant."

Marion recalled the finale of *There's a Bear in the Theater!*:

> At the end it gets even more absurd because it's like, oh, it wasn't a bear at all. I got my friend Natalie Monahan to wear a bee suit. And we paid her in beer and she comes in at the end. The Blind Melon song "No Rain" was a popular video in the 1990s, which everyone at that show would have known. And it's a little girl in a bee costume and it's all very fun and frivolous. And at the end of the show, it turns out it's just as friendly and we all sing a beautiful song. There was a bear, but it wasn't a scary bear. My friend Teddy Dunn was the bear because we paid them both in beer and they sat in the green room for two thirds of the show drinking the free beer in their costumes.

Moloney recalled that Monahan tap-danced and resembled the little girl in the music video.

Weiss remembered that they all dressed very formally:

> The guys wore shirts and ties. The women dressed up. They wore nice pants and a nice top. There was this idea that there was a formality. That this is silly, but we take it seriously. That would be the uniform of Mee-Ow. That was the costume. Every single show, every gig we did, every picture you'll see. We went to New Orleans and they schlepped their ties and shirts and the girls had a top and bottom. And again, I think it was the understanding that we're taking it very seriously. This is what we want to do and we worked really hard. I remember the boys, of course, sweating through their shirts when it was so hot in Shanley.

"It's not you, it's me," the clichéd phrase used in breakups, was featured at the time in an episode of *Seinfeld*. Weiss said, "We did have a couple in the show, Bridget and Dan, who are now married and have beautiful children. But the joke was whenever we did an improv scene, it was always trying to get them to make out. That was the game going on behind their backs."

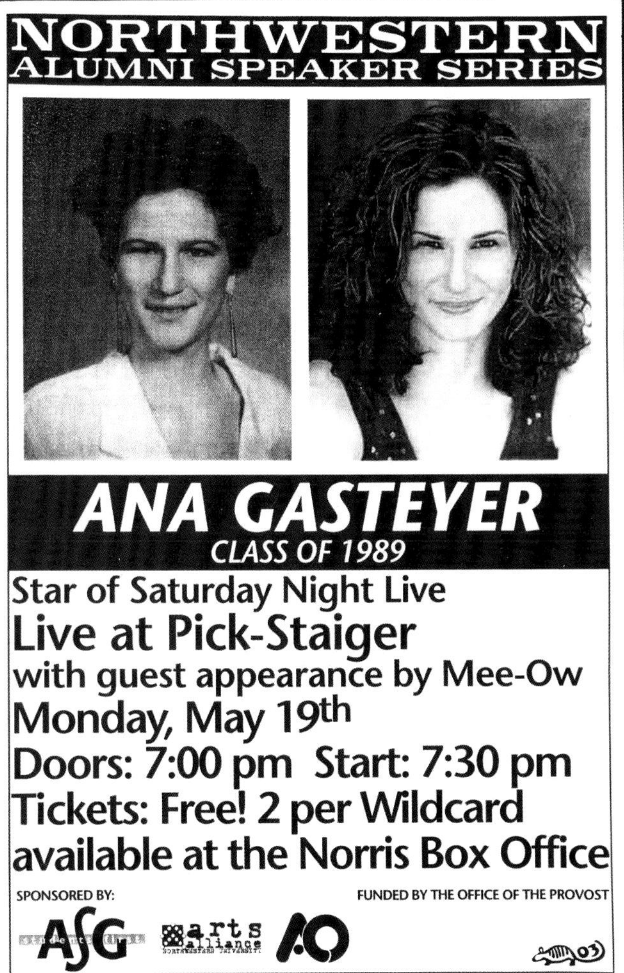

Ad from the *Daily Northwestern*

2003

2004

MEE-OW YEAR THIRTY-ONE

January 2004 Mee-Ow Show Danger On University Place

Danger on University Place

Thursday, January 22, at 8 p.m.; Friday and Saturday, January 23–24, at 8 and 11 p.m., Shanley Pavilion

Thursday, January 29, at 8 p.m., Annie May Swift Hall

It's Not You, It's Mee-Ow

Thursday, February 26, at 8 p.m.; Friday and Saturday, February 27–28, at 8 and 11 p.m., McCormick Auditorium

Returning cast member Dan Sinclair directed and performed. Other returning cast members were Briggs Hatton, who also coproduced, Jason Kessler, Bridget Moloney, and Kate Mulligan. The new cast members were John Dixon, Joe Petrilla, and Sheila Shaigany.

Danger on University Place was a response to frequent reports during the fall of 2003 and the previous school year about off-campus muggings and racial incidents on and off campus, as reported in the *Daily Northwestern*. As Moloney recalled, "There was a spate of hate crimes on campus right before then and that had been scary. But then [in one incident] the person who had found the racial slur had been then proven to have done it himself. That was a big scandal. And that inspired our show. Tensions were high. And so that's why we did it."

In a preview article in the January 22 *Daily Northwestern*, subtitled "Mee-Ow Tackles Crime, Bias, Deep-Dish Pizza," Crystal Nicholson wrote:

> The Evanston Police Department, University Police, and Northwestern's administration have all failed where student comedy group Mee-Ow has succeeded. Mee-Ow has identified the perpetrator of recent violent muggings: the Super Mario Brothers' arch-villain King Koopa.
>
> In their new show *Danger on University Place*, Mee-Ow performs eight sketches lampooning the recent trouble on NU's campus such as muggings and racial tension.
>
> "Our show is definitely edgier than last year," said Communication junior Bridget Moloney. "With respectful humor, and sometimes

THIS YEAR IN HISTORY

CIA admits Iraq had no weapons of mass destruction • Madrid train bombings • Athens Summer Olympics • EU expands, adding 10 new countries • Boston Red Sox win World Series • Dow Jones year-end close 10,783 • Average new car $22,067 • 1 gallon gas $1.88 • *Shrek 2*, *Spider-Man 2*, *Harry Potter and the Prisoner of Azkaban*, *The Incredibles* • Arcade Fire, *Funeral*; Green Day, *American Idiot*; The Killers, *Hot Fuss*; Wilco, *A Ghost Is Born*; My Chemical Romance, *Three Cheers for Sweet Revenge*

2004

disrespectful humor, we are addressing the reactions of the campus and the lack of action."

Some of the eight planned sketches of the show will comment on the actions of NU and Evanston police, including a sketch about "escort service superheroes." In a spin-off of the musical number "Cell Block Tango" from the 2002 movie musical *Chicago*, Mee-Ow performs as students imprisoned for small crimes such as noise violations and bike tickets, and also features an appearance of the alleged library hypnotist.

"There's the classic saying of truth in comedy. It's done with some sensitivity and more than sensitivity—brutal honesty," Moloney said. "Northwestern's usual problems have been eclipsed by grittier, darker realities. We felt improv sketch would be the perfect way to address them."

In addition to the eight sketches, the show contains eight improvisation games, which will be broken up by each performer singing a song from "the '80s, '90s and today," according to [Communication senior Jason] Kessler.

The improvisation games include "Carpool," in which three performers adopt audience-suggested personalities or temperaments and at the end of the sketch the carpool "driver" must guess who the other three were. In a game called "Up and Back," one performer starts a scene suggested by the audience, and then must adapt as each member steps in, changing the skit completely. Once all eight members are involved, they one by one step out, returning to a previous skit.

Although the show contains the same basic elements of past performances, this year's show is more topical.

"This show is more cohesive thematically," said the show's director, Communication senior Dan Sinclair.

In addition to on-campus muggings and discussion of bias incidents, "Danger on University Place" does not fail to emphasize the most important issues in Evanston, such as the overabundance of deep dish pizza.

"The show is basically about filling in the Lagoon and Norris getting Sbarro," Kessler said. "They just got deep dish pizza, which we felt is something we needed to address."

The Show Highlights

Moloney remembered that *Danger on University Place* began with a musical number to the tune of "Cell Block Tango" from the musical *Chicago*, saying, "[As in the song] we each said a word. Mine was *Franzia*, like the boxed wine."

Moloney also recalled performing her favorite improv games. "I had a couple of really good 'Oscar-Winning Moments,' that improv game we used to play. You'd be doing a scene, and then someone would clap and say, 'Bridget, this is your Oscar-winning moment.' And whatever had been happening, you would then deliver the speech that they would [show a] clip at the Oscars. So you had to be dramatically good, fast, whatever you were talking about. That was my ringer."

Continuing a tradition, each member of the cast sang a brief excerpt of a song. During the Shanley show, Moloney sang Bruce Springsteen's "Dancing in the Dark," and Sinclair sang Neil Diamond's "Girl, You'll Be a Woman Soon." During the McCormick show, Moloney sang "Here Comes the Hotstepper," by Ini Kamoze, and Sinclair sang David Bowie's "Space Oddity."

2005

MEE-OW YEAR THIRTY-TWO

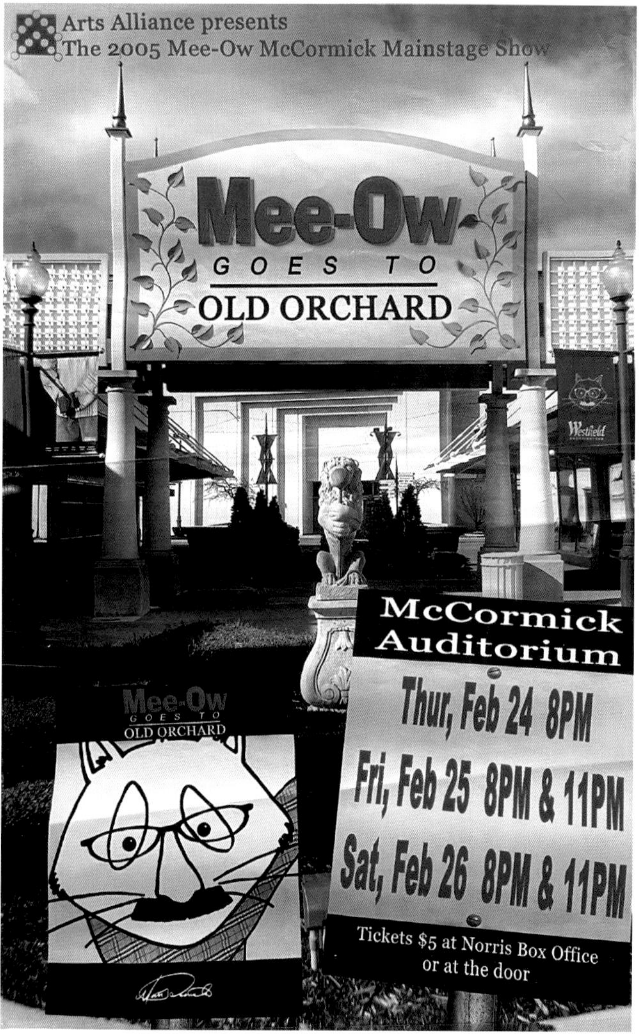

Mee-Ow Admits, Mee-Ow Has a Problem

Thursday, January 20, at 8 p.m.; Friday and Saturday, January 21–22, at 8 and 11 p.m., Shanley Pavilion

Mee-Ow Goes to Old Orchard

Thursday, February 24, at 8 p.m.; Friday and Saturday, February 25–26, at 8 and 11 p.m., McCormick Auditorium

Returning cast members Briggs Hatton and Bridget Moloney codirected and performed. Other returning cast members included Jason Kessler and Kate Mulligan. New cast members included Russ Armstrong, John Dixon, Nick Kanellis, Jessica Lowe, Peter McNerney, and Joanna Simmons.

Nick Kanellis recalled hearing about the Old Orchard Shopping Center in Skokie: "We thought it was funny that there was an outdoor shopping mall [given the weather during winter]." And Moloney explained the McCormick show title:

> By the time we chose that theme, going to Old Orchard was a high-value experience. Someone would have to give you a ride. It was kind of hard to get to. I don't remember there being a bus. This was pre-Uber and it felt really exciting and we were like, what if it's all just about how awesome it is to go to the mall? This was also pre-Evanston getting kind of mall-ified. The shopping center vibe wasn't there yet. So we were like, yeah, let's do it all about the mall, all the awesome stuff at the mall, how great it is to go to the mall. I think we were being a little ironic that our greatest love was the sort of generic commercial thing. But also we just wanted to do something about a mall.

Kanellis remembered a ritual that framed their rehearsals:

> We would begin and end every rehearsal with something called the candle. [This practice] was there when I came in and continued after I left. Everybody would sit in a circle to start

THIS YEAR IN HISTORY

Hurricane Katrina • YouTube launched • Pope Benedict XVI elected • Dow Jones year-end close 10,718 • Average new car $23,013 • 1 gallon gas $2.30 • *Star Wars: Episode III – Revenge of the Sith*, *Mr. & Mrs. Smith*, *Batman Begins*, *Charlie and the Chocolate Factory* • Gorillaz, *Demon Days*; Kanye West, *Late Registration*; Death Cab for Cutie, *Plans*; System of a Down, *Mezmerize*; The White Stripes, *Get Behind Me Satan*

rehearsal and we would light a candle and we'd pass the candle around and everybody got to put something in. Something that you wanted to burn from your day. Whatever you needed to share, to get off your chest before rehearsal began. So everybody got a chance to put something in and then we'd blow it out. And then after rehearsal was over, we would make our circle again and everybody would take something out of the candle. Something that happened in rehearsal that they wanted to remember, something that they thought was special and cool or funny, and everyone would take something out of the candle and then blow it out. It was such a great bonding experience. Having that moment to check in with each other before and after was always a really cool way to start and end.

The Show Highlights

For the Shanley show, Moloney said, "We opened to a parody of the Beatles song 'Help!' And then we stopped singing and each person did a monologue about whatever our addiction was. I think I said I was addicted to celebrity gossip."

Of the two shows, "Shanley always felt a little more raw, McCormick a little more polished," said Kanellis. "Shanley just in general had a little bit more of an underground feel to it. Senior year I did a show called *Wrestle Pocalypse* there, which felt grunge. You know, Shanley had something grunge about it. That was kind of cool."

The Shanley show had excellent attendance, despite an eleven-inch snowfall during the second blizzard of the season.

For the opening musical number of *Mee-Ow Goes to Old Orchard*, Moloney recalled, "We wrote an original song. Peter McNerney wrote the melody and we sang about going to Old Orchard. We were all going for our own personal reasons so that we'd break out into monologues about why we loved Old Orchard so much. But the opening was mid-tempo and that was a big mistake. One of my biggest artistic failures was not insisting on a more upbeat opening."

Sketches that supported the theme included "Mall Bird," about a bird trapped inside a shopping mall; one about girls identifying with their Panera restaurant food orders; and another that was pulled from the show after one performance. As Moloney explained, "John Dixon wrote a dressing room sketch we thought was really funny in rehearsals. And then it didn't play. As we say, the gag didn't work."

2006

MEE-OW YEAR THIRTY-THREE

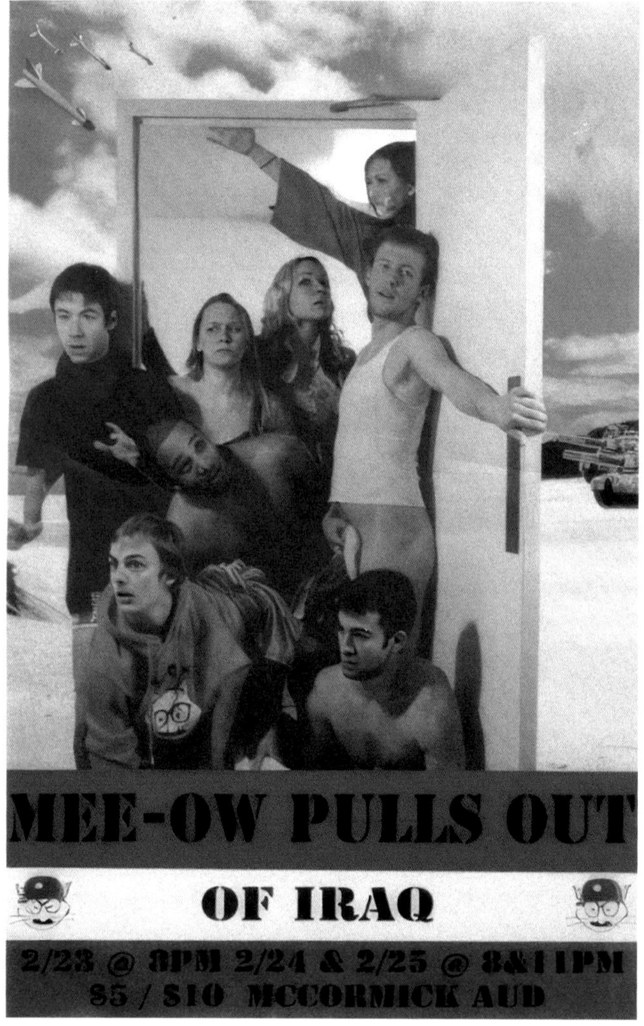

Mee-Ow Is Dead

Thursday, January 12, at 8 p.m.; Friday and Saturday, January 13–14, at 8 and 11 p.m., Shanley Pavilion

Mee-Ow Pulls Out . . . of Iraq

Thursday, February 23, at 8 p.m.; Friday and Saturday, February 24–25, at 8 and 11 p.m., McCormick Auditorium

Returning cast members Russ Armstrong and John Dixon codirected and performed. Other returning cast members included Nick Kanellis and Jessica Lowe. New cast members included Kelly O'Sullivan, Matt Sheelen, Adam Welton, and Nayla Wren.

Adam Welton remembered trying out for the Mee-Ow Show:

> They were just cracking up about my audition. Russ Armstrong had his little notebook and they were going through funny stuff that happened. Those things are managed so fast. It's improv. You're doing everything.
>
> One of the main reasons I got into Mee-Ow was the show Out Da Box. I did that my freshman year and everybody in Mee-Ow thought I was great, so they scooped me over. A lot of the Black folks were mad at me for doing Mee-Ow. But it was just a way to elevate my game. For me to expand some jokes, because in Mee-Ow you can become a dinosaur or become a salesman all in thirty seconds. Out Da Box is fantastic but you gotta step your game up a little bit. Turn it up. You can't just always be at the same kind of humor. Let's explore your mind, your art, a little bit more.
>
> Out Da Box is basically just straight sketches, no music, no improvisation, unless in-the-moment type stuff. But it's only sketches and it's mainly Black humor. You know what I'm saying? You'll hear the N-word millions of times that night. What I was enamored by as a freshman was to see that magic that happens during improv. And

THIS YEAR IN HISTORY

Google buys YouTube • Saddam Hussein executed • Dow Jones year-end close 12,463 • Average new car $23,629 • 1 gallon gas $2.59 • *The Da Vinci Code*, *Casino Royale*, *Night at the Museum*, *Cars*, *300* • Amy Winehouse, *Back to Black*; My Chemical Romance, *The Black Parade*; Red Hot Chili Peppers, *Stadium Arcadium*

2006

it's like, oh my gosh, how did they do that here in the moment, you know? And so for me to be able to translate that and take it to the next level is amazing.

I wish I could have done both. I'm sad that I had to make a choice. . . .

I was at the library and working on something on the computers. It's a small campus, people can find out where you are, and I'm not a quiet dude, you know? You kind of know where I am if I'm there. And a bunch of guys from the Mee-Ow Show in their hoodies just showed up and they're like, "You're coming with us." And so we got in the car and it's playing the Killers. We're just riding in the car, scooping up people for Mee-Ow. We had a great night. It was literally one of the best nights of my life.

I don't remember many Black men who were theater majors. I do know a few Black women who were theater majors. But as far as the audition, there weren't many Black people. I don't know who else may have auditioned, but I was the only Black guy for the entire time I was in Mee-Ow.

Juggling Mee-Ow and Titanic: Handling Busy Schedules

Jessica McKenna, at the time an incoming freshman and future Mee-Ow cast member, recalled her experience with the Titanic Players:

I definitely wanted to join Mee-Ow. All the general auditions for fall plays would happen together for all the student groups. Similarly, the Titanic Players had a shared initial improv audition with Mee-Ow and then they would hold their callbacks separately.

There was this lore that you weren't going to make Mee-Ow as a freshman, but if you could get a callback, then you'd be on their radar. It was this understanding that it was a big deal to get a callback as a freshman, because you'd probably be in front of juniors and seniors, so those juniors might cast you next year.

I ended up getting called back for both [Mee-Ow and Titanic] my freshman year, but I made Titanic. I was on that Titanic team all four years. My friend and I got chosen to train as sophomores to coach a team our junior year. And only after they picked us did they tell us, you can't audition for Mee-Ow now. It was really weird. They claimed it was a scheduling thing. But many of us were also in plays doing a thousand other things. So I ended up not auditioning for Mee-Ow my sophomore year because I wasn't allowed to by Titanic Players. But then I auditioned my junior year and made it. I was in Mee-Ow my junior and senior year. And I loved that I was in both [Titanic and Mee-Ow].

Mike [Abdelsayed] was still running [Titanic], even though he had long since graduated, and he was also trying to maybe run it more as a school within the school. I think he just didn't understand the average student's ability to balance several student groups. We're also in plays. We also sit on student theater group boards. We also do all these things.

2006

The Show Highlights

In keeping with the theme of death in the Shanley show, *Mee-Ow Is Dead*, one sketch depicted four people getting stuck in the mountains while driving. To pass the time they play the game "Marry, Kill, Kiss," in which each person says which of the other three people in the car they would marry, whom they would kill, and whom they would have sex with. The sketch took an unexpected twist at the end, as many sketches do.

Improv games included the always popular freeze tag, and a variation on the classic game "Party Quirks," set in a car. The driver has been offstage and out of earshot while the audience suggests unusual characteristics for three of the performers. When the driver returns to the stage, they must deduce the quirk of each passenger.

In addition to the band playing before the show, during intermission, and at the end, there were a few original songs as part of sketches. Also, as in previous years, each cast member sang an excerpt of a popular song with the band. They chose their songs based on audience response while singing karaoke during a winter break trip to Toronto where they participated in an improv workshop.

In a January 19 article in the *Daily Northwestern* about controversial topics in popular films, Bentley Ford wrote, "Last weekend, the lads and lasses of Mee-Ow hilariously lampooned one of the most talked-about films of the year: the infamous 'gay cowboy' movie, *Brokeback Mountain*. In the sketch, two male actors audition for the roles of Jack and Ennis, the gay cowboys of the film. Of course, the two actors must reenact the very aggressive, almost violent sex scene from the film. Hilarity ensues, and the sketch becomes one of the most memorable and successful moments of the show."

Some of the 2006 cast: Jessica Lowe, Matt Sheelen, Nayla Wren, and Adam Welton

In an article in the *Daily Northwestern* on February 23, Michael Burgner incorrectly described the structure of Mee-Ow as unchanged since its beginning, writing that "one-third improvisation, one-third sketch comedy, and one-third rock 'n' roll has been Mee-Ow's everlasting formula for success. Starting with their inauguration of McCormick Auditorium . . . their formula has not really changed—until now."

Codirector Russ Armstrong was quoted in the article, explaining that the reason for the change was to deal with contemporary and political topics, as reflected in the title of the show, *Mee-Ow Pulls Out . . . of Iraq*. He said, "With Mee-Ow there is a lot of sacredness in tradition because we've been so successful. It's hard to turn away from what you know and do something new, but we really wanted to challenge ourselves."

Reviews

In a January 12 article in the *Daily Northwestern* titled "Drop-Dead Funny," Zach Brennan wrote:

> Their latest theme of death provides an ample amount of edgy, over-the-top sketches on getting killed, coping with death and different ways to die. But this theme does not restrict the troupe to only death-related jokes, and many of the sketch and improvisational games are more zany than distasteful.
>
> "Death is sadder and scarier than it is funny, but we wanted to intrigue people," senior director and three-year Mee-Ow member John Dixon says. "We're not making fun of death, we're making light of it. We want to be risqué, not offensive. Maybe we're offensive, but (we're) not insensitive."

Fighting Stereotypes

An article by Adrienne Williams in the December 2005 issue of *BlackBoard*, Northwestern's Black student magazine, discussed masculinity and Black men in the performing arts and noted that Mee-Ow's Adam Welton had received disparaging remarks, possibly due to "a cultural insensitivity to homosexuality and emotional expression."

Ain't I a Man?

Black Male Performers Defend their Masculinity

By Adrienne Williams

"You're a theater major? Why? All theater majors are fags," the voice says.

Adam Welton gripped the telephone in disbelief. He was not sure how to address such an audacious comment.

Welton, a Communication sophomore, like most Black males in the performing arts, have family and peers who condemn the arts as a career for not being manly or lucrative. Some people attribute this behavior to a cultural insensitivity to homosexuality and emotional expression.

"By participating in the performing arts, African-American men are susceptible to a great deal of scrutiny and question," Communication sophomore

BlackBoard Magazine

The January 2006 issue of *BlackBoard* profiled Adam Welton. Medill journalism student Malena Amusa wrote:

> Not only is Welton the youngest member of Mee-Ow, he is also the only racial minority. Being an amateur and a Black man on this team has been a challenge. He wants to grow as an artist, but at the same time, peers expect him to play stereotypical Black roles that take Welton farther away from playing himself. . . . Also, he doesn't want to resort to racially stereotypical roles. He doesn't want to be typecast. "I try to make it my mission that if there is a Black joke or part, I'll try to get someone else to do it," he explains. "Trying to go against a stereotype is an added amount of pressure as a comedian."

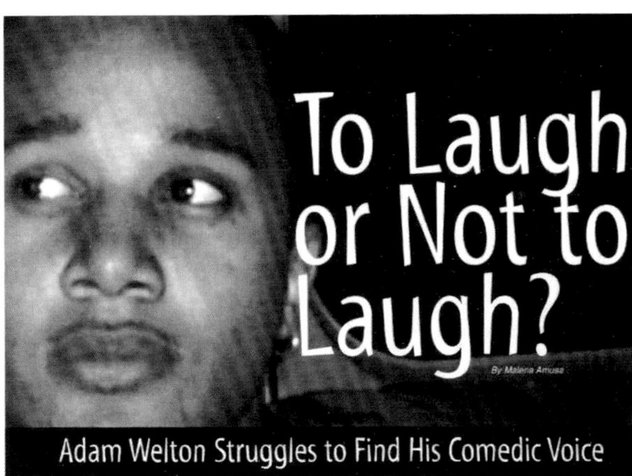

To Laugh or Not to Laugh?

By Malena Amusa

Adam Welton Struggles to Find His Comedic Voice

It's hard keeping a straight face around Adam Welton. The sophomore from Aurora, Ill., is hilarious by most standards. When he cracks a joke, his bright, caramel face contorts to form wide smiles and bulging eyes. His soft voice becomes loud and slips in and out of accents. His energy puffs up and suddenly his husky, 5-feet, 7-inch frame begins looking grander and more stately.

Welton, an aspiring comedian, says he loves making people laugh just by playing himself: a well-spoken Black man with an affinity for punch lines.

This past fall, Welton was accepted into a comedy troupe called Mee-Ow. This nationally acclaimed comedy team is reputed for having produced many famous comedians. Saturday Night Live's Anna Gasteyer, who is now starring in *Wicked*, is just one of them. Welton knew he would experience greater pressure to perform well.

"I'm just a baby in this. I can do so many voices, [but] I don't do them on stage."

As a member of Mee-Ow, Welton found he can no longer rely on the comedic personality that has made him so loved on campus.

Not only is Welton the youngest member of Mee-Ow, he is also the only racial minority. Being an amateur and a Black man on this team has been a challenge. He wants to grow as an artist, but at the same time, peers expect him to play stereotypical Black roles that take Welton farther away from playing himself.

"I'm just a baby in this," Welton says. "I can do so many voices, [but] I don't do them on stage. I just don't think about them."

During a January Mee-Ow performance, Welton tests his humor before an audience of about 100 people. In a game called Plantagonate, audience members suggest types of couples they want to see Welton and the other comedians play out. Welton and his stage partner end up with little red riding hood and the big bad wolf.

When Welton is up to perform, seconds start to tick by. Welton stays silent. His partner soon steals the scene. She jumps to the front of the small black stage. She growls and hunches her shoulders to form the body of a prowling wolf. When Welton begins playing red riding hood, he appears too timid to make a joke. His arms curl up close to his body and he nibbles his nails in feigned, girly trepidation. He squeaks polite *no thank you's* to the hungry wolf. Nobody laughs. More seconds tick by. Finally, he asks the wolf: "How come you don't have a friend sticker?" The audience laughs confused.

After a couple of shows, Welton says he felt sad because he wasn't funny enough. He kicked himself for being so generous on stage.

"I'm very giving," Welton says. "And that bleeds over into the improvising." Instead of commanding the stage, Welton retreats and lets the other comedians take over a skit.

Part of the reason is because Welton doesn't want to mess up, he says. Also, he doesn't want to resort to racially stereotypical roles. He doesn't want to be typecast.

"I try to make it my mission that if there is a Black joke or part, I'll try to get someone else to do it," he explains. "Trying to go against a stereotype is an added amount of pressure as a comedian."

But Welton thanks God for giving him the opportunity to join Mee-Ow and for blessing him with his talents. Now, he prays for the confidence he sometimes lacks as an inexperienced improvisational comedian. In the end, Welton just wants to believe in himself.

"This is just the beginning," Welton says. "God has had so much favor on my life."

Malena Amusa is a Medill senior from St. Louis, Mo. Contact her at m-amusa@northwestern.edu.

4 BlackBoard Magazine • January 2006

BlackBoard Magazine 5

2007

MEE-OW YEAR THIRTY-FOUR

Mee-Ow '08: Mee-Ow Declares Its Candidacy

Thursday, January 18, at 8 p.m.; Friday and Saturday, January 19–20, at 8 and 11 p.m., Shanley Pavilion

Mee-Ow's Anatomy

Thursday, February 22, at 8 p.m.; Friday and Saturday, February 23–24, at 8 and 11 p.m., McCormick Auditorium

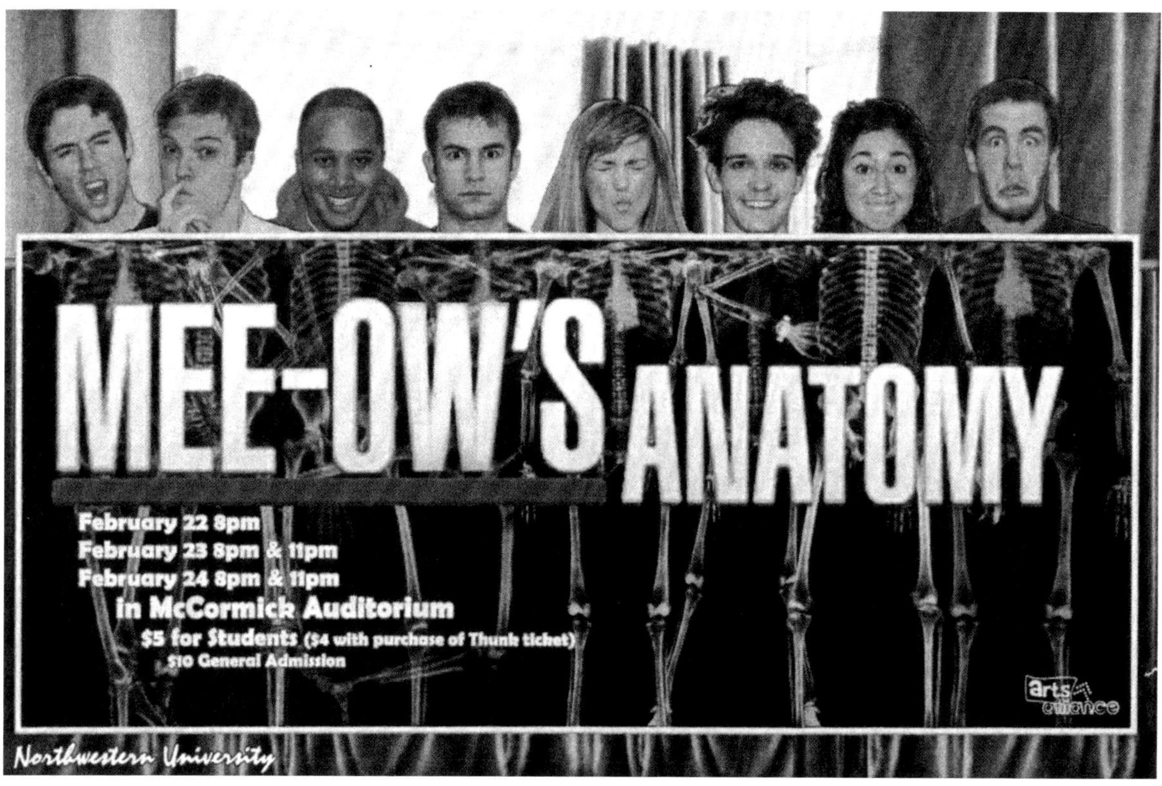

Returning cast members Nick Kanellis and Jessica Lowe codirected and performed. Other returning cast members included Matt Sheelen and Adam Welton. New cast members included Dan Bruhl, Carly Ciarrocchi, Chris Hejl, and Jack Novak.

In 2007, the Shanley show was still referred to as a preview, and the McCormick show was referred to as the mainstage show, despite being essentially two different shows. As Adam Welton described it:

2007

THIS YEAR IN HISTORY

Apple releases the iPhone • Virginia Tech shooting • Rupert Murdoch buys Dow Jones, *The Wall Street Journal* • Pakistan declares state of emergency • Great Recession begins • Dow Jones year-end close 13,265 • Average new car $23,890 • 1 gallon gas $2.80 • *Harry Potter and the Order of the Phoenix*, *Spider-Man 3*, *Shrek the Third*, *Transformers*, *Ratatouille* • Radiohead, *In Rainbows*; Arcade Fire, *Neon Bible*; Arctic Monkeys, *Favourite Worst Nightmare*

> The Shanley show was kind of like a big state school super-duper drunk fest comedy show for all the college kids. And the Louis Room [in Norris Center, where the mainstage show moved for a couple of years] is kind of like, OK, we're like actual comedians performing at Second City. This is a proper performance. That's the difference between the two vibes. Stanley's like drunk college kids. There's beer everywhere. There's standing room only. It's like that hard-core comedy club type atmosphere compared to when you're doing an actual show for the people. It's a different type of feeling. You invite the parents to the Louis Room.

Mee-Ow '08: Mee-Ow Declares Its Candidacy referred to 2008 being a presidential election year. Dan Bruhl said of the search for a theme, "I don't want to say it was competitive, because people didn't put too much weight behind any one idea, but there were a lot of ideas. Some of them are topical. We had the elections just starting up. So that totally made sense. But otherwise, I think it's a search for what can give us a good opening. Having a good theme can feed you a few good sketches."

Mee-Ow's Anatomy, the title of the McCormick show, parodied the popular hospital television program that had premiered in 2005. Welton was quoted in the *Daily Northwestern* saying, "We really love *Grey's Anatomy*, and it's a really big show right now. We thought it would be a pretty funny idea."

Rehearsals were held in the theater building, reflecting a change in the official attitude toward Mee-Ow and other student-created, student-run productions.

The Show Highlights

One of the most memorable things, Welton recalled, was when "Nick [Kanellis] did a 'SexyBack' cover [of the 2006 Justin Timberlake song], but he played Al Gore, and instead of 'I'm bringing sexy back,' he said, 'I'm bringing alternative fuel.' "

Bruhl recalled another sketch in which Kanellis was a high school teacher. "All the students are leaving class, and he says have a nice holiday [but asks] one student to stay behind. 'Hey, Bill, I've got something I want to say to you.' And then he puts on that song and does this fabulous three-minute lip sync to 'All I Want for Christmas Is You' by Mariah Carey. It's very simple, just him lip syncing and trying to seduce this high school student. You know, I hate to say it, but a lot of the sketches probably wouldn't fly today."

Reviews

In a preview of *Mee-Ow's Anatomy* in the *Daily Northwestern* on February 22, Megan Friedman described one medical-themed sketch: "It starts like a medical drama: A team of doctors reviving a patient who doesn't make it. Then it turns into a fantasy. The patient's ghost rises from the body, calling out to her grandmother that she is arriving. Then comes the punch line. Four Ghostbusters run out and suck the ghost up in a vacuum, yelling 'No heaven for you!' while singing the *Ghostbusters* theme song."

In his column on the sports page of the *Daily Northwestern* on February 28, Abe Rakov wrote a "Shout Out of the Week," recommending that other students attend the Mee-Ow Show: "NU Notes branched out from watching sports Saturday night to see *Mee-Ow's Anatomy*. If you haven't seen Mee-Ow perform, you're missing out. The group is hysterical and its shows are must-see spectacles."

2008

MEE-OW YEAR THIRTY-FIVE

DOOMSDAY: Mee-Ow Is the Winter of Our Discontent

Thursday, January 24, at 8 p.m.; Friday and Saturday, January 25–26, at 8 and 11 p.m., Shanley Pavilion

Mee-Ow Talks Down to Children

Thursday, February 28, at 8 p.m.; Friday and Saturday, February 29–March 1, at 8 and 11 p.m., Louis Room, Norris Center

MEE-OW IS THE WINTER OF OUR DISCONTENT
DOOMSDAY
SHANLEY PAVILION
JANUARY 24, 8:00 PM
JANUARY 25, 26. 8 & 11

Returning cast members Carly Ciarrocchi and Adam Welton codirected and performed. Other returning cast members included Dan Bruhl and Jack Novak. New cast members included James Daniel, Dan Foster, Jessica McKenna, and Sarah Grace Welbourn.

Jessica McKenna recalled moving the mainstage show to the Louis Room at Norris Center:

> Mee-Ow did little shows throughout the school year, like performing for a sorority or fraternity or during [new] student week. We might have gigs throughout the fall and

THIS YEAR IN HISTORY

CERN Large Hadron Collider powered up • Northern Illinois University shooting • Illinois governor Rod Blagojevich arrested • Lehman Brothers collapses • Dow Jones year-end close 8776 • Average new car $23,442 • 1 gallon gas $3.27 • *The Dark Knight*, *Kung Fu Panda*, *Mamma Mia!*, *Iron Man*, *WALL-E*, *Twilight* • Coldplay, *Viva La Vida or Death and All His Friends*; Kanye West, *808s & Heartbreak*; Kings of Leon, *Only by the Night*

2008

> spring quarter, but our real quarter was winter, where we did two shows, one in Shanley and the other in McCormick. But when I joined, we switched to the Louis Room. We thought you could make the audience feel closer. Some of us didn't like that McCormick was so *lecture hall* and it felt like the audience was far away.
>
> Shanley was still the best. Shanley felt the most like rock and roll; cram people in, low ceilings. It's the most like comedy theaters I continue to perform in. It feels like the UCB spaces. Just absolutely electric. I almost wish that we just had two weekends in Shanley, but the way that all that negotiation with all the other theater groups worked, you still had to do your second show somewhere else.

As for the inspiration behind the title *DOOMSDAY: Mee-Ow Is the Winter of Our Discontent*, "there was something changing with the CTA and a lot of talk about doomsday," McKenna explained. She was referring to the Chicago Transit Authority's multimillion-dollar budget deficit and subsequent plans to lay off employees and raise fares, which Mee-Ow turned into a pun on the line from Shakespeare's *Richard III*. "It had a great poster," she continued. "We were all in all black on the Lakefill. It was freezing."

Bruhl described the rehearsal process and the collaborative sketch-development process:

> It was like six days a week for about three months, sometimes two rehearsals in a day, from like six to eight-thirty and then again from ten to twelve. You sit in a circle and everyone put something into the middle, whatever's on their mind—upset about a girl, upset about a class, being homesick, having a stomachache. You really developed a level of comfort with your co-members. This is a frickin' boot camp. You're spending all this time with them. There's no room to butt heads, right? . . .
>
> Every rehearsal people would pitch new ideas. Some directors come from an editorial background, some directors come from a writing background, and some directors come from a production design background—costume, music, whatever. It was the same with Mee-Ow. Everyone came with a different background, and some writers were much more polished and it was much easier for them to write a ten-page sketch or whatever. Other people needed more coaching, but it was a very collaborative environment. And as you got to know the other members, you would start writing sketches. For example: "Oh, Adam does a really funny character. Why don't I write a sketch for him?"

The Show Highlights

In the opening number for *DOOMSDAY*, McKenna said, "We rewrote the words to 'It's the End of the World,' by R.E.M. Some of it was real and some of it was made up, probably news stories that are long since gone. One lyric was, 'Every song with T-Pain, and they all sound the same.' Another part was, 'Dakota Fanning has a gun. Seriously, she has a gun,' which wasn't anything. And everyone's like, 'That's not from the news.' Dakota Fanning at the time was still a child actor, like eleven or twelve."

As in previous years, each cast member sang an excerpt of a song of their choice. Welton and Ciarrocchi sang duets of the Beyoncé song "Crazy in Love" and "Ain't No Mountain High Enough," by Marvin Gaye and Tammi Terrell. Welton also sang "some Michael Jackson, some Prince."

Bruhl played the MGM lion in a sketch. "I'm not a very good actor," he said, "but I can do a good animal. I never got cast in any roles that required strong human acting, but if it was an animal, God damn it, I crushed it."

McKenna recalled one of the improv games:

> We got initials from the audience and we would make up a new game based on their initials. So J.R. would be called "Joust Reduction," a two-person scene set in the medieval period and it needs to use at least five references to plastic surgery. We would come up with it on the spot and then the audience would vote on their favorite. I believe in that show I came up with this game called "Emo Musical" where we pause and improvise music in the emo style. I still do that. I do a ton of musical improv. It's my whole job.

Bruhl recalled a joke his mother loved: "It was in 'World's Worst.' That's a game we did where we say, 'Tell us any category and we'll tell you the world's worst version of that.' So someone said the 'world's worst school mascot,' and I said, 'The pencils. We're number two! We're number two!' My mom always brings up that as her favorite."

In another sketch, McKenna remembered, she and Dan Foster wrote about what might have happened if Hillary Clinton won in 2008, if she had gotten the presidential nomination instead of Obama: "At this point, we didn't know yet who was going to get the nomination. So it was a two-person scene where Hillary has won the election. She's the new president. And Bill Clinton comes in the Oval Office and he just is sort of passive-aggressively talking about her decorating choices. 'You know, when I was here, we had this chair over here.' And she's like, 'Bill, I'm really busy.' "

Bruhl wrote an eerily prescient sketch: "It was about the University of Phoenix having a frat party where everyone was at home and on their computers. We were poking fun at the idea of doing college remotely."

And McKenna described the zaniness of a sketch called "Talking Down to Children." She said, "It was really colorful and bright. I think that was the first time we played [the improv game] "Oxygen Deprivation," where someone had to have their head in a bucket of water until they were tagged back in the scene, which was a mess. That was a really fun show."

Reviews

In a letter to the editor of the *Daily Northwestern* (January 29), junior Tami Lieberman took issue with a sketch from the Shanley show. She wrote:

> While I am a fan of comedy, Mee-Ow and exploring new comedic styles and boundaries, I was extremely put off by a written sketch on Saturday night.
>
> Mee-Ow set a controversial tone from the beginning of the show. Controversy is a great comedic tool: What makes us uncomfortable and what makes us laugh are closely related. I have never before made demarcations in what is too controversial in comedy, but now I can make at least one—a non-improvised comedy sketch should never be entirely about rape.
>
> The sketch opened with a lone woman on stage and a man with headphones on slowly approaching her. As he came up behind the woman, she looked nervous and tried to get away. The guy lifted her such that her legs straddled his waist and mock-raped her, humping on the stage as she screamed "no" and "stop." The scene cut, and the guy with the headphones looked at the audience and said, "If you can't hear her say no, it's not rape," or something very close to that. The sketch ended there, the lights cut and the music started.
>
> There was no clarification, no debriefing about the reality of rape, no follow-up joke and no laughter.
>
> Why isn't this funny? Maybe it's because mimicking rape on stage is too graphic. Maybe it's because as a SHAPE peer educator, I'm sensitive to the subject. But I think it's something else.
>
> At its core, it isn't a joke—it's a defense used by rapists over and over again. It has been used in the past and, on some college

> campus somewhere, in fact, someone is probably using it now.
>
> The lighthearted tone with which Mee-Ow addressed rape perpetuates the idea that rape is not a serious issue. It was irresponsible for Mee-Ow to use that punch line without addressing its falsehood.

Ciarrocchi's response was published two days later as a letter in the *Daily Northwestern* on January 31. She wrote:

> In the sketch, a girl standing by herself is approached by a boy, tiptoeing, hands raised in a Scooby-Doo Monster-esque fashion, wearing huge headphones and under an overly dramatic red light. The boy grabs the girl and pretends to advance on her against her will as she yells "No! Stop!" Shortly after, they both freeze, and a voice-over is heard: "If you can't hear her say no, it isn't rape. Bose." Blackout. The sketch was a parody of the popular Bose sound-canceling headphones commercials, taking its comedy from a situation heightened beyond reality.
>
> Mee-Ow goes through a long process of choosing sketches for each show. When we pick the sketches, we consider the balance of our overall show, including levels of controversy and intellectualism, and some sketches are not put in based on our feeling that they are not in good taste or are too offensive. No sketch goes into the show that any member of Mee-Ow is uncomfortable with or against. Not all sketches are in every show—some sketches are rotated in and out for each performance. "Bose" was a sketch that appeared in every performance based on the strong audience response it received every single night.
>
> Throughout the history of comedy, from Aristophanes to Shakespeare to Larry David and George Carlin, controversial, edgy and sometimes outright dark subjects have had a presence in performances that have made people laugh. We sincerely apologize if we have offended anyone, our intention was not to highlight the popular defense used by rapists, but to parody the Bose headphones commercials.

2009

MEE-OW YEAR THIRTY-SIX

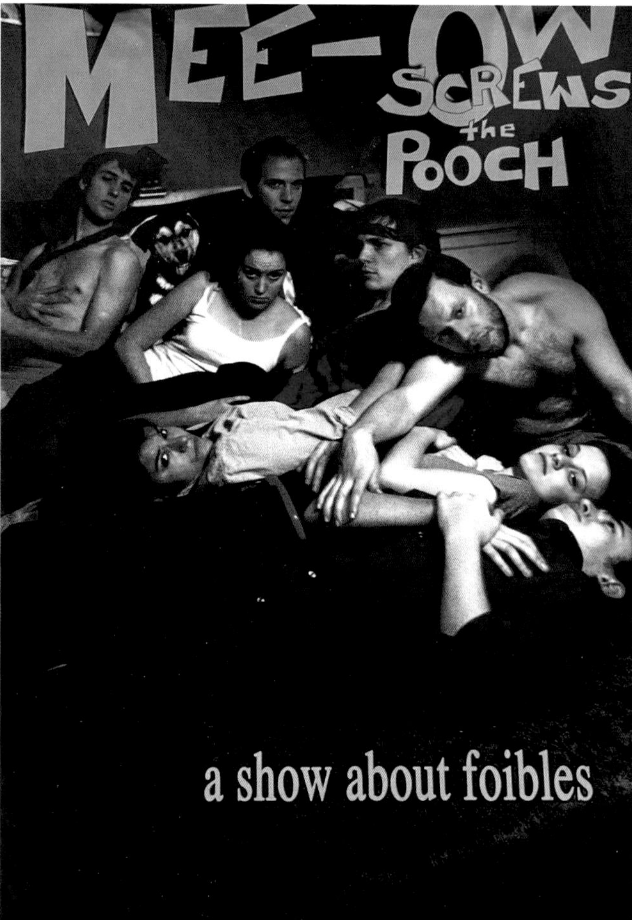

Mee-Ow Screws the Pooch

Thursday, January 22, at 8 p.m.; Friday and Saturday, January 23–24, at 8 and 11 p.m., Shanley Pavilion

Mee-Ow Presents Dr. Pepper's Homely Joke Brigade

Thursday, February 26, at 8 p.m.; Friday and Saturday, February 27–28, at 8 and 11 p.m., Louis Room, Norris Center

Returning cast members Jack Novak and Sarah Grace Welbourn codirected and performed. Other returning cast members included James Daniel and Jessica McKenna. New cast members included Jen D'Angelo, Tim McGovern, Joel Sinensky, and Conner White.

Tim McGovern explained how he learned that he was cast in Mee-Ow:

> The year before I was cast, I wrote, directed, and performed a one-man version of *Lord of the Rings*. I did all three books in like forty-five minutes and put it all on YouTube and it was one of the most rewarding things I had ever done. I felt like my comedic sensibilities were better and so I was really excited for the Mee-Ow auditions. I listened to the *Rocky* song maybe a few hundred times, trying to get in a positive space. I am very self-deprecating, very hard on myself, but I can easily say that after walking out of that callback, I was like, I don't really imagine anybody else who could have gotten that. I failed before at this. Having failed, I felt like I had some sort of clarity.
>
> I was talking to Nick Kanellis, who had been on the show and who was one of my idols and, for a summer when I was interning at *Conan* in New York, we did a two-person improv show together. He was a huge mentor to me. He was like, "How'd it go?" And I was like, "I don't know what to expect," and then they came knocking on my door. Jack and James sat me down and I'm thinking, *this is not it.* I was in nodding mode, just agree to what they're saying, let them leave, cry in private. They told me, "You had a great audition.

THIS YEAR IN HISTORY

Captain Richard Phillips rescued • Michael Jackson dies • Barack Obama inaugurated • Financial crisis continues • Dow Jones year-end close 10,428 • Average new car $23,245 • 1 gallon gas $2.35 • *Avatar*, *Harry Potter and the Half-Blood Prince*, *2012*, *Up*, *Angels & Demons* • Florence + The Machine, *Lungs*; Arctic Monkeys, *Humbug*; Mumford & Sons, *Sigh No More*; Lady Gaga, *The Fame Monster*

2009

> Maybe next year." And I was like, "Oh, OK." And they left, and then they bum-rushed the apartment and told me I was in. . . . I was given a bottle of champagne, I think. And then we had to let all the others know. Nobody else got that fake letdown. I stayed up all night and we got to talk to all the other alums who had moved on to Los Angeles. I was so excited, and I felt an enormous pressure to justify my existence on the team. But once I started doing small shows, it just felt right, like I was doing what I had wanted to do for two years.

In an article in the *Daily Northwestern* on January 22, titled "Screwing the Pooch," Jen D'Angelo wrote ironically about how terrible it was to be in Mee-Ow:

> It really is not all that much fun to be in Mee-Ow. The people are, for the most part, terrible, the pay is abysmal and the hours are just too much. I get really tired of sitting around in rehearsal with seven extremely unpleasant individuals and talking about mundane things day in and day out. I wish I could describe to you how unbearable it is, but there really just aren't enough words to do so.

The Show Highlights

McGovern remembered especially an injury he sustained in a Pinocchio skit at the Shanley show:

> It was a lot more close quarters. It was a little turbulent. I remember my first night of the performance, my good friend now—I say "good friend" because I'm going to level some serious accusations against him. The sketch written by Jen D'Angelo is about the reality of your puppet coming to life. And I play Jiminy Cricket at the very end. Joel [Sinensky] playing Geppetto was terrified of not only Pinocchio, but of this "cockroach" Jiminy Cricket. He was supposed to fake punch me and say "Ah! A cockroach!" and then punch me through the air. And he landed one right in my temple. And I started bleeding and I had to wear a Band-Aid for the rest of the show's run there. I had a huge rhino-like swelling there. So he could probably sue me for defamation, but I have witnesses. So it really explores the gritty reality of this horror film called *Pinocchio*.

In other sketches from the Shanley show, McGovern recalled:

> I played a creepy guy where I go behind Sarah Grace Welbourn and I put my hands around her eyes and she thinks that it's someone she knows and it's just a complete stranger.
>
> We also did a cat version of all the different medical dramas that were on. They were all combined and I remember playing a character like House, and someone had to tell me, "Yeah, just play him really world-weary." And apparently it made sense.

McGovern recalled *Mee-Ow Presents Dr. Pepper's Homely Joke Brigade* in the Louis Room as being a "really fun conceptual show. It was a lot more experimental than I think some members wanted, but it turned out great because it was turning us into a Beatles-like comedy group with our own musical acts, our own musical personas. I played a Ringo-like character. It could have been a blend of all four based on the accent that I was doing. We decked out the Louis Room, and wrote musical numbers [including] a musical

2009

interlude before intermission. We did 'One Day More' from *Les Mis* and it was 'One Sketch More.' And there was a fog machine."

Continuing a tradition, the cast each sang short excerpts of popular songs. McKenna recalled, "Sometimes people would do duets and that would be helpful to move the pace along. It became a little self-indulgent, that all eight people get to have their rock star moment. It would be fun as long as the songs were fun and people would legitimately get up and dance, which I think happened more in Shanley than in the Louis Room show, just given the Shanley vibe."

Why Mee-Ow?

Jessica McKenna spoke about the need for Mee-Ow and other student theater productions at Northwestern:

It just seemed like the same ten kids got to do every University Theatre production, which is why student theater was really important. I think that spirit of why Mee-Ow started was still alive when I was there. Definitely there was a little bit of "Make more opportunity for us or we're going to do it ourselves. You let four hundred of us in [as theater students] and you put the same ten people in plays. At a certain point the center isn't going to hold." I think that Northwestern attracts the type of student who's just like, "All right, I'll do it myself."

You could feel that sort of lifeblood in Mee-Ow, especially in Shanley, as you're breaking every crowd law and it's a party in there. Hopefully, you're speaking a comedic language to just your peers. And there's no other goal that you need to reach besides starting from a place where making the other seven people in Mee-Ow laugh and then seeing how that translates to making a bunch of your peers laugh and [not about] impressing the faculty. It didn't even feel competitive once you were on. It was competitive to get on it, but in my experience, it felt very like an ensemble. I think that is probably what other directors have said. That was by design. You wanted funny people, but you wanted funny people who are going to work as a team and not feel like it was some sort of showcase for your stardom. It was very pure in that way, which is great.

2009

This weekend ... don't be in England.
DR PEPPERS
HOMELY JOKE
BRIGADE
MEE·OW
IN DR PEPPERS HOMELY JOKE BRIGADE
THE LOUIS ROOM
THURSDAY, FEB 26 @ 8 PM
FRIDAY, FEB 27 @ 8 PM & 11 PM
SATURDAY, FEB 28 @ 8 PM & 11 PM

2010

MEE-OW YEAR THIRTY-SEVEN

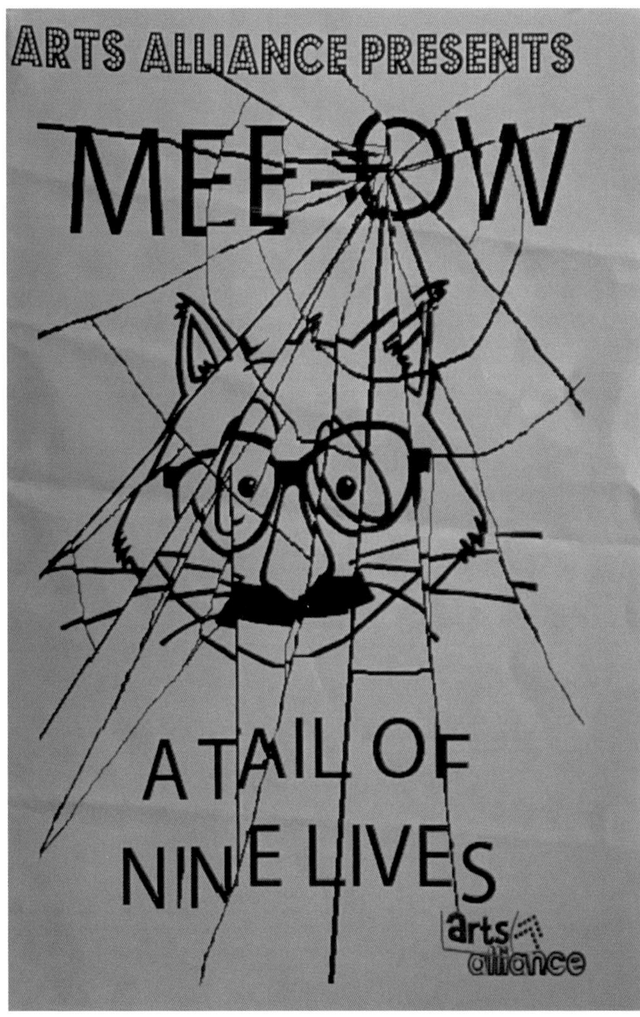

The Mee-Ow Show: A Tail of Nine Lives

Thursday, January 28, at 11 p.m.; Friday and Saturday, January 29–30, at 8 and 11 p.m., Shanley Pavilion

The Mee-Ow Kids Solve a Murder at Chuck Fuffalo's

Thursday, February 25, at 11 p.m.; Friday and Saturday, February 26–27, at 8 and 11 p.m., Louis Room, Norris Center

Returning cast members Jen D'Angelo and Tim McGovern codirected and performed. James Daniel was the only other returning cast member. New cast members included Aaron Eisenberg, Nick Gertonson, Ryan Nunn, Isabel Richardson, Marie Semla, and Josh Waytz. McGovern said, "We had to orchestrate, I think, five people. And it does take a lot of coordinating to grab and bag people. But we did it. And, you know, it was so much fun to be on the other end. It's kind of like planning Christmas for kids. You get to be on the other side of it and still get as much fun out of the experience."

The Show Highlights

"We made fun of the set direction" of the Shanley show, McGovern said. "It was just like a clock and a swirl on the wall. And that was pretty much it. [laughs] We made fun of it so much. It looked like someone had Rip Van Winkled after getting hired as a set designer and woke up fifteen minutes before. It was like, 'What can I hastily paste on the walls of Shanley?' "

McGovern explained the premise of the Louis Room show, *The Mee-Ow Kids Solve a Murder at Chuck Fuffalo's*:

> We created this theme park full of jokes. Essentially all the rides had themes and it was kind of this Scooby Doo–like carnival with this mysterious Chuck Fuffalo who goes missing. They did a great job of turning up the production value for that show. It was amazing. We also knew that we were going to do another conceptual show following the year before when we did *Dr. Pepper's Homely*

2010

THIS YEAR IN HISTORY

BP Deepwater Horizon oil spill • Affordable Care Act enacted • Burj Khalifa opens • Ongoing financial crisis and recession • Vancouver Winter Olympics • Arab Spring protests begin • Dow Jones year-end close 11,578 • Average new car $24,898 • 1 gallon gas $2.79 • *Toy Story 3*, *Harry Potter and the Deathly Hallows—Part 1*, *Inception*, *Despicable Me* • Kanye West, *My Beautiful Dark Twisted Fantasy*; Arcade Fire, *The Suburbs*; The Black Keys, *Brothers*; Janelle Monáe, *The ArchAndroid*

Ryan Nunn, Nick Gertonson, Aaron Eisenberg, Isabel Richardson, and Tim McGovern

Choosing Northwestern

Cast member Aaron Eisenberg recalled why he chose Northwestern:

My dad was at Northwestern from '74 to '78 as a Medill student. I heard about Mee-Ow at first from him. I always knew I wanted to go to school for theater. I knew Northwestern. I was very college oriented, focused on getting into my dream school, and that would have been Northwestern. You can really find your niche at Northwestern. We were painting with a very broad brush in high school. If you were a theater kid that counts for the whole scope. So you're hanging with the musical kids—even if you're not a great singer—or the serious actors. I grew up in New Jersey, right outside of New York City, and so I was seeing my first improv shows, long-form improv shows, Upright Citizens Brigade, around 2005 or '06. And I knew that Northwestern in particular had comedy alumni that didn't just do one thing but were what you would call multi-hyphenate in the industry that I'm in. So writer, director, actor, producer, and that was really all I needed to hear. Then the rest was just me crossing my fingers and hoping that I would get in. And then once I got in, hoping that I would get on Mee-Ow.

> *Joke Brigade*. We were like, let's do something like that again. And we did and it was so much fun. We had a whole through line. So there was a plot to it as well. Normally with Mee-Ow shows it's just random sketches. It was great.

Another sketch featured Nick Gertonson playing a fifteen-year-old boy trying to date the fifteen-year-old daughter of Chris Hansen, the host of the 2004–07 television series *To Catch a Predator*. Upon meeting Gertonson, the performer playing Hansen says, "You want to tell me what you're doing here?" as if he is catching a predator.

"Rondald" introduced a character played by Eisenberg who looked for clues that might solve the big Scooby Doo–type mystery that was the theme of the Chuck Fuffalo show.

"Party Bones" featured Ryan Nunn playing someone with "party bones disease." All he could do was dance.

Each cast member again sang an excerpt from a song of their choice. Nunn sang "Cousins," by Vampire Weekend; Richardson sang "P.Y.T. (Pretty Young Thing)," by Michael Jackson; Semla sang "I Wanna Dance with Somebody (Who Loves Me)," by Whitney Houston; Daniel and Eisenberg sang a duet of "Good Girls Go Bad," by Cobra Starship; Waytz sang "Ain't Too Proud to Beg," by the Temptations; Gertonson sang the theme song to the animated show *Carmen Sandiego*; and McGovern and D'Angelo sang a duet of "Proud Mary," by John Fogerty.

JUSTIN BARBIN

6 Onward to the Fiftieth Anniversary and Beyond

2011–2024

By its fourth decade, Mee-Ow had become a reason why aspiring writers and performers decided to attend Northwestern. Given the success of Mee-Ow alumni, Northwestern was now seen as "*the* comedy career college." Along with the rest of their contemporaries, members of Mee-Ow moved into social media, creating and posting promotional videos.

In 2021, for the first time since its inception, Mee-Ow did not perform for a live audience due to the nationwide lockdown during the COVID-19 pandemic. Mee-Ow made use of Zoom for auditions and rehearsals and posted sketches online before returning to Shanley and McCormick the following year to the energy and excitement of the live crowd.

As they closed in on the show's fiftieth anniversary, the authors of this book interviewed Mee-Ow alumni across the country about the show that had so deeply affected their lives. The stories they heard were incredible.

You're holding them in your hands.

Facing page (*top to bottom*): Jake Curtis, Joey Lieberman, and Julianne Lang in the 2018 Mee-Ow Show *Take Mee-Ow to the Ball Game*

2011

MEE-OW YEAR THIRTY-EIGHT

Mee-Ow Is Dating a Monster

Thursday, January 27, at 11 p.m.; Friday and Saturday, January 28–29, at 8 and 11 p.m., Shanley Pavilion

Glee-Ow: Mee-Ow Sells Out!

Thursday, March 10, at 11 p.m.; Friday and Saturday, March 11–12, at 8 and 11 p.m., McCormick Auditorium

Returning cast members Aaron Eisenberg and Marie Semla codirected and performed. Other returning cast members included Nick Gertonson, Ryan Nunn, and Isabel Richardson. New cast members included Danielle Calvert, Sam Fishell, Caroline Goldfarb, and Tucker May.

Glee-Ow: Mee-Ow Sells Out! parodied the popular television series *Glee*, which focused on a high school glee club.

In a January 27 article in the *Daily Northwestern*, Emma Lehmann quoted Eisenberg on the theme of *Mee-Ow Is Dating a Monster*: "With Valentine's Day right around the corner, we thought what better (than) to put on a show about relationships and their downfall. But there's so much more than that, too. We have everything in this show from Air Bud to Cleopatra."

Eisenberg reflected on the collaboration during the show: "You feel very adult and at the same time, biologically you're not fully there yet. People have—egos isn't the right word. But the art of collaboration is a practice that takes time. And I've found at least in writing with my brother professionally, one of the nicest things about writing with your own family is that you can be as honest as possible, and you do not have to surrender the quality of an idea in order to preserve the relationship."

The Show Highlights

Eisenberg wrote a sketch about a monster in the closet that was a metaphor for closeted people: "It was a monster that didn't know how to come out. It had a good relationship with a little girl who would tell her parents that there's a monster in my closet. And it was deeply closeted. The sketch ended with the monster embracing his true self. It was a very sweet sketch."

THIS YEAR IN HISTORY

Fukushima nuclear disaster • Occupy Wall Street protests • Osama bin Laden killed • "Don't Ask, Don't Tell" repealed • Dow Jones year-end close 12,218 • Average new car $25,482 • 1 gallon gas $3.53 • *Harry Potter and the Deathly Hallows—Part 2, Pirates of the Caribbean: On Stranger Tides, Kung Fu Panda 2, The Hangover Part II, Cars 2, Fast Five* • The Black Keys, *El Camino*; Adele, *21*; Foo Fighters, *Wasting Light*; Kendrick Lamar, *Section.80*; Drake, *Take Care*

2011

Social Media

The first Facebook post by the Mee-Ow Show appears to have been on February 1, 2011. The post was an album titled "Picking Sketches for 'Dating a Monster'" and included twelve photos of cast members and one photo of notecards with the names of sketches taped to a wall. Each of the notecards had hash marks that appeared to indicate votes by the cast members, with "Air Bud" in first place with nine votes and "Whack Swan" in second with seven votes.

From this time forward, announcements about auditions and show dates appeared on social media, starting with Facebook and later including Instagram.

Nick Gertonson posted a promotional video to Vimeo that began with a clip from the 1963 film based on the musical *Bye Bye Birdie*, showing birds landing on telephone wires. The video transitioned into the cast lip-syncing to the song "The Telephone Hour" from the film. Then it showed cast member Tucker May appearing dead on the floor in front of a couch, which the others sat on or stood behind. The video ended with the dialogue, "What happened to Tucker?" "He had a hot date." "Mee-Ow is dating a monster!" A graphic with the title of the show and dates and times of performances then appeared.

2012

MEE-OW YEAR THIRTY-NINE

Dr. Faustus Mee-Owstus

Thursday, January 26, at 11 p.m.; Friday and Saturday, January 27–28, at 8 and 11 p.m.; Shanley Pavilion

Three's Company, Ten's Mee-Ow

Thursday, February 23, at 10 p.m.; Friday and Saturday, February 24–25, at 8 and 11 p.m.; Louis Room, Norris Center

Returning cast members Nick Gertonson and Caroline Goldfarb codirected and performed. Other returning cast members included Sam Fishell and Tucker May. New cast members included Matthew Hays, Drigan Lee, Amina Munir, Emily Olcott, Austin Perry, and Brendan Scannell.

Gertonson said that Sarah Sherman auditioned for the 2012 show but didn't get in, only because she was a freshman. She was listed in the 2013 program as the scenic designer, but never appeared in a Mee-Ow Show. She was a four-year member of the Titanic Players. In October 2021, Sherman became a featured player on *Saturday Night Live*, and was promoted to Repertory Status in 2023.

In a preview article in the *Daily Northwestern* on February 23, Chelsea Peng wrote that this was "the group's first ten-member ensemble in three decades. Drawing inspiration from and recreating the 'Three's Company' stage, complete with risers for the audience, the TV-themed show will feature a live band, sketches, pre-written blackouts and improvisation games."

The Show Highlights

For *Three's Company, Ten's Mee-Ow*, the set re-created the look of the *Three's Company* stage, complete with risers for the audience in the Louis Room. The TV-themed show included the usual live band, sketches, blackouts, and improv games.

In the *Daily Northwestern* article on February 23, Peng quoted Gertonson as saying, "What we're playing with in the show are TV tropes. We've

THIS YEAR IN HISTORY

Hurricane Sandy • Sandy Hook school shooting • Aurora, Colorado, movie theater shooting • London Summer Olympics • World does not end despite Mayan calendar • Queen Elizabeth II's Diamond Jubilee • Dow Jones year-end close 13,104 • Average new car $25,545 • 1 gallon gas $3.64 • *The Avengers*, *Skyfall*, *The Dark Knight Rises*, *The Hunger Games* • Kendrick Lamar, *Good Kid, M.A.A.D City*; Fiona Apple, *The Idler Wheel*; Lana Del Rey, *Born to Die*; Jack White, *Blunderbuss*

2012

got a couple sketches that make fun of TV shows that are on right now and a couple set up as talk shows."

Peng also quoted codirector Caroline Goldfarb about how ensemble members make each other laugh, usually with a dirty sex joke, which, Peng explained, they make "plenty of use of" in *Three's Company, Ten's Mee-Ow*. Goldfarb said, "We have a super dirty show. You're in for a good, maybe perverted time, but you won't feel like a cheap whore. You'll feel classy, Eliot Spitzer, all the stops are being pulled out on you."

Social Media

Codirector Nick Gertonson posted two promotional videos to Vimeo.

The video promoting *Three's Company, Ten's Mee-Ow* used the theme song of the 1989–98 television sitcom *Family Matters*. The video emulated the style of the opening of a sitcom of that era, introducing and establishing each member of the cast as they engaged in different activities around the house. The video ended with the entire cast running through a park hand in hand, then cut to the group assembled on a couch.

The video promoting *Dr. Faustus Mee-Owstus* showed the entire cast sitting on a large couch, drinking beer and watching the dramatic 2008 film *The Hurt Locker*. The video starts cutting between a television showing the movie, and the cast watching. Every time something serious, dangerous, or dramatic happens in the movie, the cast laughs. Then Tucker May, who is sitting in a chair next to the couch, tells everyone to come watch a video on his laptop. He shows them a scene that is suddenly interrupted by a bare-chested, blue-faced, screaming man. One of the cast members points out the resemblance to Drigan Lee, who is confused. Then the screaming figure interrupts the video. The scene changes to a shot of the cast watching Nick edit the video. He turns to the rest of the cast and says, "I think we got it!" Caroline Goldfarb replies, "I don't know. It's so like conceptual and douchey. I feel like we need to make it something simple, like us dancing or something." The video cuts to the cast dancing, then pulls back until the image becomes the screen of a television. The video pans left to show a lamp and a rabbit figurine. Then that image pulls back to become the screen of a laptop floating in the air in a nighttime shot of a cemetery. Over this image the words "Dr. Faustus Mee-Owstus" appear, along with the dates and place of the show. The video ends with Drigan Lee again appearing bare-chested in blue face and screaming.

2013

MEE-OW YEAR FORTY

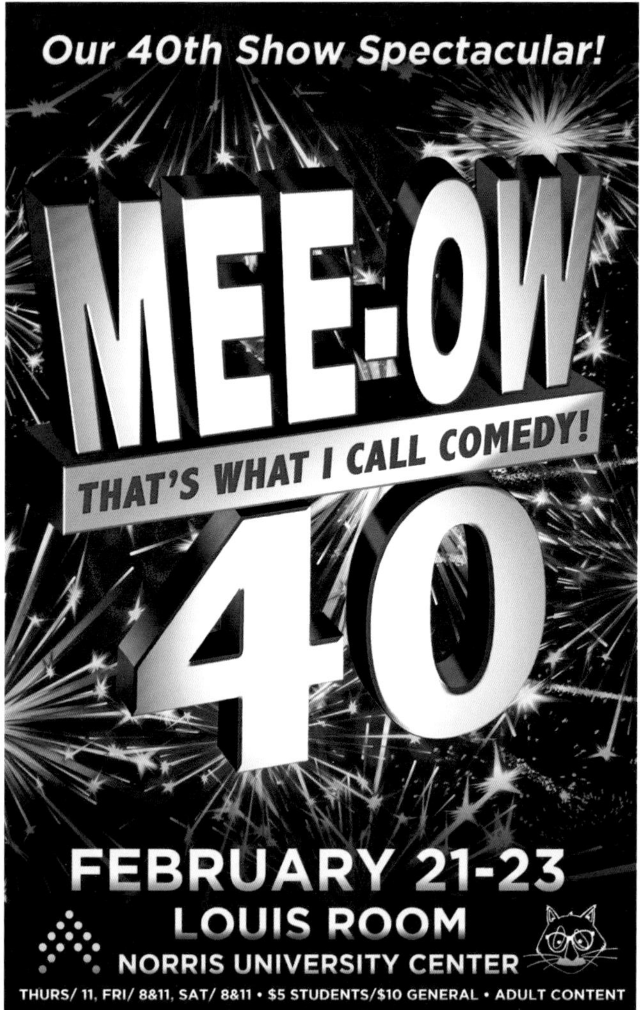

Our 40th Show Spectacular!
MEE-OW
THAT'S WHAT I CALL COMEDY!
40
FEBRUARY 21-23
LOUIS ROOM
NORRIS UNIVERSITY CENTER
THURS/ 11, FRI/ 8&11, SAT/ 8&11 • $5 STUDENTS/$10 GENERAL • ADULT CONTENT

Mee-Ow Presents The Great Catsby

Thursday, January 24, at 11 p.m.; Friday and Saturday, January 25–26, at 8 and 11 p.m., Shanley Pavilion

Mee-Ow That's What I Call Comedy! Vol. 40

Thursday, February 21, at 11 p.m.; Friday and Saturday, February 22–23, at 8 and 11 p.m., Louis Room, Norris Center

Returning cast members Sam Fishell and Emily Olcott codirected and performed. Other returning cast members included Matthew Hays, Amina Munir, and Brendan Scannell. An October 8, 2012, Facebook post in the Mee-Ow group announced, "Congratulations to our new members: Emma Cadd! Pat Buetow! Gaby Febby [Febland]! Michael Janak! We're thrilled!"

The title of the Shanley show parodied the film version of *The Great Gatsby* that opened in May 2013, directed by Baz Luhrmann. *Mee-Ow That's What I Call Comedy! Vol. 40* parodied the title of a long-running music compilation series called *Now That's What I Call Music!*, which released its fortieth volume just two years earlier. The show was again held in the Louis Room to accommodate the expected larger audiences.

The Show Highlights

Fishell and Olcott opened *The Great Catsby* by speaking directly to the audience.

> Sam: Welcome to Mee-Ow's *The Great Catsby*! We are so excited that you guys are here.
>
> Emily: A few quick things before we get started. There are three exits in Shanley should there be an emergency. Two behind you, and one behind the set.
>
> Sam: The show contains some adult content, so please be advised.
>
> Emily: And one last thing. We provided some hand sanitizer and Kleenex at the door because we know it's flu season.

THIS YEAR IN HISTORY

Barack Obama's second inauguration • Boston Marathon bombing • NSA admits illegally collecting emails • Lance Armstrong admits doping • Dow Jones year-end close 16,577 • Average new car $25,446 • 1 gallon gas $3.53 • *Frozen*, *Despicable Me 2*, *The Hunger Games: Catching Fire*, *Gravity*, *Man of Steel*, *Thor: The Dark World*, *Fast & Furious 6* • Kanye West, *Yeezus*; Daft Punk, *Random Access Memories*; Lorde, *Pure Heroine*; Chance the Rapper, *Acid Rap*; David Bowie, *The Next Day*

2013

Choosing Northwestern

Cast member Michael Janak recalled why he chose Northwestern, and how he heard about the Mee-Ow Show:

A lot of colleges would come to my performing arts high school in Dallas to audition people. We wouldn't have to go to them. My parents, my family all went to Texas A&M. Everyone I knew in Texas went to a state school. I wanted to leave Texas. And I wanted to do theater. My teacher said, "A good way to figure out the school you want to go to is find somebody whose career you want and see where they went to school." The person whose career I wanted was Seth Meyers. So I said, I want to write for *SNL*. And he went to Northwestern. That's how I knew what Northwestern was. So I auditioned for the Cherubs music program as a classical music voice singer and went to Northwestern over the summer.

It's beautiful during the summer and I just fell in love with the place. So I said, this is it. So it's those three things. I'd been there. I knew Seth Meyers went there. And they didn't require an audition. But once I got accepted, I'm doing my research. All of these *SNL* alums come out of here, so where are their improv classes, where's the curriculum for it? And it wasn't there at all. And there was no improv class. There was no comedy class that I could see. So I knew from day one I wanted to be on Mee-Ow. Before I ever went to Northwestern, before I knew anything about it, I wanted to be on Mee-Ow.

> Sam: Yes, we love to joke around up here, but the one thing we don't joke about is our health. So, please, take care of yourselves. After all, the flu is highly contagious—

This immediately transitioned into the opening number about catching the "Jazz Flu."

The performances of *Mee-Ow That's What I Call Comedy! Vol. 40* in the Louis Room required the construction of a set and bringing audience seating into the empty space. The simple backdrop behind a raised platform was bright green covered with orange triangles. The Mee-Ow logo that prevailed from about 2005—a cat wearing Groucho glasses—was centered at the top of the backdrop and flanked by doors.

Janak recalled a sketch he wrote about Waa-Mu: "The musical theater kids for Waa-Mu the year before had done a musical number called something like 'Go Wildcats' where these theater kids are trying to be football players and be like jocks on the bleachers. And they would have all these songs about 'the game' and it was just so cringey. So I wrote this sketch making fun of that, like 'we're going to win the match' and using all the wrong terminology. The whole joke was just that it was a parody of how bad Waa-Mu is."

Janak also remembered a sketch he performed called "A Day in the Life of a Sea Captain." While the band played and sang Beyoncé's song "Halo," he mimed standing at the wheel of a ship for a couple of minutes, stopping to mime getting a cup of coffee, then returning to the wheel. Suddenly the ship was struck, and he mimed being thrown about, being trapped and struggling to get out, bailing water, and eventually drowning with his body being tossed about underwater, until he settled on the bottom of the sea.

2013

Continuing a tradition, each cast member sang a song with the band. Janak recalled:

> I think about my Mee-Ow songs all the time because I wish I'd done different songs. I still sometimes when I'm listening to music think, *That would have been a really good song.* I sang this song for *The Great Catsby* called "My Body," by Young the Giant. It was like a song I liked that I thought would show off my voice, but that's actually not what you're supposed to do. You're supposed to choose a song that gets people up and into it. For my second song, I sang "Teenage Dream," by Katy Perry, which I think is a great song, except for the fact they told me afterward that Tucker May had done it the year before, so both of my songs were a mess. Sam and Emily did a duet of "Superstition" by Stevie Wonder, and everyone loved it. The people who had been there before knew to sing a song that gets people up, that the people know the lyrics to.

Social Media

Codirector Sam Fishell posted a promotional YouTube video on February 16, 2013. The forty-three-second video showed the entire cast sitting as a group with deadpan expressions. Then, at nineteen seconds, it briefly showed them wearing each other's clothing, and at twenty seconds, it showed them in apparent stages of undress, tastefully covered with pillows or blankets and wearing conical party hats. A link to the video was posted in the Mee-Ow Facebook group, announcing, "And for those of you who need a more carnal persuasion . . ."

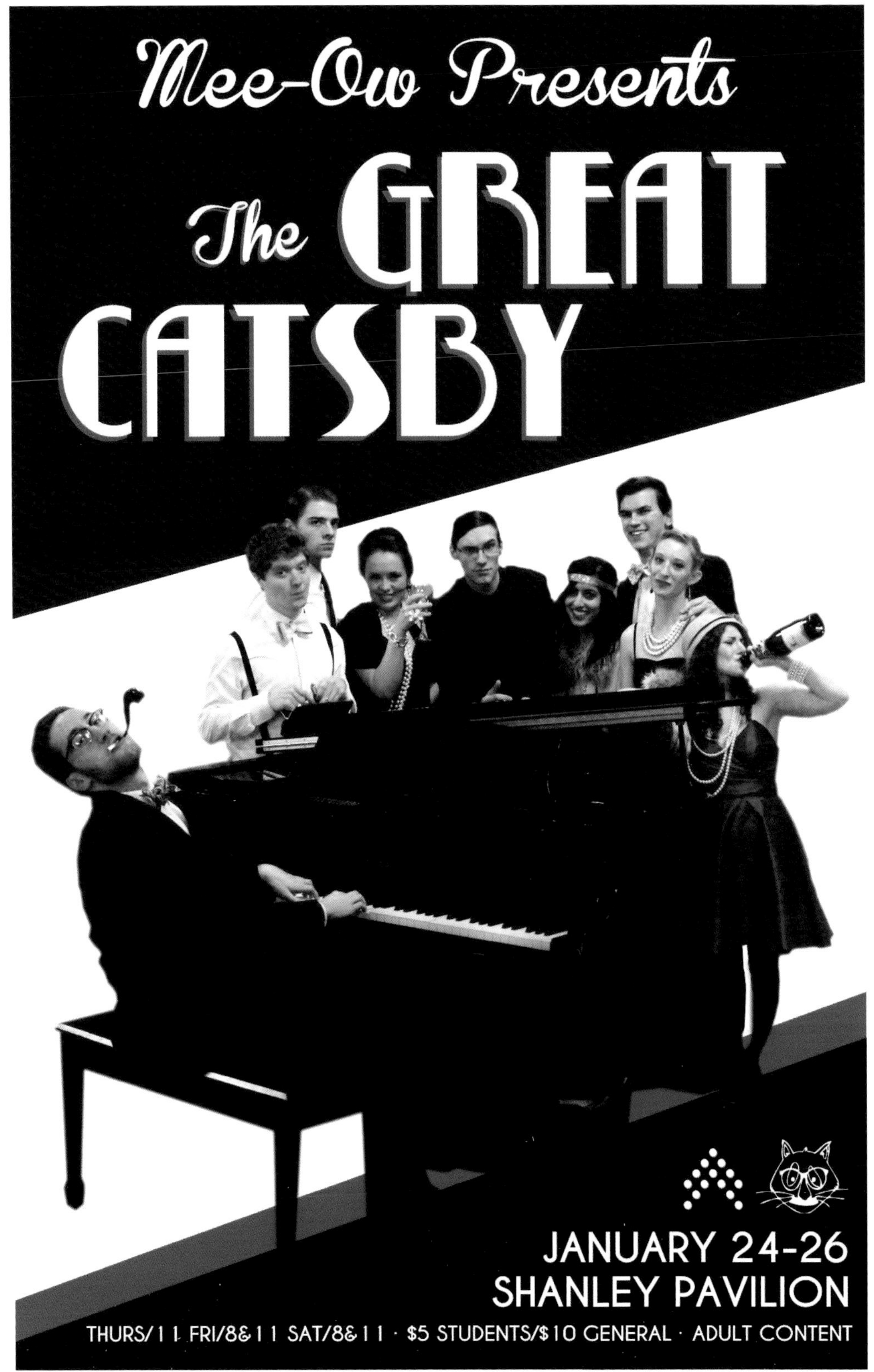
Mee-Ow Presents
The GREAT CATSBY
JANUARY 24-26
SHANLEY PAVILION
THURS/11 FRI/8&11 SAT/8&11 · $5 STUDENTS/$10 GENERAL · ADULT CONTENT

2013

2014

MEE-OW YEAR FORTY-ONE
(THE FORTIETH ANNIVERSARY SHOW)

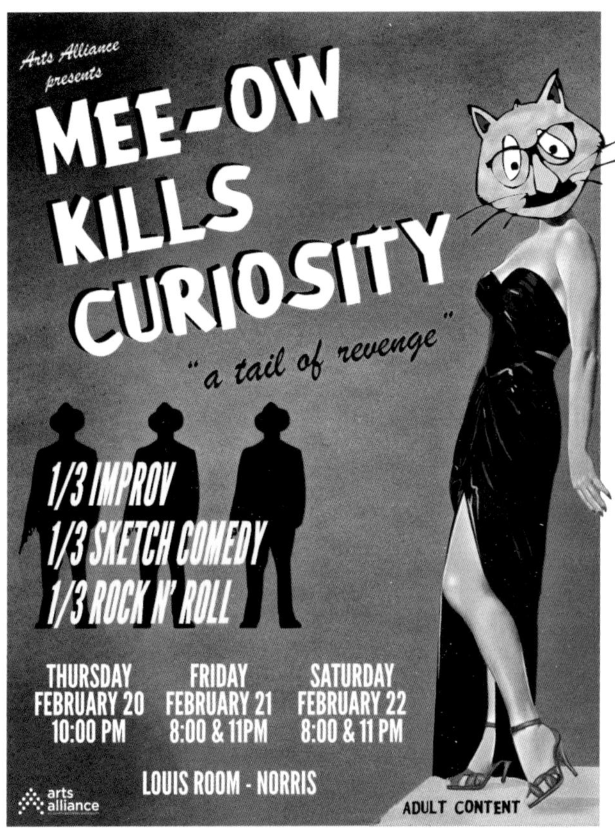

You're Invited to Mee-Owy-Kate and Ashley's Sleepover Party

Thursday, January 23, at 10 p.m.; Friday and Saturday, January 24–25, at 8 and 11 p.m., Shanley Pavilion

Mee-Ow Kills Curiosity: A Tail of Revenge

Thursday, February 20, at 10 p.m.; Friday and Saturday, February 21–22, at 8 and 11 p.m., Louis Room, Norris Center

Returning cast members Emma Cadd and Amina Munir codirected and performed. Other returning cast members were Pat Buetow and Gaby Febland. The new cast members were announced on Facebook on October 7, 2013: "Mee-Ow is proud and delighted to announce its newest cast members: Nick DiMaso! Scott Egleston! Jack Olin! Laurel Zoff Pelton! We're purring with excitement!"

The singers were announced in a Facebook post on December 7, 2013: "The Mee-Ow Band is incredibly excited to announce our SINGERS for this year's shows! Jon Schneidman will be rocking Shanley Pavilion January 23–25, and Betsy Stewart will dominate the Louis Room February 20–22. Thanks to everyone who auditioned!"

Mary-Kate and Ashley Olsen were child actors who continued their careers as teens and then became successful fashion entrepreneurs. As preteens they released a series of ten direct-to-video productions titled *You're Invited to Mary-Kate & Ashley's . . .*, the first of which, in 1995, was *You're Invited to Mary-Kate & Ashley's Sleepover Party*. Given the rereleases and popularity of these videos, they would have been familiar to Northwestern students.

In contrast, the noirish mystery theme of *Mee-Ow Kills Curiosity* evoked an older style of entertainment, while the title inverted the old saying "Curiosity killed the cat."

The Show Highlights

The opening night of *You're Invited to Mee-Owy-Kate and Ashley's Sleepover Party* offered cookies

THIS YEAR IN HISTORY

Ebola outbreak in West Africa • Sochi Winter Olympics • Russia annexes Crimea, faces sanctions • Islamic State offensive in Iraq, US launches air campaign • One World Trade Center in NYC opens • Dow Jones year-end close 17,823 • Average new car $24,979 • 1 gallon gas $3.37 • *Guardians of the Galaxy*, *The Hunger Games: Mockingjay—Part 1*, *Captain America: The Winter Soldier* • St. Vincent, *St. Vincent*; D'Angelo and the Vanguard, *Black Messiah*; Spoon, *They Want My Soul*; Lana Del Rey, *Ultraviolence*; FKA Twigs, *LP1*; Taylor Swift, *1989*

2014

for sale, as well as "being given away to lucky audience members! Because what's a sleepover party without snacks, right?"

Mee-Ow Kills Curiosity was again in the Louis Room. The backdrop of the raised platform stage was primarily green, a shade between forest green and olive green, with a painted marbling effect. The now traditional Mee-Ow cat logo was again centered at the top of the backdrop, but in keeping with the theme of the show, X's were painted over the eyes of the cat in the manner indicating that a cartoon character is dead. Doors were inset in the backdrop on both sides of the stage. As in all Louis Room performances, audience seating was brought in.

Social Media

In a conversation on Facebook, someone commented, "No one uses Facebook anymore, Mee-Ow." Codirector Amina Munir replied, "Mee-Ow has an Instagram!"

Alex Gold produced a video by Tom Mason and Brandon Green and posted it to Vimeo to promote *You're Invited to Mee-Owy-Kate and Ashley's Sleepover Party*. The eighty-second video featured the entire cast dressed in brightly colored '80s styles, with period-appropriate accoutrements, dancing to "Aaron's Party (Come Get It)," by Aaron Carter. The video then shows each cast member with superimposed graphics of their name and a check mark in the "invitation accepted" box. The video concludes with the entire cast dancing the Macarena, an '80s fad.

A YouTube video by Mee-Ow videographers Tom Mason and Brandon Green promoting *Mee-Ow Kills Curiosity* was a black-and-white film noir that introduced the cast in '40s-style clothing, with a fast-paced jazz soundtrack. The camera moved through hallways and a stairwell, concluding with the entire cast standing over the chalk outline of a body. The ending featured a voice-over by Humphrey Bogart from the movie *In a Lonely Place*, a 1950 American film noir directed by Nicholas Ray. A link to the video was posted on the Mee-Ow Facebook page.

Following the show, the codirectors for the next year were announced in a Facebook post that also invited petitions for producers.

2015

MEE-OW YEAR FORTY-TWO

Mee-Ow Presents THE TRUTH

Thursday, January 22, at 10 p.m.; Friday and Saturday, January 23–24, at 8 and 11 p.m., Shanley Pavilion

The 87th Annual AcadeMEE-OWards

Thursday, February 19, at 8 p.m.; Friday, February 20, at 8 and 11 p.m.; Saturday, February 21, at 10 p.m., McCormick Auditorium

Returning cast members Nick DiMaso and Emma Cadd, who also directed the previous year, codirected and performed. Other returning cast members included Scott Egleston and Jack Olin. In an October 6, 2014, Facebook post, Mee-Ow announced the new cast members Ben Gauthier, Alex Heller, Chanse McCrary, Natalie Rotter-Laitman, and Anne Sundell.

Chanse McCrary recalled how themes were chosen:

> Usually when we were picking themes, we picked both themes at the same time. And themes for us went all the way through the show, stuff like the sketches, the design, everything is around the theme. So when we pick the themes at the same time, usually based on the space, that would really impact our theme. The way someone described it—I think it was Emma Cadd—you have a grungy show and you have a pretty show. The grungy show is where you're gross, you're nasty. You're in Shanley. The grungy show for us was *THE TRUTH* and the nice show was *AcadeMEE-OWards*. The difference is the grungy show people are up onstage willingly. They're like, yes, we know this place. We have to have a little bit of finesse. We have to have a little class. We're at the Academy Awards. We're in suits. We're in dresses. We're glammed up. And it also helped us write. Since [the two shows] were almost within the same month, we had to get them as different as possible. That's really where the glam and the grunge came into play because we're writing gross. We're writing weird. And then we're writing smarter and more conventional sketch comedy in the glam shows.

THIS YEAR IN HISTORY

US resumes diplomatic relations with Cuba • Charlie Hebdo shooting, Paris • Islamic State destroys cultural heritage sites in Iraq, Syria • Greece defaults on 1.6 billion euro debt to IMF • Volkswagen emissions scandal • Space X lands reusable rocket • Dow Jones year-end close 17,425 • Average new car $25,194 • 1 gallon gas $2.45 • *Furious 7, Avengers: Age of Ultron, Minions, Spectre, Inside Out* • Kendrick Lamar, *To Pimp a Butterfly*; Carly Rae Jepsen, *E•MO•TION*

2015

The publicity photo for *Mee-Ow Presents THE TRUTH* shows the cast wearing aluminum foil hats, as an apparent commentary about conspiracy theories.

The 87th Academy Awards ceremony, presented by the Academy of Motion Picture Arts and Sciences, honored the best films of 2014 and took place on February 22, 2015. *The 87th Annual AcadeMEE-OWards* took place just beforehand, on February 19–21.

Social Media

A promotional video was posted to YouTube by Mee-Ow videographer Tom Mason on January 19, 2015. It showed silhouetted cast members on a white background, each speaking about conspiracy theories. Then the background changed to a scrolling image of symbols. The video ended with the show information and credits. The background music was by the Philip Glass Ensemble.

The Show Highlights

The backdrop of the set for *Mee-Ow Presents THE TRUTH* resembled the wall of a conspiracy theorist, with photos and newspaper clippings connected by red lines indicating the linkages of a grand plot. The cat logo was formed by a negative space in the backdrop that also included spray-painted messages and concrete blocks on the floor.

McCrary described a sketch he wrote about the Pokémon character Jigglypuff:

> Her power is that when she sings everyone falls asleep. But she wants to be a pop star, but she can't because every time she sings, everyone falls asleep. So I had a sketch where she's competing on *The Voice* during the blind auditions [when the judges start facing away from the competitor]. They can't even see the Jigglypuff if they're already asleep. For three minutes she just sang her name because that's all she does. This thing is kind of a theater of the absurd. The gag is she's just going to keep going until someone turns around and no one ever turns around because the judges are all asleep.

A recurring bit had McCrary in different wigs: "It was like for a cruise, but I had a wig on and I played this wack character. Then for the rest of the show, the gag was I just kept having different wigs on. It was so stupid, so easy. And it was like, 'Oh, he's got a different wig!' Memorable moment. The wigs kept getting worse and kept getting more disheveled. Then it's like 'He has a mustache now. What's going on?' "

McCrary said that the cast sang songs as in previous years, but this year was different: "You usually sang verse, chorus . . . but we were in rehearsals and they're like, 'We're going to do the bridge.' So then we sang verse, chorus, bridge, last chorus. And the band got into it, and then I got into it, and then the whole audience could feel it. And you were just like, *yeah, this is what we're going for.*" McCrary sang "a song unfortunately by Macklemore. But it was very fun."

In previous years, the sequence was often a single song between sketches. However, this inhibited the audience's ability to dance during the songs, because by the time they had gotten up to dance, they had to find their seats again. So the sequence this year had three songs between a sequence of sketches and improvs to create a longer time for the feel of a dance party. These multiple dance breaks were replaced a couple of years later with a single, longer dance break in lieu of an intermission.

2016

MEE-OW YEAR FORTY-THREE

Arts Alliance presents...
Speak Mee-Ow or Forever Hold Your Peace
THURS FEB 18, 10 PM* • FRI FEB 19, 8 & 11 PM • SAT FEB 20, 8:30 & 11 PM
1/3 IMPROV, 1/3 SKETCH, 1/3 ROCK 'N ROLL • MATURE CONTENT
$5 STUDENTS, $10 GENERAL ADMISSION • SHANLEY PAVILION
*PAY WHAT YOU CAN

Save the Date
Shanley Pavilion
2.18-2.20

Ctrl Alt Mee-Ow

Thursday, January 21, at 10 p.m.; Friday and Saturday, January 22–23, at 8 and 11 p.m., Shanley Pavilion

Speak Mee-Ow or Forever Hold Your Peace

Thursday, February 18, at 10 p.m.; Friday, February 19, at 8 and 11 p.m.; Saturday, February 20, at 8:30 and 11 p.m., Shanley Pavilion

Returning cast members Jack Olin and Natalie Rotter-Laitman codirected and performed. Other returning cast members included Chanse McCrary and Ben Gauthier. In a Facebook post, Mee-Ow announced new cast members Will Altabef, Isabella Gerasole, Dan Leahy, Caroline Reedy, and Eva Victor.

For the first time, both the January and February shows were in Shanley Pavilion. An article in the *Daily Northwestern* the previous year (April 28, 2015) explained that a tripling of the number of groups requesting spaces at Norris University Center required the reallocation of space.

In addition, the management of Norris might have been reluctant to book performances in McCormick Auditorium due to damages to the facility during a 2014 performance of *Merrily We Roll Along* by Spectrum Theatre Company, a student group that focuses on addressing social and political issues in their theater productions. As reported in the *Daily Northwestern*, Spectrum Theatre was fined $12,000 by the Office of Student Conduct, "for space violations including for some of the cost of a ripped projector screen." To pay the fine, Spectrum raised money from "other student groups, friends, family and the greater NU community," using an Indiegogo campaign.

The Show Highlights

In a preview article by Juliet Freudman in the *Daily Northwestern* on January 21, Rotter-Laitman spoke about *Ctrl Alt Mee-Ow*. "Ctrl Alt Mee-Ow will explore themes of technology, innovation, keyboards, mouses, screens," she explained. "The set design, lighting and props will habituate into a haven of technology . . . this weekend,

THIS YEAR IN HISTORY

Zika virus outbreak • Panama Papers leaked • Pulse nightclub shooting • Pokémon Go launched • Donald Trump, Hillary Clinton nominated • Chicago Cubs win World Series • Ebola vaccine approved • Dow Jones year-end close 19,763 • Average new car $25,451 • 1 gallon gas $2.20 • *Batman v Superman: Dawn of Justice*, *Deadpool*, *Suicide Squad* • Frank Ocean, *Blonde*; David Bowie, *Blackstar*; Kanye West, *The Life of Pablo*; Beyoncé, *Lemonade*; A Tribe Called Quest, *We Got It From Here . . .*

2016

providing a modernistic venue for the performance to unfold."

The article continued, quoting Olin, "Many of Mee-Ow's shows are intended to provide humor, but the group also focuses on highlighting conversations and issues affecting the NU community. In the past the group has performed sketches related to race and sexuality."

Gerasole recalled of the opening number: "Everyone was waiting for how the sketch would turn into the opening dance. For *Ctrl Alt Mee-Ow* we danced to 'WTF' by Missy Elliott. We got a dance major to come and choreograph the song in the years that I was on it. Horrific dance. Actually, that's not true. Chanse was really good, and Natalie was pretty good, too. But with everyone else it was like the poor dance major's eyes just kept getting wider and wider."

The last improv game of *Ctrl Alt Mee-Ow* was "O2 Deprivation," aka "The Most Dangerous Game." The person who is not actively in the game submerges their head fully in a bucket of water and does not come up for air until someone switches out with them. Because of the water that spills on the floor, this is always the final improv game.

Speak Mee-Ow or Forever Hold Your Peace evoked a garden wedding, and the opening sketch showed a marriage ceremony, but everyone kept objecting. This then turned into the opening dance number.

Gerasole recalled: "I remember Natalie wrote this really funny *Sisterhood of the Traveling Pants*–themed sketch. She was describing the different body shapes of the girls and it was something like a pencil or slender objects, like a blade of grass. And then the last girl, who was me, was 'clock.' Made me laugh."

Social Media

On January 18, 2016, Mee-Ow publicity director David Brown posted a video on YouTube promoting *Ctrl Alt Mee-Ow*. The video parodied a computer or software company product announcement and capabilities video and began with the words "Coming Soon . . ." in a sans serif type on a white background, parodying Apple videos.

Each cast member, wearing an identical, high-collared, zip-front jacket, was framed in a medium shot on the right side of the screen in front of a white limbo backdrop. Each spoke in stereotypically vague terms about the "product benefits" of the unnamed offering. The video ended with a graphic of the keyboard "ctrl" and "alt" keys, plus an additional key labeled "mee-ow," and the dates, times, and location of the show, plus the cost of tickets.

Gerasole also recalled how Olin and Rotter-Laitman worked together:

> Jack would write these sketches that would just make no sense to anyone except him. And yet they somehow came to be crowd favorites. He wrote one about two Amish kids on Rumspringa. You would read it on paper and you'd be like, "What the hell is going on here?" But then he would be like, "No, the inflections are supposed to be like this." . . . And then it would turn out to be the funniest sketch. He was just so kind and really funny and a great listener. And Natalie is just a total powerhouse. She's still doing comedy in New York, doing a lot of stand-up. But her improv just blew me away. And they worked so well with each other. It was a very relaxed environment, but we still managed to get everything done. Yeah. I had a great time.

2017

MEE-OW YEAR FORTY-FOUR

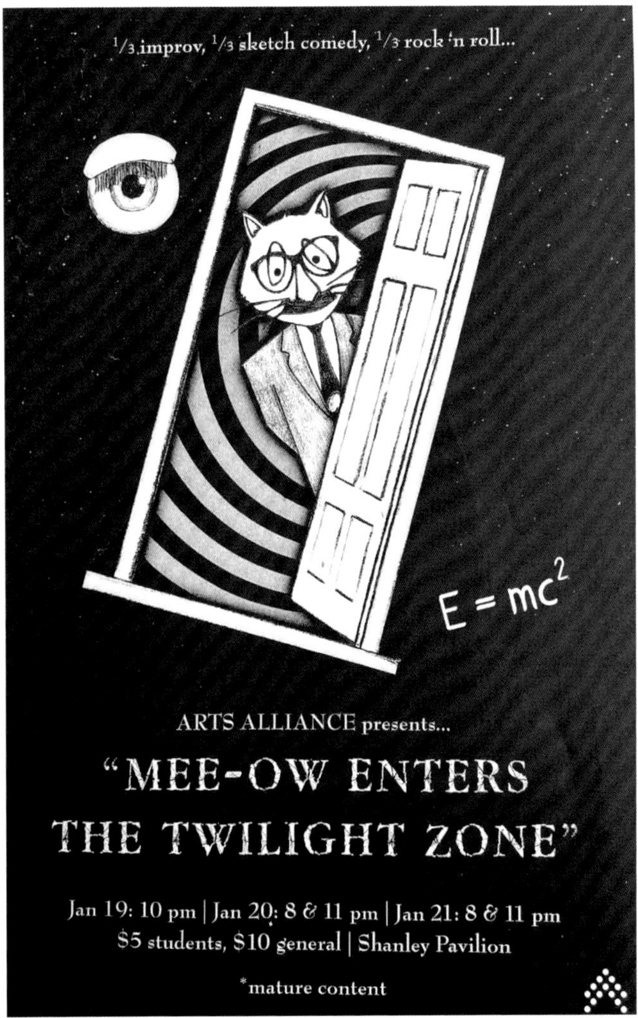

Mee-Ow Enters the Twilight Zone

Thursday, January 19, at 10 p.m.; Friday and Saturday, January 20–21, at 8 and 11 p.m., Shanley Pavilion

Mee-Ow's Anatomy

Thursday, February 16, at 10 p.m.; Friday and Saturday, February 17–18, at 8 and 11 p.m., Shanley Pavilion

Returning cast members Ben Gauthier and Isabella Gerasole codirected and performed. Other returning cast members included Will Altabef and Dan Leahy. In a Facebook post on October 3, 2016, Mee-Ow announced their new cast members Maya Armstrong, Devyn Johnson, Allie Levitan, Nabeel Muscatwalla, and Harry Wood.

Mee-Ow's Anatomy was a parody of the popular, long-running television medical drama series *Grey's Anatomy*.

Mee-Ow Enters the Twilight Zone was an homage to the long-running television series created by Rod Serling. The shows featured fantasy, science-fiction, dystopian, supernatural, suspense, and horror themes to illuminate moral and social issues, and usually ended in an unexpected twist. But there was more to the story of choosing that name and theme. Gerasole explained:

> After the 2016 election, everyone on campus was very torn up about Trump being elected. It was recent enough that we were like, we have to address this in some way. But we don't want the show to be about that. We want this to kind of be a release for the students, because we would have to turn people away every night. The room would be so packed that Devyn was always the one who was stressed about the fire code, about there being too many people in here. We would, I think, get it up to like a hundred and eighty. And that was too many people anyway. People just wanted to come and have a good time. So we were like, how can we marry those two feelings? So we entered the Twilight Zone.

THIS YEAR IN HISTORY

#MeToo movement • Donald Trump inaugurated • Women's March on Washington • Supreme Court decision implements travel bans • FBI investigation into election hacks • NFL anthem protests • Removal of Confederate monuments • Dow Jones year-end close 24,719 • Average new car $25,565 • 1 gallon gas $2.79 • *Get Out*, *Wonder Woman*, *It*, *Okja*, *Dunkirk*, *Atomic Blonde* • Lorde, *Melodrama*; SZA, *Ctrl*; Lana Del Rey, *Lust for Life*; Kendrick Lamar, *DAMN.*

2017

Choosing Northwestern

Londoner Jake Curtis recalled how he decided to come to Northwestern:

I started doing improv in London [with] a guy who had been at Second City in Chicago and then moved to London. And I just fell in love with it. From like fifteen to eighteen it was pretty much all I did. So then when I was looking for schools to apply to, I knew I wanted to go somewhere in America and I Googled "best improv universities in America" and a thing came up talking about Mee-Ow and Titanic and Northwestern. I was like, deal. I'm in. In hindsight, it was just some dude's list. Maybe I shouldn't have made the biggest decision of my life at that point based on some blog. But I did. But also one of the people who I improvised with in London had been in Boom Chicago, in Amsterdam. I remember talking to him and saying, "Oh, I was thinking about Northwestern." He goes, "Oh, you should do Mee-Ow. My friend Seth was in this group." It took me like till the next day to work out he was talking about Seth Meyers. It was an exciting thing for me, the idea that improv and comedy would be something that was seen as significant by a university and by the students there. There's wonderful comedy in England, but it's still really considered more of a fanciful hobby. The idea that you could go somewhere where there were these real stalwart, legacy groups of comedy was very appealing to me.

I got into Northwestern in the fall of 2016, and coming in I was definitely a little cocky about my comedy stuff I'd been doing, maybe not with the chops to back it up. I've been working with a few improv groups and some groups up in Canada and I was feeling very excited. Then I found out a few weeks in that I had missed the Mee-Ow auditions. I cursed my administration skills. I got into Titanic freshman year and some of the other comedy-based groups. My sister visited the weekend of Mee-Ow, and so I went to see Mee-Ow with my sister freshman year and I just loved the show. It was a wonderful show. The writing, the improv, the dancing was great. But especially what I just loved was that it felt like they were taking it seriously and it felt like they were holding each other accountable to the idea [that] a show should be something that an audience is not forced to like but likes involuntarily, instead of performed with a sort of air of "we're all students, so be nice to us."

The Show Highlights

The black-and-white backdrop for *Mee-Ow Enters the Twilight Zone* featured a variation of the opening graphic of concentric white-on-black rings from season three of the *Twilight Zone* television series, which aired in 1961 and 1962. For the Mee-Ow set, a white outline of a black silhouette of the cat's head Mee-Ow logo was surrounded by concentric white outlines increasing in size.

Armstrong recalled the opening number: "It was Izzy and Ben trying to run away from terrible, ridiculous things that were happening, one of which being Donald Trump running for president. It ended with demonic ghouls capturing them."

The set of *Mee-Ow's Anatomy* resembled a doctor's examination room, with white walls, anatomical posters, an eye chart with silhouettes of the cat's head logo instead of letters of the alphabet, and the Mee-Ow cat's head logo placed atop a drawing of a doctor in a lab coat. Armstrong recalled a blackout sketch where

2017

"someone was in the hospital with a heart monitor beeping. Then eventually everyone joined in and was singing and rapping and dancing to the beat of the monitor."

In keeping with the structure of one-third sketch, one-third improv, and one-third rock-and-roll format that had become the Mee-Ow tradition, the band would play before and after the show, with an extended dance break in lieu of an intermission. They would also play interstitial music between sketches, blackouts, and improvs. Sometimes the interstitials would be stretched to a full minute to give those cast members who opted to do so the opportunity to sing with the band, hearkening back to a time in which every cast member sang a solo.

Ben Gauthier wrote "such a funny sketch, the pen pal sketch," Gerasole recalled:

> It was Will Altabef and he is, oh my God, one of the funniest people I have ever met. His mom really wanted him to be an actor, and he's a lawyer. I don't know if his mother would appreciate me saying that, but suffice to say he was so funny and we also did improv together, and he was the star of this sketch that Ben wrote. A young kid was a pen pal with a Cold War dictator named Pyotr. The sketch was their exchange of letters. Ben was an amazing writer and still is. Ben was the kid and Will was the dictator Pyotr. I came out at the end. And then I think I became pen pals with Pyotr and killed him and usurped him.

Gerasole also remembered a show where the band member Lorenzo Gonzalez-Lamassonne, on electronics and vocals, repeatedly interjected a specific piece of music: "There was one show that had an electronic keyboard and there was a drop that they would do in between each sketch that was the song 'Fuck Donald Trump' [also known as FDT by YG & Nipsey Hussle]. And then one night they just kind of went crazy and played it every time in between the sketches and blackouts."

Band leader Alex Warshawsky chose the Mee-Ow Show singers Ogi Ifediora and Aiden

JUSTIN BARBIN

The 2017 cast: Muscatwalla, Leahy, Armstrong, Gauthier (*obscured*), Gerasole, Johnson, Altabef, Levitan, and Wood

Fisher. As Gerasole recalled, "Ogi came in and sang 'Here Comes the Sun' for the audition, and I just burst into tears. She was amazing."

Reviews

Future cast member Jake Curtis recalled:

> I saw both shows in Shanley and they were great except they were too long. I remember seeing it going, "That's great, if they let me in, I'm going to tell them to make it shorter." And I did, ultimately. In my first year, we reduced the length by an hour from the year before when they were three and change. They threw in every sketch. They had two dance breaks and an intermission. That was the big issue. I said, "That's ridiculous." No one wanted to dance by the third one, especially on the kind of parents' nights. The [early] show usually had a lot of family coming. . . . The first time I went to see Mee-Ow was the middle of winter and it was freezing and there was snow. Nabeel was a friend of mine and he was in it, so he'd saved me two seats. I show up like twenty minutes before and there's just like two hundred people freezing in the cold, shivering. You get to know the comedy crowd, and this wasn't them. These were like random people. And so I was like, "Oh, that's so cool. These people are actually giving time from their lives to go see this college thing." This isn't like, "Please come. If each of us brings two friends we'll do this." It was like these people have reached the point and worked hard enough to have this kind of crowd. And that excited me. I thought that's where I want to get to. I want to be in the show and I want to direct this show. I told myself it was happening.

JUSTIN BARBIN

Devyn Johnson and Allie Levitan

2018

MEE-OW YEAR FORTY-FIVE

ARTS ALLIANCE AT NORTHWESTERN UNIVERSITY PRESENTS

1/3 improv. 1/3 sketch comedy. 1/3 rock n roll!

DIRECTED BY DEVYN JOHNSON AND NABEEL MUSCATWALLA
PRODUCED BY ALEX SCHWARTZ | SHANLEY PAVILION

Take Mee-Ow to the Ball Game

Thursday, February 1, at 8 p.m.; Friday, February 2, at 10 p.m.; Saturday, February 3, at 7 and 10 p.m., McCormick Auditorium

The Mee-Owstery Machine

Thursday, March 1, at 8 p.m.; Friday and Saturday, March 2–3, at 7 and 10 p.m., Shanley Pavilion

At the beginning of October 2017, Mee-Ow announced auditions on Facebook. The Facebook post linked to a YouTube video on the NU Arts Alliance channel of returning cast members and codirectors Devyn Johnson and Nabeel Muscatwalla cracking up while trying to introduce each other.

Maya Armstrong was the other returning cast member. The new cast members were Makasha Copeland, Jake Curtis, Jake Daniels, Julianne Lang, Amara Leonard, and Joey Lieberman.

In addition to the usual improv games in groups during the first audition and scene work during the callbacks, the applicants were required to submit a "Mee-Ow Writing Supplement." The categories of the supplement included:

1. Tell us about your hot new startup.
2. Give us three superheroes/supervillians that don't exist.
3. What is your horcrux, and where would you hide it?
4. Tell us about a character you'd like to write a sketch about.
5. Write a three-line scene.

Jake Curtis recalled his audition:

> Just before [auditions] I'd been in Canada doing this fifty-hour improv-a-thon that a group called Die-Nasty does up there every year. You go there and you stay up and improvise for fifty hours and the crowd cycles out every two hours and you play one character. So it's a thirty-person cast and they have a caller who calls who's going to be in the scene. So you don't have to be locked

THIS YEAR IN HISTORY

PyeongChang Winter Olympics • March for Our Lives gun violence protest • Syrian civil war continues • US withdraws from Iranian nuclear agreement, reimposes sanctions • US imposes tariffs on Chinese goods, withdraws from UN Human Rights Council • Trump administration disbands pandemic response team • *Washington Post* journalist Jamal Khashoggi murdered • The Camp Fire in California • Dow Jones year-end close 23,327 • Average new car $25,507 • 1 gallon gas $2.79 • *Black Panther*, *Bohemian Rhapsody* • Car Seat Headrest, *Twin Fantasy*; Kacey Musgraves, *Golden Hour*

2018

> in onstage the whole time. You play one character on one big arc for fifty hours and you slowly go crazy. And I played this kind of metrosexual German character called Klaus wearing tight spandex shorts and a tight spandex jacket. And I remember I did it for fifty hours and it was crazy. And then I get on the plane, fly back, and Mee-Ow auditions were like three days later. And so I remember I showed up and we did a bunch of games and I felt like I was doing fine. And [in the callbacks] the final game was "Yearbook Photo." They would get you in for a yearbook photo and someone would fake a snap and you pretend to be members of a club and you're basically just monologuing as members of whatever this yearbook group was. And I remember they were like, "Try a character you're comfortable with because you're going to have to stay in it for a moment." And I just remember I was like, "Oh, I'm ready." I was still sleep deprived and I just remember switching into my German self and it went really well. I remember feeling pretty confident by the end of that. I was really obsessed. I mean, I still am, but I was really analytically obsessed with improv at that point. I remember sitting in the audience and kind of mentally giving critiques and notes to everyone and trying to weigh it up really as hard as I could. I remember leaving, and in the most emotionless way possible, thinking, I'm pretty sure I've added up the numbers and I'm going to get in.

On learning that he had been cast:

> We all went over and had pizza at Devyn Johnson's house and all the old cast members from the year prior called us on the phone, which was exciting for me because they were all my heroes and I fancied two of them. So the fact that they were calling me felt nice. I remember it was really nice that I got in with two of my friends who I'd already performed with. And I remember this joyful feeling of "we have three years of this." Like we are locked in. We were all sophomores. We get to invest into this and it's going to stay, which I think was a lovely feeling immediately that this can become a family. I remember I walked home with Nabeel that night and just felt [great].

The Show Highlights

The backdrop of *Take Mee-Ow to the Ball Game* was painted to resemble the signage of Wrigley Field, the home of the Chicago Cubs.

The backdrop of *The Mee-Owstery Machine* emulated the look of the Mystery Machine van from the cartoon *Scooby-Doo.* The blue and green backdrop featured the name of the show in orange letters in the same style, and the Mee-Ow cat's head logo was painted brown to resemble the Great Dane cartoon dog.

Of the two shows and venues, Curtis said, "McCormick I have mixed feelings about. It was cool to get to do such a big show there and with such technical proficiencies. But Shanley was a bigger energy and it was easier to fill, so it was lovely. It felt like you got the big lugging one out of the way. And then Shanley was the reward."

He described one of the "intricately overwritten sketches" he wrote during jury duty:

> I ended up having a song in the show that was all perfectly done to the rhythm and rhyme of an old R. Kelly song about a booty call. It was like one of those sexy R&B, back-and-forth songs with a guy calling up a girl and being like, "Hey, like it was pretty cool,

> you want to hang out again?" But then she didn't know who it was. She kept being like, "Oh Jim from . . . Yeah . . . Jim . . . the brown hair?" And he's like, "I've got blond hair." But it was all sung and rhymed and Nabeel is an incredible singer. And so I wrote that knowing that he could pull it off if I got it in the show. The other singer was Amara Leonard, who is also a wonderful singer. We were blessed with musical theater performers. For me, comedy song sketches are always my favorite. And I sadly can't sing.

Curtis also recalled the opening sketch of *Take Mee-Ow to the Ball Game*, which he wrote with Devyn Johnson: "It was two lawyers going to a baseball game and they get put on the kiss cam and kind of awkwardly kiss and then it goes away. And then the kiss cam comes back and they have to kiss again. And they're getting into this increasingly heated work argument about a lawsuit. And they keep just having to make out in between the argument. And it involved a lot of kissing. And I remember my dad came to the show and he gave a thumbs up from the audience."

Of the opening sketch for *The Mee-Owstery Machine*, he said: "I was such a try hard. It was my first year. I was like, I can build this funny costume. And I spent my own money to build this costume. I got a chest plate and then cut a hole in the middle and put a realistic doll face in it, so I just had a face in my belly. And then I wore a mask that covered up my own face. So I just looked like someone with a face in his belly. And so I was like the Scooby-Doo villain in that."

Armstrong recalled a sketch that parodied a Northwestern advertisement and "devolved into us talking about the corrupt institution that we all attend." The ad included the Northwestern tagline "AND is in our DNA."

Another sketch featured Copeland as Dora the Explorer and Armstrong as a child following Dora. Then Dora started telling the child terrible things to do.

Reviews

The February 27, 2018, podcast episode produced by the *Daily Northwestern* was titled "Wildcats Go Mee-Ow." Hosts Marisa Hattler and Natalie Shilati interviewed Johnson and Muscatwalla, and "also talked to students on campus about their experiences watching the show."

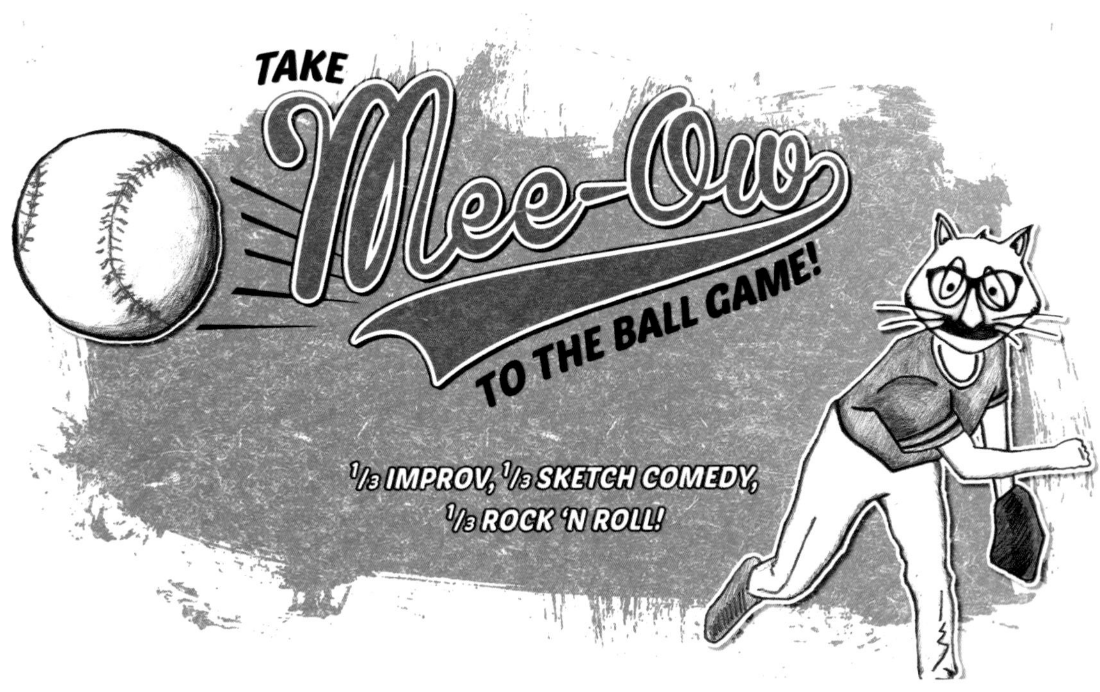

Colbert Hosts a Gala

In April 2018, Northwestern's School of Communication hosted a fundraising performance for a new MFA program in acting. The gala, called "A Starry Night," took place in the new Ryan Fieldhouse. The host of the evening was Stephen Colbert '86, '11 H. The show was written by Shelly Goldstein '79 (Mee-Ow '78). In attendance and performing were Communication alumni including Ana Gasteyer '89 (Mee-Ow '88, '89), Kathryn Hahn '95, Richard Kind '78, Harry Lennix '86, and Seth Meyers '96 (Mee-Ow '96). As reported in the *Daily Northwestern* on April 22, 2018, "Past and present Mee-Ow comedians joined forces to revive sketches from previous years." In addition to the performances, the weekend included reunions, workshops, and exhibits.

Dana Olsen (Mee-Ow '77, '78, '79, '80) recalled a vintage sketch performed at the gala:

About five years ago when they did this whole dedication of the new field house, they brought in all these famous alumni that had scored big on Broadway and everything. They put Mee-Ow in the show. It was the wrong room to do comedy because it was this huge field house and it wasn't intimate. Anyway, we tried doing the Philosophy OD sketch because it's big and broad. [The sketch] was originally Stew Figa [Mee-Ow '76, '77] and Kyle Heffner [Mee-Ow '76, '77, '78]. Figa was the telephone operator at a philosophy OD clinic. And Kyle calls him up and he's freaking out because he's been reading Hegel and Nietzsche and he feels like he has absolutely no value and no purpose to his life and he wants to end it all. Kyle's going, "I feel like I want to die! I feel like I want to die!" And Figa goes, "What have you been reading?" [Kyle replies,] "Hegel and Nietzsche!" Figa's like, "Oh my God!" And he has to talk him down. And eventually he goes, "Do you have a television set?" And Kyle replies, "Yes." Figa says, "Turn it on. Can you tune in *Green Acres*?" "Yes!" "Do you [see] Fred Ziffel?" That starts to bring him down a little bit. [Figa says,] "Stick your finger in your eye." And Kyle sticks his finger in his eye and screams in pain and Figa goes, "OK, so, you know you exist." There are all these like great philosophical references. It's a perfect college sketch. It's a great sketch that was in the '76 show. Predated my time but I know it well.

JIM PRISCHING

2019

MEE-OW YEAR FORTY-SIX

Presented by NU Arts Alliance & Mee-Ow Comedy

Jaclyn Orlando, Producer
Jake Daniels & Maya Armstrong, Directors
Jacob Galdes & Oliver Holden-Moses, Band Directors

In Mee-Owdieval Times

Thursday, January 31, at 8 p.m.; Friday, February 1, at 10 p.m.; Saturday, February 2, at 7 and 10 p.m., McCormick Auditorium

In Mee-Owmoriam

Thursday, February 28, at 8 p.m.; Friday and Saturday, March 1–2, at 7 and 10 p.m., Shanley Pavilion

Returning cast members Maya Armstrong and Jake Daniels codirected and performed. The other returning cast members were Makasha Copeland, Jake Curtis, and Amara Leonard. The new cast members included Willa Barnett, Edson Montenegro, Jasmine Sharma, and Ross Turkington. Armstrong recalled:

> In the fall we'd meet once a week and go over sketches, and then in the winter, it would pick up and we would be rehearsing four hours a day, five days a week, Sunday through Thursday. And every day you bring in two sketches, or one sketch could be worth two or three blackouts. Writing five days a week, every single day, trying to churn things out and realizing that some things are going to be stinkers and that the stinkers are the most fun for the people in the room. And having a safe environment for people to indulge you in your weirdest, funniest, most probably indefensible comedic instincts is always great.

The Show Highlights

Jake Curtis described the opening sketch for *In Mee-Owdieval Times*: "We were all playing medieval people in different parts of McCormick. It was a big mess of three lines here and three lines there and three there and no one laughed. And then we would open with a dance and then jump straight into the first improv games."

"We were all pretending to be on horses," Armstong added. "Ross Turkington took the lead on that opening because he's such a nerd about medieval history. I'm pretty sure it was his title [for] the show."

2019

THIS YEAR IN HISTORY

US leaves Intermediate-Range Nuclear Forces Treaty • New Zealand mosque shootings • WikiLeaks cofounder Julian Assange arrested • El Chapo sentenced • Trump impeached • COVID-19 first reported in Wuhan, China • US Space Force established • Dow Jones year-end close 28,538 • Average new car $26,340 • 1 gallon gas $2.79 • *Avengers: Endgame*, *Captain Marvel*, *Joker* • Tyler, the Creator, *Igor*; Lana Del Rey, *Norman Fucking Rockwell!*; Billie Eilish, *When We All Fall Asleep, Where Do We Go?*

JUSTIN BARBIN

Amara Leonard, Edson Montenegro, Jake Curtis, Maya Armstrong, Makasha Copeland, unidentified audience member, and Jake Daniels

Curtis described the opening sketch he wrote for *In Mee-Owmoriam*: "It was lots of people gossiping at a funeral and having different conversations. There was a real coffin in the middle. One person was trying to steal something from the coffin and one person was flirting. I wrote little bits for everyone, but it all weaved into one thing. It was a little macabre. And then we all went into the dance and it was a fun one."

Curtis wrote and performed a country song that appeared to begin as a love song.

> We did the first show in McCormick and I'd come out in the darkness and start strumming a guitar, which always got a laugh. I was like, it's the easiest laugh I'm going to get. I would ask, "Who's looking for love?" I'd get someone up onstage and sit and then romantically serenade them. This whole song was like, "I love you. But there's still just one thing I need to hear from you, like three words, sing it to me." And then the chorus was: "Bush. Did. 9/11. Say Bush. Did. 9/11. Three little words that would send me to heaven. And say Bush. Did. 9/11." And then I would just pause and I would lean the mic towards them [laughs]. And then I would stand up and get the audience to start standing up. And on the third chorus, I would say, "Now, everybody!" and the house lights would come up and like five hundred people would start chanting, "Bush. Did. 9/11."

Curtis explained a sketch he wrote for Armstrong:

> She just killed it as a priest. She'd get the whole audience to stand up and say, "Praise the Lord" [gestures with arms above his head]. And then she would say, "The offerings he brings down upon you" [brings upraised hands down to his head]. And she would start getting them to do the YMCA [gestures to the song by the Village People]. Like "Point to the east to Jerusalem." And she was screaming and she just commanded everyone. . . . I was relieved with that show. We're trying to fill McCormick, make it a big spectacle, because I think it can at its best be a spectacle more than a comedy show.

Reviews

In an article in the February 3, 2019, issue of *North by Northwestern*, Navpreet Dhillon wrote:

> The cast engaged the crowd throughout the entire show. Whether the actors were performing in the aisles or calling on crowd members for suggestions for the improv exercises, Mee-Ow made sure to keep the crowd actively involved. The show also featured dance breaks in which more than half of the crowd joined them on stage for a sweaty and loud dance party while Honey Butter and some cast members performed.
>
> *Mee-Owdieval* showcased the wide variety of talent from the cast. They performed light-hearted skits parodying President Morton Schapiro and filled the auditorium with their and the crowd's voices while singing "Bush did 9/11."
>
> *Mee-Owdieval* was undoubtedly a hit, as expected.

Northwestern University's culture and arts publication, *Scene + Heard*, founded in 2014, published the article "Five Reasons You Can't Miss *In Mee-Owmoriam*," written by Lexi Vollero, in the February 28, 2019, online issue:

> Someone's gotta step up and say it: your Northwestern experience is incomplete until you get yourself to a Mee-Ow show. Self-described as "one-third improv, one-third sketch comedy, and one-third rock n' roll," the comedy group has been a bright light in the dark, dreary Evanston winter since 1974. They focus their energies on two shows during winter quarter and serve it to you à la *SNL*. Imagine an episode of *Saturday Night Live* grounded in audience participation and tailor-made to fit the collective sense of humor on campus, complete with quirky Northwestern inside jokes and some mild roasts (in good fun) that we can all relate to.

JUSTIN BARBIN

The 2019 cast: (*back row*) Jasmine Sharma, Jake Daniels, Maya Armstrong, Amara Leonard, Willa Barnett, Jake Curtis, and Makasha Copeland; (*front*) Edson Montenegro and Ross Turkington

2019

JUSTIN BARBIN

Jasmine Sharma, Willa Barnett, Jake Curtis, Amara Leonard, and Edson Montenegro

JUSTIN BARBIN

Maya Armstrong, Edson Montenegro, and Jake Curtis

2020

MEE-OW YEAR FORTY-SEVEN

America's Next Top Mee-Owdel

Thursday, January 30, at 9 p.m.; Friday, January 31, at 10 p.m.; Saturday, February 1, at 7 and 10 p.m., McCormick Auditorium

Mee-Owddle School Dance: Unchaperoned

Thursday, February 27, at 9 p.m.; Friday and Saturday, February 28–29, at 7 and 10 p.m., Shanley Pavilion

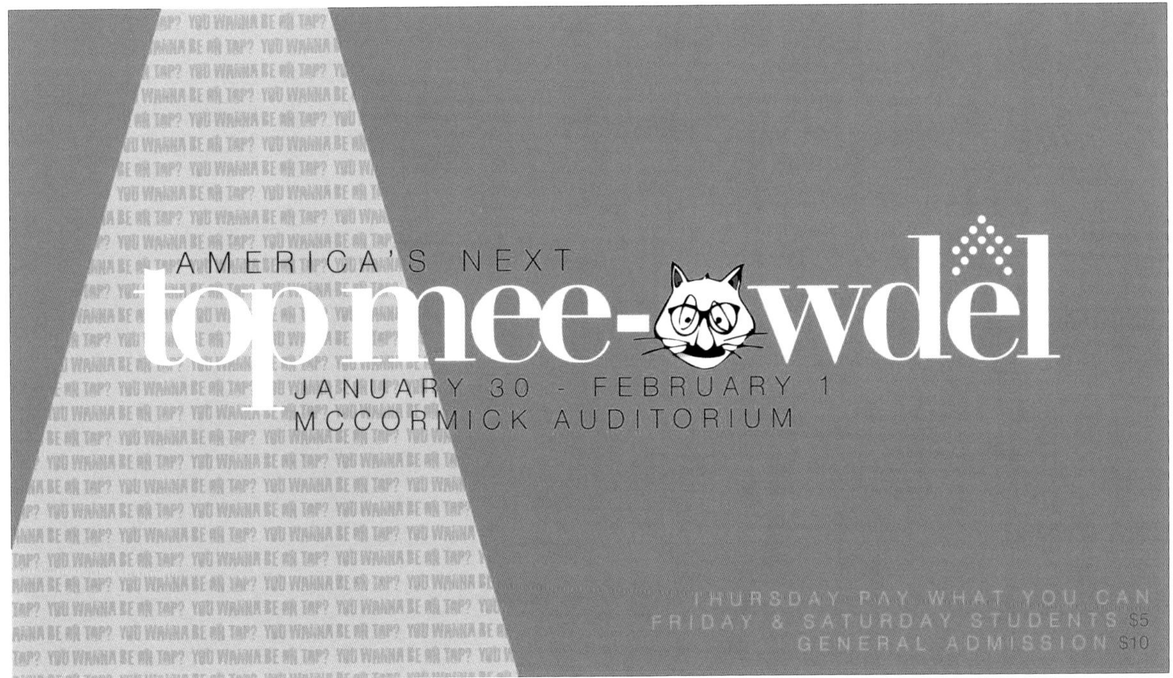

Returning cast members Jake Curtis and Ross Turkington codirected and performed. Other returning cast members included Willa Barnett and Jasmine Sharma. The new cast members were Arshad Baruti, Sydney Feyder, Carly Griffin-Fiorella, Carden Katz, and Graham Kirstein. Singers were announced on Facebook as Christina Carty and Emily Somé.

Curtis explained his approach as director:

> The show won't work unless we can make everyone feel safe and happy in the room. That's the only thing we can do. That's got to be priority number one for us. We would take people aside outside of rehearsals

THIS YEAR IN HISTORY

Trump claims COVID-19 "totally under control" • US withdrawal from Afghanistan begins • WHO declares COVID-19 pandemic • Stock market crash • Pandemic lockdowns • US suspends funding of WHO • George Floyd murder, widespread protests • FDA issues emergency use authorization for COVID-19 vaccine • Dow Jones year-end close 30,606 • Average new car $27,567 • 1 gallon gas $2.24 • *Tenet*, *Dolittle*, *Bad Boys for Life* • Phoebe Bridgers, *Punisher*; Taylor Swift, *Folklore*; The Weeknd, *After Hours*; Dua Lipa, *Future Nostalgia*

2020

and check in with everyone as much as we could. We would have a talk with them if we felt like the way they were acting wasn't helping. Because sometimes people's body language can be giving off a rough energy, or [we'd say], "Hey, sometimes when you phrase feedback like this, it's kind of tough to take or sounds a bit like you're attacking the person." So to really keep a watchful eye on the way we were talking, on the way we were approaching things, on the way sketches were coming about, on the way we were treating our cast members. Because when you're rehearsing for forty hours a week, you can't rely on good behavior. Everyone's getting down to a pretty depraved version of themselves. It does need a watchful eye and that's the role of the director. These are talented, funny people. They'll come up with great material if they can. It's your job to clear the way of obstacles. . . .

There was a time during COVID—which was obviously just such a tough time for Mee-Ow and any group—where they lowered the rehearsal time, which made sense. I was still around that year and got to see that it really affected the way the people engaged. You saw people start questioning the seriousness and commitment to the group because it's this all-or-nothing thing. I think by being able to put your all into it, you're able to treat yourself like a professional and say, I'm going to make this good. Because it's so easy when making any comedy thing to go halfway and get embarrassed and kind of bail, or to just tell yourself it'll be funnier on the day. Mee-Ow really allowed me to be like, "No, this is what I want to do. One day I want someone to pay me for this. I'm going to really work at it."

Why Freshmen Are Almost Never Cast in Mee-Ow

Jake Curtis explained:

That was one of our rules because we felt it was too intense of a commitment to ask from a freshman realistically and kindly, and also too much of a commitment that they were signing up for four years of Mee-Ow without having really seen a Mee-Ow show. That's not really a good decision. Most of the years I was on Mee-Ow at least seven out of the nine people intended to work somehow in media, performance, writing. There was always a couple who were like, "I'm really funny and then I'm going to be a lawyer." But for most people if you were going to commit so much time, you're probably only going to do that because really that's what you want to do. Because it did damage your academics and it damaged your social stuff. So, it had to be the thing you really wanted to do.

Choosing the names of the shows was a creative early morning process. The title *America's Next Top Mee-Owdel* parodied the popular television competition show, and *Mee-Owddle School Dance: Unchaperoned* parodied the adolescent ritual of middle school dances while incorrectly implying that those were always closely chaperoned.

According to Curtis, everyone "really kind of stepped up [their writing]" following the first show. "And it was a lovely thing when you feel people really start to get more of a grip on themselves as writers. We were talking, we were doing more like writing-exercise things, trying to get people going, working together. So people just started bringing these really strong sketches. I remember night after night, just being really excited."

The Show Highlights

Entering McCormick Auditorium, the audience saw the primarily white set of *America's Next Top Mee-Owdel*. Panels covered in a random pattern of rectangular, wavy-textured blocks were set at angles with inset, draped doorways framing the cat's head Mee-Ow logo centered at the top above a curtained doorway. The floor had a taped "runway" in white outlined in black.

For the opening sketch, the cast began at the back of McCormick Auditorium. Curtis recalled, "We all model-walked down the big stairs of McCormick and then we were all pop culture figures. One guy was Pete Buttigieg, because it was when he was kind of relevant in that two months while he was running for president. It was tough to fill McCormick with enough energy, so I think everyone was a little disappointed with how the shows had felt. We had one or two really great ones."

This year included a single dance break in lieu of an intermission, a format that has continued. As Curtis explained,

> We thought, let's bring the band into as many of the sketches and songs as we can, because it's ridiculous that we do an hour and a half show with ten incredible musicians sitting down watching. So why don't we try doing like funny song moments in between the sketches, just like little ten-second musical bits, playing fun theme songs or relevant songs to the sketch, ironic songs for the sketch that just happened. Like we'd have one dude playing the solo from [the 2014 film] *Whiplash* and then another one of the band did a J. K. Simmons impression like, "Not quite my tempo!" They'd play the SpongeBob theme song and the whole audience would sing along. We did that and had them play in more sketches. And we started adding some musical improv games to the improv sections. During the one dance break we would each do a song.

Kirstein, whom Curtis described as one of the most talented performers he had seen in Mee-Ow, played a priest in a sketch written by Curtis (who remarked that he "wrote too many priest sketches").

> He would get everyone to stand up and hold hands and promise to the person next to them, "You can stand with my faith," and they would repeat, "You can stand with my faith." And he would say, "You can walk with my faith," and they would repeat, "You can walk with my faith." Then he said, "You can sit on my faith." And the audience said, "You can sit on my faith." Then he would get the whole crowd going: "Sit on my faith! Sit on my faith!" It was only a moderately funny sketch on paper. The emphasis on having to be a strong performer is really something that differentiated [Mee-Ow] when we were doing it. It makes it such a different experience because I know what I write will be done well.

The opening of *Mee-Owdle School Dance: Unchaperoned* depicted a middle school dance. Later, Curtis and Sharma performed a parody of the Billy Joel song "We Didn't Start the Fire" called "We Didn't Just Forget You," about celebrities who should be in jail, with a slideshow of the names of each of the celebrities.

Katz wrote and performed a sketch revolving around the Hasbro Bop It! game, which is a device with motion-sensing technology that issues random commands to the players, such as *Drink it*, *Hammer it*, or *Sing it*, which the players have to act out. The commands get faster as the game proceeds. As Curtis described it:

> The game said, "Bop it" and he bopped it, "Pull it" and he pulled it. It said, "Pick it up" and he reached into a box and picked up a toy gun. And then it said, "Fire" and he fired the toy gun. And then he walked off. The lights went dark and the audio came over the speakers saying, "President John F. Kennedy was shot today in Dallas, Texas," and the whole audience went, "Ooooh!" That's what I love with Mee-Ow, [when] the audience buys it enough that you get a big reaction. They're there for it.

2020

Sydney Feyder and Arshad Baruti in a promotional video

Graham Kirstein, Carden Katz, Willa Barnett, and Ross Turkington in a promotional video

2021

MEE-OW YEAR FORTY-EIGHT

Due to the COVID-19 pandemic, the Mee-Ow Show was not performed for an in-person audience. In lieu of in-person shows, recorded sketches and live online improv were presented. The proposed title of an unproduced web series was *Get Mee-Owt of My Head!!*

Preserving the Mee-Ow Culture

The seniors in the cast were concerned that the lack of a live performance as well as the extra preparation and changes to process required to put the show together in a new format would keep them from teaching the newer cast members how to make the Mee-Ow Show work. So in addition to online auditions and the usual initiations of new cast members, Mee-Ow held rehearsals on Zoom from 6 to 10 p.m., five days per week. They wrote sketches and chose a show title. Although they were never able to post a full show online, they continued the process in order to pass on the institutional memory of how to create and produce Mee-Ow to the cast who would return the following year.

In March 2020, about ten days after the final Mee-Ow Show performance that year, the university shut down all in-person classes and live performances due to the COVID-19 pandemic, as was done at universities across the country.

In an article in the *Daily Northwestern* on April 4, 2022, Nora Collins described the timeline of the university's response. Between March 11 and 13, 2020, the university began to transition to online classes and announced its first COVID-19 case. "University President Morton Schapiro announced all Spring Quarter classes will be held remotely for at least three weeks and Spring Break would be extended by one week."

One week later, it was announced that "all undergraduate professors must make finals optional. Governor J. B. Pritzker issued a 'stay-at-home' order for the state. . . . Commencement ceremonies and graduation-related events were held online for the Class of 2020. The University announced it intends to hold in-person graduation ceremonies for the Class of 2020 in Spring 2021. . . . Administrators announced updated plans for Fall Quarter 2020, stating first- and second-year undergraduates are not allowed on campus and are discouraged from moving to the Evanston area during Fall Quarter."

For the first time since 1974, there was no in-person, public performance of the Mee-Ow Show.

In the midst of uncertainty about the duration of the shutdown and limitations, Mee-Ow had to get creative.

Returning cast members Arshad Baruti, Carly Griffin-Fiorella, and Jasmine Sharma codirected and performed. Other returning cast members included Willa Barnett and Carden Katz. The new cast members—Sam Buttress, Anelga

THIS YEAR IN HISTORY

January 6 insurrection attack • Second Trump impeachment • Biden inaugurated • US rejoins Paris Climate Agreement • Russian military on Ukraine border • US ends Afghanistan operations • James Webb Space Telescope launched • COVID-19 deaths worldwide hit 5 million • Dow Jones year-end close 36,338 • Average new car $30,113 • 1 gallon gas $3.13 • *Spider-Man: No Way Home*, *No Time to Die*, *Shang-Chi and the Legend of the Ten Rings* • Tyler, the Creator, *Call Me If You Get Lost*; Weezer, *OK Human*

Hajjar, and Emily Pate-Somé (who was the singer the previous year)—had been announced in a post on Facebook on October 5, 2020. Zoom "meet and greets" and auditions were announced on Facebook. These were held due to the prohibition of in-person meetings because of the pandemic.

> *Welcome to a brand new year of Mee-Ow! Big stuff coming up . . . so keep reading.*
>
> *Zoom meet and greets will be on Friday, September 25th. There will be 3 sessions:*
>
> > *- 10:00 a.m.*
> >
> > *- 6:00 p.m.*
> >
> > *- 10:00 p.m.*
>
> *Links to the zoom meetings will be posted that Friday!*
>
> *A Google form application will be posted to this event page on Thursday, September 24th, but all materials will be due on Friday, Oct 2nd by midnight . . . which makes it the 3rd? Who knows!*
>
> *If you want to get a head start, applications will ask you for:*
>
> > *- 2 original sketches*
> >
> > *- A self-tape of 30 seconds of what you think is funny. That can mean sitting in silence, a bad pick up line, or eating cereal*
> >
> > *- A short form of *fun!* questions*

On February 18, 2021, producer Lily Feinberg introduced a Zoom video that was posted to the YouTube channel of the Office of Student Organizations & Activities (SOA). In this recorded Zoom, the cast of Mee-Ow performed improv games live as a part of SOA's virtual Mardi Gras event.

On May 16, 2021, Mee-Ow posted: "Exciting news, Mee-Ow Nation! Each day this week, we will be releasing a new sketch that we filmed this year over Zoom! Keep an eye out here for the first one tomorrow at 7 p.m. If you enjoy them, please clap! No matter where you are, just clap and we will hear it 😼. That's all for now Mee-Ow Kingdom, stay perfect!"

As it turned out, the first video sketch was posted May 18, 2021, on Facebook. The beginning featured a Mee-Ow logo in the style of the MTV logo, with a large M, similar to the MTV M, and EE-OW where the letters TV appear.

"Trix" was a blackout sketch done via Zoom in which Hajjar asks Buttress about the meaning of the word "dominatrix." The sketch was written by Katz and edited by Baruti.

The second sketch was posted with the message, "Happy Tuesday . . . have you guys seen Bridgerton yet?"

"Bridgerton," another blackout sketch via Zoom, featured a central figure who instructs the writers of the popular television show *Bridgerton* to "spice up" the scripts for the first season, which presumably is yet to be filmed. One of the writers, whose camera is not on, suggests many of the sex scenes that actually occur on the show. The sketch was written and directed by Sharma and edited by Baruti.

2022

MEE-OW YEAR FORTY-NINE

How Do They Pee in Mee-Owter Space?

Thursday, January 27, at 7 p.m.; Friday and Saturday, January 28–29, at 7 and 10 p.m., Shanley Pavilion

Mee-Ow You See Me

Thursday, February 24, at 9 p.m.; Friday, February 25, at 10 p.m.; Saturday, February 26, at 7 and 10 p.m., Shanley Pavilion

Returning cast members Sam Buttress and Carden Katz codirected and performed. The other returning cast members included Anelga Hajjar and Emily Somé. The new cast members were Liv Drury, Justin Kuhn, Orly Lewittes, Alondra Rios, and Jared Zavala.

Liv Drury explained how she was notified that she was cast. "I got a phone call from Carden [Katz], who said, 'Oh, we still are deciding between improv people. We need you to come and do one last round of auditions at Sam's house.' And I was like, 'OK.' And then we showed up and they were like, 'We've got to hurry up! We've got another group coming!' And then they faked an argument and they're like, 'You're on the show!' "

How Do They Pee in Mee-Owter Space? spoofs one of the questions most frequently asked by children of astronauts. A Facebook post promoting the show stated, "One small step for mee, one large step for ow-kind." *Mee-Ow You See Me* parodies *Now You See Me,* a 2013 film about a team of magicians who use their skills to commit bank robberies and are pursued by the FBI.

Buttress described the challenges of the rehearsal process and writing of the show during the continuing pandemic. "Fall quarter after casting, we only met once a week and did improv mostly, and had one meeting where people brought in sketches. And then beginning the first Monday of winter quarter, we were rehearsing four hours, five nights a week. The first week was on Zoom and then we did a week in someone's basement, but some people were still on Zoom. Then we were in person for a while, and then a couple of people got sick and we were back on Zoom for a while."

2022

THIS YEAR IN HISTORY

Beijing Winter Olympics • Russia invades Ukraine • COVID-19 deaths worldwide top 6 million • SCOTUS overturns *Roe v. Wade* • Europe heat waves • January 6 Committee votes to prosecute Trump and John Eastman • Elon Musk buys Twitter • Dow Jones year-end close 33,147 • Average new car $32,596 • 1 gallon gas peaked at $4.49 • *Top Gun: Maverick*, *The Batman* • Bad Bunny, *Un Verano Sin Ti*; Beyoncé, *Renaissance*; Taylor Swift, *Midnights*; Harry Styles, *Harry's House*; Megan Thee Stallion, *Traumazine*

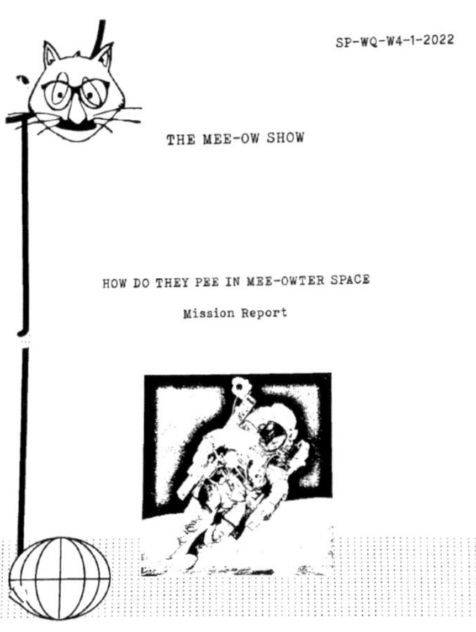

Jared Zavala in Mee-Owter space and the show program

Hajjar continued, "This quarter in particular, 6 to 10 p.m. you're writing sketches and really working, and I had to restrict how much I was partying because I didn't want to get COVID before the show. I was like, I'm not partying until the show is over."

"Because you don't want to give [COVID] to your friends in Mee-Ow," Buttress added.

Fortunately, no one was sick during the show.

Due either to an oversight in scheduling or to the Norris Center's continued policy response to the increased number of groups wanting space, both Mee-Ow Shows were again in Shanley Pavilion. Of the differences performing in the two spaces, Buttress said, "They still do the dance party at McCormick. Everybody gets on the stage, but it just feels less like a dance floor. There's something inherent in Shanley, because I've done other shows in Shanley, and I've gone to Shanley shows—that because it's not of Northwestern itself, it feels more almost grungy, like people feel like they are on the same level and that they can play and have more fun than in more institutional rooms like in Norris. There it feels like, yeah, we're dancing, having fun, but within the confines of the institution."

Drury added, "Yeah. It feels like nobody at university can touch you in Shanley. You can say whatever you want. We always say that every [year's] show paints the floor for their show. We always think, how much smaller has Shanley gotten over the years?"

New this year was the use of the mobile payment system Venmo to pay for admission at the door. Mee-Ow requested that the Arts Alliance approve this method of payment.

2022

Emily Somé, Sam Buttress, and Anelga Hajjar

JUSTIN BARBIN

The Show Highlights

Both shows began with a series of sketches based on the theme, and transitioned into a musical number featuring the entire cast.

Mee-Ow You See Me opened with Hajjar introducing herself as Alex Russo, the character portrayed by Selena Gomez on the 2007–12 television series *The Wizards of Waverly Place*. She set up the first magic act, "Pontificus the Escaper," followed by "Todd the Magnificent." Todd's ex-girlfriend shouted from offstage, "Not so magnificent in the sack!" They then argued. The next magic act was "Goob the Mindbender," who couldn't proceed with her act because, as she tearfully announced to the audience, her dog was just put down at the vet. She tried to continue, but each thing she did reminded her of her dog. After Alex Russo reminded the audience that no children were allowed onstage, she introduced the next magic act as "Richard Parker," played by Lewittes on the shoulders of Buttress wearing an extra-long trench coat and entering the stage as two children pretending to be an adult. The next act was "Pedronius the Wise" with her ventriloquist dummy, which led into the opening dance number featuring the entire cast.

Another sketch included Drury and Katz as Australian wildlife experts in a parody of TV host and conservationist Steve Irwin, "The Crocodile Hunter." Wearing Australian slouch hats, khakis, and binoculars, they viewed a series of photos on an onstage monitor. They spoke in thick Aussie accents, analyzing the behavior of junior high school students who were using the social media app Snapchat.

Another featured Drury behaving badly, but excusing her behavior by saying, "I'm on my period." Every time another cast member came onstage and commented on her increasingly outrageous bad behavior, the other cast members would say, in unison, "But she's on her period." No one in the sketch reacted squeamishly to this information, so the punch line was when Hajjar announced she was going through menopause and the other cast members, in unison, said, "Ewww!"

One tightly written and well-rehearsed sketch featured Buttress and Lewittes as best-friend dock workers who know each other so well that they say phrases simultaneously. The scene ended with a transition to a dance break with the audience, held in lieu of intermission.

2022

JUSTIN BARBIN

The opening musical number: Drury, Kuhn, Rios, Hajjar, Lewittes, Somé, and Katz

JUSTIN BARBIN

Sam Buttress and Orly Lewittes as dock workers

2023

MEE-OW YEAR FIFTY

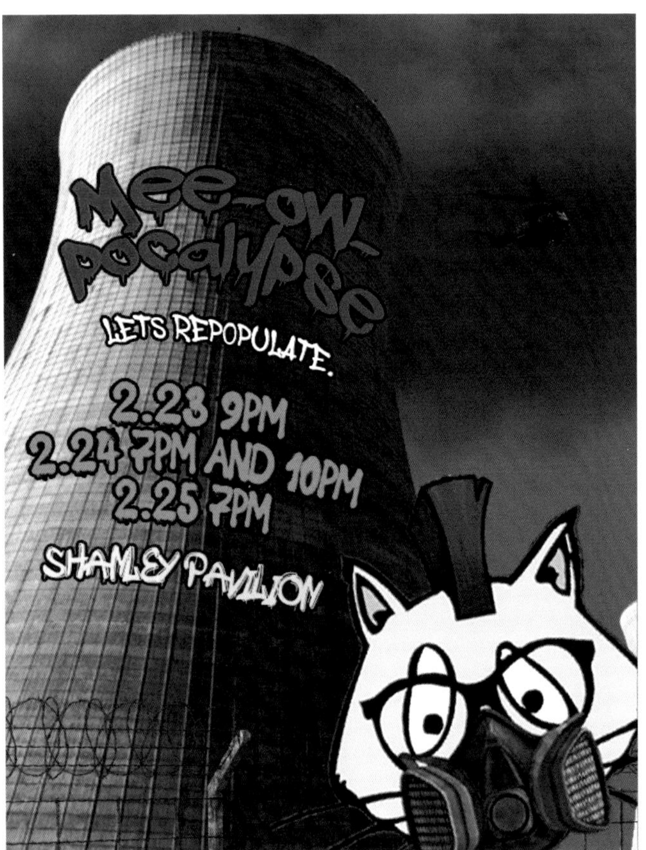

Mee-Owgic Mike's Last Dance

Thursday, January 26, at 9 p.m.; Friday, January 27, at 7 and 10 p.m.; Sunday, January 28, at 7 p.m., McCormick Auditorium

Mee-Owpocalypse: Let's Repopulate

Thursday, February 23, at 9 p.m.; Friday, February 24, at 7 and 10 p.m.; Saturday, February 25, at 7 p.m., Shanley Pavilion

Returning cast members Liv Drury and Anelga Hajjar codirected and performed. The other returning cast members included the previous year's codirector Sam Buttress, Orly Lewittes, and Alondra Rios. New cast members were announced on Instagram on October 16, 2022, and included Brenden Dahl, Arjun Kumar, and Ferd Moscat.

The movie *Magic Mike's Last Dance* was just about to be released. Buttress said he saw the trailer a few weeks before it was time to name the show.

> I was too busy to see it when it came out, but I was like, this looks like so much fun. It's people splashing around onstage and doing their sexy dances. And I really like Channing Tatum. I feel like every once in a while I just pick a movie that's coming out to be really into and it happened to be this. Then I realized, oh, Magic Mike could be Mee-Owgic Mike. I originally wanted to call it "Mee-Owgic Mike's Second to Last Dance," because his last dance would be a few weeks later when the movie came out. But then everyone else agreed that was perhaps too wordy.

"Something kind of funny happened this time around," Hajjar said of the naming process.

> The way we pick the show themes is that we meet at our last rehearsal in fall quarter, because winter quarter, we're really just writing and having writers' room rehearsals. But fall quarter, we have a final rehearsal where we just pitch show titles and names. And really the only requirement is that it feels exciting for us. Also, we're only going to have

THIS YEAR IN HISTORY

Jair Bolsonaro supporters storm Brazilian congress • US shoots down spy balloons • Ohio train derailment • King Charles III coronation • Oct. 7 Hamas attack on Israel • Dow Jones year-end close 37,690 • Average new car $31,410 • 1 gallon gas $3.52 • *Barbie*, *Oppenheimer*, *John Wick: Chapter 4* • Hozier, *Unreal Unearth*; Bob Dylan, *Shadow Kingdom*; Miley Cyrus, *Endless Summer Vacation*; Olivia Rodrigo, *GUTS*

2023

> one sketch really that pertains to the show title, which would be our opener. Then we just need a set. We need to give something to our set designer that is the overarching theme of the show. Can you make a set that evokes Magic Mike or evokes apocalypse? So something kind of funny happened this year where we named the first show thinking that *Magic Mike's Last Dance* would be more in the zeitgeist. And yet, nobody was even caring about that movie. But then we did *Mee-Owpocalypse* just because we were like, that's fun. We do our performances in Shanley Pavilion, which is literally like a glorified bomb shelter. And it feels appropriate to make it look like an apocalypse scene. But [the Netflix series] *The Last of Us* was getting a lot of traction, so people thought that was us having a finger on the cultural pulse. But that just happened to be convenient.

As in the previous year, every cast member was expected to bring in two sketches per day, and the development process was five rehearsals a week for eight weeks.

The Show Highlights

Entering McCormick Auditorium, the audience saw the stage set for *Mee-Owgic Mike's Last Dance*, which included a lighted platform with a black backdrop with a graphic of the Mee-Ow cat logo, tilted to the left and outlined in lights, next to a graphic of a martini glass tilted to the right. A door outlined in lights was stage left, and the simple set included several vertical flats for entrances and exits.

The show opened with a popular song performed by the band and singers to an appreciative audience. Then the lights dimmed. After the obligatory announcements about exits and a dance break, the band began playing "Lady Marmalade," with its recurring lyric, "Voulez-vous coucher avec moi?," first made famous by the group LaBelle (who performed it at Northwestern in 1975). The lights outlining the cat logo and the door flashed and changed color in time with the music.

The lights came up onstage for the opening, title-themed sketch, written by Drury and Hajjar, who said, "We thought Magic Mike was a perfect framing for everyone in the cast to have a featured little moment." Lewittes and Moscat sat on two chairs facing the audience, talking about their disappointment with the strippers they'd seen at this strip club. Hajjar announced over the speakers, "The hottest lineup of dancers this evening. There won't be a dry seat in the house." Then Buttress dressed as a construction worker and Kumar as a real estate agent danced onto the stage, proclaiming that they were "looking to spoil a girl rotten." Moscat recognized them as the TV hosts of *Property Brothers*. Buttress and Kumar made suggestive, double entendre statements about properties and construction while giving lap dances.

Hajjar announced and played as the next dancer. As she entered, Lewittes shouted, "Mom?" Hajjar then lectured Lewittes about being at a strip club, using parental clichés, such as "If all your friends did it . . ." and "Don't make me turn this car around."

The next stripper announced was Drury as actor Timothée Chalamet, who was portrayed as unsuited to being a stripper.

The offstage announcer said, "Do you like amateur porn? Watching real couples go at it? Then get ready for our real-life, hot sexy couple, Zeke and Marianna!" Dahl and Rios entered through the lighted door stage left in mid-argument with each other about having tried to conceive for the

2023

last ten months. When Moscat said, "Aren't we supposed to be getting a lap dance over here?" Dahl and Rios moved over to the two chairs and kept arguing while lap dancing. They resolved their argument, hugged, and left the stage.

Lewittes said, "You know what would get me going? A group of eight hot, hot strippers." Then the stage lights turned red, all the cast donned their Mee-Ow jackets, the band started playing "Candy Shop" by 50 Cent, and the entire cast started a dance in the style of the movie *Magic Mike.*

Drury said that the opening of *Mee-Owpocalypse* "had less of a framing device. It was more just like different vignettes of different people in the apocalypse, but still had everyone featured for a moment. They were kind of unrelated. Sam played a zombie who was the zombie of Anelga's ex-boyfriend. Arjun and Orly played these friends in a bunker. Arjun played a character who was just really out of breath from all the running in the apocalypse. Two of our other members played like influencer types, and I played like somebody who got left behind." Hajjar chimed in, "Yeah, we were mapping the pandemic onto an apocalypse with influencers."

The opening sketch concluded with a dance number featuring the entire cast.

Reviews

Selena Kuznikov wrote of *Mee-Owgic Mike's Last Dance* in the *Daily Northwestern*, "Opening with a performance from the Mee-Ow band to get the crowd pumped up, the group smashed its first two-hour long show of the weekend."

The program cover, designed by Nick Hollenbeck, parodying the movie *Magic Mike's Last Dance*

2024

MEE-OW YEAR FIFTY-ONE
(THE FIFTIETH ANNIVERSARY SHOW)

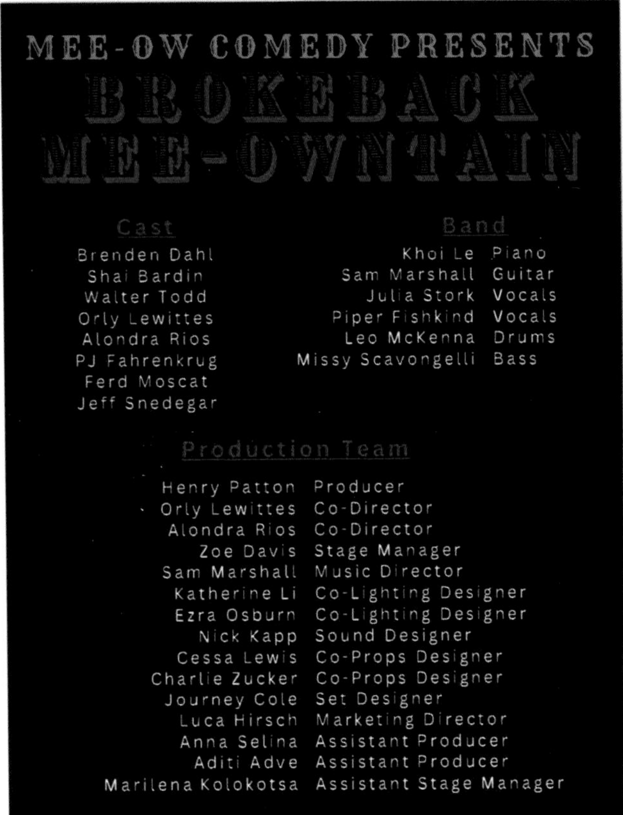

Mee-Owd Life Crisis: Mee-Ow Turns 50!

Thursday, January 25, at 9 p.m.; Friday, January 26, at 7 and 9:30 p.m.; Saturday, January 27, at 8 p.m., McCormick Auditorium

Brokeback Mee-Owntain

Thursday, February 22, at 9 p.m.; Friday, February 23, at 7 and 10 p.m.; Saturday, February 24, at 8 p.m., Shanley Pavilion

Returning cast members Orly Lewittes and Alondra Rios codirected and performed. The other returning cast members included Brenden Dahl and Ferd Moscat. New cast members were announced on Instagram on October 24, 2023, and included Shai Bardin, PJ Fahrenkrug, Jeff Snedegar, and Walter Todd.

The January shows were titled *Mee-Owd Life Crisis: Mee-Ow Turns 50!* in recognition of the show's fiftieth anniversary. The February show's title, *Brokeback Mee-Owntain*, was a pun on the groundbreaking 2005 film starring Heath Ledger and Jake Gyllenhaal as two cowboys who fall in love. Predictably, in the parody, there were lots of sexual references and easy punchlines.

But the funniest sketches weren't about that.

The Show Highlights

The opening sketch of *Mee-Owd Life Crisis* was a series of quick vignettes of stereotypes about fifty-year-olds, including mentions of adult diapers, back pain, pill organizers, dysfunctional marriages, obsolete technology, and menopause, that then transitioned into the now traditional dance number featuring the entire cast.

Sketches included "Acceptance Speech," written by Moscat, about a Tony Award acceptance speech; "Cobb Salad," written by Lewittes, about three women at lunch; "Eyeliner," by Bardin, about a man at a makeup sales counter buying a gift for his girlfriend; "Interpreter," by Rios, about a ten-year-old boy interpreting for his Spanish-speaking mother, who receives phone calls from a bank, a veterinarian, a lawyer, the mother's lover, and a clinic; "Word Problems," written by Lewittes, about a middle-school math class; and "Saw," a

2024

Shai Bardin (*left*); Orly Lewittes and Brenden Dahl (*below*)

parody of the horror film, with the perpetrator as an aspiring stand-up comedian.

The show also included short blackouts about a couple at a fertility doctor's office; one of the elves finding Santa's name on the naughty list; and "Slut Strands," by Bardin, in which a woman and an Orthodox Jew separately primp in front of bathroom mirrors, using the same gestures.

For *Brokeback Mee-Owntain*, the band started promptly and played popular music, country and western, and classic rock for six minutes, warming up and exciting the crowd. The two singers were in excellent voice, belting out tunes including "Jolene" and "Southern Nights."

The first song the band played was "Sweet Home Alabama." The audience reaction indicated that they took this for an intentional commentary on the Alabama Supreme Court decision earlier in the week, ruling embryos to be children. However, the producer said that this was not the case.

The opening sketch was a collection of alternating vignettes, including one depicting the cowboys from *Brokeback Mountain* and their concerns about their camp diet, a stereotypical can of beans. This transitioned into an opening dance with the entire cast, while the band played "Save a Horse (Ride a Cowboy)."

The first improv of the evening was "New Choice."

Highlights of the show included a sketch about a boss who invites an up-and-coming employee to share some excellent scotch to celebrate. The boss keeps talking about how exceptional the scotch is, but has an increasingly negative, physical adverse reaction every time he takes a sip. This was one of the few examples of highly physical comedy.

Another sketch depicted a funeral where friends of the deceased each spoke about how much they loved her, but also talked about her flaws.

In one sketch, Todd asks farmer Dahl for directions. Dahl responds in a thick Southern country accent, giving directions in folksy phrasings. Finally, a frustrated Todd Googles directions on his phone. Google responds with directions that repeat the farmer's folksy gibberish.

A sad, touching, and hopeful sketch had Fahrenkrug as a character wearing a pig nose and lipstick who says only "oink," crying in a restroom while other girls go in and out dropping phrases such as "sweating like a pig," leaving her in tears. Finally, one girl says, "When pigs fly," and Fahrenkrug smiles. The band breaks into the upbeat tune "Fight Song."

Clever wordplay featured in a sketch that also commented on a current political issue by depicting a school principal telling the teaching staff that because of the "don't say gay bill," there would be "no more homo stuff." Bardin, as the English teacher, jumps up, saying, "I teach homophones." She then uses poster boards on an easel to ask for clarification of homophones, such as "Do you mean 'allowed' or 'aloud'?" every time the principal says something.

One recurring punch line featured Bardin breaking into the Grace VanderWaal song "I Don't Know My Name," while playing a ukulele.

And yes, there were dick jokes too.

The cast certainly knew their audience, who found the entire show enormously entertaining.

The last show of this fiftieth-anniversary year joyfully concluded with the entire cast taking bows to enthusiastic applause and the directors receiving flowers from the cast and thanking their producer, as well as Joseph Radding, one of the authors of this book, for his participation in the beginnings of the Mee-Ow Show.

JAY TOWNS

PJ Farhrenkrug, Jeff Snedegar, Walter Todd, Orly Lewittes, and Ferd Moscat

2024

JAY TOWNS

Shai Bardin teaches homophones in a skit skewering "Don't Say Gay" bills

JAY TOWNS

Walter Todd and Brenden Dahl (*left*); Alondra Rios (*right*)

JAY TOWNS

PJ Farhrenkrug

JILL FOOTLICK

7 The Legacy, Influence, and Future of the Mee-Ow Show and Its People

Our intention was never simply to catalog the names, dates, and places of Mee-Ow's history. We were, instead, looking for what insights we could glean from the stories, documents, scripts, programs, data, and minutiae of Mee-Ow, and especially the first-person, contemporaneous account of participants, taken together as a whole. Here we reflect on the legacy and influence of Mee-Ow, and on its possible futures.

Facing page, the 1985 cast: (*top*) Dermot Mulroney, Beth Bash, and Romy Rosemont; (*middle*) Allyson Rice and Craig Bierko, in baseball cap; (*bottom*) Richard Kaplan, Richard Radutzky, and Karen Schiff

The Mee-Ow Show began as a way to honor the intellectual contributions of students. They would have control over their work from conception through execution.

The entrepreneurial mindset of the creators of the first Mee-Ow Show endured and proliferated. Mee-Ow participants and other students formed their own improv groups, theater companies, sketch groups, and other enterprises.

"We'll make it ourselves into what *we* think it should be" could be the subtitle of this book. That approach persists, as students write, create, perform, film, and record their own works without waiting for permission.

This creative spirit has always been at odds with regimentation and limitation, which are unfortunately and paradoxically often found in a university. But creativity is not at odds with discipline, and the Mee-Ow creators have often demonstrated exemplary discipline and collaboration in their approach to their work. This discipline is not externally imposed, however. Rather, it is born out of a sense of mutual respect and responsibility to the group endeavor.

As Mee-Ow evolved into its now recognizable format as a sketch comedy and improv show, that original purpose matured into a collaborative and dedicated enterprise. As that happened, Mee-Ow became a professional launching pad for the careers of hundreds of entertainment professionals. It also became clear that the skills of collaboration, listening, communication, storytelling, and improv were important tools for many Mee-Ow alums whose careers were in other professions.

Scholars have studied the interaction and balance between formal structures (an organization's rules and regulations) and informal structures (social relationships and networks) that define the creative potential of an organization. While these studies generally have focused on commercial organizations, their observations apply here, because the limitations of the formal structures of the university gave rise to the fellowship of Mee-Ow, which in turn developed its own formal and informal structures. And, possibly in response, or at least in recognition, the university developed additional infrastructure and formal programs of study.

The social relationships and networks that Mee-Ow developed have been one of the keys to its enduring success.

The recurring question throughout its history is how Mee-Ow retained the rebellious impulse that led to its creation, while also growing into a recognized institution.

In many ways the story of Mee-Ow is the story of creativity during the tumultuous last quarter of the twentieth century and the uncertain first quarter of the twenty-first.

A Few Surprises

In the process of researching and writing, we've talked with more than a hundred Mee-Ow alums, including cast, crew, staff, and musicians. We also spoke with Mee-Ow-adjacent people, whose paths intersected with Mee-Ow. We originally thought we were writing a history; we found something else.

We discovered that the story of Mee-Ow has reflected the larger concerns of society. Mee-Ow has at times been political, satirical social commentary ranging from national to local issues—absurdist, downright silly, and sometimes touching. But always funny and memorable.

We expected the many conversations we've had with people from throughout Mee-Ow's history to be reflective, or perhaps even nostalgic. What we did not expect were the conversations that were regretful, or painful, or cathartic, or healing, or restorative.

We also discovered how frequently the Mee-Ow Show has reinvented itself, sometimes by recreating what had been done before. Perhaps this book can serve as a source of ideas and inspiration to future casts and creators, as history has so frequently done.

As we've pointed out to several people, their participation in Mee-Ow was when they were undergraduates, mostly between the ages of seventeen and twenty-two. Looking back on your life at that age should be done with kindness, with a willingness to forgive yourself for decisions you would not make with hindsight and the wisdom of age.

JUSTIN BARBIN

Orly Lewittes singing with the Mee-Ow Show band in 2022; Noah Rabinovitch (bass), Tabor Brewster (drums), and Sam Marshall (guitar)

Many people told us that the Mee-Ow Show was one of the most meaningful experiences of their lives. For some, Mee-Ow helped set the course of their professional career. For others, there were skills they learned that they applied to professions unrelated to performing or show business. And for many, their closest, lifelong friendships are the ones they made in Mee-Ow.

Those friendships and the expansive network of alums are one of the most important and enduring legacies of the Mee-Ow Show.

Recurring Themes

Several recurring themes have continued in sketches and shows throughout the years, beginning with the very first show. These include political satire (sketches about Nixon, the Bush presidencies, Trump, war, patriotism, media fearmongering), social commentary (sexism, homophobia), local issues (campus life, Evanston), the absurdity of life, wordplay (title puns, phrasal overlap portmanteaux, "New Choice" improv), parodies of popular culture ("Who's on First," "Schlepardy," sitcoms, movies, magic shows), physical and rambunctious humor ("Cartwheels and Somersaults," "O2 Deprivation"), and high-energy, witty improvisation. Music has also been an important component of Mee-Ow, from the thirteen-piece orchestra of the first show and the pianists who were regarded as integral members of the cast, to the solos sung by the cast with the band and the rock-and-roll bands and singers that now represent one third of the show.

Influence

Many of the Mee-Ow alums we interviewed said the show launched their career, and often their professional collaborations, and was certainly the vehicle through which they discovered their confidence. Many other groups arose, either inspired by or in reaction to Mee-Ow, which over time became a small and elite company of performers. These groups include those on campus (The No Fun Mud Piranhas, Out Da Box, The Titanic Players, Griffin's Tale, The Bix, The Blackout, NSTV) as well as professional groups (The Practical Theatre, Boom Chicago, Whose Line Is It Anyway, Story Pirates). Mee-Ow alums have also contributed to *Saturday Night Live* as performers and writers, and as improv performers in Upright Citizens Brigade, iO, and Second City. Many professionals began mastering their own writing process at Mee-Ow.

The University Redeemed

The mismatch between what the university promises its students and the reality of the student experience partially inspired the rebellious creativity that led to the creation of the Mee-Ow Show. However, Mee-Ow cannot claim to be solely responsible for the improvements in infrastructure, performance opportunities, and instructional programming that have occurred over the years, including a Comedy Arts module for Radio/Television/Film students that includes Mee-Ow as a recommended student group. Certainly, many of the newer generations of faculty since the inception of Mee-Ow have embodied that same creative energy and entrepreneurial spirit, so much so that by the turn of the new century, Northwestern was, in the words of Kristen Schaal, "a great, creative, lovely place to be. There were so many student productions, student groups. If you wanted to be a performer or work onstage, or if you wanted to be involved in a production, you could."

Institutional Memory and Reinvention

Certainly the first few years of Mee-Ow were a creative exploration. Although the focus of the show soon became sketch comedy, its content and format continued to evolve, first with the addition of improv, and later with the reintroduction of a house band. It was only after decades that the current format of one-third sketch, one-third improv, and one-third rock and roll, along with the expectation that codirectors would also write and perform, became established.

Every few years, the creators of the show have introduced changes to the audition process (an application package, separate band and singer auditions) or the writing process (a required number of sketches brought in rather than solely developed through improv).

While the current practice of casting a sophomore, two juniors, and a senior in addition to the returning cast does provide for a certain amount of institutional memory, it still allows for change over time. A change made one year is repeated and soon becomes "the way it's always been done."

The More You Do, the Better You Get (if you're paying attention)

The antidote to Sturgeon's law, "90 percent of everything is crap," is simply to do more, especially for creative people. A corollary is, "While doing more, you have to pay attention. Otherwise you'll continue to produce crap."

Mee-Ow cast members have consistently expressed the revelation that the demands of writing every day resulted in their improved capacity for, and facility with, writing. The additional motivation of the camaraderie of Mee-Ow, and the unwillingness to let down the rest of the cast, has also been consistent throughout the decades.

Diversity, Equity, and Inclusion

Mee-Ow has, at times, reflected the larger society. At other times, it has been ahead of societal changes. The early years of the Mee-Ow Show were often referred to in retrospect as a "boys' club," as was the comedy scene of the 1970s in general. This description, condoning a "boys will be boys" mentality, downplays the often-blatant misogyny that relegated women to supporting and "decorative" roles based on the erroneous assumption, prevalent at the time, that women were not funny.

Certainly, Julia Louis-Dreyfus challenged that assumption in 1980. The first woman to direct Mee-Ow was Romy Rosemont in 1985, the twelfth show. And the shows have tackled gender issues over the years. Women have not only been integral members of the casts, they have been leaders.

While theater has a long tradition of welcoming LGBTQ+ people, it has not always been so in comedy. Machismo was often part of the aforementioned "boys' club" of the early days of Mee-Ow, even though the larger Northwestern community was welcoming. Then in the 1980s, possibly in reaction to a new wave of Reagan conservatism in the country, and also in response to the emerging AIDS crisis, people became more guarded about their identities. Even some people who had been "out of the closet" in the '70s went back in, out of a sense of self-protection. As the mood of the country in the '90s shifted back, and

LGBTQ+ activists became more outspoken, the Mee-Ow Show also more openly dealt with subjects of gender identity and sexual orientation. The early 2000s again saw a wave of conservatism, but this time people were not willing to quietly "recloset" themselves. People were out for good, and for the good, bringing their voices and viewpoints to comedy and to Mee-Ow.

While the first Mee-Ow Show had a Black man in the cast, Obie Story, it wouldn't be until 1982 that another Black man, George Steven "Steve" Beavers, was in the cast. And it wasn't until 1991 that the first Black woman, Daniele Gaither, would join Mee-Ow.

Finally, when the directors of Mee-Ow came to recognize that the show did not reflect the diversity of the student body because of who was choosing to audition, they began an outreach effort to encourage all interested students to audition and participate. These consistent efforts have proven successful, and today's casts and staff are consistently diverse.

Friendships

An enduring legacy of Mee-Ow is the lifelong friendships that were forged during the show. As many Mee-Ow alumni have commented, the long, intensely collaborative process that goes into creating the show can, and often does, establish bonds that last for decades. Many of these friends have even found themselves professionally collaborating long after graduation.

Resilience and the Enduring Spirit of Rebellion

At least once per decade during its fifty years, there has been a possibility that the Mee-Ow Show would not continue. Despite the obstacles facing the show, including budgets, the content of sketches, objectionable (to some) show titles, and a pandemic, students have always found a way to keep the show going. The resilience and rebelliousness of the cast and creators have been essential qualities of Mee-Ow since its beginning.

One of the questions that must be asked of any enterprise that began as a rebellion is whether the same spirit will continue once it becomes an institution. It has become clear that rebellion is inherent in comedy and satire, since no institution seen to be "punching down" is ever perceived as funny. Rather, it is satirizing the foibles and peccadilloes of established authority that people find entertaining. Except, of course, those in authority, and their reaction to being satirized is often even funnier, or sadder, or both.

Creative Entrepreneurship

One of the engines of creativity at Northwestern has been the several dichotomies inherent in the student body. There have been, and continue to be, a large number of students on scholarship, in contrast to the wealthy, often legacy, students whose families could donate enough to name a building; the liberal arts students on the south campus and the tech students on north campus; and back in the day, the Greeks versus the "freaks." With all those differences in the student body, Northwestern has not only been an informative place, but an enlightening one, as a university should be. Exploring those differences often sparked conversations, new ways of looking at the world, and new ideas. This combination of ideas from different disciplines and different points of view in new applications is one functional definition of creativity. When creativity is combined with intelligence and aspiration, the results are often exciting and groundbreaking.

The Future of Mee-Ow

Mee-Ow had two establishing principles from its inception. First, all students from any field of study were welcome to apply to participate. Second, there would be no interference, editing, imposed censorship, or control by faculty or administration. Despite whatever changes will inevitably occur, from the increased use of technology to even the unlikely possibility that Shanley Pavilion will finally and regretfully be condemned, the students will continue to define what the Mee-Ow Show is. Without interference. Without censorship. And *with* collaboration.

And that, as Kristen Schaal has said, is a "great, creative, lovely place to be."

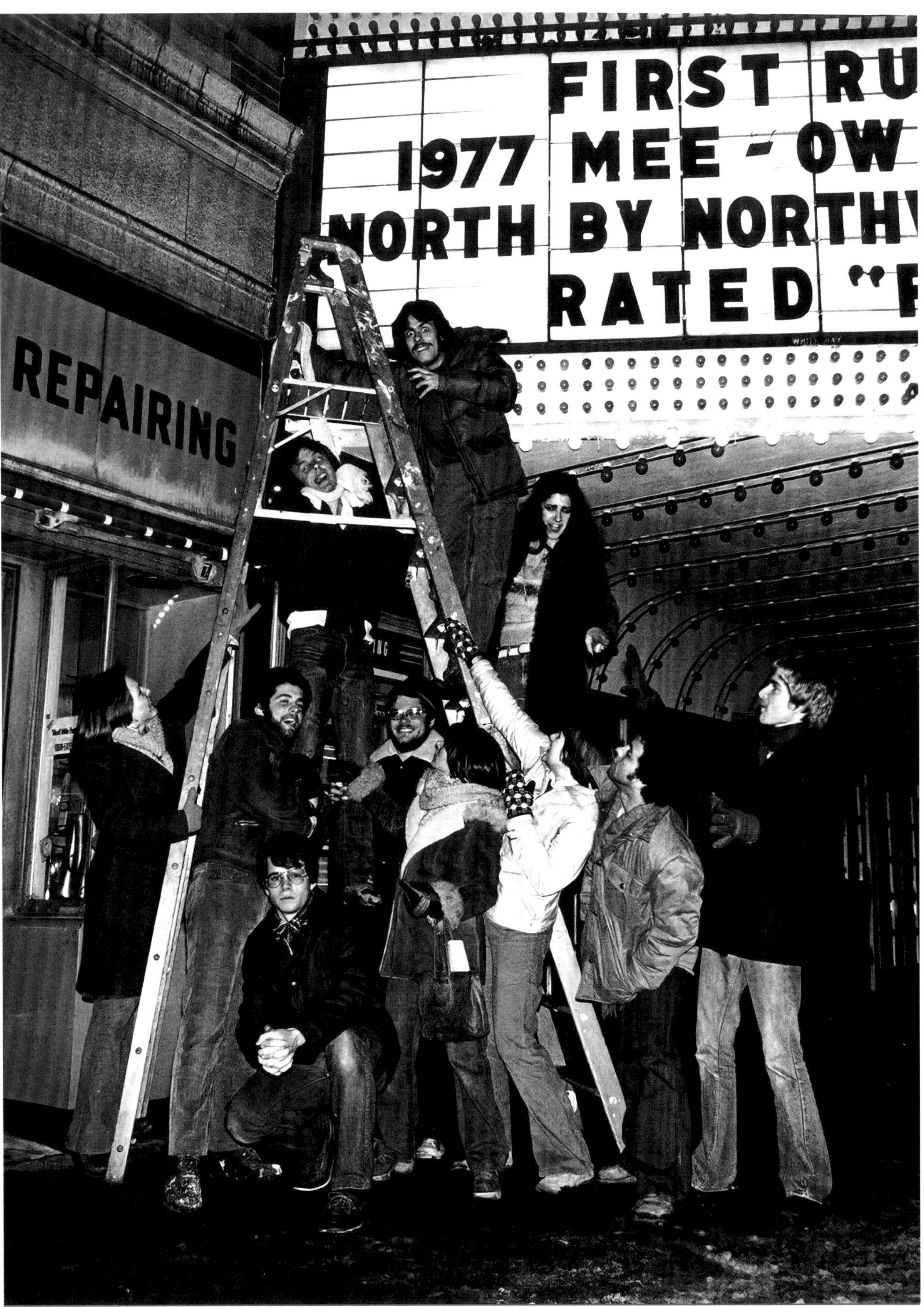
FIRST RU
1977 MEE-OW
NORTH BY NORTH
RATED "
REPAIRING

8 In Their Own Words

Notable Alumni on Their Mee-Ow Experience

This book was based in large part on more than a hundred interviews with fifty years of Mee-Ow cast and crew members from all over the country—their stories, in their own words. The comments in this chapter are excerpts from some of those interviews. In all the talk of performance and production, behind the scenes and in front of the curtain, what came shining through is what the experience of Mee-Ow meant to people. Professionally, but also personally. First, as students, and then as those students grew older—they went out into the world and found where they fit, where their voices mattered, and where they could make a contribution to the world.

However wonderfully weird and wild it may be.

Facing page, the 1977 cast: (*kneeling*) Tom Virtue; (*standing*) Janie Fried, Jeff Lupetin, pianist Jim May, Betsy Fink, Cindy Milstein, Kyle Heffner, and Peter Bales; (*on ladder*) Dana Olsen, Allison Burnett, and Suzie Plaksin

Kyle T. Heffner '78
(Mee-Ow '76, '77, '78)

Actor. Cast in *Young Doctors in Love*, his first film role, by Northwestern alum Garry Marshall '56. Films include *Flashdance, The Woman in Red, Runaway Train, When Harry Met Sally*.

> "Mee-Ow was actually the propellant that led me into getting my first film role."

Allison Burnett '79 (Mee-Ow '77)

Screenwriter, film director, novelist. Wrote and directed the films *Ask Me Anything* and *Another Girl*, based on his novels.

> "You have a choice. You can rage at circumstance . . . or you get humble and you adapt. You have to improvise in life."

Dana Olsen '80
(Mee-Ow '77, '78, '79, '80)

Actor, film producer, screenwriter. Cocreator of *Henry Danger*; written works include *George of the Jungle, The 'Burbs*, and *Inspector Gadget*.

> "It was great, because once I got into Mee-Ow then I knew I found what I wanted to do."

Shelly Goldstein '78 (Mee-Ow '78)

TV writer-producer and successful cabaret performer. Appearances at The Gardenia in Los Angeles and London's Pizza on the Park.

> "If you want to be in comedy, you better get to Northwestern and you better be in the Mee-Ow Show. You know, that's pretty damn cool. I'm real glad it's on my life résumé. You built something really amazing that has affected American comedy."

Julia Louis-Dreyfus '83, '07 H
(Mee-Ow '80, '81)

Actor. *Saturday Night Live* cast member 1982–1985; starring roles in *Seinfeld, The New Adventures of Old Christine*, and *Veep*. Eleven Emmy Awards; Golden Globe Award; nine Screen Actors Guild Awards; five American Comedy Awards; two Critics' Choice Television Awards; Hollywood Walk of Fame star; Television Academy Hall of Fame in 2014; Mark Twain Prize for American Humor, 2018, presented by the Kennedy Center as America's highest comedy honor.

> "Mee-Ow was really for me a life changer. Complete life changer, really."

The 1980 cast: (*front row*) John Goodrich, Paul Barrosse, Julia Louis-Dreyfus, Rush Pearson, and Judy Pruitt; (*back row*) Mike Markowitz, Ken Marks, Dana Olsen, and Rod McLachlan

John Cameron Mitchell '85

(Mee-Ow '84)

Actor, playwright, screenwriter, and director. Served as writer, director, and star of the 1998 stage musical and 2001 film *Hedwig and the Angry Inch*. Appeared as Joe Exotic in the Peacock limited series *Joe vs. Carole* (2022); appeared in the Netflix series *The Sandman* (2022).

> "The disciplined anarchy of Mee-Ow was really important for me to get out of my classical state of mind and even get out of the closet . . . because I had confidence for the first time."

Dermot Mulroney '85 (Mee-Ow '84, '85)

Actor. *My Best Friend's Wedding, The Family Stone*. Jury Special Prize, Torino International Festival of Young Cinema (1990); Best Actor, Seattle International Film Festival (1992); Artistic Achievement Award, Philadelphia Film Festival (2007).

> "It's because of the Mee-Ow Show that I sit here today in a parking lot on a production and that people still use me not just for that guy they mistook me for when it began in Hollywood, which was just an edgy kid, but rather the kind of guy I really am, as you know, which is a foolish comedian. I was spotted by the local agent [at Mee-Ow] that led to this, that, and the other thing. And that is for real. Straight back to you guys [who started Mee-Ow]. In terms of legacy, I never undervalue the experience. And I've always known that it was a huge part of my skill set and in its own way, a stepping stone out of Chicago and right away starting an early career as a kid. Oh, gosh, I've got such gratitude to you guys deep down for sure."

Craig Bierko '85 (Mee-Ow '85)

Actor. *The Music Man, Cinderella Man, Scary Movie 4*. Nominated for the Shorty Award for Humor (2014); *Entertainment Weekly*'s 100 Most Creative People in Entertainment "It" List, 2003; Sexiest Broadway Star—*People* (2000); Theatre World Award (winner, 2000); Broadway.com Audience Awards (winner, 2000). Nominated for the Tony Award for Best Actor in a Musical, Drama Desk Award for Best Actor in a Musical, and Outer Critics Circle Award for Best Actor in a Musical, all for *The Music Man* in 2000.

> "I don't know that I would have considered my training absolutely complete had it not been for Mee-Ow . . . This I can tell you honestly, hand to God, I would not be the person or the actor I am without this experience. It was elemental. This was the reason I was going to Northwestern. And considering what Northwestern is, that's really saying something."

John Lehr '88 (Mee-Ow '86, '87, '88)

Film and television actor and comedian. Off-Broadway, one-man show *The Lehr Curse: A Series of Comedic Lectures*. Cocreator, executive producer, and star of *Quick Draw*. One of the original Geico Cavemen in the series of popular commercials.

> "[Mee-Ow] changed my life. Doing that show really opened up this idea of, oh my God, I could do this. I can do this with my life. And I have basically been doing improv ever since."

Dan Patterson (Mee-Ow '86)

British television producer and writer. Cocreator and producer of the British and American versions of the improvisation show *Whose Line Is It Anyway?* Also cocreated and produced the British satirical panel show *Mock the Week*.

> "I think in any life you look back at an early magical period where suddenly everything changed and you suddenly went, this is what I want to do. And I think part of that for me was the Mee-Ow Show . . . I think the Mee-Ow Show is an incredible institution that has really powered so much of American comedy in terms of the people that have come out of it, whether performers, directors, producers, all sorts of people, arts people, stage writers, creatives."

Ana Gasteyer ’89 (Mee-Ow ’88, ’89)

Actor and comedian. *Saturday Night Live* cast member 1996–2002. Starred in the sitcoms *Suburgatory*, *People of Earth*, and *American Auto*, and the film *Mean Girls*.

> “Like many people who did Mee-Ow, the second I found it and did it, I was like, aha, my thing, my tribe, my people, the other mutant weirdos on the planet who think the way I do.”

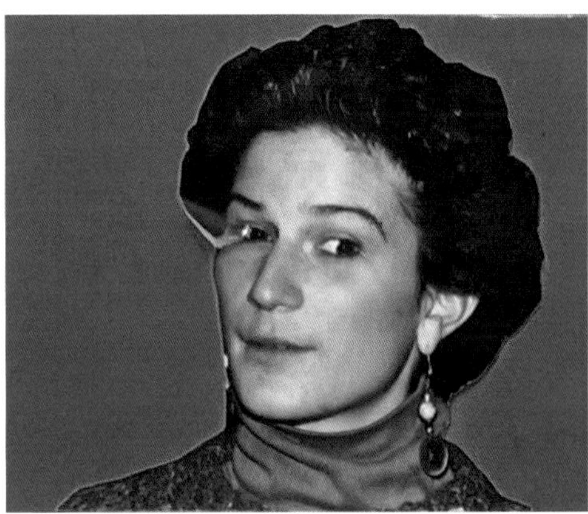

J.P. Manoux ’91 (Mee-Ow ’89, ’90, ’91)

Actor. Appeared in over 100 different television series, 90 commercials, and 40 films, including recurring characters on HBO series *Veep* and PopTV series *Swedish Dicks*. Voice and motion-capture performance for eight video games, competed on six TV game shows, read two original pieces for *All Things Considered* on National Public Radio. 2018 Moth StorySLAM winner (Los Angeles).

> “I remember thinking [Mee-Ow] was the most stimulating and important thing in my life, at that time.”

Jon “Pep” Rosenfeld ’90 (Mee-Ow ’90)

Founder and current artistic director of Boom Chicago in Amsterdam, the English-language improv and sketch comedy theater that served as a comedy grad school for Seth and Josh Meyers, Jordan Peele, Ike Barinholtz, Heather Anne Campbell, and many others.

> “The Mee-Ow Show made me what I am today.”

Jean Villepique ’95 (Mee-Ow ’92, ’93, ’94, ’95)

Actor. *BoJack Horseman*, *A.P. Bio*, *Up All Night*, and *30 Rock*; The Second City.

> “[The Mee-Ow Show] gave me my voice. It gave me the chance to practice making mistakes a lot. Putting myself in situations where I don’t know what’s happening. And your friends, the people you work with, you build these relationships and do those trust falls and all that stuff, because you practice knowing you will be supported whatever you do. That’s so rare.”

Anjali Bhimani ’94 (Mee-Ow ’93)

Stage, film, television, and voiceover actor. Known for her roles as Symmetra in the video game *Overwatch* and Rampart in the video game *Apex Legends*. Long-time collaborator with Mary Zimmerman. Appeared in the TV series *All My Children*, *Law & Order*, *The Sopranos*, and *Modern Family*.

> “In life, not just as a performer, but in life, to be comfortable being uncomfortable . . . to trust in yourself enough to handle anything. To trust that no matter what happens you will land on your feet. And improv is such a great training ground for that.”

Ed Herbstman ’95 (Mee-Ow ’93, ’94, ’95)

Film and television actor, writer, improviser, and teacher. Actor in the films *The Big Sick* and *Hustlers* and the TV series *Manifest*. Cofounder of Magnet Theater in New York City.

> “I was really just interested in what school has the best improv group. That’s all I cared about. [Mee-Ow] is the thing that hooked me. And I thought, that’s what I want to do. Applied to Northwestern, got in, and pretty much organized my college experience around my Mee-Ow experience. . . . And I knew that if I went to Northwestern, I could do the Mee-Ow Show and I could continue studying at Improv-Olympic in the city with Del Close, which is what I did all four years of school. And then when I graduated, I got into the Second City touring company.”

Seth Meyers '96, '16 H

(Mee-Ow '96)

Host, *Late Night with Seth Meyers*. *Saturday Night Live* cast member 2001–2014 and its head writer and news anchor of *Weekend Update,* 2006–2014. Writers Guild of America Award for Comedy/Variety Series or Special (2007, 2009, 2010, 2015); Peabody Award (2009); Primetime Emmy Award for Outstanding Original Music and Lyrics (2011); Writers Guild of America Award for Comedy/Variety—Sketch Series (2017); Critics' Choice Television Award for Best Talk Show (2020).

> "Everything kind of sprung for me out of doing Mee-Ow. I remember the last show we did our senior year, and just thinking I'm going to do this until somebody tells me to stop. This is too much fun."

Heather Anne Campbell '00

(Mee-Ow '97, '98, '99, '00)

Writer, comedian, improv comedy performer, actor, voice actor, video-game journalist, podcaster, photographer. *Saturday Night Live* (2010–11), *Whose Line Is It Anyway?* (2013–22), *The Eric Andre Show* (2014–16), and *Rick and Morty* (2022–present).

> "If it hadn't been for Mee-Ow, I wouldn't have done Boom Chicago, which was founded by Mee-Ow people. Then I wouldn't have started a sketch show at UCB, which is how I got to *Saturday Night Live*. And now today, literally today, I'm in a writers' room with Jess Lacher, who was in the [Mee-Ow] show in the year 2000. It just keeps giving. When you hear people talk about the good old days, it's always a little sad. The Mee-Ow Show feels different because it wasn't like something that I did and then never touched again. It's literally still touching my life."

Kristen Schaal '00 (Mee-Ow '99, '00)

Actor, voice artist, writer, and comedian. Known for roles in *Flight of the Conchords, Bob's Burgers, Gravity Falls,* and *The Last Man on Earth*. Appeared on *The Daily Show, The Hotwives of Orlando, 30 Rock,* the *Toy Story* movies (3 & 4), and *Wilfred*.

> "Mee-Ow is so special and in such a specific environment of everyone being able to rehearse and make stuff at the same age, at the same time, with no distractions. Not to make money, not to get more famous than the other person, just to create a piece of art together, to learn how to make comedy together."

Appendix: The People Who Made Mee-Ow

Cast, Staff, and Band Members, 1974–2024

1974 Just in Time

EXECUTIVE BOARD

Creators/Producers: Josh Lazar, Paul Warshauer
Director: Jeff Wilson
Music Director: George Lisle
Technical Director: Chris Rusch
Lighting Designer: Roy Lamberton
Costume Designer: Karen Wheeler
Assistant Director: Wendy Gajewski
Special Effects: Wally Olden
Public Relations: Chris Rector
Production Coordinator: Obie Story

STAFF

Stage Managers: Dan Guss, Stu Rosenthal
Sound Engineers: Scott Kerlin, Peter Lucas
Surrealist-in-Residence: Joseph Radding
House Manager: Linda Sills
Properties: Ellen Burkes
Scenic Consultant: Lee Brodsker
Makeup: Jeff Segal
Asst. to the Director: Terry Blum

STAGE CREW

Paul Adler
Mike Andlers
Mike Higgens
Thierri Riek
Bob Rogoff

TECHNICAL LIGHTING CREW

David Gellman
Catheryn Lamberton
Mark Mongold
Peter Rudoy
Keith Wheeler

COSTUME CREW

Rissa Fine
Shelly Gilbert
Nubie Richardson

CAST

Terri Blum
Devan Carter
Bob Chimbel
Sue Cibrario
Carol Cling
Sue Devero
Ken Elliott
Ron Ensel
Jonathan Fox
Meredith Freeman
Debbie Gaber
Wendy Gajewski
Nancy Gordon
Sandy Grimsley
Holly Hartle
Bill Hindin
Steve Humphrey
Marla Jones
Randy Kaplan
Robbie Karnofsky
Dusty Kay
Rick Kotrba
Jerry Larkin
Josh Lazar
Barb Mallorie
Kevin McDermott
Wendy Nadler
Bill Nuss
Rod Oram
Alan Perkins
Russ Pishnery
Tom Reese
Sandy Richens
Patti Rubin
Debbie Sauer
Joe Schuster

Suzanne Sciez
Obie Story
Wendy Taucher
Jeaninee Tortelli
Lisa Wershaw

ORCHESTRA

Dave Boruff: Alto Sax, Clarinet, Flute
Susie Fox: Flute, Piccolo
Kevin Hosten: Flute, Piccolo, Alto Flute
Peter Kallish: Guitar
George Lisle: Electric Piano
Malcolm MacDonald: Guitar, Bass
Harvey "Hubcap" Moshman: Vibes, Percussion
Mike Privitera: Drums
Bruce Reed: Trombone
Mark Running: Trumpet, Flugelhorn
Daryl Stehlic: Trumpet, Flugelhorn
Janet Steidl: Oboe, English Horn
Benjy Stemple: Tenor Sax, Bass Guitar

ARRANGERS

Dave Boruff
Dan Guss
William Jay
Peter Kallish
George Lisle
Mark Running
Daryl Stehlic

LYRICISTS AND COMPOSERS

Bob Chimbel
Robert Elisberg
Dan Guss
Phil Rosenberg

ACCOMPANISTS

Jon Fox
Steve Humphrey
Jeanne Masschelin
Judy Miller
Lynn Soderdahl

1975 What Did You Expect?

CAST

Carol Appleby
Mike Bonner
Eloise Jane Coopersmith
Betsy Fink
Thomas Fitzgerald
Wendy Gajewski
David Garrett
Neal Gold
Roy Alan Hine
Michelle Holmes
Laurie Karon
Curtis Katz
Dusty Kay
Kathy Kirshenbaum
Kitty Knecht
Rick Kotrba
Charlie Lucci
Jeff Lupetin
Jane McClary
Brad Mott
Lisa Nesselson
Bill Nuss
Karen Alison Pepper
Keith Reddin
Scott Rothburd
Wendy Taucher

STAFF

Executive Producer: Ira Deutchman
Produced and Directed: Dusty Kay, Bill Nuss
Sketches: Curtis Katz, Dusty Kay, Rick Kotrba, Bill Nuss, Keith Reddin
Music and Lyrics: Bob Chimbel, George Lisle, Lisa Nesselson, Karen Alison Pepper, Scott Rothburd
Music Director: Karen Alison Pepper
Assistant Music Director: Scott Rothburd
Set Design: Chris Rusch
Technical Director: Alan Novick
Choreography: Wendy Taucher
Lighting Design: Dean Taucher
Comedy Coordinator: Rick Kotrba
Costume Design: Sue Eggleston
Stage Manager: Mike Sicotte
Production Manager: Neal Gold
Show Sound: Mark Guncheon
Dance Captain: Carol Appleby
Publicity Chair: Steve Caulk
Publicity Staff: Bill Flanagan, Kathy Gabel, Sue Ireland, Jim Montemayor, Alan Perkins
Production Assistants: Shelly Gilbert, Helene Sanders
Rehearsal Pianist: Bruce Martz
Script Supervisors: Dusty Kay, Rick Kotrba, Bill Nuss
Stage Crew/Set Construction: Thierry Rick, Tim Wilson
Faculty Advisor: Irving J. Rein
Uncredited tech crew: Drew McCoy, Mark Mongold, Mike Secotte

ORCHESTRA

Conductor: Stuart Hirsch
Tim Aiken: Drums
Charles Key: Trumpet
Malcolm MacDonald: Guitar
Bruce Martz: Piano
Gary Onstad: Tenor Saxophone
Tim Paternode: Bass
Mark Running: Trumpet
John Swiatek: Alto Saxophone
Steve Todd: Trombone
Gail Ytterberg: Flute

1976 Spirit, My Ass

CAST

Peter Bales
Stew Figa
Betsy Fink
Kyle T. Heffner
Jeff Lupetin
Keith Reddin
Alice Tell

EXECUTIVE STAFF

Executive Producers: Mike Baron, Bill Nuss
Producers: Dusty Kay, Bruce Martz
Director: Dusty Kay
Comedy Coordinator: Keith Reddin
Lighting Designer: Dean Taucher
Costume Designer: Sara Berg
Technical Director: John Mathes
Stage Manager: Lisa Hightower
A&O Board Theatrical Events Chair: Bill Flanagan
Publicity Chair: "Odd Todd" Benson
Script Supervisor: Dusty Kay
Faculty Advisor: Sid Miller
Stage Photographer: Charles Seton

1977 North by Northwestern

CAST

Peter Bales
Allison Burnett
Betsy Fink
Janie Fried
Kyle T. Heffner
Jeff Lupetin
Cindy Milstein
Dana Olsen
Suzie Plaksin
Tom Virtue
Jim May: Piano

EXECUTIVE BOARD

Producers: Peter Bales, Bill "Killer" Flanagan
Director: Peter Bales
Lighting: Ken Belkhof, Paul Zucker
Settings: Cindy Milstein, Paul Zucker
Associate Producer: Melanie Barker
Assistant Director: Rachel Lederman
Publicity: Mark Ganshirt
Costumes/Props: Anne Greenberg
Scripting: Robert Mendel
Choreography: Bridget McDonough
Mime Consultant: "The Hands" Rand Whipple
Technical Director: Paul Zucker
Stage Manager: Sherry Krsticevic
Stage Crew: Anne Greenberg, Randy Oppenheimer, Charles Talbert
House Manager: William Springer
Executive Producers: Michael Baron, Stew Figa
Faculty Advisor: Sid Miller

1978 In Search of the Ungnome

CAST

Paul Barrosse
Jerry Franklin
Shelly Goldstein
Ken Marks
Jane Muller
Dana Olsen
Rush Pearson
Tina Rosenberg
Bill Wronski
Larry Schanker: Piano

EXECUTIVE BOARD

Producer: Melanie Barker
Director: Kyle T. Heffner
Associate Producer: Steve Jarvis
Assistant Director: Meryl Friedman
Script Assistants: Bill Aiken, Terry Aronoff, Ira Besserman
Technical Director: Catherine Martineau
Stage Manager: Dave Silberger
Set Design: Meryl Friedman, Kyle T. Heffner, Catherine Martineau
Lighting Design: Ron Mahla
Choreography: Bridget McDonough
Publicity Staff: Melanie Barker, Steve Jarvis, Debby Regen
Technical Staff: Claudia Crown, Jim McCuthen, Frank McGovern, Raymond Shinn
Wardrobe: Ellie Rossenfeld
Props: Dave Silberger
Faculty Advisor: Sid Miller
Arts Alliance Chairs: Phyllis Johnson, Bill Melamed
A&O Board Chair: Johnny Levin
Orgy of the Arts President: Rob Mendel

1979 But Is It Art?

CAST

Bill Aiken
Paul Barrosse
Winnie Freedman
John Goodrich
Barb Guarino
Althea Haropulos
Dana Olsen
Rush Pearson
Larry Schanker: Piano

STAFF

Producers: Ira Besserman, Anne Greenberg
Directors: Meryl Friedman, Dana Olsen
Technical Director/Set and Lighting Designer: Margaret Nelson
Stage Manager: Dave Silberger
Script Consultant: Bill Aiken
Film Director: Joe Labritz
Publicity Directors: Terry Aronoff, Connie Gray
Graphics Artists: Dave Gardner, John Goodrich
Script Assistants: Paul Barrosse, Rush Pearson, Dori Solomon, Alan Wolfson
Assistant Stage Manager: Tricia Galin
Cameraman: Dean St. John
Photographer: Robert Sabal
Publicity Committee: Gini Greer, Laura Matalon, Lisa Montgomery, Vicki Pomerance, Libby Schmidt, Rob Wright
Faculty Advisor: Lou Castelli
Arts Alliance Board: Eileen Gill, Anne Greenberg, Wiley Hausam, Kim Johnson, Rob Mendel, Alan Ziter

1980 Ten Against the Empire

CAST

Paul Barrosse
John Goodrich
Julia Louis-Dreyfus
Rod McLachlan
Mike Markowitz
Ken Marks
Dana Olsen
Rush Pearson
Judy Pruitt
Larry Schanker: Piano

STAFF

Coproducers: Eileen Gill, Dave Silberger
Director: Dana Olsen
Set Designer: Dan Fechtner
Lighting Designer: Laura A. Sunkel
Graphic Artists: David Gardner, John Goodrich
Film Director: Casey Fox
Stage Manager: Roy Henley
Master Electrician: Amy Lindberg
Tech Director: Ralf Hestoft
Publicity Director: Bob Ravasio
Assts. to the Producers: Drew Brown, Nancy Prahofer
Asst. to the Director: Tricia Galin
Script Assistant/Writer: Althea Haropulos
Props Mistress: Suzie Gilligan
Publicity Staff: Gary Brano, Vance Freyman, Judy Kaplan, Joan King, Elyce Zahn
Technical Staff: Lenore Martin
Photographer: Ralf Hestoft

1981 Candy from Strangers

CAST

Bekka Eaton
John Goodrich
Mark Lancaster
Bill Lopatto
Julia Louis-Dreyfus
Mike Markowitz
Ken Marks
Rod McLachlan
Sandy Snyder
Larry Schanker: Piano

STAFF

Producer: Dave Silberger
Director: Ken Marks
Music Director: Larry Schanker
Assistant Director: Tricia Galin
Shortstop: Don Kessinger
Set Designer: Tara Jean
Tech Director: A. E. Gallagher
Lighting Designer: William (BK) Kelly
Stage Manager: Cory Powers
Interpretation Dept. Chair: Lilla Heston
Publicity Directors: Mike Blum, Jeff Semmerling
Assistant Producer: Mike Roy
Props, et al: Suzie Gilligan
Script Assistants: Garland Cunningham, Stephen Marvel, Laura Matalon
Graphic Artists: John Goodrich, Bruce Norris, Jennifer Stewart
House Manager/Flautist: Norda Mullen
Master Electrician: Garland Cunningham
Spot Operators: Joe Galvin, Lorri Platex
Board Operator: Jane Tanya Beresford
Lighting Technician: Rich Shandross
Faculty Advisor: Bud Beyer
Photographer: Mike Heeger
Bartender: James Foley
Chauffeur: K. Winston Snedegar

1982 'Till the Cows Come Home . . . Where ARE Those Damn Cows?

CAST

Steve Beavers
Rob Chaskin
John Goodrich
Chris Hueben
Mark Lancaster
Laura Matalon
Sarah Partridge
Susan Wapner

STAFF

Producer: Tricia Galin
Director: John Goodrich
Video Director: Ralph Beliveau
Music Director: Bill Martens
Set Designer: Cory Powers
Technical Director/Lighting Designer/Stage Manager: Keith Berner
Publicity Director: Alison Lyon
Assts. to the Producer: David Rochlin, Diane Singer
Asst. to the Director: Patrick Trettenero
Graphic Artist: John Goodrich
Assistant Lighting Designer: Craig Jackson
Assistant Stage Manager: Bob Burcham
Scenic Painter: Becky Katz
House Manager: Michelle Olson
Photographers: Mike Heeger, Kelly Sheehan
A/V Technician: Bob Sassenrath
Sound Engineer: Marty Wilde
Assistant Sound Engineer: David Hemmings

THE MEE-OW SHOW DORCHESTRA: AND THE AND THE ANDTHES

Mike Blum: Keyboards
Steve Jarvis: Drums
Bill Martens: Bass Guitar
Rush Pearson: Rhythm Guitar, Vocals
Peter Van Wagner (The Riffmaster): Lead Guitar

1983 Wake Up, Yo Tinheads

CAST

Taylor Abbott
Mark Gunnion
Tami Hinz
Chris Hueben
Sue Klein
Ellen Kohrman
Mark Lancaster
Michael Simon

STAFF

Producer: Craiglet
Codirectors: Chris Hueben, Mark Lancaster
Music Director: Steve Huffines
Production Manager: Sraa
Space Designer: Cory Powers
Lighting Designer: Emily Bristor
Stage Manager: Anne Marie Paolucci
Assistant Stage Manager: Genevieve Overholser
Publicity Director: Mindy Ginsburg
House Manager: Priscilla Vail
Program Cover Design: Nathan Kaatrud
Graphic Artists: John Goodrich, Priscilla Vail
Poster Production: Peter Shott
Photographer: Kelly Sheehan
Individual Portraits: Gail Butensky
Animator: Cindy Moran, Eric Scholl
Board Operator: Gary Winters
Script Assistants: Karen Cooper, Barry Hamill, Jim McMasters
Faculty Advisor: David Downs

1984 Escape from Baltic Avenue

CAST

Karen Cooper
Jesse Dabson
Eric Gilliland
Kelley Hughes
Richard Kaplan
Wendi Messing
John Cameron Mitchell
Dermot Mulroney
Richard Radutzky
Romy Rosemont

STAFF

Producer: Mark Brogger
Director: Eric Gilliland
Assistant Director: Mitchell Bass
Scenic Design: Daniel Gene Guyette
Lighting Design: Mike Vermillion
Assistant Producer: Kurt Moore
Stage Managers: Steve Juergens, Sara Winikoff
Publicity: Mindy J. Ginsburg, Lisa Kelley
Public Relations: Martha Ross
Publicity Staff: Toni Gallagher, David Martin, Becky Schnur, Lisa Sperling
House Manager: Joe Hershberger
Master Electrician: Todd Grinnell
Lighting Assistant: Mark Leland
Photographer: Kelly Sheehan
Poster Design: David Steinberg

THE BAND

Fran Banich
Eric Mandel
Mark Mulé
Brian Schmidt

1985 Local an' Aesthetic

CAST

Beth Bash
Craig Bierko
Richard Kaplan
Dermot Mulroney
Richard Radutzky
Allyson Rice
Romy Rosemont
Karen Schiff

STAFF

Producer: Mark Brogger
Director: Romy Rosemont
Stage Manager: Liz Kruger
Assistant Director: Stuart Feldman
Set Designer: Daniel Guyette
Lighting Designer: Todd Grinnell
Technical Director: Larry Welzen
Master Electrician: Joe Szadowski
Assistant Stage Manager: Sue Petsche
Publicity Directors: Dan Fisher, Mary Jane Herman
Public Relations: Kenny Chodock, Lori Cozen, Debbie Decker, Jamie Goldman, Cathy Hammond
Photographer: Jill Footlick
Production: Grace Kahng, Robert Ramsey
Lighting: Barry Gribbon

THE BAND

Fran Banich
Eric Mandel
Mark Mulé
Brian Schmidt

1986 Oedipuss 'n Boots

CAST

Mollie Allen
Dave Clapper
Jon Craven
Andy Hirsch
Lisa Houle
Jessica Hughes
John Lehr
Barry Levin
Catherine Newman
Chris Pfaff

STAFF

Producer: Elizabeth Kruger
Director: Dan Patterson
Assistant Director: Stuart Feldman
Associate Producer: Shannon Dobson
Staff Writer: Mark Walker
Set Designer: Derek Anderson
Lighting Designer: Barry Gribbon
Technical Designer: Larry Welzen
Stage Manager: Kathryn Ware

Assistant Stage Managers: Andrea Goodman, Mark Walker
Publicity Directors: Ken Chodock, Nancy Friedman
Publicity Staff: Gary Dorfner, Cathy Hammond, Amy Meyers
Public Relations: Lisa Harrison, Hilary Kahn, Mark McGowan
Graphic Artist: Dave Martin
Sound Engineer: Mark Laxen
Assistant Lighting Designer: Martha Ann Bozeman
Photographer: Katrina Sarson
Tickets/Program: Dan Pink

PIANISTS

Adam Fields
Ron Jackson

THE BAND

Andrew Hagerman
Alan Lerner
Bob Spector
Eric Sproull

1987 Eating Mee-Ow

CAST

Mollie Allen
Bo Blackburn
Marc Goldsmith
Melanie Hoopes
Lisa Houle
John Lehr
Catherine Newman
Jerry Saslow

STAFF

Producer: Eric Goodman
Director: Jonathan Craven
Associate Producer: Jessica Hughes
Associate Director: Leelai Demoz
Lighting Designer/Stage Manager: Jennifer Kunin
Lighting: Mark Griswald
Sets: Dave Clapper, Chip Yates
Technical Director: Richard Mone
Publicity Coordinator: Anne Read
Publicity Staff: Hane Christofersen, Toni Gallagher
Public Relations: Rachel Anderson
Properties: Dawn Hillman
Field Manager: Steve Conley
Photographer: Jill Footlick
Graphic Guru: Mike Whetstone

ACCOMPANIST

Matt Wolka

DR. BOB AND THE FOKAKTAH BLUES BAND

Dave Anderson
Adam Grant
Greg Hinderyckx
Eric Karten
Larry Natkin
T.B. Weeks
Temple Williams III

1988 Mee-Ow Tse-Tung

CAST

Betsy Braham
Jill Cargerman
Tim Ereneta
Stu Feldman
Ana Gasteyer
Jessica Hughes
John Lehr
Jerry Saslow

STAFF

Producer: Jennifer Kunin
Director: Jessica Hughes
Associate Director: Michael Rohd
Stage Manager: Tristan Lemons
Assistant Stage Manager/Props: Lisa Kenner
Set Director: John Carroll
Set Design Concept: Jim Mail
Lighting Designer: Nathan Turner
Photographer: David Catlin
Publicity: Jennifer Flamhaft, Ann Obenchaing
Public Relations: Ana Petrovic
Production Assistant: Kathleen Fabiny
Artist: Tim Maloney

ACCOMPANIST

Matt Wolk

THE BAND

Lionel Cole
Frances Epsen-Devlin
Geoff Fisher
Fred Hemke Jr.
Sarah Hummon
Thom Russo
John Scholvin

1989 Salvador's Deli

CAST

Bo Blackburn
Jill Cargerman
Ana Gasteyer
Mary Jackman
Eric Letzinger
J.P. Manoux
Philip Pawelczyk
Spencer Shapiro

STAFF

Producer: Tristan Lemons
Director: Tim Ereneta
Associate Director: Emilie Beck
Associate Producer: Caroline Hockaday
Asst. to the Director: Ian Deitchman
Stage Manager: Lisa Kenner
Business Manager: Charlie Schroder
Publicity Coordinator: Elisabeth Weiss
Publicity: Lisa Giblin
Set Designer: Michael Mehler
Technical Director: Ken Schaefle
Technical Assistant: Jim Mail
Lighting Designer: Robert Mestman
Light Wizard: Deb Sullivan
Props: David Ketchman
Ticket Manager: Vanessa Taylor
Runners: J.J. Davidson, Carolyn Manetti, Betsy Thomas
Artist: Chip Yates

Video/Photography: Jim Dennen
Button Designer: Rick Qualliotine

THE MEE-OW SHOW HOUSE BAND: FREE DELIVERY

Ron Baslow
Jerome Brown
Dave Fischer
John Goodman
Becca Kaufman
Kameron Steele
Wendy Wilf

1990 Sunday Eating Pork with George

CAST

Jason DeSanto
Kate Fry
Lillian Hubscher
J.P. Manoux
Philip Pawelczyk
Greg Rice
Jonathan Rosenfeld
Spencer Shapiro

STAFF

Producer: Ira Ungerleider
Director: Jill Cargerman
Associate Director: Suzanne Bukinik
Associate Producer: Stephanie Howard
Set Designer: Dan Jackson
Lighting Designer: Deborah Sullivan
Stage Manager: Martha Christensen
Assistant Stage Manager: Jenny Berner
Technical Director: David Cushing
Publicity Director: Noel Rihm
House Manager: Rebecca Sacks
Production Assistant: Robin Underleider
Poster Design: Chip Yates
Mee-Ow Video Producer: Daniel Weintraub
Show Videographer: Matthew Richter

THE BAND: MR. KRINKELBEIN AND THE SHANGHAI NUNS

Steve Bennshoff
Mike Conroy
Tim Fidler
Steve Jo
Scott Smith

1991 Lawrence of Your Labia (previews)

Are You There, God? It's Mee-Ow (mainstage)

CAST

Lesley Bevan
George Brant
Daniele Gaither
Rachel Hamilton
Mark Kretzmann
Bruce McCoy
Jon Mozes
Kirsten Nelson

STAFF

Producer: Peter Glawatz
Director: J.P. Manoux
Assistant Director: Lara Dieckmann
Stage Manager: Lillian Hubscher
Associate/Assistant Producer: Rebecca Herman
Set Designer: David Cushing
Assistant Set Designer: Allison Hill
Lighting Designer: Patrick Chan
Assistant Lighting Designer: Elaine Molinaro
Assistant Stage Manager: Libby Beyreis
Technical Queen: Kirsten Nelson
Music Director: Matt Heaton
Publicity Director/Graphic Designer: Scott Dougherty
House Manager: Kim McGaw
Ticket Manager: Andrea Goldstein
Video Producer: Jennifer Savage
Electrician: Michele Huitema
Production Assistants: Andrea Goldstein, Stacy Hallal, Kim McGraw, Peter Mueller, Laura Stover

THE MEE-OW HAUS BAND: BIG SAUSAGE

Mark Chou: Keyboards
Matt Heaton: Music Director, Guitar
Kevin O'Donnell: Drums
Enrique Ramirez: Bass
Ted Sidey: Saxophones

1992 Dental Damn Yankees (previews)

It's a Wonderful Life Sentence (mainstage)

CAST

Lesley Bevan
Scott Duff
Anne Eggleston
Daniele Gaither
Chris Grady
Mark Kretzmann
Bruce McCoy
Jean Villepique

STAFF

Producer: Darren Turbow
Director: Lillie Hubscher
Assistant Director: Lara Siegal
Stage Manager: Jason Levine
Associate Producer: Brad Bruskoffer
Set Designer: Alison Kay Hill
Lighting Designer: Benjamin Shields
Technical Director: Adam Bilsky
Publicity Director: Jonathan Goodon
Graphic Designer: Scott Dougherty
Publicity Staff: Tim O'Brien
Tour Director: Andrea Goldstein
House Manager: Kimberly McGaw
House Staff: Diane Tinker
Video Codirectors: Justin McKinley, Douglas Palmer

THE MEE-OW SHOW HAÜS BAND: BABY FISH MOUTH
Pete Coviello: Alto Sax
Dave Dieckmann: Guitar
Kevin O'Donnell: Drums
Enrique Ramirez: Bass
Ted Sidey: Music Director, Tenor and Soprano Sax

1993 When I Think about You, I Touch Mee-Ow (previews)

The Tao of Mee-Ow (mainstage)

CAST
Colby Beserra
Anjali Bhimani
Ed Herbstman
Abby Kohn
Ethan Sandler
Deborah Stern
Paul Vaillancourt
Jean Villepique
Amanda Weier
Dan Weiss
Adrian Wenner

STAFF
Producer: Brad Bruskotter
Director: Paul Vaillancourt
Stage Manager: Laurie Sales
Set Designers: Tara Knel, Dan Weiss
Technical Director: David Glassman
Publicity Director: Deanne Benos
Graphic Designer: Kevin O'Donnell
House Manager: Diane Tinker
Video Producers: David Gioiella, Andy Smith

THE MEE-OW BAND: SPICY SMOKED SNACK
Joshua Abrams: Bass
Kenneth Horowitz: Guitar, Vocals
Kevin O'Donnell: Drums

1994 Politically Erect (previews)

Teach Mee-Ow to Love Again (mainstage)

CAST
Jill Alexander
Ed Herbstman
Louise Lamson
Ethan Sandler
Jean Villepique
Amanda Weier
Dan Weiss
Adrian Wenner
Jason Winer

STAFF
Producer: Jeanne LaPlante
Director: Ed Herbstman
Lighting Designer: Justin Anderson
Assistant Lighting Designer: Joel Watson
House Manager: Bob Hanscum
Publicity Manager: Veronica Seet
Assistant Publicity Managers: Aaron Brown, Jason Hill, Melissa Meloro, Missy Near
Technical Assistant: Lis Dunmeyer
Stage Manager: Corey Rosen
Assistant Stage Manager: Sarah Finch
Assistant Producer: Tamara Krinsky
Chicago Tour Director: Saskia Young
Caricature Artist: Gregory Nussbaum
Sound Designer: Tony Gama-Lobo
Assistant Sound Designer: Karl Fenske
Videographer: Dave Gioella
Technical Director: Dave Glassman

THE BAND: SIDESHOW BOB
Joshua Abrams: Bass
Bill Cantrell: Trombone
Rob Gehrka: Percussion
Paul Leschen: Piano
John Sandfort: Saxophone

1995 Pope Fiction (previews)

For Whom the Bell Curves (mainstage)

CAST
Jill Alexander
Ed Herbstman
Rob Janas
Louise Lamson
Liv Oslund
Jean Villepique
Dan Weiss
Adrian Wenner

STAFF
Producer: Saskia Young
Codirectors: Jean Villepique, Adrian Wenner
Assistant Producer: Melissa Meloro
Stage Manager: Missy Near
Tour Director: Stephanie March
Production Coordinator: Matt Gilmore
Set Designer: Dan Weiss
Lighting Designer: Patricia Gaborik
Assistant Stage Managers: Sara Levavy, April Shapiro
Videographer/Assistant Tour Director: Matt Sherman
House Manager: Cary Brothers
McCormick Publicity Directors: Jen Chambers, Michelle Mikolajczak
Documentarian: Dave Gioella
Graphic Designer: Chris Schweiger
Publicity Staff: Dave Glassman, Kristin Mochnick, Apphia Parsons
Music Director/Pianist: Paul Leschen

1996 Mee-Ow Say Tongue (previews)

It's a Wonderful Lie (mainstage)

CAST
Jill Alexander
Peter Grosz

Jen Horstman
Rob Janas
Laura McKenzie
Seth Meyers
Ryan Raddatz
Robin Shorr
Sarah Yorra

STAFF (MEE-OW SAY TONGUE)

Director: Jill Alexander
Producer: Melissa Meloro
Tour Director: Saskia Young
Stage Manager: Alison Sneed
Technical Director: John Hackett
Assistant Director: Jeremy Fleck
Assistant Producer: Erin West
Assistant Stage Manager: Noah Falk
House Manager: Kat Schutzman
Lighting Designer: Andrew Coveler
Props Coordinator: April Shapiro
Co-Publicity Chairs: Heather Landy, Kristen Mochnick
Graphic Designer: Sam Lieb
Sound Technician: Chris Darnielle
Photographer: Kirsten Sorton
Videographer: Brian Morris
Publicity Team: Matt Dudley, John Kostrey, Michelle Mikolajczak
Tech Godsend: Emlyn Saunders
Production Assistant: Andrew Lanchoney

STAFF (IT'S A WONDERFUL LIE)

Director: Jill Alexander
Producer: Melissa Meloro
Tour Director: Saskia Young
Stage Manager: Alison Sneed
Technical Director, Set Designer: John Hackett
Assistant Director: Jeremy Fleck
Assistant Producer: Erin West
Assistant Stage Manager: Noah Falk
House Manager: Kat Schutzman
Lighting Designer: Andrew Coveler
Props Coordinator: April Shapiro
Co-Publicity Chairs: Heather Landy, Kristen Mochnick
Graphic Designer: Sam Lieb
Sound Technician: Chris Darnielle
Photographer: Kirsten Sorton
Videographer: Jonathan Hoenig
Sound Technician: Libby Minarik
Publicity Team: Matt Dudley, John Kostrey, Michelle Mikolajczak
Tech Godsend: Emlyn Saunders
Production Assistant: Andrew Lanchoney
Staff Member for a Week: Andrea Spitz

THE BAND

Marshall Greenhouse: Drums
Jason Kanakis: Guitar *(It's a Wonderful Lie)*
Dan Lipton: Music Director, Keyboards
Zach Seldess: Guitar *(Mee-Ow Say Tongue)*
Ian Thompson: Bass

1997 Apocalypse Mee-Ow (previews)

The Mee-Owtsiders (mainstage)

CAST

Jill Alexander
Liz Cackowski
Heather Campbell
Josh Meyers
Ryan Raddatz
Jamey Roberts
Robin Shorr
David Terry

STAFF

Producer: Libby Minarik
Director: Jill Alexander
Assistant Director: Lauren Bishop
Assistant Producers: Michael Kraskin, Brooke Sadowsky
Music Director: Ian Thompson
Lighting Designer: Andrew Coveler
Properties Designer: April Shapiro
Technical Director: Chad Emigholz
Stage Manager: Ethan Alter
Graphics Designer: Patrick Kalyanapu
Tour/PR Directors: Stephanie Rapp, Heather Schmucker
Publicity Director: Jamie Geller
Fundraising Director: Cecile-Anne Sison
Master Electrician: Paul Bongaarts
Videographers: Cathryn Humphris, Debbie Kraus
Additional Graphics: David Iserson
Production Assistants: Peter Duffy, Nikki Faust, Jeanna Fazzalaro, Patrick Gagnon, Dori Graff, Jessica Kingery, Jeff Leister

THE BAND

Brian Cohen: Sound Technician
Paul Giallorenzo: Keyboard
Marshall Greenhouse: Drums
Jason Kanakis: Guitar
Bevin Ryness: Vocals
Ian Thompson: Bass

1998 Get in Touch with Your Pussy (previews)

Hell No, Mee-Ow Show! (mainstage)

CAST

Liz Cackowski
Heather Campbell
Luke Hatton
Josh Meyers
Jamey Roberts
Robin Shorr
Justin Spitzer
David Terry

STAFF

Producer: Libby Minarik
Director: Ryan Raddatz
Assistant Producers: Jaime Morgenstern, Sara Rosen

Stage Managers: Ethan Alter, Michelle Weber
Lighting Designer: Andrew Coveler
Props Director: April Shapiro
Technical Director: Chad Emigholz
Master Electrician: Paul Bongaarts
Sound Technician: Brian Cohen
Publicity Directors: Jessica Kingery, Brooke Sadowsky
Assistant Publicity Director: Claire Yoon
Graphics Designer: David Iserson
Charlie: Ed Herbstman
Production Assistants: Sarah Angelmar, Steve Bassman, Liz Blood, Lauren Flans, Lauren Markofsky
Uncredited protestors (Hell No, Mee-Ow Show!): Jeff Leister, Scott Wilson

THE BAND

Tom Barrett: Guitar
Marshall Greenhouse: Drums
Jason Kanakis: Guitar *(Get in Touch with Your Pussy)*
Marco Paguia: Piano
Kathryn Parsons: Vocals
Ian Thompson: Band Director, Bass

1999 That Was Then, This Is Mee-Ow (previews)

The Last Mee-Ow Show Ever (mainstage)

CAST

Dave Asher
Liz Cackowski
Heather Campbell
Luke Hatton
Jamey Roberts
Kristen Schaal
Michael Sinclair
Scott Speiser

STAFF

Producer: Jaime Morgenstern
Codirectors: Liz Cackowski, Jamey Roberts
Technical Director: Dave Weyburn
Assistant Technical Director: Sean Morse
Lighting Designer: Dennis Kiilerich
Assistant Lighting Designer: Laura Evans
Master Electricians: Tim Berger, Christian Rehder
Lighting Crew: Steve Hall, Joe Morrow, Jin Sakakibara, Kensuke Suzuki, Dan Weaver
Sound Designer: Scott Wilson
Properties Designer: Jessica Kingery
Assistant Properties Designer: Lindsey Stephens
Graphic Designer: Heather Campbell
Web Page/Program Designer: Graham Walker
Set Designers: Gary Ashwal, Heather Campbell, Jaime Morgenstern, Dave Weyburn
Mee-Ow Alumni Coordinators: Rush Pearson, Paul Warshauer
Stage Manager: Michelle Weber
Assistant Stage Manager: Laurel Felt
Head of Production Team: Stephen Sassman
Production Team: Jen Bender, Darren Grodsky, Lindsey Stephens, Graham Walker, Rani Waterman, Trina Wong
House Manager: Jeff Porter

THE BAND: THE CLEVELAND STEAMERS

Ben Bokor: Drums, Percussion
Peter Jablonowski: Bass
Sam Kleiner: Guitar
Merritt Lyon: Drums, Percussion
Marco Paguia: Music Director, Keyboards
Jennie Wilke: Vocals

2000 Don't Tread on Mee-Ow (previews)

Mee-Ow on Ice (mainstage)

CAST

Heather Campbell
Lauren Flans
Ryan Harrison
Luke Hatton
Jess Lacher
Matt McKenna
Kristen Schaal
Scott Speiser

STAFF

Director: Luke Hatton
Producers: Heather Campbell, Karyn Meltz
Assistant Tech Director: Molly Meacham
Assistant Light Designer: Laura Evans
Light Crew: Steve Hall, Joe Morrow, Kensuke Suzuki, Jim Wirth
Production Assistants: Owen Douglas, Brad Jorsch, Kristen Kolada, Shannon Mok, Steve Settles, Mike Sherman, Janice Tsai
Web Page Designers: Jeff Harper, Brad Jorsch, Janice Tsai
Photographer: Jessica Kingery
Graphics: Heather Campbell
Zamboni Driver: Mike Sherman

THE BAND: SWEET SWEET CANDY

Jeremy Bass: Guitar
Jason Dolinger: Drums
Ethan Goldman: Tenor Sax
Pete Jablonowski: Band Director, Bass
Sam Kleiner: Guitar
Jamie Newman: Vocals
Jonathan Sanford: Alto Sax

2001 Sesamee-ow Street (previews)

Les Mee-Owsérables (mainstage)

CAST

Drew Callander
Laura Grey
Ryan Harrison
Jess Lacher
Dan Mahoney
Martha Marion
Matthew McKenna
Lee Overtree

STAFF

Codirectors: Ryan Harrison, Matthew McKenna
Coproducers: Aleksandra Kostovski, Jess Lacher
Stage Manager: Micaela Hester
Assistant Producers: Mark Arnot, Liz Lyons
Assistant Stage Manager: Michael Sherman
Lighting Designer: Laura Evans
Assistant Lighting: Megan Caldwell
Set Designer: Blake Longacre
Technical Director: Nate Doud
Assistant Technical Directors: Cheryl Conkling, Sam Roberts
Sound Designer: David Feldman
Assistant Sound: Dan Schulman
Master Electrician: Steven Hall
2nd Master Electrician: Dan Weaver
Electrician: Edna Flores
Color Consultant: Dan Weaver
Costume and Props Designer: Shannon Mok
Band Director: Pete Jablonowski
Publicity/Program Designer: Joel Richlin
Webmaster: Jan Ice Tsai
Assistant Webmaster: Jeffrey Cheng
Graphics Designers: Jess Lacher, Joel Richlin
Photographer: Ayako Okano

THE BAND: THE MONKEY BUTLERS

Jeremy Bass: Guitar, Vocals
Ethan Goldman: Tenor and Soprano Saxophones
Jeff Gutierrez: Saxophone
Bice Holden: Vocals
Pete Jablonowski: Bass
John Ostrowski: Drums, Percussion
Tim Requarth: Keyboard

2002 Seven Minutes in Heaven (previews)

Mee-Owd to Be an American (mainstage)

CAST

Laura Grey
Ryan Harrison
Jess Lacher
Dan Mahoney
Martha Marion
Kate Mulligan
Lee Overtree
Frank Smith

STAFF

Coproducers: Martha Marion, Dory Weiss
Codirectors: Laura Grey, Dan Mahoney
Stage Manager: Eliot Monaco
Technical Director: Gary Ashwal
Set Designer: Gary Ashwal
Lighting Designer: Patrick Frank
Sound Designer: Ryan Hinshaw
Assistant Lighting Designers: Martha Jackson, Joanna Simmons
Assistant Producers: Caroline Davis, Sarah Peters, Debbie Schreiner
Photographer/Publicity Chair: Alex Sherman
Poster Designers: Cassandra Kegler, Jess Lacher
Program Designer: Joel Richlin

ACCOMPANIST

Michael Mahler

THE BAND: SASQUATCH

Jeremy Bass: Vocals, Guitar
Ethan Goldman: Sax
Jeff Gutierrez: Sax
Aaron Kotler: Keyboard
Geoff Kraly: Bass
John Ostrowski: Drums
Sari Schwartz: Vocals

2003 Mee-Ow Saves Christmas (previews)

There's a Bear in the Theater! (mainstage)

CAST

Chris Gorbos
Briggs Hatton
Jason Kessler
Martha Marion
Alex Marlin
Bridget Moloney
Kate Mulligan
Dan Sinclair

STAFF (MEE-OW SAVES CHRISTMAS)

Producer: Dory Weiss
Codirectors: Martha Marion, Kate Mulligan
Technical Director/Set Designer: Kenneth Ferrone
Lighting Designer: Tom McGrath
Stage Manager/Choreographer: Ben Sinclair
Sound Designer: Ryan Hinshaw
Assistant Producers: Claudia Ballard, Chris Sachs
Program Cover Design: Greta Lee
Program Design: Chad Young

STAFF (THERE'S A BEAR IN THE THEATER!)

Producer: Dory Weiss
Codirectors: Martha Marion, Kate Mulligan

Technical Director/Set Designer: Kenneth Ferrone
Lighting Designer: Tom McGrath
Stage Manager: Tom McGrath
Sound Designer: Ryan Hinshaw
Assistant Producers: Claudia Ballard, Jack Sachs, Emily Weiss
Bear: Teddy Dunn
Uncredited surprise appearance as the Bee: Natalie Monahan
Uncredited lighting operator: Ben Sinclair

THE BAND: JUNK IN THE TRUNK

Jeff Gutierrez: Saxophone
Casey Kannenberg: Guitar and Vocals
Aaron Kotler: Keyboard
Geoff Kraly: Bass
Terris Ransom: Trombone and Vocals
Leah Wagner: Vocals
Kobie Watkins: Drums

2004 Danger on University Place (previews)

It's Not You, It's Mee-Ow (mainstage)

CAST

John Dixon
Briggs Hatton
Jason Kessler
Bridget Moloney
Kate Mulligan
Joe Petrilla
Sheila Shaigany
Dan Sinclair

STAFF

Director: Dan Sinclair
Coproducers: Briggs Hatton, Jack Sachs
Stage Manager: Morgan Beck
Sound Designer: Nick Kanellis
Production Assistant: Kate Kountzman
Publicity Designer: Felipe Lima
Assistant Producer: Jessica Lowe
Lighting Designer: Alex Robins

2005 Mee-Ow Admits, Mee-Ow Has a Problem (previews)

Mee-Ow Goes to Old Orchard (mainstage)

CAST

Russ Armstrong
John Dixon
Briggs Hatton
Nick Kanellis
Jessica Lowe
Peter McNerney
Bridget Moloney
Joanna Simmons

STAFF

Codirectors: Briggs Hatton, Bridget Moloney

THE BAND: CAPTAIN TEABAG

Patrick Droppleman: Keyboards
Brendan Fox, John Johnson, Greta Lee: Vocals
Brad Jepson, Nick West: Bass
Nate Linkon: Saxophone
Jake Nissly: Drums

2006 Mee-Ow Is Dead (previews)

Mee-Ow Pulls Out . . . of Iraq (mainstage)

CAST

Russ Armstrong
John Dixon
Nick Kanellis
Jessica Lowe
Kelly O'Sullivan
Matt Sheelen
Adam Welton
Nayla Wren

STAFF

Codirectors: Russ Armstrong, John Dixon
Producer: Nikki Zaleski
Lighting Designer: Aaron Weissman
Lighting/Sound Advisor: Alec Thorne
Set Designer: Hannah Hodak
Sound Designer: Jack Sachs
Public Relations: Ginger Davis
Assistant Producer: James Seifer
Stage Manager: Josiah Jenkins
Technical Directors: Joe Lofting, Ruth Orme
Publicity: Carly Ciarrocchi, Jordan McDole
Tropical Themes and Arrangement Manager: Dan Foster
Fundraising Director: Mary Healy
Graphics Designer: Evyn Williams
Preparatory Research Director: Conor White

THE BAND

Phillip Floyd: Saxophone
Brad Jepson: Trombone
Jon Johnson: Guitar
Max Krucoff: Drums
Sean McCluskey: Piano
Pranidhi Varshney: Vocals
Nick West: Bass

2007 Mee-Ow '08: Mee-Ow Declares Its Candidacy (previews)

Mee-Ow's Anatomy (mainstage)

CAST

Dan Bruhl
Carly Ciarrocchi
Chris Hejl
Nick Kanellis
Jessica Lowe
Jack Novak
Matt Sheelen
Adam Welton

STAFF

Codirectors: Nick Kanellis, Jessica Lowe
Producer: Lindsey Dorcus
Assistant Producer: Chuck Filipov
Lighting Designer: Alec Thorne
Assistant Lighting Designers: Lindsay Fritchman, Samuel B. Prime
Set Designer: Rie Ma
Publicity: Emma Olson
Stage Manager: Jessica McKenna
Graphics Designer: Andrew Karas
Sound Technician: Brad Kolsky
Sound Board Operator: Chuck Filipov

THE BAND: SEDUCTION GROOVE

Andrew Haynie: Sax, Gold Clarinet
Brad Jepson: Trombone, Electric Triangle
Janelle Kroll: Vocalist
Max Krucoff: Drumset
Fritz Schenker: Keyboard, Accordion, Percussion
Rump of Steel Skin: Guitar, Vox
Truth: Bass

2008 DOOMSDAY: Mee-Ow Is the Winter of Our Discontent

Mee-Ow Talks Down to Children

CAST

Dan Bruhl
Carly Ciarrocchi
James Daniel
Dan Foster
Jessica McKenna
Jack Novak
Sarah Grace Welbourn
Adam Welton

STAFF

Codirectors: Carly Ciarrocchi, Adam Welton
Producer: Zora Senat

THE BAND

Catherine Brookman: Vocalist
Janelle Kroll: Vocalist

2009 Mee-Ow Screws the Pooch

Mee-Ow Presents Dr. Pepper's Homely Joke Brigade

CAST

Jen D'Angelo
James Daniel
Tim McGovern
Jessica McKenna
Jack Novak
Joel Sinensky
Sarah Grace Welbourn
Conner White

STAFF

Codirectors: Jack Novak, Sarah Grace Welbourn
Producer: Katie Halpern
Assistant Producers: Chase Altenbern, Johanna Middleton
Stage Manager: Chase Altenbern
Set Designer: Andrew Karas, Kyle Warren
Lighting Designer: Jeff Glass
Lighting Assistant: Tina Frank
Sound Designer: Dave Sumberg
Graphic Designer: Evan Twohy
Publicity Chair: Danielle Gaines
Publicity: Justin Barbin, Maddy Bloch, Naomi Brodkin, Max Cove, Breanne Ward
Photographer: Justin Barbin

2010 The Mee-Ow Show: A Tail of Nine Lives

The Mee-Ow Kids Solve a Murder at Chuck Fuffalo's

CAST

Jen D'Angelo
James Daniel
Aaron Eisenberg
Nick Gertonson
Tim McGovern
Ryan Nunn
Isabel Richardson
Marie Semla
Josh Waytz

STAFF

Producer: Tracey Cook
Codirectors: Jen D'Angelo, Tim McGovern
Assistant Producers: Michael Janak, Ben Ratskoff
Stage Manager: Dave Collins
Assistant Stage Manager: Nicole Silverberg
Technical Director: Matt Dealy
Master Electrician: David Griffin
Set Designer: Phoebe Brooks
Lighting Designer: Dan Lazar, Andrew Tolbert
Sound Designer: Dave Sumberg
Graphic Designer: Max Cove
Publicity Chair: Naomi Brodkin
Publicity Team: Anna Ciamporcero, Darrin French, Tristan Powen, Em Reit, Ed Wasserman
Fundraising Chairs: Drigan Lee, Lucas McMahon
Fundraising Team: Ben Estus, Brendan Scannell, Jeremy Shpizner
Build Team: Emilia Barrosse, Max Fagelson

THE BAND

Jed Feder: Drums
Mike Johnson: Guitar

Charles Meuller: Guitar
Carly Robinson: Singer
Zach Spound: Keyboard
Danny Yadron: Bass

2011 Mee-Ow Is Dating a Monster

Glee-Ow: Mee-Ow Sells Out!

CAST

Danielle Calvert
Aaron Eisenberg
Sam Fishell
Nick Gertonson
Caroline Goldfarb
Tucker May
Ryan Nunn
Isabel Richardson
Marie Semla

STAFF

Codirectors: Aaron Eisenberg, Marie Semla
Producer: Jeremy Shpizner

THE BAND

Jed Feder: Drums
Jane Hurh: Singer
Zack Spound: Keyboard

2012 Dr. Faustus Mee-Owstus

Three's Company, Ten's Mee-Ow

CAST

Sam Fishell
Nick Gertonson
Caroline Goldfarb
Matthew Hays
Drigan Lee
Tucker May
Amina Munir
Emily Olcott
Austin Perry
Brendan Scannell

STAFF

Codirectors: Nick Gertonson, Caroline Goldfarb
Assistant Producer: Liz Steelman
Stage Manager: Jake Pollock
Lighting Designer: Ford Altenbern
Assistant Lighting Designer: Rachel Shapiro
Master Electrician: Brannon Bowers
Sound Designer: Ray Rehberg
Props Designers: Alex Barontini, Emma Cadd, Scott Egleston
Scenic Design Team: Corinne Bass, Ryan Hynes, Mitch Johnston, Kylie Mullins
Driver: Pager Anderson
Graphic Design and Promo Video: Nick Gertonson
Production Assistants: Maggie Fish, Izzy Garcia, Ellen Groble, Claire Huntington, Bridget McNamara, Francesca Mennella, Dylan Pager

THE BAND

Sam Altman: Vocalist
Alex Goldkang: Saxophone
Cameron LeCrone: Drums
Jeremy Levine: Keyboard
Aaron Messing: Trumpet
Charles Mueller: Music Director, Guitar
Nic Park: Bass
Thom Schwartz: Trombone

2013 Mee-Ow Presents The Great Catsby

Mee-Ow That's What I Call Comedy! Vol. 40

CAST

Pat Buetow
Emma Cadd
Gaby Febland
Sam Fishell
Matthew Hays
Michael Janak
Amina Munir
Emily Olcott
Brendan Scannell

STAFF (MEE-OW PRESENTS THE GREAT CATSBY)

Producer: Francesca Mennella
Codirectors: Sam Fishell, Emily Olcott
Assistant Producer: Wes Humphrey
Stage Manager: Will Sonhein
Assistant Stage Manager: Ben Bailey
Light Designer: Bobby Ramirez
Assistant Light Designer: Jack Olin
Sound Designer: Conor Keelan
Assistant Sound Designer: Elsa Gay
Scenic Designer: Sarah Sherman
Set Designers: Alex Goodman, Katy Piotrowski, Nikolaj Sorensen
Technical Directors: Emily Baldwin, Elliot Hornsby
Props Team: Savannah Couch, Nathan Lamp
Publicity Director: Maggie Fish
Publicity Team: Justin Connolly, Shannon Grogans, Jessie Klueter, Sam Mueller, Cate Walters
Fundraising/Production Assistants: Summer Benowitz, Michael Fleischer, Shaina Wagner
Graphic Designer: Juli Del Prete

STAFF (MEE-OW THAT'S WHAT I CALL COMEDY! VOL. 40)

Producer: Francesca Mennella
Codirectors: Sam Fishell, Emily Olcott
Assistant Producer: Wes Humphrey
Stage Manager: Will Sonhein
Assistant Stage Manager: Ben Bailey
Light Designer: Bobby Ramirez
Assistant Light Designer: Jack Olin
Sound Designer: Conor Keelan
Assistant Sound Designer: Elsa Gay
Scenic Designer: Sarah Sherman
Set Designer: Katy Piotrowski
Assistant Set Designers: Alex Goodman, Nikolaj Sorensen
Technical Directors: Emily Baldwin, Elliott Hornsby

Heads of Props: Savannah Couch, Nathan Lamp
Props Team: Matt Dial, Josh Issler
Publicity Director: Maggie Fish
Publicity Team: Justin Connolly, Sam Mueller, Cate Walters
Fundraising/Production Assistants: Summer Benowitz, Michael Fleischer, Shain Wagner
Production Assistant: Max Kramer
Graphic Designer: Michael Janak

THE MEE-OW SHOW BAND

Michael Abbey: Bass *(Mee-Ow That's What I Call Comedy!)*
Lillie Cummings, Eliza Palasz: Vocals *(Mee-Ow That's What I Call Comedy!)*
Hallye Webb: Vocals *(The Great Catsby)*
Cameron Lecrone: Drums
Jeremy Levine: Keyboard
Aaron Messing: Trumpet *(Mee-Ow That's What I Call Comedy!)*
Max Paymar: Saxophone, Keyboard, Backing Vocals
Nick Platoff: Trombone *(Mee-Ow That's What I Call Comedy!)*
Zach Puller, Will Steiger: Guitar

2014 You're Invited to Mee-Owy-Kate and Ashley's Sleepover Party

Mee-Ow Kills Curiosity: A Tail of Revenge

CAST

Pat Buetow
Emma Cadd
Nick DiMaso
Scott Egleston
Gaby Febland
Amina Munir
Jack Olin
Laurel Zoff Pelton

STAFF

Producer: Alex Gold
Codirectors: Emma Cadd, Amina Munir
Assistant Producer: Julie Busch
Stage Managers: Wes Humphrey, Eva Victor
Assistant Stage Manager: Isabel Thompson
Scenic Designer: Matt Moynihan
Lighting Designer: Bobby Ramiraz
Sound Designer: Matt Cassoli
Marketing Director: Ryan Kearney
Fundraising Director: Shaina Wagner
Outreach Director: Cory Goldman
Graphic Designer: Ian Robinson
Promotional Videographers: Brandon Green, Tom Mason
Production Assistants: Dana Balkin, Ben Bass, Avril Dominguez, Liam Feroli, Dominque French, Isabella Gerasole, Kyle Largent, Allie Levitan, Daniel Liu, Rachel Marchant, Hale McSharry, Sam Mueller, Harry Wood

THE BAND

Alex Beer, Will Steiger: Guitar
Cameron Lecrone: Music Director, Drums
Charles Mueller: Bass
Max Paymar: Keyboards
Jon Schneidman: Vocals
Betsy Stewart: Vocals

2015 Mee-Ow Presents THE TRUTH

The 87th Annual AcadeMEE-OWards

CAST

Emma Cadd
Nick DiMaso
Scott Egleston
Ben Gauthier
Alex Heller
Chanse McCrary
Jack Olin
Natalie Rotter-Laitman
Anne Sundell

STAFF

Codirectors: Emma Cadd, Nick DiMaso
Producer: Mallory Harrington
Assistant Producer: Seth Rosner
Stage Manager: Caroline Reedy
Assistant Stage Manager: Devyn Johnson
Scenic Designer: Axel Mark
Assistant Scenic Designers: Yianni Kinnas, Kate Kowalski
Lighting Designer: Raphael Grimes
Assistant Lighting Designer: Courtney Quinn
Sound Designer: Jim Alrutz
Assistant Sound Designer: Juliet Roll
Sound Engineer: Aissa Guerra
Props Designer: Justin Shannin
Assistant Props Designers: Grant Lewis, Nick Tiffany
Publicity Director: Michael Fleischer
Assistant Publicity Director: Margot Zuckerman
Outreach Directors: Liam Feroli, Angelina Strohbach
Fundraising Director: Mahek Tulsiani
Graphic Designer: Maria Fernandez-Davila
Videographer: Tom Mason

THE BAND: PHANTOM J AND THE GALACTIC BOOTY

Tommy Carroll: Band Leader
Lady Contagion: Saxophone
Lord Zarquad: Guitar
Vice Admiral Seitan: Guitar
Maryjane Indica: Keyboard
Maryjane Sativa: Keyboard
Bass Dragon: Bass
Phantom J: Drums
Kipwa Chunk: Vocals
Darth Vapor: Vocals

Jessie Klueter: Vocals (Louis Room)
Jared Corak, Drew Tildon: Vocals (Shanley)

2016 Ctrl Alt Mee-Ow

Speak Mee-Ow or Forever Hold Your Peace

CAST

Will Altabef
Ben Gauthier
Isabella Gerasole
Dan Leahy
Chanse McCrary
Jack Olin
Caroline Reedy
Natalie Rotter-Laitman
Eva Victor

STAFF

Producer: Devon Levy
Codirectors: Jack Olin, Natalie Rotter-Laitman
Publicity Director: David Brown

THE BAND: STOP FIGHTING!

Tommy Carroll: Drums
Josh AleXander Crowder: Rap and Backup Vocals
Leo Galbraith-Paul: Keys
Marion Hill: Synths and Backup Vocals
Grace Kennedy: Vocals *(Speak Mee-Ow)*
Karl Maher: Guitar
Jessie Pinnick: Lead Vocals *(Speak Mee-Ow)*
Sage Ross: Backup Vocals
Matthew Wang: Lead Vocals *(Ctrl Alt Mee-Ow)*
Alex Warshawsky: Bass

2017 Mee-Ow Enters the Twilight Zone!

Mee-Ow's Anatomy

CAST

Will Altabef
Maya Armstrong
Ben Gauthier
Isabella Gerasole
Devyn Johnson
Dan Leahy
Allie Levitan
Nabeel Muscatwalla
Harry Wood

STAFF (MEE-OW ENTERS THE TWILIGHT ZONE!)

Producer: Devon Levy
Codirectors: Ben Gauthier, Isabella Gerasole
Set Design: Luke Miller
Lighting Design: Sara Torres
Sound Design: Jeremy Gubman
Props Design: Chase Doggett
Technical Director: Becca Schwartz
Stage Manager: Margot Zuckerman
Choreographer: Michaela Kastelman
Music Director: Alex Warshawsky

CREW (MEE-OW ENTERS THE TWILIGHT ZONE!)

Assistant Producer: Rachel Cantor
Assistant Lighting: Chloe Fourte
Assistant Props: Arianna Cu, Amanda Lifford, Julia Tesmond
Assistant Stage Managers: Katie Adler, Jack Goss
Board Operators: Jack Goss, Alex Schwartz
Fundraising/Outreach Director: Liz Coin
Assistant Fundraising: Hannah Collins, Evan Nixon
Publicity Director: Dawn Rafal
Assistant Publicity: Matt Zients
Videographer: Liz Coin
Video Editor: David Brown
Graphic Designer: Adam Turkel
Photographer: Justin Barbin
Production Assistants: Mat Benson, Athena Chen, Mahito Henderson, Katia Podtynov, Jesse Rudnick, Alex Schwartz, Yiting Wang, Jane Yun
Producer Support: Emma Brick

STAFF (MEE-OW'S ANATOMY)

Producer: Devon Levy
Codirectors: Ben Gauthier, Isabella Gerasole
Set Design: Nate Brown
Lighting Design: Benji Solomon
Sound Design: Chloe Fourte
Props Design: Amanda Lifford, Julia Tesmond
Technical Director: Becca Schwartz
Stage Manager: Margot Zuckerman
Choreographer: Kayla Griffith
Music Director: Alex Warshawsky

CREW (MEE-OW'S ANATOMY)

Assistant Producer: Rachel Cantor
Assistant Lighting: Grace Alexander
Assistant Props: Arianna Cu
Assistant Stage Managers: Katie Adler, Jack Goss
Board Operators: Jack Goss, Alex Schwartz
Fundraising/Outreach Director: Liz Coin
Assistant Fundraising: Hannah Collins, Evan Nixon
Publicity Director: Dawn Rafal
Videographer/Editor: David Brown
Graphic Designer: Adam Turkel
Photographer: Justin Barbin
Production Assistants: Mat Benson, Athena Chen, Mahito Henderson, Katia Podtynov, Jesse Rudnick, Alex Schwartz, Yiting Wang, Jane Yun
Producer Support: Emma Brick

THE BAND: MOONLIGHT PALACE

Curtis Boysen: Drums
Aiden Fisher, Ogi Ifediora: Vocals
Leo Galbraith-Paul: Synths
Lorenzo Gonzalez-Lamassonne: Electronics, Vocals
Victor Lalo: Guitar
Julius Tucker: Keys
Alex Warshawsky: Band Leader, Bass

2018 Take Mee-Ow to the Ball Game

The Mee-Owstery Machine

CAST

Maya Armstrong
Makasha Copeland
Jake Curtis
Jake Daniels
Devyn Johnson
Julianne Lang
Amara Leonard
Joey Lieberman
Nabeel Muscatwalla

STAFF

Producer: Alex Schwartz
Codirectors: Devyn Johnson, Nabeel Muscatwalla
Set Design: Mahito Henderson, Sydney Thomas
Lighting Design: Jonah Pazol
Sound Design: Riina Dougherty
Props Design: Danny Callahan, Jess Mordacq
Stage Manager: Madeline LeFevour
Choreography: Christopher Flaim
Music Direction: Ryan Savage

CREW

Assistant Stage Managers/Board Operators: Izzie Lienen, Serena Salgado
Assistant Sound Designer: Noelle Torres
Assistant Props Designers: Kaitlyn Poindexter, Haley West, Jane Yun
Publicity Director: Claudia Sierra
Graphic Designer: Adam Turkel
Production Assistants: Kristine Liao, Katie Russell, Natalie Shilati, Claudia Sierra, Sarah Springhorn

THE BAND: TUESDAYS ARE FOR BILLIARDS

Meryl Crock, Bria Kalpen, Lizzie Zhang: Vocals
Dimitris Goulimaris: Auxiliary Percussion
Conor Jones: Lead Guitar
Ben Krege: Bass
Alejandro Paredes: Keyboard
Luke Peterson: Drums
Ryan Savage: Band Leader, Synth
Gabriel Shelhorse: Synth, Rap Vocals
Slade Warnken: Rhythm Guitar, Vocals

2019 In Mee-Owdieval Times

In Mee-Owmoriam

CAST

Maya Armstrong
Willa Barnett
Makasha Copeland
Jake Curtis
Jake Daniels
Amara Leonard
Edson Montenegro
Jasmine Sharma
Ross Turkington

STAFF

Producer: Jaclyn Orlando
Codirectors: Maya Armstrong, Jake Daniels
Stage Manager: Lily Feinberg
Set Designer: Quinn Stiefbold
Lighting Designer: Mark Biedke
Sound Designer: Casey Wells
Sound Engineer: Sharlene Burgos
Lighting Board Operator: Kevin Cox
Marketing Director: Nicole Andonova
Assistant Producer: Billy O'Handley
Props Master: Henry Lang
Production Manager: Jane Emma Barnett
Technical Director: Nate Brown
Business Manager: Katia Podtynov
Choreographer: Gabriella Green

THE BAND: HONEY BUTTER

Band Leaders: Jacob Galdes, Oliver Holden-Moses
Band Members: George Estey, Peter Hoerenz, Austin Klewan, Dan Peters, Sam Wolsk
Mee-Ow Singers: Morgan Buckley, Nicole Rinne

2020 America's Next Top Mee-Owdel

Mee-Owddle School Dance: Unchaperoned

CAST

Willa Barnett
Arshad Baruti
Jake Curtis
Sydney Feyder
Carly Griffin-Fiorella
Carden Katz
Graham Kirstein
Jasmine Sharma
Ross Turkington

STAFF

Producer: Jackie Orlando
Codirectors: Jake Curtis, Ross Turkington

THE BAND: THE GIANT PEACHES

Darsan Swaroop Bellie: Drums
Christina Carty, Emily Pate-Somé, Taj Smith: Singers
AJ Denhoff: Band Leader, Bass
Jamie Eder: Band Leader, Guitar
Clay Eshleman: Piano

2021 Get Mee-Owt of My Head!!

(Due to the COVID-19 pandemic, the Mee-Ow Show was not performed for an in-person audience. In lieu of in-person shows, recorded sketches and live online improv were presented. The proposed title of an unproduced web series was *Get Mee-Owt of My Head!!*)

CAST

Willa Barnett
Arshad Baruti
Sam Buttress
Carly Griffin-Fiorella
Anelga Hajjar
Carden Katz
Emily Pate-Somé
Jasmine Sharma

STAFF

Producer: Lily Feinberg
Codirectors: Arshad Baruti, Carly Griffin-Fiorella, Jasmine Sharma

2022 How Do They Pee in Mee-Owter Space?

Mee-Ow You See Me

CAST

Sam Buttress
Liv Drury
Anelga Hajjar
Carden Katz
Justin Kuhn
Orly Lewittes
Alondra Rios
Emily Somé
Jared Zavala

STAFF (HOW DO THEY PEE IN MEE-OWTER SPACE?)

Coproducers: Grant Albright, Kate Bowman
Codirectors: Sam Buttress, Carden Katz
Stage Manager: Jordan Panzier
Set Designer: Jessie Vallan
Lighting Designer: Annie Horowitz
Music Codirectors: Tabor Brewster, Clay Eshleman
Props/Costume Designer: Katherine Tuohy
Business Manager: Lily Forbes
Graphic Designer: Nick Hollenbeck
Sound Designer: Bea Stewart
Assistant Sound Designer: Evan Trotter-Wright
Lightboard Operator: Cooper Silverman
Soundboard Operator: Goldie Beck

STAFF (MEE-OW YOU SEE ME)

Coproducers: Grant Albright, Kate Bowman
Codirectors: Sam Buttress, Carden Katz
Stage Manager: Jordan Panzier
Set Designer: Sammy Koolik
Lighting Designer: James Hovet
Music Codirectors: Tabor Brewster, Clay Eshleman
Props/Costume Designer: Katherine Tuohy
Business Manager: Lily Forbes
Graphic Designer: Nick Hollenbeck
Sound Designer: Evan Trotter-Wright
Assistant Sound Designer: Nick Kapp
Lightboard Operator: Cooper Silverman
Soundboard Operator: Goldie Beck

THE BAND

Riva Akolawala: Vocals
Tabor Brewster: Drums
Clay Eshleman: Keyboard
Dana Hinchcliffe: Vocals
Sam Marshall: Guitar
Noah Rabinovitch: Bass

2023 Mee-Owgic Mike's Last Dance

Mee-Owpocalypse: Let's Repopulate

CAST

Sam Buttress
Brenden Dahl
Liv Drury
Anelga Hajjar
Arjun Kumar
Orly Lewittes
Ferd Moscat
Alondra Rios

STAFF (MEE-OWGIC MIKE'S LAST DANCE)

Codirectors: Liv Drury, Anelga Hajjar
Producer: Julia Kruger
Stage Manager: Henry Patton
Set Designer: Jessica Vallan
Sound Designer: Nick Kapp
Lighting Designer: Katherine Li
Choreographer: Shira Hirsch
Prop Designer: Amelia Reyes-Gomez
Graphic Designer: Nick Hollenbeck
Assistant Producer/Assistant Stage Manager: Cooper Silverman

STAFF (MEE-OWPOCALYPSE: LET'S REPOPULATE)

Codirectors: Liv Drury, Anelga Hajjar
Producer: Julia Kruger
Stage Manager: Henry Patton
Set Designer: Sunnie Eraso
Sound Designer: Nick Kapp
Lighting Designer: Katherine Li
Assistant Lighting Designer: Julia Marshall
Choreographer: Mika Parisien
Prop Designer: Amelia Reyes-Gomez
Graphic Designer: Nick Hollenbeck
Assistant Producer/Assistant Stage Manager: Cooper Silverman

THE BAND

Tabor Brewster: Band Director, Drums
Piper Fishkind: Singer

Khoi Lee: Keyboard
Sam Marshall: Guitar
Noah Rabinovitch: Bass
Sarika Rao: Singer
Jackson Spellman: Trombone (*Mee-Owgic Mike's Last Dance*)
Julia Stork: Singer
Jason Zhu: Saxophone (*Mee-Owgic Mike's Last Dance*)

2024 Mee-Owd Life Crisis: Mee-Ow Turns 50

Brokeback Mee-Owntain

CAST

Shai Bardin
Brenden Dahl
PJ Fahrenkrug
Orly Lewittes
Ferd Moscat
Alondra Rios
Jeff Snedegar
Walter Todd

STAFF

Codirectors: Orly Lewittes, Alondra Rios
Producer: Henry Patton
Stage Manager: Zoe Davis
Music Director: Sam Marshall
Co-Lighting Designers: Katherine Li, Ezra Osburn
Sound Designer: Nick Kapp
Co-Props Designers: Cessa Lewis, Charlie Zucker
Set Designer: Journey Cole
Marketing Director: Luca Hirsch
Assistant Producers: Aditi Adve, Anna Selina
Assistant Stage Manager: Marilena Kolokotsa

THE BAND

Piper Fishkind: Singer
Khoi Lee: Keyboard
Sam Marshall: Guitar
Leo McKenna: Drums
Missy Scavongelli: Bass
Julia Stork: Singer

Every effort has been made to ensure the accuracy of these credits. Information was obtained from show programs, where available, and was often highly idiosyncratic. Apologies for any names that have been inadvertently omitted or misspelled. Names are generally given as they appeared in the program. Many Mee-Ow actors later went on to adopt stage names in their professional careers or changed their names for other reasons. For example, Fran Banich became Fran Banish; Barry Levin became Barry Neal; Wendy Nadler became Davis Alexander; Philip Pawelczyk became Phil Pavel; Suzie Plaksin became Suzie Plakson; Scott Rothburd became Scott Harlan; and Spencer Shapiro became Spencer Kayden.